XML and Java

from scratch

Nicholas Chase

201 West 103rd Street,
Indianapolis, Indiana 46290

XML and Java from scratch

International Standard Book Number: 0-7897-2476-6

Library of Congress Catalog Card Number: 00-108361

Printed in the United States of America

First Printing: February 2001

01 00 99 4 3 2 1

Associate Publisher
Dean Miller

Acquisitions Editor
Michelle Newcomb

Technical Editor
Andrew H. Watt

Development Editor
Victoria Elzey

Managing Editor
Thomas Hayes

Project Editor
Karen S. Shields

Copy Editors
Kay Hoskin
Geneil Breeze

Indexer
Kelly Castell

Proofreader
Maribeth Echard

Team Coordinator
Cindy Teeters

Interior Designer
Karen Ruggles

Cover Designer
Rader Design

Production
Darin Crone
Liz Patterson
Gloria Schurick

Overview

Contents

Foreword

Welcome to *Jesse Liberty's Programming from scratch* series. I created this series because I believe that traditional primers do not meet the needs of every student. A typical introductory computer programming book teaches a series of skills in logical order and then, when you have mastered a topic, the book endeavors to show how the skills might be applied. This approach works very well for many people, but not for everyone.

I've taught programming to more than 10,000 students: in small groups, large groups, and through the Internet. Many students have told me that they wish they could just sit down at the computer with an expert and work on a program together. Rather than being taught each skill step by step in a vacuum, they'd like to create a product and learn the necessary skills as they go.

From this idea was born the *Programming from scratch* series. In each of these books, an industry expert will guide you through the design and implementation of a complex program, starting from scratch and teaching you the necessary skills as you go.

You may want to make a *from scratch* book the first book you read on a subject, or you may prefer to read a more traditional primer first and then use one of these books as supplemental reading. Either approach can work: Which is better depends on your personal learning style.

All the *from scratch* series books share a common commitment to showing you the entire development process, from the initial concept through implementation. We do not assume you know anything about programming: *from scratch* means from the very beginning, with no prior assumptions.

While I didn't write every book in the series, as series editor I have a powerful sense of personal responsibility for each one. I provide supporting material and a discussion group on my Web site (`www.libertyassociates.com`), and I encourage you to write to me at `jliberty@libertyassociates.com` if you have questions or concerns.

Thank you for considering this book.

Jesse Liberty

from scratch Series Editor

Dedication

To the woman who is my universe
My wife, Sarah
Thank you for being you

Acknowledgments

So many people have gotten me to this point that it's impossible to thank everyone.

I'd like to thank Michelle Newcomb at Pearson for all her patience and shepherding, as well as Victoria Elzey and Sean Dixon for their expertise and advice. Thanks also to Karen Shields, Cindy Teeters, and Mandie Frank for all their help, and to Benoît Marchal and everyone else who helped to refine this particular vision. Thanks especially to Andrew Watt for his diligence in tracking down the details.

I'd also like to thank Rob Faller, Thom Dupper, Chuck Waterhouse, Dan Mackay, Jay Donaldson, and the rest of the crew at Site Dynamics Interactive Communications for understanding my crazy schedule.

Thanks to Melanie Moser for the help when I needed it. You're a good friend.

And finally, thanks to my wonderful wife Sarah for understanding what a project like this takes—and standing by me anyway, and my son Sean for understanding why all those weekends had to be rescheduled.

About the Author

Nicholas Chase has been involved in Web site development for companies such as Lucent Technologies, Sun Microsystems, and Oracle Corporation. He got his first email account in 1989, and before immersing himself in the Web, he was a physicist, a high school teacher, a low-level radioactive-waste facility manager, an online science fiction magazine editor, a multimedia engineer, and an Oracle instructor. He is currently the chief technology officer of Site Dynamics Interactive Communications in Clearwater, Florida. He is also the author of *Active Server Pages 3.0 from scratch*. He enjoys watching sunsets with his lovely wife Sarah and their teenage son Sean.

Tell Us What You Think!

As the reader of this book, *you* are our most important critic and commentator. We value your opinion and want to know what we're doing right, what we could do better, what areas you'd like to see us publish in, and any other words of wisdom you're willing to pass our way.

As an associate publisher for Que, I welcome your comments. You can fax, email, or write me directly to let me know what you did or didn't like about this book—as well as what we can do to make our books stronger.

Please note that I cannot help you with technical problems related to the topic of this book, and that because of the high volume of mail I receive, I might not be able to reply to every message.

When you write, please be sure to include this book's title and author as well as your name and phone or fax number. I will carefully review your comments and share them with the author and editors who worked on the book.

Fax: 317-581-4666

Email: feedback@quepublishing.com

Mail: Associate Publisher
Que
201 West 103rd Street
Indianapolis, IN 46290 USA

Introduction

Unless you've been living under the proverbial rock for the last few years, you're probably aware that the World Wide Web has been transforming society. Because you're looking at this book, you're probably also aware that the "language" of the Web is HTML, or Hypertext Markup Language. But, what you might not be aware of is how important those last two words really are.

What Is a Markup Language?

A markup language is a way of describing content—for instance, to help indicate how you want it to look. You might have specific tags, in this case indicated by < and >, that mean certain things. If you want bold, you might use `<b>`. For italic, you might use `<i>`. But the important thing is that the reader (or more likely, the program being used by the reader) understands what those tags should mean.

This is how HTML came to rule. It wasn't just a markup language. It was a markup language that had been through a process of standardization through public discussion and a recommending body, the W3C; it was an agreed-upon markup language. Because of that, every browser knew that `<b>` meant bold, `<i>` meant italic, and `<h1>` meant it was a very important header, so you should make it prominent somehow.

Notice the difference between formatting markups and content markups. Bold and italic tags are self-explanatory, and describe only formatting. A header tag, on the other hand, describes the content itself. Although it's generally agreed that a header should be big and bold, the tag merely points out that the content is important. The formatting—making the header bold or large—follows from that.

In fact, in early Web pages, there was very little actual formatting. If you wanted to point out important information, you would mark it as `<strong>` or `<em>` (for emphasis).

This system worked pretty well in the beginning, but as more and more people started building sites, they wanted greater control over how that content would look, so they began favoring the formatting tags (such as `<center>`) over the markup tags (such as `<code>`). In addition, the first content authors didn't much care how their pages looked, as long as they were usable. When designers entered the mix, however, form became at least as important as content. (Some might even say that, for a time, it was more important!)

To accommodate this, new tags began to find their way into the language, so they needed to be added to the next version of browsers. Sometimes a tag would be supported in one browser but not another, such as the `<marquee>` tag in Microsoft Internet Explorer or the `<layer>` tag in Netscape.

In addition, as more people started writing Web pages, they became more and more lax in following the standards. Browsers adjusted, allowing authors to "get away" with it.

And as if that weren't enough, the whole idea of a markup language was getting lost. Few people used tags like `<strong>` anymore. Even header tags, the last bastion of content markup, were being supplanted by the new `<font>` tag, which allows much finer control over appearance. This abandonment of content markup has played havoc with search engines and other applications that need to understand the structure of a document. Whereas in older documents authors could assign a higher relevance to words contained in a heading, with the newer documents that didn't use that convention, they were missing even this rudimentary context information.

XML, or Extensible Markup Language, solves many of these problems. It's similar in form to HTML, using < and > to set tags off from the rest of the document—there's even an XML version of HTML, called XHTML—but there are important differences between the two.

The Overly Tolerant Browser

It's been said that as much as 50% of the code in today's browsers is there to compensate for bad practice in writing Web pages. An XML document, on the other hand, must be "well-formed." For instance, all start tags must have an end tag, and sections can't overlap. For instance, the code

```
<b>This section <i>is</b> very important</i>.
```

is illegal in HTML, but many modern browsers render it just fine. A browser can't be so lenient with XML, however.

Separation of Content and Presentation

Part of the reason that this can't be done in XML is that the formatting is completely separate from the nature of the content. If we look at this sentence from an XML standpoint, we might tag it like this:

```
<sentence>
   <subject>This section</subject>
   <verb>is</verb>
   <adjective>very important<adjective>
   <punctuation>.</punctuation>
<sentence>
```

In this case, we're defining what everything is, not how it should look. So, unlike the previous code sample, in which `is` was part of both the first and the last part of the sentence (formattingwise), this sample now puts it on its own.

Of course, this means that we have to tell the browser how we want to display this sentence, because tags such as `sentence` and `verb` don't carry any meaning on their own—they are not part of HTML, so a browser doesn't know what to do with them. Fortunately, there are several ways to add styles to content so that a browser knows that `subject`s should be italicized, `verb`s should be bold and italicized, and so on.

Retrieving and Repurposing Information

By classifying data according to its purpose and not just how we want it to look, we're also providing a way for a computer program to analyze it. For instance, if we have an XML file listing a few dozen furniture items, we can use an application to do any of the following:

- Analyze or manipulate the data (for example, to total prices or adjust inventory)
- Display different pages for different browsers (for example, Netscape versus Internet Explorer versus a Web phone or other system)
- Share data with another system (for example, between a company and a vendor)
- Repurpose the data for a completely different medium (for example, printing an electronic list as a paper catalog)

The Project

Throughout the course of this book, we're going to build a Web site and application for ChaseWeb Furniture—a fictitious catalog furniture company. All the information on products, prices, vendors, and so on is stored in XML.

We start by building some simple product pages using Cascading Style Sheets (CSSs) and XML Stylesheet Language (XSL), and then we look at Document Type Definitions (DTDs) and parsers, which describe what an XML document should contain and make sure it does, respectively. These first few chapters will talk only about XML and won't take on any programming.

Then, after we're comfortable with the basic building blocks, we start looking at Java, and how it's used with XML. We learn about processors, and how they're used, among other things, to make our XML pages accessible to any browser, not just those that understand XML.

From there we move on to actual programming, using Java servlets to manipulate orders taken off the Web site. In doing this, we actually look at three APIs, or Application Programming Interfaces (which is just fancy wording for a set of instructions). There are the Document Object Model (DOM), the Simple API for XML (SAX)—and circumstances when one might be preferable over the other—and JDOM. We also work with Namespaces, a standard that allows us to combine data from different sources (such as vendors, in this case) without leading to confusion.

Finally, because many of the applications we're going to build with XML are currently being done with databases, we learn to use Java to access our legacy SQL databases in conjunction with XML.

The final section looks at using XML in other environments, such as PDAs or a paper catalog. We also get a glimpse of some of the emerging standards.

System Requirements

Although a good amount of time is spent discussing the server side as opposed to the client, or browser side, you should be able to do everything in this book on your very own machine because this book uses Java for the server-side development. This includes things that are normally done with a Web server.

The basic software (all of which is available to download free) that you need for this book consists of the following:

- Netscape 6 (Preview Release 1 is used in this book) or Microsoft Internet Explorer 5

- Java Development Kit (J2SDK, also known as JDK1.2)
- JavaServerTM Web Development Kit (JSWDK)
- Xalan
- Xerces
- JDOM
- XQL

All of these are freely downloadable from the Web. Locations and instructions for downloading are covered as each piece is used.

To run these applications, you need the following:

- Windows 95, Windows 98, Windows 2000, Windows NT 4.0, or Red Hat Linux 6.1
- Pentium or equivalent
- 133MHz
- 32MB of RAM

The Netscape 6 application also runs on the Macintosh, but some of the server-side applications do not. If, however, you have access to a server where you can run these applications and you just want the browser, the system requirements are as follows:

- Mac OS 8.5, Mac OS 8.6, or Mac OS 9
- 200MHz PowerPC 604 or G3
- 48MB of RAM

About This Book

This book is different from the usual technical book for a number of reasons. First, we don't assume that you know anything at all about the topic. You don't even have to know HTML. Experience always helps. So, if you have experience in Java or another programming language, you'll be able to get through the book a bit faster. However, even if you have no experience, anything you need to know will be explained as we go along.

Second, rather than a series of disconnected examples, this book follows a single project from beginning to end. You will be able to see not just how all of the pieces fit together, but also where they all came from.

A number of indicators are used throughout to help you along. For instance, when code samples are provided, they look like Listing I.1.

Listing I.1—Sample Code Generally Looks Like This

```
0:  <?xml version="1.0" encoding="ISO-8859-1" ?>
1:
2:  <xsl:stylesheet
2a:    xmlns:xsl="http://www.w3.org/XSL/Transform/1.0">
3:
4:  <xsl:template match="/">
5:     <html>
6:        <head>
7:           <title>Welcome to Vanguard Furniture!</title>
8:        </head>
9:        <body>
10:          <xsl:apply-templates/>
11:       </body>
12:    </html>
13: </xsl:template>
14:
15: </xsl:stylesheet>
```

The important thing here is that the numbers are NOT part of the code. They're only there so that we can refer to particular lines. Also, sometimes, because we can only fit so many characters on a line, we'll have to break a line in the listing. In that case, we'll try to indicate it with a letter, as we did with lines 2 and 2a. Sometimes, however, a line is just too long to break reasonably, and you see ➥ at the head of the line indicating that both lines should be one.

Also, throughout the book you'll see other features we've added to help you along.

EXCURSION

What Is an Excursion?

Sometimes there will be a topic that really should be discussed, but doesn't really fit in with the flow of what we're talking about at that time. Instead of doing without it, we break that out into an excursion so you can come back to it without disrupting your learning curve.

Notes contain side information that doesn't really need an excursion.

Geek Speak—A term that's not generally well known, so we define it separately.

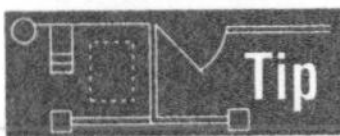

Tips provide advice and ways to make your programming life easier.

Along the way we point out issues that can make your life considerably more difficult and help you avoid them.

Also, we'll occasionally refer to code elements such as tags (`<DIV></DIV>`) or Java (`public`) within the text, in which case they'll be monospaced.

So, that's all you need to know right now. Ready to dive in? Let's go!

Chapter 1

In this chapter

- *Walking Before We Run: HTML and XHTML*
- *Controlling Presentation: Cascading Style Sheets*
- *Delving Deeper into CSS2*
- *Converting Our Content to XML*
- *Next Steps*

Vendor Pages: Styling XML with Cascading Style Sheets

If you're anything like me—and you probably are, or you wouldn't be reading this book—you're anxious to get your hands dirty and actually see something happen. We're going to do that right here in Chapter 1.

This book will chronicle the building of a Web site for the ChaseWeb Furniture Company using XML, so we're going to start by building introductory pages for our imaginary vendors. In doing that, we'll start by explaining how HTML works, for those of you who may not be familiar with it. If you already know HTML, great! Feel free to skip ahead to *Controlling Presentation: Cascading Style Sheets*, where we'll look at using CSS to influence the presentation of not just HTML, but also actual XML content.

This will get us ready for Chapter 2, "Product Pages: Transforming XML in the Browser Using XSL," where we'll use Extensible Stylesheet Language, or XSL, to transform and format XML in the browser.

Walking Before We Run: HTML and XHTML

The best way for us to see immediate results is to look at a markup language with which you might be familiar, Hypertext Markup Language, or HTML. To do that, we're going to take a look at one of ChaseWeb Furniture's vendors, Crazy Marge's Bed Emporium. But before we do, let's look at some of the basics of HTML.

HTML was developed as a way for different users and software programs to understand enough about a document to display it properly. For instance, if I were to type

```
<center>Crazy Marge's Bed Emporium</center>
```

virtually any Internet browser would understand that the text information between the open tag (<center>) and the close tag (</center>) was to be centered on the page.

In essence, that's all there is to HTML right there. Tags enclose content, which is then displayed as the tags have specified. Of course, if it were really that simple, there wouldn't be so many HTML books on the market! The fact is that this is an immensely powerful way of passing information to the browser.

For instance, tags can be nested, which means that one set can be contained within another. If we wanted, we could emphasize that this was Crazy Marge's Bed Emporium (in case there were a surplus of Bed Emporiums, I suppose) by putting her name in bold using the <b> and </b> tags, like this:

```
<center><b>Crazy Marge's</b> Bed Emporium</center>
```

Seeing this in action is easy. All we need to do is to type the text in any text editor (such as Notepad or Simpletext) and save the file with an extension of .html or .htm. I called mine marge.html. After you have the file, open your favorite browser, such as Netscape Navigator or Microsoft Internet Explorer, and, choosing File/Open, call up your new HTML file. A window similar to Figure 1.1 should appear.

Figure 1.1

Formatting content in HTML is relatively straightforward.

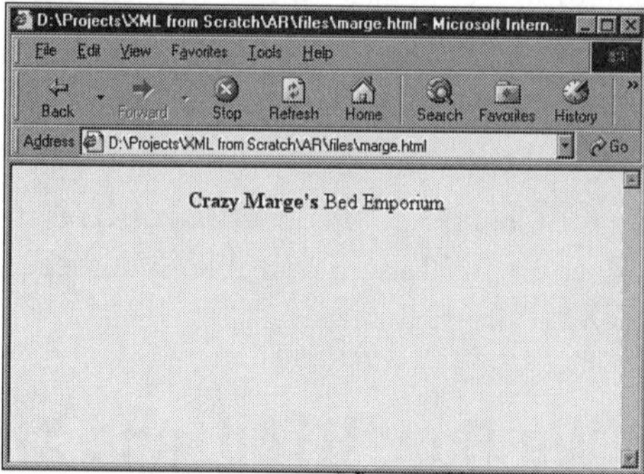

Now, most of today's browsers will render this text all by itself, but in actuality that's terrible form. HTML can do more than just presentation, after all. It can also help to describe the structure of a document. For instance, our single-line HTML page should actually read more like Listing 1.1.

Listing 1.1—A Traditional HTML Page

```
0: <html>
1:     <head>
2:         <title>Crazy Marge's Bed Emporium</title>
3:     </head>
4:     <body>
5:         <center><b>Crazy Marge's</b> Bed Emporium</center>
6:     </body>
7: </html>
```


(Remember, the line numbers are not part of the page. They're just there so we both know which lines I'm referring to.)

In this case, on lines 0 and 7, we're letting the browser know that it's dealing with an HTML document. (Although for many years that was obvious—what else would it be?—these days there are actually other choices, such as `<xml></xml>`.) More than that, by using the `<body></body>` tags, we've designated the start and end of a specific element of information—the page content.

Element—An element is a discrete unit of information. An element can be as simple as a name or a description, or it can be more complex, perhaps containing child elements of its own. For instance, in the previous listing,

```
<center><b>Crazy Marge's</b> Web Emporium</center>
```

is a child of the

```
<body></body>
```

element.

Within that HTML document, there are actually two sections, the head and the body. The head section contains the title (which you should now notice in the title bar of your browser's window) and other items, such as scripts or style sheets. In fact, for the most part, everything but the actual content generally goes into the head section, and the content itself goes into the body section.

EXCURSION

Presentation Versus Content

If you're unfamiliar with HTML, you might find this emphasis on structure a little odd. After all, isn't HTML intended to define how the content should look? Actually, no. HTML was originally intended to define the structure of the document, which the browser would use to decide how to display it. The advent of XML brings us back in that direction, and we'll expound on it when we get to *Controlling Presentation: Cascading Style Sheets*, but it's good to keep it in the back of your head as you familiarize yourself with HTML itself.

Of course, we can't just drop all our content onto the page and expect the browser to do the rest. Let's try it with Listing 1.2 and see what happens:

Listing 1.2—Our Content on the Page

```
<html>
    <head>
        <title>Crazy Marge's Bed Emporium</title>
    </head>
    <body>
        <center><b>Crazy Marge's</b> Bed Emporium</center>

        We never have a sale because we've got the lowest
        prices in town!  Come in today and shop around. If
        you can find lower prices anywhere Crazy Marge will
        shave her husband's head!!!

        We have all kinds, all sizes.  Don't see what you
        want?  Don't worry.  We customize orders!

        Sleepeazy Mattresses
        $300 per set, any size
        Free pillows with every set

        CozyComfort Mattresses starting at only $99.99
        Queen: $159.00
        King:  $209.00
        Free sheets with every set

        Floataway Waterbeds
        15 different styles to choose from with free delivery --
        we'll take your old mattress as a trade in!

        This week only:  Round beds with rotating motors
        starting at a price that will make your head spin.
        Just talk to Crazy Marge.  She'll tell you all about
        it!

    </body>
</html>
```

The lines in boldface just indicate what has been added since the previous listing. They do not need to be in bold in your code.

Now, while that's perfectly readable to you and me, it's not so readable to the average browser. In fact, it displays like Figure 1.2.

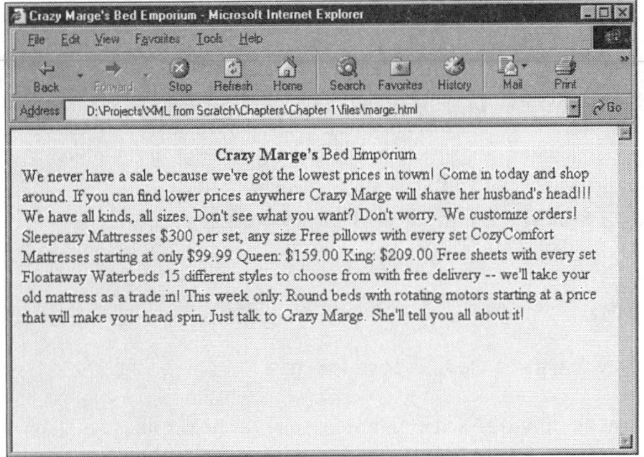

Figure 1.2

Just putting text into a document isn't enough to make it look good.

So, what can we do about it?

Well, because this isn't a book on Web design, we won't be getting into too much detail about the HTML itself, but there are a few tags that you should know about before we move too much farther. They are

- **<h1>**—Headers actually come in six varieties, with <H1> signifying the largest and most important, and <H6> specifying the smallest and least important. They're often used to set off titles or subheadings.
- **<p>**—Paragraph tags are used to designate paragraphs, and to create blank lines between items.
- **
**—A cousin to the paragraph tag, the line break does just what it says, creating a line break in the midst of content.
- **<b>** and **<i>**—The bold and italic tags are used for actual formatting of content.
- **<ul>** and **<ol>**—Many times a Web page author wants to create a list of items. The unordered list and ordered list tags normally contain multiple list items, designated by the **<li>** tag.
- **<center>**—The center tag can be used to center anything from a single line to an entire page of content.
- **<hr>**—The horizontal rule tag actually creates a line within the page, usually to separate different areas of content.
- **<table>**—Tables are usually used for lining up specific items, such as the data in a spreadsheet. A table has rows (enclosed in **<tr>** tags) and cells within rows (enclosed in **<td>** tags).

Considering that HTML 4.0 has dozens of distinct tags, that's hardly a comprehensive list, but it's enough to get us started.

If we were to mark up Crazy Marge's ad copy, we'd wind up with something like Listing 1.3 and Figure 1.3.

Listing 1.3—The Initial Markup of Crazy Marge's Ad Copy

```
<html>
<head>
    <title>Crazy Marge's Bed Emporium</title>
</head>

<body>

<h1>Crazy Marge's Bed Emporium</h1>

<p>We never have a sale because we've got the
lowest prices in town!  Come in today and shop
around. If you can find lower prices anywhere
Crazy Marge will shave her husband's head!!!</p>

<p>We have all kinds, all sizes.  Don't see what
you want?  Don't worry.  We customize orders!</p>

<b>Sleepeazy Mattresses</b><br />
$300 per set, any size<br />
<i>Free pillows</i> with every set<br />
<br />
<b>CozyComfort Mattresses</b> starting at only $99.99<br />
Queen: $159.00<br />King:  $209.00<br />
<i>Free sheets</i> with every set<br />
<br />
<b>Floataway Waterbeds</b><br />
<i>15 different styles to choose from</i> with free
delivery -- we'll take your old mattress as a trade
in!<br />

<p>This week only:  Round beds with rotating motors
starting at a price that will make your head spin.
Just talk to Crazy Marge, she'll tell you all about
it!</p>

</body>
</html>
```

Now let's take a good hard look at what we've done here, because there's much more going on behind the scenes than you might think.

The first thing to notice is the syntax we're using for our break tags, `<br />`. Although all the other tags we've worked with come in pairs, such as `<b></b>` or `<h1></h1>`, the traditional break tag in HTML was `<br>`, without a closing tag. XHTML, which will eventually replace HTML, however, doesn't allow for a single tag all by itself, and even though we're not strictly conforming to XHTML syntax here, it's a good idea to avoid doing things we know will cause problems later. For that reason, we need to either use our break tag as `<br></br>`, which looks kind of odd to those familiar with the old way of doing things, or `<br />`, which is the XML abbreviation for it. We'll see more of this in Chapter 2, "Product Pages: Transforming XML in the Browser Using XSL," and we'll talk about the coming of XHTML in Chapter 9, "Other Applications for XML (SOAP)."

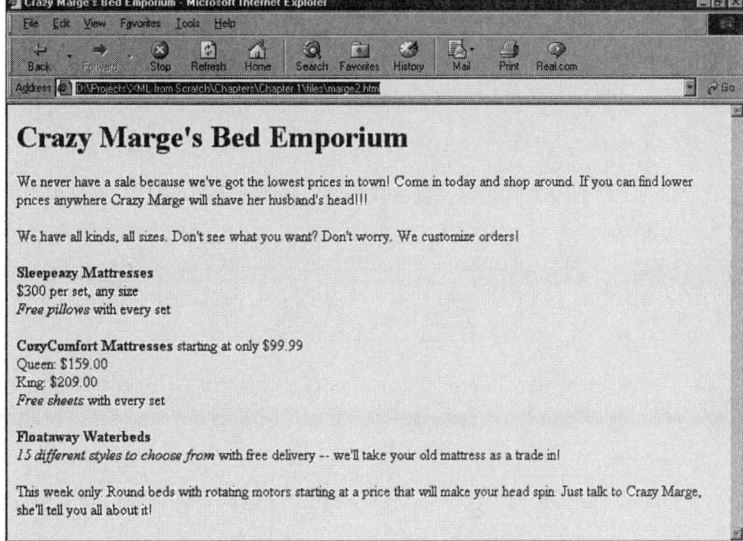

Figure 1.3

Adding just a few presentation-related tags makes our pages much more legible.

The next thing we need to notice is that whitespace and line breaks happen where we tell them to, not where they are in the file itself. For example, there are four line breaks in the text on lines 9 through 12, but they don't show in Figure 1.3. On the other hand, putting a break tag in the middle of line 22 splits it on the page.

Here we see the first fundamental rule about authoring Web pages: HTML ignores whitespace. In some ways, this is a very good thing, because we can write pages and not worry about inadvertent line breaks, because they'll be ignored. As long as we place line breaks where we need them to be, everything is fine.

But this brings up the question: If we didn't put a line break after the header, why did the browser render it as separate from the paragraph below it?

The answer lies in the way that tags have been designed in HTML itself. Some tags, such as `<i>` or `<b>`, are designed to be rendered inline—that is, within the line that contains them. Others, such as `<h1>` or `<p>`, are designed to be rendered as a block, which means that nothing appears on the same line as they do. So, we can put a header anywhere, and it will always appear on its own line.

So, does that mean that the presentation, or the way that HTML tags are rendered, is chiseled in stone? Happily, the answer is "no."

Controlling Presentation: Cascading Style Sheets

Although the vast majority of those authoring Web pages today don't remember this, early browsers actually gave users a small amount of control over how Web pages were displayed. For instance, a Web page author could use the (now almost forgotten) `<strong>` tag to designate that something is important, as in

```
Don't forget to <strong>notify us of changes!</strong>
```

In most cases. this tag was rendered as bold, but the early browsers, such as Mosaic, allowed the user to choose to display it as, perhaps, red or italic. This function was lost as newer browsers gave authors control over presentation, or at least as much control as HTML would allow. HTML wasn't perfect, but at least if the author set text as bold, it was likely to be rendered that way.

But what if the author wanted text to be not just bold, but also 16pt Arial, instead of whatever the browser's default was? The `<font>` tag was born out of this desire to stretch the presentational limits. The author could now write a passage such as

```
Don't forget to <font face="Arial" size="16pt">notify us of changes!</font>
```

That would certainly do it, but we've lost something here: Although a human can look at the rendered sentence and pick out the piece that's important, a program couldn't. All it knows is that some of the sentence is being rendered differently from the rest of the sentence.

This was one of the major reasons for the development of XML. The structural nature of HTML was all but gone, replaced by a preoccupation with presentation. What was needed was a way to separate the two, allowing an author to concentrate on content while a designer controlled the presentation.

Fortunately, there's a middle ground called Cascading Style Sheets. A style sheet allows an author to mark up content properly and then specify how each item should be displayed based on what it is.

Let's say that we wanted to apply the earlier styling to all the names of items that Crazy Marge is selling. Because they're all in bold now, we can use style sheets to tell the browser how we want bold items to be displayed, as in Listing 1.4.

Listing 1.4—Adding Style Information to the Bold Tag

```
0: <html>
1: <head>
2:     <title>Crazy Marge's Bed Emporium</title>
3:
4:     <style>
5:         b {
6:             font-family:Arial;
7:             font-size:16pt;
8:             color:red ;
9:             font-weight:bold;
10:          }
11:    </style>
12:
13:</head>
14:
15:<body>
16:
17:<h1>Crazy Marge's Bed Emporium</h1>
18:
19:<p>We never have a sale because we've got the
20:lowest prices in town!  Come in today and shop
21:around. If you can find lower prices anywhere
22:Crazy Marge will shave her husband's head!!!</p>
23:
24:<p>We have all kinds, all sizes.  Don't see what
25:you want?  Don't worry.  We customize orders!</p>
26:
27:<b>Sleepeazy Mattresses</b><br />
28:$300 per set, any size<br />
29:<i>Free pillows</i> with every set<br />
30:<br />
31:<b>CozyComfort Mattresses</b> starting at only $99.99<br />
...
```

The ellipsis at the end of the code listing is not part of the page. The ellipsis is just there to show you that there's more text we're not showing.

After we've done this, we see that all the text that we marked with `<b></b>` tags is styled, as in Figure 1.4.

Let's take a look at what we've done to add the style information on lines 4 through 11.

First of all, we notice that all the style information is embedded within the `<style>` `</style>` tags, so the browser knows what to do with it. Otherwise, it would just be text to display. Instead, the browser looks down the list of selectors so that it knows what content will need styling. In this case, we have just one selector, for the <b> tag.

Figure 1.4

By applying the proper style, we can control what a tag looks like.

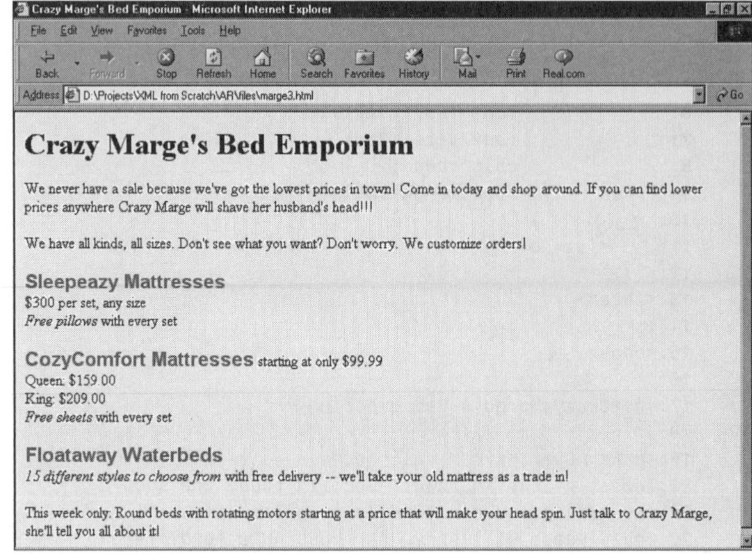

Selector—A selector, such as b in Listing 1.4, tells the browser what tags to look for when applying a style.

The information in the brackets is the style information. The current standard, CSS2, actually lists more than 100 properties that can be used, although no browser supports all of them. In fact, for the most part, no two browsers support the same set, and definitely not the same way. In the section "Delving Deeper into CSS2" later in this chapter, we'll take a look at those properties, but first let's look at how we can apply them. Making a few changes to the file, shown in Listing 1.5, can change the entire page, as shown in Figure 1.5.

EXCURSION

All Browsers Are Not Created Equal

With the advent of the so-called browser wars, there has been a great deal of debate over which browser is "best." Each generation of browsers seems to leapfrog its competitor either in terms of functionality or standards-compliance. For a long time, Microsoft Internet Explorer 5 had the greatest amount of support for CSS, but it doesn't always adhere strictly to the standard. At the time of this writing, the just-released Netscape 6 has the greatest amount of support for CSS2, and many of the properties shown here will have an effect only in it.

What this all means is that not all the items we're going to see in this chapter are going to work in all browsers, so if you decide to use them in your Web site, make sure to test your pages in the target browser for your audience. CSS was originally designed to degrade gracefully, meaning that if the browser didn't understand it, the text would still be readable, but if you rely on advanced features such as positioning, you might wind up with a document that's unreadable on older browsers.

In any case, the inability to see all of these properties is not a showstopper. If you have trouble getting your browser to recognize something, just move on. It won't hamper your ability to use the rest of the book.

Listing 1.5—Styling the Entire Page—Or Just Selected Parts

```
0: <html>
1: <head>
2:     <title>Crazy Marge's Bed Emporium</title>
3:
4:     <style>
5:
6:         *  { font-family: Arial, Helvetica, sans-serif; }
7:
8:         h1, p { text-decoration: underline; }
9:
10:    </style>
11:
12:</head>
13:
14:<body>
15:
16:<h1>Crazy Marge's Bed Emporium</h1>
17:
...
```

The first thing to notice is that we have removed the original styling, because the bold tags are fine the way they are. What we've done instead, on line 5, is to tell the processor (in this case, the browser) that this instruction applies to all parts of the document, and not just any specific elements.

Wildcard—Just as in poker, a wildcard can be used to represent anything, or in this case, everything. Because every tag matches it, every tag has the style applied.

Sans-serif—A sans-serif font does not have crosslines at the ends of letters. For instance, Times New Roman is a serif font, whereas Arial is a sans-serif font, as in Figure 1.6.

Figure 1.5

Changing a few lines changes the entire appearance of the document.

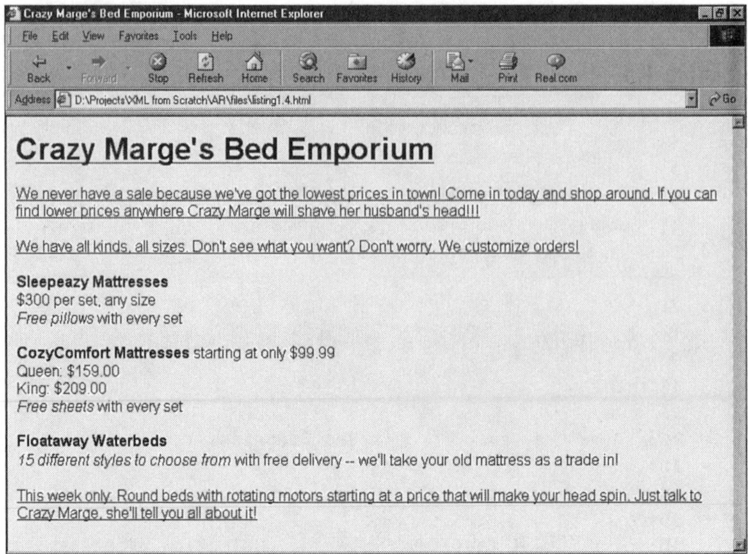

Figure 1.6

Fonts are either serif or sans-serif.

But let's look at what we're actually telling it to do. After all, we have three designations for this property on line 6, and, of course, only one font can be displayed at a time. In fact, what the browser does in this case will depend on what fonts the user has available on his or her local machine. The first choice is Arial, so if that's installed and available, that's what's going to be used. If it's not available, the browser will try to find Helvetica, and if that's not available either, it will choose any available sans-serif font.

So, that takes care of our default styling. Now, if we look at lines 8 through 10, we're applying a style to two different types of tags—the paragraph tags and the header tags. We can list as many different tags as we like, as long as they're separated by commas. There's just one problem with this. The style is going to apply to all instances of those tags, whether we want it to or not. What if we just wanted to highlight the heading and the specials at the bottom of the page?

Fortunately, we can do this using classes, as we'll see in Listing 1.6.

Listing 1.6—Using Classes for Styles

```
0:<html>
1:<head>
2:    <title>Crazy Marge's Bed Emporium</title>
3:
4:    <style>
5:
6:        *  { font-family: Arial, Helvetica, sans-serif; }
7:
8:        .highlight { text-decoration: underline; }
9:
10:    </style>
11:
12:</head>
13:
14:<body>
15:
16:<h1 class="highlight">Crazy Marge's Bed Emporium</h1>
17:
18:<p>We never have a sale because we've got the
19:lowest prices in town!  Come in today and shop
20:around. If you can find lower prices anywhere
21:Crazy Marge will shave her husband's head!!!</p>
22:
23:<p>We have all kinds, all sizes.  Don't see what
24:you want?  Don't worry.  We customize orders!</p>
...
39:<p class="highlight">This week only:  Round beds with
40:rotating motors starting at a price that will make your
41:head spin.  Just talk to Crazy Marge, she'll tell you
42:all about it!</p>
43:
44:</body>
45:</html>
```

What we've done is create a class of elements—in this case, things that we wanted to highlight in some way. By placing the class designation in the tag, we're telling the browser that we want to apply any styles for this class. In the style sheet on line 8, we place a `.` before the class name to let the browser know that this is a class, and that it shouldn't be looking for a tag named `highlight`.

In this way, we can be very specific about which elements should have certain styles applied to them. In this case, we've added an underline, as in Figure 1.7.

Figure 1.7

Using classes gives us more control over where styles are applied.

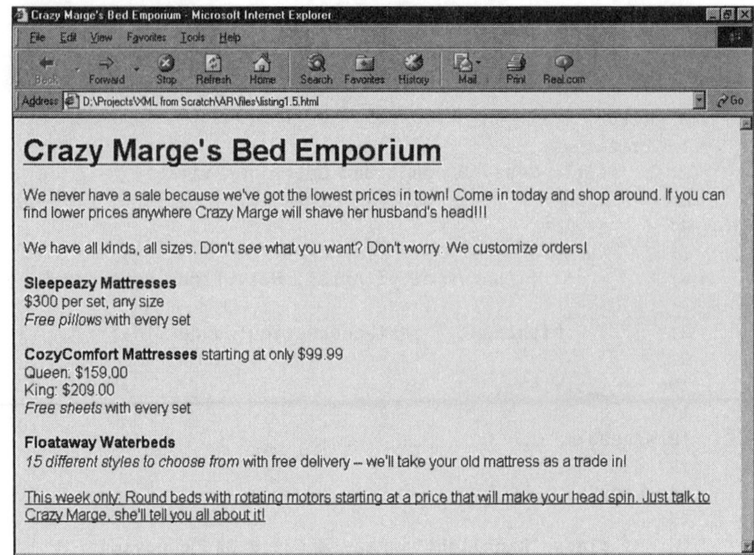

There are a number of other ways to specify which elements we want to style, so let's make a few changes to our page to demonstrate them. Then, we're going to use Crazy Marge's special of the week to demonstrate a number of CSS2 properties, so let's go ahead and add it to its own `<div>`. The `<div></div>` tag is often used to separate out various elements so they can be treated individually. In this case, we're going to nest the special inside a `<div>`, as in Listing 1.7. We'll also add an `id` to the paragraph so we can reference it individually.

Listing 1.7—Putting the Weekly Special in Its Own DIV

```
<i>15 different styles to choose from</i> with free
delivery -- we'll take your old mattress as a trade
in!<br />

<div>
<p class="highlight" id="weeklyspecial">This week only:  Round beds with
rotating motors starting at a price that will make your
head spin.  Just talk to Crazy Marge, she'll tell you
all about it!</p>
</div>

</body>
</html>
```

Now we can look at two other types of descriptors.

First, we have a nested element. In this case, we would say that the `<p>` is the child of the `<div>`, and that the `<div>` (naturally enough) is the parent of the `<p>`. We would also say that the <p> is the descendant of the <div>. This will become much more important later on when we're working with straight XML, but it still applies now.

To apply the highlight style only to the special, we could actually use the descendant selector, like so:

```
div p { text-decoration: underline; }
```

In this case, the browser would look for any <p> element that is contained within a <div> at any level. This means that it would be selected even if it were the child of a child of the <div>. To select the <p> only if it's the actual child of the <div>, we would use the child selector, as in the following:

```
div > p { text-decoration: underline; }
```

This is going to select ONLY <p> elements that are the direct children of a <div>.

We can also select sibling elements. For instance, if our <DIV> also contained another element, as in Listing 1.8, we could use the sibling selector:

Listing 1.8—Using the Sibling Selector

```
<html>
<head>
    <title>Crazy Marge's Bed Emporium</title>

    <style>

        * { font-family: Arial, Helvetica, sans-serif; }

        h3 + p { text-decoration: underline; }

    </style>

</head>
...
delivery -- we'll take your old mattress as a trade
in!<br />

<div>
<h3>The Weekly Special</h3>
<p class="highlight" id="weeklyspecial">This week only:  Round beds with
rotating motors starting at a price that will make your
head spin.  Just talk to Crazy Marge, she'll tell you
all about it!</p>
</div>

</body>
</html>
```

We can also use the id that we added earlier. To reference an id, we use the # sign in the descriptor:

```
#weeklyspecial { text-decoration: underline; }
```

An id doesn't have to be unique to an element. In fact, ids are similar to classes in the way that they can be used. For the sake of humans who will be reading your code later, however, it's better to use ids for single elements and classes for groups of elements.

Finally, we can specify that we just want the weekly special by combining the element and the class. Both the header and the special are part of the highlight class, but only the special is a <p> element. We can specify that it's the one that we want using

```
p.highlight { text-decoration: underline; }
```

This will select only <p> elements that are part of the highlight class.

So, let's recap. By using a style sheet, we can tell the browser which styles we want to apply (using declarations and properties) and where we want it to apply them (using a number of different descriptor types). These two simple principles give us an enormous amount of power over the presentation of a document.

Delving Deeper into CSS2

Cascading Style Sheets can be used for a whole lot more than just adding color or underlines to a section of text. They can be used for positioning elements on the page, adding borders, specifying properties that were previously relegated to desktop publishing, such as leading and kerning, or even to control how a page is read aloud by audio applications. Let's take a look at some of these more advanced features.

First things first: Where does the "Cascading" part of Cascading Style Sheets come from?

Cascading Style Sheets can be extraordinarily useful based on the fact that a single style sheet can be applied to multiple documents. For instance, we could set up an entire Web site using a style sheet, and when we wanted to change the look, all we'd have to do is change the style sheet and the site would change—but not the way we currently have them set up.

In order for our style sheet to be accessible from more than one document, we're going to have to make it external to the page, and then link the page to it. We'll do this by taking the style information and putting it into a file called, in this case, vendor.css, as in Listing 1.9.

Listing 1.9—The External Style Sheet

```
 *  { font-family:Arial, Helvetica, sans-serif; }

.highlight { text-decoration: underline; }
```

Notice that the <style></style> tags are not included in this file. The browser will know what to do with the contents based on how we link it to the file, as in Listing 1.10.

Listing 1.10—Linking to an External Style Sheet

```
0:<html>
1:<head>
2:    <title>Crazy Marge's Bed Emporium</title>
3:
4:    <link rel="stylesheet" href="vendor.css" type="text/css">
5:
6:</head>
7:
8:<body>
9:
10:<h1 class="highlight">Crazy Marge's Bed Emporium</h1>
11:
12:<p>We never have a sale because we've got the
...
```

On line 4, we link our page to the external style sheet, and the browser takes it from there. Any changes that we make to the style sheet will show in this page—or any other page that links to this sheet.

EXCURSION

URLs, URIs, and Other Locations

The purpose of the <link> tag is to let the browser know where to find the style sheet. It just so happens that we put the `vendor.css` file in the same directory as the HTML page, so all that was necessary was the name of the file. There's nothing that says that we have to be that limited, however.

`href` is short for Hypertext Reference. Although all we see here is the filename, this is actually the URI for the file. A URI is a Universal Resource Identifier, which consists of a URL, or Universal Resource Locator, and a URN, or Universal Resource Name. It just happens that nobody really uses the URN yet, so most people consider a URI and URL to be the same, but that won't always be the case.

This means that while what we have here is a relative URL—meaning relative to the current file—if we wanted to, we could actually link to a style sheet that was on a different computer altogether. For instance, we could have had a link such as the following:

```
<LINK rel="stylesheet"
href="http://www.primaryoutpost.com/stylesheeets/vendor.css"
type="text/css">
```

In this case, we could actually reference this style sheet from anywhere, as long as we were connected to the Web.

Whenever we talk about locating a file or other resource, we will be talking about using URIs to indicate their location, so we have the option to specify a full URL as we've done before.

Now that we know how to link our style sheets to our documents, let's take a look at some of the things that we can do with them. As I said before, there are more than 100 different properties, but we'll just look at some of the more common ones. If you want the complete list, it can be found at `http://www.w3.org/TR/REC-CSS2`.

Color

Because many of the CSS2 properties center around `color`, let's take that one first. The `color` property of any object (including the page itself) can be set using either the established color names such as `red`, `blue`, `green`, and so on. It can also be set using the RGB hex values, where the first two digits are the value of red from 0 to 255 (or FF), the second two digits are green, and the third two digits are blue. For instance, pure blue would be 0000FF, black is 000000, white is FFFFFF, and a light orange might be FFBB66. For those who prefer to stay away from hex values, we can also use the decimal values. For instance, to set the color of an element to green, we could use

```
color: rgb(0,255,0)
```

Background

One of the oldest improvements to graphical browsers was the capability to control the background of a page, first by setting it to a specific color, and then by adding an image to be displayed behind the page content. With CSS2, this property still stands, but we now have a great deal more control over how we use it.

The most common use for the background set of properties is for the background of the page, so the most logical place to put them in the style sheet is in the body tag. A simple `body` element might look like Listing 1.11.

Listing 1.11—Adding Background Information

```
body {
      background-image: url(cwimage.jpg);
      background-color: gray;
      background-attachment: fixed;
      }
```

The first thing to note is the format of line 1. Although we have so far used the HTML notation, which was similar to `href="cwimage.jpg"`, we're now using the CSS2 notation. What we're saying is that we want to add a background image, and it can be found at the specified URL. Note also that in CSS2 the quotation marks here are optional.

Let's look at what these statements are doing. First, the browser is looking for the file `cwimage.jpg` in the same directory as the style sheet. Next, it's setting the background color to `gray`. (Of course, you will see it only if the background image isn't found, or if it's transparent.) The last property, `background-attachment`, is fairly new. In this case, it tells the browser that if the user scrolls, the page content should move but the background image shouldn't.

The background properties and their values are

- **`background-color`**—Can be set using the same values as the color property. The default value for this property is `transparent`.
- **`background-image`**—Can be set to a URL, as shown previously, or to `none`, which is the default.
- **`background-repeat`**—Can be set to one of four values: `repeat`, `repeat-x`, where the image will be repeated horizontally, but not vertically, `repeat-y`, where the image will be repeated vertically, but not horizontally, and `no-repeat`, where it will just be rendered once. This can be helpful if you're using a background image to display a graphic at the top of the page, but you don't want it to be repeated if the page gets very long. The default is `repeat`.
- **`background-attachment`**—Can be set to `scroll` or `fixed`. The default value, which will be used if this property isn't specified, is `scroll`.
- **`background-position`**—Can be used to adjust the position of the background image. For instance, using a rule of

  ```
  background-position: 50% 50%;
  ```

  results in the shifting of the background image as shown in Figure 1.8. This property can also be set using pixel values, as in

  ```
  background-position: 100 75
  ```

One nice thing about the background properties is that they can be applied to more than just the page itself. They can actually be applied to any block-level element (as opposed to an inline element), such as a header or paragraph. For instance, we can set the background on the `<div>` that we placed around the weekly special, as in

```
div { background-image: url('cwimage.jpg'); }
```

The results are shown in Figure 1.9.

Figure 1.8

CSS2 gives us control over where background images are placed.

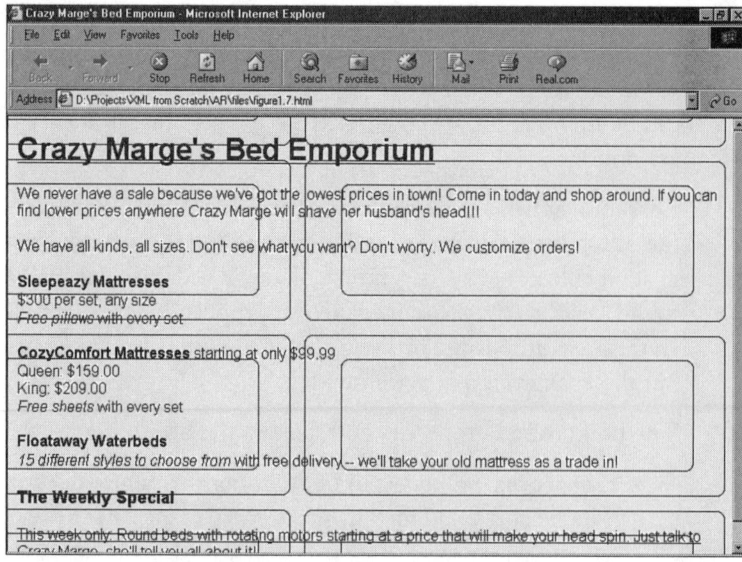

Figure 1.9

Backgrounds can be applied to any block-level element, such as a `<div>`.

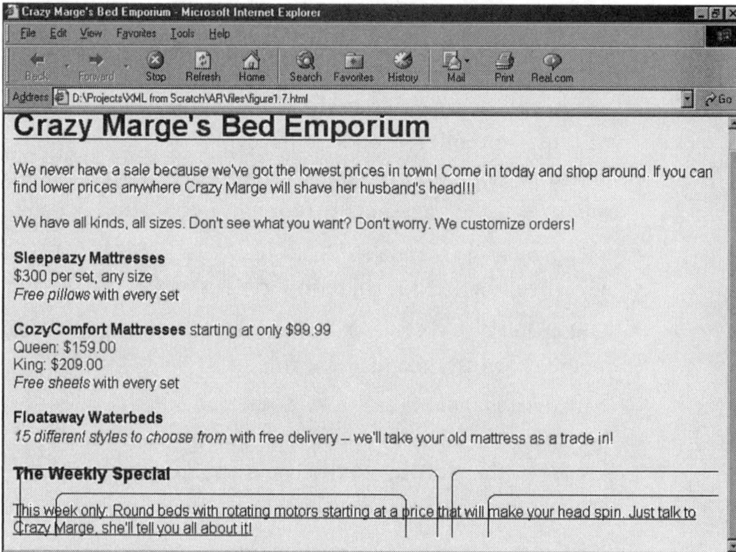

Finally, you can actually use shorthand to specify all of these properties at once by adding them to the background property in order. So the rule

```
div { background: blue url(cwimage.jpg) no-repeat scroll; }
```

is perfectly valid.

1

Border

Border properties can actually be added to any element, including inline elements such as <b> or <i>. In fact, as Web page authors we have a great deal of control over the borders of specific areas. Not only can we can set the width and color of a border, we can set it to one of 10 different styles. We can even control each of the four sides individually, in case we wanted to only partially enclose an area or, more likely, use them for decorative effect.

The `border` properties include the following:

- **`border-style`**—Actually made up of the `border-top-style`, `border-right-style`, `border-bottom-style`, and `border-left-style`. Each of these can be set to any of the following values: none, `hidden`, `dotted`, `dashed`, `solid`, `double`, `groove`, which looks like the border has been carved into the page, `ridge`, where it looks like it's jutting out of the page, `inset`, where the entire element seems to be embedded in the page, and `outset`, where the entire element appears to be jutting out of the page.

  We can use `border-style` as a shortcut for specifying all four properties. For instance the following sets are equivalent:

Shorthand	***Longhand***

`border-style: solid;`	`border-top-style: solid;`
	`border-right-style: solid;`
	`border-bottom-style: solid;`
	`border-left-style: solid;`

`border-style: solid dashed;`	`border-top-style: solid;`
	`border-right-style: dashed;`
	`border-bottom-style: solid;`
	`border-left-style: dashed;`

`border-style: solid dashed inset outset;`	`border-top-style: solid;`
	`border-right-style: dashed;`
	`border-bottom-style: inset;`
	`border-left-style: outset;`

  The default value for `border-style` is none, so unless we set it or one of the four properties it's shorthand for to a different value, no border will appear, no matter how we set the other properties.

- **`border-color`**—This property is shorthand for `border-top-color`, `border-right-color`, `border-bottom-color`, and `border-left-color`. The actual color values are the same as for the color property. They can also be set either individually or as a group, similar to `border-style`. The default value is `black` (unless we have set the `color` property).

- **`border-width`**—Shorthand for `border-top-width`, `border-right-width`, `border-bottom-width`, and `border-left-width`. These values can either be set to a specific width, such as 5px (or 5 pixels), or to `thin`, `medium`, or `thick`. The default value is `medium`.
- **`border-top`, `border-right`, `border-bottom` and `border-left`**—These are actually shorthand properties that represent width, style, and color. For instance, we can set the right border to be `thick`, `inset`, and `red` using

```
border-right: thick inset red;
```

  If any of these values are missing, the default value will be used.
- **`border`**—The `border` property is also shorthand—in this case, for `border-width`, `border-style`, and `color`. So, if we modified the `border-right` definition slightly, we could set these values for all four sides, using

```
border: thick inset red;
```

Positioning Elements

One of the most common uses for CSS is to position elements on the page. To that end, CSS provides a number of properties to give us control over where elements will appear. Most of them will make reference to the bounding box, or the container in which the element appears.

What this container actually is depends on whether the element has been nested. For instance, the weekly special `<div>` on our Crazy Marge page is contained in the body of the page, so the container for it will be the page itself. The `<p>` in the `<div>`, however, would have the `<div>` as its container.

CSS2 defines the following position-related properties:

- **`position`**—Before we can make any decisions on where we want something to appear, we need to decide what we're using as a reference point. Position can have one of four values: `fixed`, where the element is placed on the page and doesn't move even if user scrolls the page, `absolute`, where placement is calculated with respect to the containing block, `static`, where the element is placed without reference to any positioning properties, and `relative`, where placement is calculated with respect to the `static` position. The default value is `static`.

- **`top, left, bottom, right`**—These properties are essentially margins. A setting of 100px for `top` will move the element down 100 pixels from the top of the reference point (either the containing block or the `static` position, as determined by the `position` property). `Left` will move the element with respect to the left of the reference point. `Bottom` and `right` actually help to set the size, by setting their respective sides of the element relative to the bottom and right of the containing box.
- **`height, width`**—These properties explicitly set the `height` and `width` of an element. They can be set to a specific length, such as a certain number of pixels, or to a percentage. Percentages are set with regard to the containing block.
- **`clear`**—This property can be used to help determine the flow of a document. As opposed to actually setting the position of an element, `clear` is used to place it relative to another block. For instance, if we had an image immediately previous to our element, the property

  ```
  clear: left;
  ```

  would make sure that our element was positioned under it, as opposed to next to it. The acceptable values are `left`, `right`, `both` and the default value, `none`.
- **`z-index`**—The `z-index` determines the stacking level of an element. If several elements occupy some or all the same space, those with higher `z-levels` will appear in front of those with lower `z-levels`. The default value is `auto`.
- **`margin`** and **`padding`**—Shorthand for `margin-left`, `margin-top`, `margin-bottom` and `margin-right`, and `padding-left`, `padding-top`, `padding-bottom` and `padding-right`, respectively. `Margin` sets the spacing around the outside of the element, as shown in Figure 1.10, whereas `padding` sets the spacing around the inside of the element, as shown in Figure 1.11.

  `Margin` and `padding` can be set as absolute lengths or as percentages of the containing block.

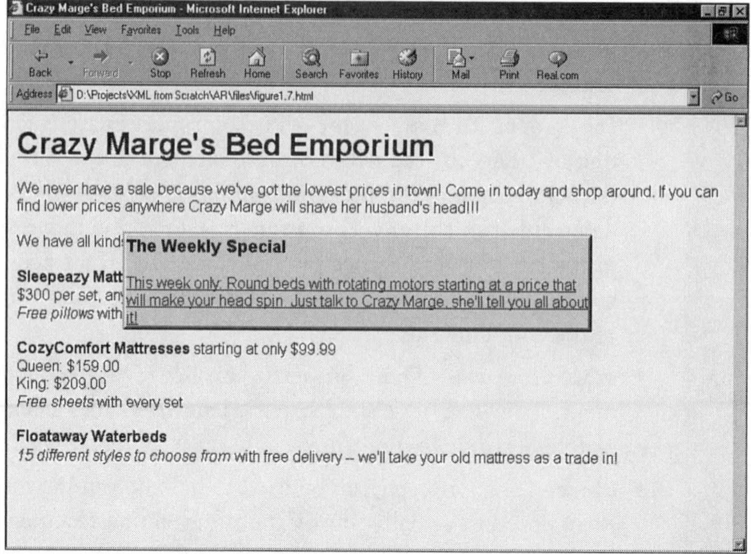

Figure 1.10

Margin sets the spacing around the outside of an element.

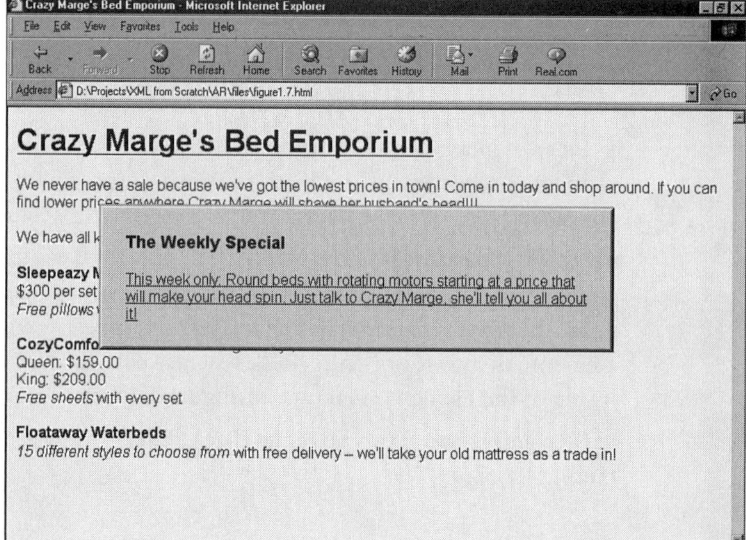

Figure 1.11

Padding sets the spacing around the inside of an element.

Text Properties

In some ways, font manipulation was the genesis of style sheets, so it's not surprising that font properties are perhaps the most common, and most commonly used. They are

- **`font-family`**—The `font-family` represents what most people think of as the font name, such as Times New Roman or Chicago. As we discussed earlier in this chapter, `font-family` can be set to either a specific font or a generic font type.
- **`font-size`**—The size of text can be determined in different ways. The most common is a length value, such as 12pt. Fonts can also be set as `smaller` or `larger` than the rest of the text in their containing block. Finally, text can be set to an absolute size. The absolute size values for text can vary from application to application, but the CSS2 standard suggests values of `xx-small`, `x-small`, `small`, `medium`, `large`, `x-large` and `xx-large`.
- **`font-style`**—The values for this property are `normal`, which is the default, and `italic` and `oblique`, which mean almost the same thing, in that they are both slanted fonts. The difference lies in how specific fonts are registered, but for everyday use, they are essentially identical.
- **`font-weight`**—This property is most commonly used to set a font to be bold or normal, but in actuality, we can use it to set the weight of a font relative to the text around it. For instance, if the parent text is `bold`, we can set an element to be `bolder`, and it will be even darker. We could also set it to be `lighter`, and the browser will make the adjustment. The accepted values for `font-weight` are `normal`, `bold`, `bolder`, `lighter`, `100` (the lightest), `200`, `300`, `400`, `500` (the default), `600`, `700`, `800`, and `900` (the darkest).
- **`text-align`**—Can be set to `left`, `right`, `center` or `justify`, which will stretch the text so each line fills the entire width of the box. The default is typically `left`.

CSS2 allows us to set the `direction` property to its default, `ltr`, or left to right, for languages such as English, or `rtl`, or right to left, for languages such as Hebrew. The default value for `text-align` will be affected by the setting for this property.

- **`text-decoration`**—This is the property that allows Web page authors to remove the underline from links in their pages. The default value is `none`. Other acceptable values, which can be used together, are `underline`, `overline`, `line-through`, and `blink`.

The use of `blink` is extremely tempting for first-time Web authors, but it is generally accepted that this property should rarely, if ever, be used. More than the extremely rare, exceptionally relevant use (and perhaps even that) will instantly brand you as a rookie. More importantly, it is extremely difficult on the eyes, and might actually drive people away from your site.

- **`text-indent`**—Designates the indentation for the first line of a box such as a paragraph. The value can represent a percentage of the width of the box, or it can be a length value. In CSS2, the units for length values are `pt` for points, `pc` for picas, `px` for pixels, `em`, which represents the width of the m character in the given font, and `ex`, which represents the width of the x character in the given font. The default is `0px`.
- **`text-transform`**—Using the values of `capitalize`, `uppercase`, and `lowercase`, we can use `text-transform` to change the case of entire elements. The default value is `none`, which will leave the text unaffected.
- **`white-space`**—This value is perhaps the most underused. One of the first things that we discussed about HTML was the fact that it ignores whitespace in the page. This property allows us to turn off that behavior. By setting the value to `pre`, we force the browser to preserve the whitespace that was in the original HTML file. By making the first declaration in our style sheet

```
*   {
    font-family:Arial Helvetica sans-serif;
    white-space:pre;
    }
```

  we make the browser display the page with whitespace separating paragraphs.

  We can also use the `white-space` property to prevent the browser from breaking lines in the middle, as it normally does, by setting `white-space` to `nowrap`. The default value is `normal`.

List Item Properties

Before we discuss list item properties, we need to define what a list item is. As we mentioned earlier, one of the capabilities of HTML is the `ordered` or `unordered` list. An example of each is provided in Listing 1.12, which appears as Figure 1.12.

Listing 1.12—Ordered and Unordered Lists

```
<html>
<head>
    <title>Listing ChaseWeb Furniture Vendors</title>
```

Listing 1.12—continued

```
3: </head>
4:
5: <body>
6: <h3>An Unordered List</h3>
7: <ul>
8:     <li>Conners Chair Company</li>
9:     <li>Crazy Marge's Bed Emporium</li>
10:    <li>Wally's Wonderful World of Furniture</li>
11:</ul>
12:
13:<h3>An Ordered List</h3>
14:<ol>
15:    <li>Conners Chair Company</li>
16:    <li>Crazy Marge's Bed Emporium</li>
17:    <li>Wally's Wonderful World of Furniture</li>
18:</OL>
19:
20:</body>
21:</html>
```

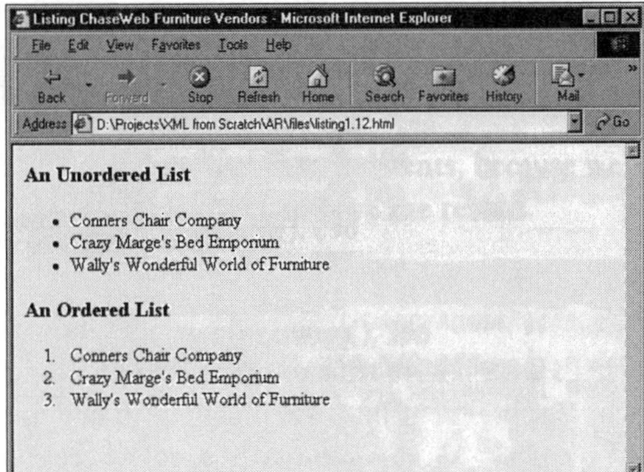

Figure 1.12

Shown here are examples of ordered and unordered lists.

The two lists, on lines 8 through 12 and lines 15 through 19, are virtually identical, except for the type of list designated on lines 8 and 15. In both cases, the content is specified as `<li>`, or list items.

There is a set of properties that applies only to elements that are displayed as list items such as those here:

- **`list-style-type`**—This property is extremely useful for displaying long, multilevel, outline content. It allows us to specify which type of indicators a list should use. The appropriate values are `disc`, `circle`, `square`, `decimal`,

`decimal-leading-zero`, `lower-roman`, `upper-roman`, `lower-greek`, `lower-alpha`, `lower-latin`, `upper-alpha`, `upper-latin`, `hebrew`, `armenian`, `georgian`, `cjk-ideographic`, `hiragana`, `katakana`, `hiragana-iroha`, `katakana-iroha`, and `none`. The default value is `disc`.

We can set different types of lists to use different `list-style-types`. For instance, we can set our unordered list to use square icons, while we set the ordered list to use uppercase Roman numerals using the following style rules:

```
ul { list-style-type: square; }
ol { list-style-type: hebrew;}
```

This results in a display like Figure 1.13.

Figure 1.13

Users can manipulate list types.

- **`list-style-position`**—This property determines how the browser handles a situation where the list item runs to more than one line. The default value is `outside`, where subsequent lines are indented to line up with the text on the first line. We can also set this value to `inside`, where subsequent lines line up with the icon or marker. (Actually, the icon or marker is brought inside to line up with the text, hence the name.)
- **`list-style-image`**—This value gives us the opportunity to specify an actual graphic to use instead of the default circles and squares the browser would normally use. For instance, the style rule

  ```
  li { list-style-image: url(listbutton.jpg); }
  ```

  forces the browser to display our listbutton image instead of the normal disc, as in Figure 1.14.

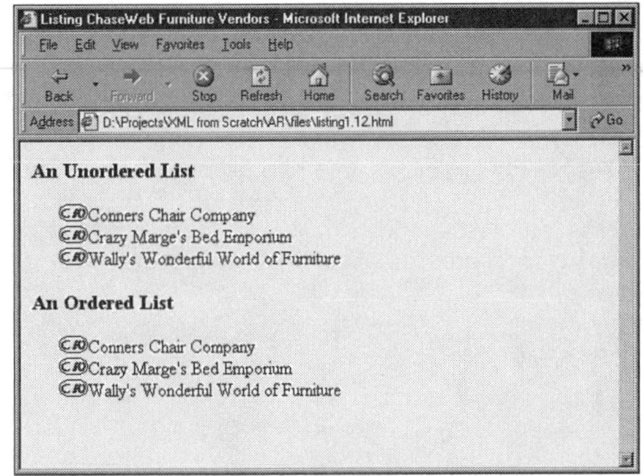

Figure 1.14

List-style-image allows us to specify an image to use instead of the normal disc.

- **`list-style`**—This is a shorthand property, where we can specify, in order, `list-style-type`, `list-style-position`, and `list-style-image`.

Tables

Before we move on to a few of the most general properties, we need to take a look at one more type of item that we discussed earlier: tables.

Tables are a convenient way to organize information on the page into rows and columns. In this case, let's take a look at a few of our vendors and what they sell. In Listing 1.13, we set up the table.

Listing 1.13—Displaying Information in a Table

```
<html>
<head>
    <title>Listing ChaseWeb Furniture Vendors</title>
</head>
<body>

<table border="1">
    <tr>
        <th>Vendor</th>
        <th>Chairs</th>
        <th>Sofas</th>
        <th>Beds</th>
    </tr>
    <tr>
        <td>Conners Chair Company</td>
        <td>yes</td>
        <td>yes</td>
        <td>no</td>
    </tr>
    <tr>
```

Listing 1.13—continued

```
20:         <td>Crazy Marge's Bed Emporium</td>
21:         <td>no</td>
22:         <td>no</td>
23:         <td>yes</td>
24:     </tr>
25:     <tr>
26:         <td>Wally's Wonderful World of Furniture</td>
27:         <td>yes</td>
28:         <td>yes</td>
29:         <td>yes</td>
30:     </tr>
31:</table>
32:
33:</body>
34:</html>
```

An HTML table is perhaps one of the best examples of parent and child elements. The table, which starts on line 6 and ends on line 31, is the parent to four rows, which start on lines 7, 13, 19, and 25. Each of the rows is parent to four table data cells. The browser takes all that information and displays it as in Figure 1.15.

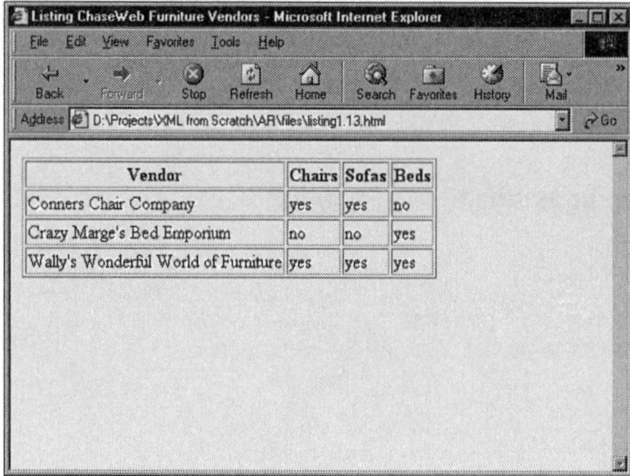

Figure 1.15

Information can be displayed in a table.

In this case, I've turned on the border on line 6 so it's a little clearer to see, but many people use tables solely for formatting purposes, so they leave the border off.

Display and Inheritance

All the style rules we have looked at so far—and all those we haven't, in fact—are affected by two very important properties.

The first of these is the `display` property. `Display` is the very foundation of how an element will be seen. As we mentioned earlier in the chapter, some elements, such as

`<p>` and `<h1>`, are block elements, and some, such as `<b>` or `<i>`, are inline elements. All this is controlled through the `display` property.

The `display` property also controls which properties might apply to a particular element. For example, the `list-style-image` property only applies to elements that have a display value of `list-item`. For all other elements, that property would be ignored.

In general, there are three types of values for the `display` property.

The most commonly used values are `inline`, where the element is rendered within the block that contains it, `block`, where it creates its own block on the page, and `list-item`, which allows the browser to treat the element as a list item element. Also in this category is `none`, which completely removes the item from the page. The element is not hidden; we can't refer to it because it's not there at all.

Next are the table-related values, `table`, `inline-table`, `table-row-group`, `table-header-group`, `table-footer-group`, `table-row`, `table-column-group`, `table-column`, `table-cell`, and `table-caption`.

Finally, there are more advanced values that are not, as a rule, implemented in current browsers: `run-in` and `compact`, which will behave differently depending on how they're used, and `marker`, which enables the author to add content to the page based on the style sheet.

Inheritance

The other important aspect of CSS that doesn't appear to have come up yet is inheritance. Notice that I said that it didn't appear to have come up. In fact, we've been dealing with it all along. Almost every property we've talked about is generally inherited. This means that whatever the value is for an element's parent, that is what it will be for the element itself. That's why when we nest italic (`<i>`) inside a section that's bold, the section becomes bold AND italic.

This makes a lot of sense when you think about it: After all, with more than 100 properties, it would be impossible to worry about making sure that every one of them was set all the time. True, many properties have default values, but if you had a document several layers deep, keeping track of which properties should be in effect and which shouldn't would be a daunting task.

So, in general, an element inherits all the properties and values of its parent. If the element itself has its own values for a property, those values override the inherited values.

Converting Our Content to XML

The nice thing about all this is that by using CSS2 properties for our elements, we can completely control how they're displayed—to the extent that it's supported by the browser, of course.

But in all of this talk about presentation, the structure of the content is getting lost. Sure, a human can look at the page and pick out the meaning of each item, but to a computer, the vendor name is no different from the body of the advertisement; they're both just text to be displayed.

One `<p>` is just like the others, and the fact that text is enclosed in `<b></b>` tags means nothing, structurally.

Fortunately, all this control has given us an advantage: Because we're determining the presentation using properties anyway, there's no reason that we even have to use HTML.

Instead, we can take our page of information and mark up the content itself using XML, and then use CSS to control how the browser renders it.

Our XML Structure

Designing the structure of an XML document happens one of two ways. Sometimes, we have a concept of what it is we want to do, or to document, and from there we can build a structure for our content. This normally involves design concepts that we'll get into in Chapter 3, "Defining the Data Structure: Document Type Definitions, XML Schema, and Parsers."

The second way it happens is a situation like the one we have now: We have content, and we want to make XML out of it. In this case, we look at the logical types of information that we have, and we try to make some sense out of it.

Looking at the page, we have the following types of information:

- Vendor Name
- Advertisement
- Products
- Starting prices
- Product descriptions
- Product prices
- Giveaways
- Weekly Special

That's not to say that all these items are present for every product we're going to sell. In fact, some of the information doesn't have to do with products at all. All of it, however, pertains to the vendor, so it all goes together. We'll probably need several revisions as we take a look at things, so let's take a first stab at it, as in Listing 1.14:

Listing 1.14—The First Try for an XML Version of the Page

```
<vendor>
    <vendor_name>Crazy Marge's Bed Emporium</vendor_name>
    <advertisement>
        We never have a sale because we've got the lowest
        prices in town!  Come in today and shop around. If
        you can find lower prices anywhere Crazy Marge will
        shave her husband's head!!!

        We have all kinds, all sizes. Don't see what you
        want?  Don't worry. We customize orders!
    </advertisement>

    <product_name>Sleepeazy Mattresses</product_name>
    <price>$300</price>
    <product_desc>per set, any size</product_desc>
    <giveaway>Free pillows with every set</giveaway>

    <product_name>CozyComfort Mattresses</product_name>
    <starting_price>starting at only $99.99</starting_price>
    <product_desc>Queen</product_desc><price>$159.00</price>
    <product_desc>King</product_desc><price>$209.00</price>
    <giveaway>Free sheets with every set</giveaway>

    <product_name>Floataway Waterbeds</product_name>
    <giveaway>
        15 different styles to choose from with free
        delivery -- we'll take your old mattress as a trade in!
    </giveaway>

    <weekly_special>
        This week only:  Round beds with rotating motors
        starting at a price that will make your head spin.
        Just talk to Crazy Marge, she'll tell you all about it!
    </weekly_special>
</vendor>
```

Now, none of the content has actually changed. We haven't even changed the order in which it appeared. What we have done, however, is to define the structure of the information using XML tags. That structure looks like Figure 1.16.

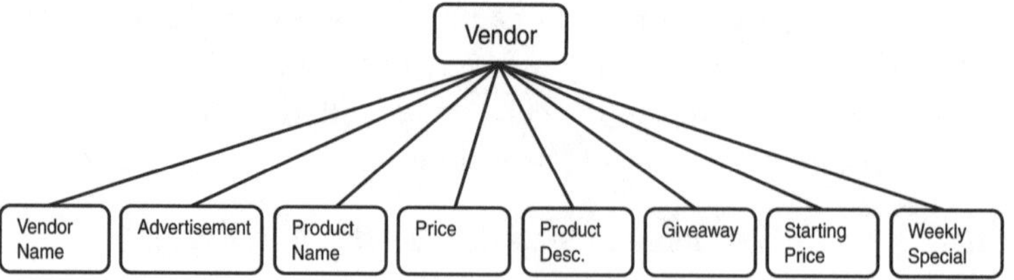

Figure 1.16

Our initial structure is pretty simple, with everything a child of the vendor.

Not bad for a first try, but there are a couple of problems with this structure. As far as the data is concerned, every product description is on the same level as any other product description. The same situation exists for prices. The problem with this is that there's no way to know which price or description goes with which product. We'll need to fix that.

On the presentation end, while the advertisement is correct from a data standpoint, the two distinct paragraphs are going to cause us difficulty later, when we want to treat them as two separate elements.

What we need to do is find a way to put elements together into logical groupings. That brings us to Listing 1.15.

Listing 1.15—Separating Product Information

```
<vendor>
    <vendor_name>Crazy Marge's Bed Emporium</vendor_name>
    <advertisement>
        <ad_sentence>
            We never have a sale because we've got the lowest
            prices in town!  Come in today and shop around. If
            you can find lower prices anywhere Crazy Marge will
            shave her husband's head!!!
        </ad_sentence>

        <ad_sentence>
            We have all kinds, all sizes. Don't see what you
            want?  Don't worry. We customize orders!
        </ad_sentence>
    </advertisement>

    <product>
        <product_name>Sleepeazy Mattresses</product_name>
        <item>
            <price>$300</price>
            <product_desc>per set, any size</product_desc>
        </item>
        <giveaway>Free pillows with every set</giveaway>
    </product>

    <product>
```

Listing 1.15—continued

```
25:        <product_name>CozyComfort Mattresses</product_name>
26:        <starting_price>starting at only $99.99</starting_price>
27:        <item>
28:            <product_desc>Queen</product_desc>
29:            <price>$159.00</price>
30:        </item>
31:        <item>
32:            <product_desc>King</product_desc>
33:            <price>$209.00</price>
34:        </item>
35:        <giveaway>Free sheets with every set</giveaway>
36:    </product>
37:
38:    <product>
39:        <product_name>Floataway Waterbeds</product_name>
40:        <giveaway>
41:            15 different styles to choose from with free
42:            delivery -- we'll take your old mattress as a trade in!
43:        </giveaway>
44:    </product>
45:
46:    <weekly_special>
47:        This week only:  Round beds with rotating motors
48:        starting at a price that will make your head spin.
49:        Just talk to Crazy Marge, she'll tell you all about it!
50:    </weekly_special>
51:</vendor>
```

What we've done here is to group individual pieces of content together into distinct elements. For instance, all the content on lines 16 through 21 is now part of a single product, as is the content on lines 25 through 35, and 29 through 43.

Taking that a step further, we need to recognize that within each product grouping, we can have several items, and we've delineated them on lines 17 through 20, 27 through 30, and 31 through 34.

What we've done is separate out the individual products, and also the subproducts within them, so that we can deal with them programmatically. Let's take a look at the new structure, as shown in Figure 1.17.

Well, that's a bit closer. Now that we have our content, I think we're ready to start working on the presentation.

Our goal here is going to be to produce the same vendor information page we had before, only directly with XML and CSS2 instead of with HTML.

Figure 1.17

A more detailed structure is shown.

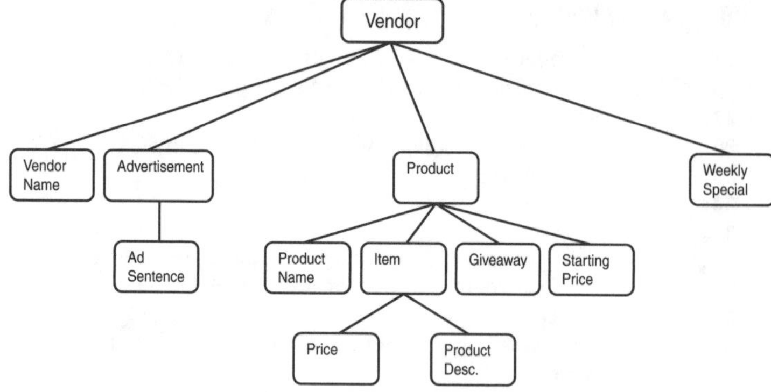

EXCURSION

Why Bother with XML and CSS?

If we can do all of this presentation work with HTML, it might seem a little silly to go through the work of duplicating that functionality with XML and CSS. The fact is, however, that these are important concepts, for a couple of reasons.

First, it's important to realize that we can manipulate the actual content in lots of ways without actually changing it. It's impossible to stress the separation of content and presentation too much.

Second, one of the most powerful features of XML is our ability to manipulate it in ways we haven't even thought of using. In Chapter 9, "Other Applications for XML (SOAP)," we'll look at taking these same concepts and using them to output our XML for different media. For instance, rather than serve a traditional Web page, we can convert our XML to a PDF document, which will be displayed on any browser precisely the way we intended it to, even if the browser doesn't understand XML at all.

We'll start by creating the XML page and the style sheet, and then we'll add to the style sheet as we go along. Our starting page is shown in Listing 1.16.

Listing 1.16—Combining XML with a Style Sheet

```
<?xml version="1.0"?>
<?xml-stylesheet href="vendor.css" type="text/css"?>

<vendor>
    <vendor_name>Crazy Marge's Bed Emporium</vendor_name>
    <advertisement>
        <ad_sentence>
            We never have a sale because we've got the lowest
            prices in town!  Come in today and shop around. If
            you can find lower prices anywhere Crazy Marge will
            shave her husband's head!!!
        </ad_sentence>
        <ad_sentence>
```

Listing 1.16—continued

```
            We have all kinds, all sizes. Don't see what you
            want?  Don't worry. We customize orders!
        </ad_sentence>
    </advertisement>

    <product>
        <product_name>Sleepeazy Mattresses</product_name>
        <item>
            <price>$300</price>
            <product_desc>per set, any size</product_desc>
        </item>
        <giveaway>Free pillows with every set</giveaway>
    </product>

    <product>
        <product_name>CozyComfort Mattresses</product_name>
        <starting_price>starting at only $99.99</starting_price>
        <item>
            <product_desc>Queen</product_desc>
            <price>$159.00</price>
        </item>
        <item>
            <product_desc>King</product_desc>
            <price>$209.00</price>
        </item>
        <giveaway>Free sheets with every set</giveaway>
    </product>

    <product>
        <product_name>Floataway Waterbeds</product_name>
        <giveaway>
            15 different styles to choose from with free
            delivery -- we'll take your old mattress as a trade in!
        </giveaway>
    </product>

    <weekly_special>
        This week only:  Round beds with rotating motors
        starting at a price that will make your head spin.
        Just talk to Crazy Marge, she'll tell you all about it!
    </weekly_special>
</vendor>
```

As we have mentioned previously, no browser does everything. At the time of this writing, this functionality was not yet fully implemented in Netscape 6, so we've been using Microsoft Internet Explorer 5.5 (with the exception of Figure 1.13 which is best viewable in Netscape). If you have trouble getting functionality to work, it is most likely because of the browser you're using.

Now that we're working strictly in XML, we needed to change the format a little bit. First of all, we're now working with an *.xml file—in this case, `marge.xml`—instead of an HTML file. This way the browser knows it needs to treat things a bit differently. Also on line 0 we are telling the browser not only that we're dealing with XML, but also which version. One line 1, we have a slightly altered syntax from the `<link>` tag that is XML's way of retrieving the style sheet, which is shown in Listing 1.17.

Listing 1.17—The Beginning Style Sheet

```
* {
font-family:Arial, Helvetica, sans-serif;
}
```

Taking a look at what we have in Figure 1.18, we see that we've lost everything we had gained as far as presentation is concerned. We'll start by recovering the basic structure of the document.

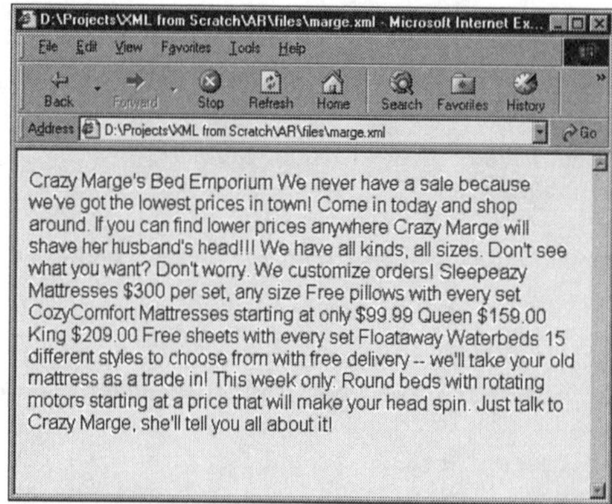

Figure 1.18

Now that we've removed all HTML clues, the browser treats the entire document as one big text block.

To start out, let's set the major elements to be shown as blocks, as in Listing 1.18.

Listing 1.18—Setting Elements As Blocks

```
* {
   font-family:Arial, Helvetica, sans-serif;
   }

vendor_name {
    display: block;
    }

advertisement {
    display: block;
    }
```

Listing 1.18—continued

```
product {
    display: block;
    }

weekly_special {
    display: block;
    }
```

All we did was set the `display` property for the first child level of elements, `vendor_name`, `advertisement`, `product`, and `weekly_special`, so there won't be much difference at this point, as we can see in Figure 1.19.

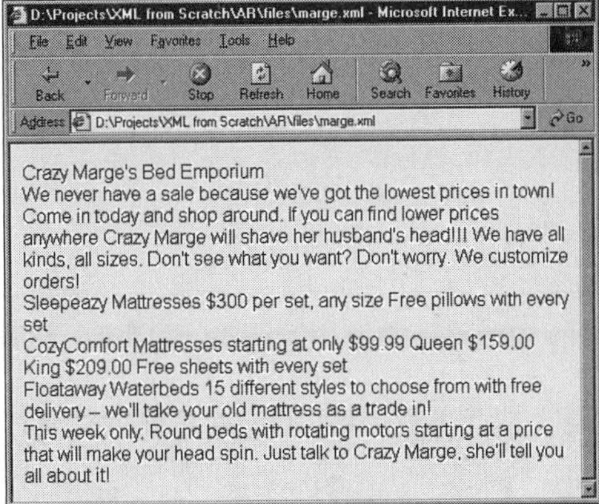

Figure 1.19

First we separate the elements into blocks.

Now let's start adding some formatting, and separating some of the elements that still need to become blocks, as in Listing 1.19.

Listing 1.19—Adding Formatting and Correcting Problems

```
*  {
    font-family:Arial, Helvetica, sans-serif;
    }

vendor_name {
    display: block;
    font-weight: bold;
    font-size: x-large;
    }

advertisement {
    display: block;
    margin: 20px 0px;
    }
```

Listing 1.19—continued

```

product {
    display: block;
    margin: 20px 0px;
    }

product_name {
    display: block;
    font-weight: bold;
    }

item {
    display: block;
    }

giveaway {
    display: block;
    }

weekly_special {
    display: block;
    margin: 20px 0px;
    }
```

This actually gets us pretty close, as we can see in Figure 1.20.

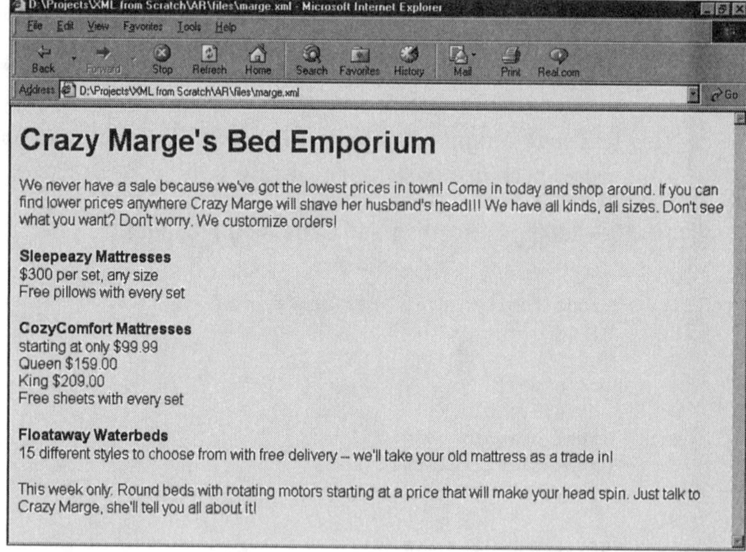

Figure 1.20

We are getting closer...

But we still need to separate out the individual paragraphs under the advertisements. Also, we have two new problems.

First, because we set the product names as blocks, we have no way to make the starting price appear on the same line, where it was before. To solve this problem, we'll have to make the product name an inline element as in Listing 1.20. This is less of a problem than it seems, however, as the items that appear below it are already block elements, so only the starting price will wind up on the same line.

The second problem is a bit tougher to solve. In our original file, the first part of the giveaway, which mentioned the item itself, was in italic, and the second part, which offered more information, was normal. Because this is currently a single element, we have no way to accomplish this directly with the style sheet.

What we have here is a common occurrence. Granted, we didn't take an inordinate amount of time defining the structure of our XML file, but even if we had, it would have been inevitable that after we started working with it, we discovered things that had been left out. This is why it is so important to test the structure as we go along. Programmers are not the only ones who can be tripped up by skipping this vital step!

To solve this problem, we'll go back to the original XML file and make the changes in Listing 1.21. We'll also add the relevant formatting to the style sheet in Listing 1.20.

Listing 1.20—The Final Style Sheet

```
*  {
    font-family:Arial, Helvetica, sans-serif;
    }

vendor_name {
    display: block;
    font-weight: bold;
    font-size: x-large;
    }

advertisement {
    display: block;
    margin: 20px 0px;
    }
ad_sentence {
    display: block;
    margin: 10px 0px;
    }

product {
    display: block;
    margin: 20px 0px;
```

Listing 1.20—continued

```
    }

product_name {
    display: inline;
    font-weight: bold;
    }

item {
    display: block;
    }

giveaway {
    display: block;
    }

giveaway_item {
    font-style: italic;
    }

weekly_special {
    display: block;
    margin: 20px 0px;
    position: absolute;
    top: 200px;
    left: 300px;
    width: 300px;
    border-style: outset;
    border-width: 5px;
    background-image: url(vfimage.jpg)
    }
```

Listing 1.21—The Final XML File

```
<?xml version="1.0"?>
<?xml-stylesheet href="vendor.css" type="text/css"?>

<vendor>
    <vendor_name>Crazy Marge's Bed Emporium</vendor_name>
    <advertisement>
        <ad_sentence>
            We never have a sale because we've got the lowest
            prices in town!  Come in today and shop around. If
            you can find lower prices anywhere Crazy Marge will
            shave her husband's head!!!
        </ad_sentence>
        <ad_sentence>
            We have all kinds, all sizes. Don't see what you
            want?  Don't worry. We customize orders!
        </ad_sentence>
    </advertisement>

```

Listing 1.21—continued

```
    <product>
        <product_name>Sleepeazy Mattresses</product_name>
        <item>
            <price>$300</price>
            <product_desc>per set, any size</product_desc>
        </item>
        <giveaway>
            <giveaway_item>
                Free pillows
            </giveaway_item>
            <giveaway_desc>
                with every set
            </giveaway_desc>
        </giveaway>
    </product>

    <product>
        <product_name>CozyComfort Mattresses</product_name>
        <starting_price>starting at only $99.99</starting_price>
        <item>
            <product_desc>Queen</product_desc>
            <price>$159.00</price>
        </item>
        <item>
            <product_desc>King</product_desc>
            <price>$209.00</price>
        </item>
        <giveaway>
            <giveaway_item>
                Free sheets
            </giveaway_item>
            <giveaway_desc>
                with every set
            </giveaway_desc>
        </giveaway>
    </product>

    <product>
        <product_name>Floataway Waterbeds</product_name>
        <giveaway>
            <giveaway_item>
                15 different styles to choose from
            </giveaway_item>
            <giveaway_desc>
                with free delivery -- we'll take your
                old mattress as a trade in!
            </giveaway_desc>
        </giveaway>
    </product>

```

Listing 1.21—continued

```
    <weekly_special>
        This week only:  Round beds with rotating motors
        starting at a price that will make your head spin.
        Just talk to Crazy Marge, she'll tell you all about it!
    </weekly_special>
</vendor>
```

While we were in the file tweaking for the giveaways and advertisements, we also made the weekly special more prominent, by moving it to an otherwise empty area of the page. The final result is shown in Figure 1.21. And with absolutely no HTML tags!

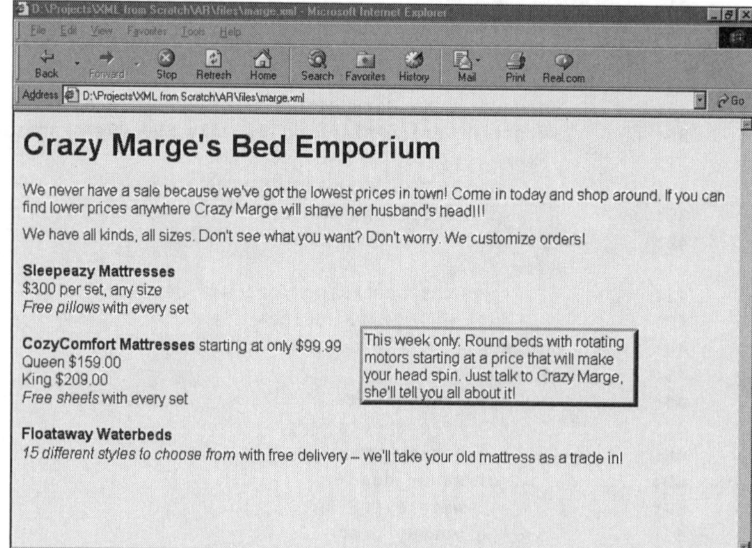

Figure 1.21

The final result of styling our XML data is shown here.

Next Steps

In this chapter, we learned the basics of a markup language by examining HTML in the creation of a listing page for one of our sites' vendors. We then used Cascading Style Sheets to influence the presentation of that HTML. Finally, we converted our HTML page into XML, and used CSS to create a Web page without any HTML, separating content from presentation.

In the next chapter, "Product Pages: Transforming XML in the Browser," we're going to take this concept of separation one step further, as we look at an even more powerful way of styling XML: Extensible Stylesheet Language, or XSL. Where

Cascading Style Sheets allow us to change the way data looks, XSL will actually give us the opportunity to affect the data itself, changing the order, making lists, even adding links to other pages based on the data. All of this will allow us to create much fuller listings for our vendors, linking to pages that display the products they offer for sale.

In this chapter

- *The Two Faces of XSL*
- *Trees: The Basic Structure of XML*
- *Well-Formedness*
- *Building the Style Sheet*
- *Getting Specific—Using XPath*
- *Looping and Sorting*
- *Adding Elements and Attributes*
- *Conditionals*
- *Next Steps*

Chapter 2

Product Pages: Transforming XML in the Browser Using XSL

Chapter 1 talked about markup languages in general and HTML and XML in particular. Specifically, we discussed the separation of content and presentation.

One of the ways we did that was to take our HTML content, which was rich in presentation but didn't give us a lot of information about the content, and change it to XML, which told us everything we needed to know about the content but nothing about the presentation. We then used Cascading Style Sheets (CSSs) to control the presentation of our XML elements.

In this chapter, we take this a step further. Extensible Stylesheet Language, or XSL, allows you to do everything you could do with CSSs and much more.

The Two Faces of XSL: XSL Transformations and XSL Formatting Objects

XSL is actually a pair of potential standards, XSL Transformations or XSLT (version 1.0 of which is already a full W3C Recommendation, and version 1.1 of which has been proposed), and XSL Formatting Objects, or XSLFO. Each is designed to do a different task when it comes to XML data.

XSLT allows us to take XML content and literally transform it into something else, whether that something else is an HTML page, a text file, or even another XML document. We can choose the content we want to display, add content, or even reorder the content that is there. XSLT can work in conjunction with CSS by converting XML to HTML and adding CSS style information to those tags, or by simply creating the page to which CSS information is later applied.

XSLFO is similar to CSS. In fact, not only does it do the same thing as CSS, it is based on CSS and uses essentially the same attributes and values as its predecessor. So, why do we need it? Why not use CSS exclusively?

One of the strengths of XML is the fact that it can be used on many different platforms and not just a browser. Because of this, you could easily find yourself in a situation where your environment understands XML, but the HTML that contains or refers to the style information means nothing.

XSL Formatting Objects become part of the "result tree" you end up with after a transformation and can be processed by any application that supports them.

Getting Ready

At the time of this writing, only one major browser supports XSLT. That browser is Microsoft Internet Explorer 5 and 5.5. As installed, however, it uses an older working draft of the Recommendation. Using the Recommendation requires downloading the latest version of MSXML3.

Installing MSXML3

Although it should be straightforward to download and install MSXML3, there have been numerous reports of systems that cease all XSL processing after it has been installed. Users have two options:

- Install MSXML3 in "side-by-side" mode, which is the default, making sure to back up `c:\windows\system\MSXML.DLL` first. If this file is corrupted and XSL processing stops, replacing it with the backup should allow you to at least use the following option.
- Keep the default installation and use the working draft. Most of the information covered in this chapter is the same for both, and we'll note the one exception where it's not. Later, when we move to processing XSLT on the server instead of the client, we can use the Recommendation in its entirety, producing XHTML pages so that we don't need to worry about browser support for XSL when we build our applications.

Installation of MSXML3 involves the following steps:

1. Make sure that you have the Windows Installer on your machine. It can be downloaded from

   `http://www.microsoft.com/msdownload/platformsdk/instmsi.htm`

   Install this software, close the browser, and restart it.

2. Download the software. We are using the release version of MSXML3 with Microsoft Internet Explorer 5.5 It can currently be found at

   `http://msdn.microsoft.com/xml/c-frame.htm?/xml/general/xmlparser.asp`

If you have a previous version of MSXML installed, you may want to upgrade at this point, as some of the results we'll be seeing in this chapter differ with each version.

3. Make a backup copy of `c:\windows\system\MSXML.DLL`, as mentioned previously.
4. Run the downloaded file by double-clicking the msxml3.exe file.
5. In some cases, this might not complete the installation, as the default is "side-by-side mode," which leaves the old DLL intact. You will be able to tell when you run the following test. If you find that you don't see the results of the test, you may need to run an additional installation file, `xmlinst.exe`. It can be downloaded from

   `http://msdn.microsoft.com/downloads/default.asp?URL=/code/sample.asp?url=/msdn-files/027/001/469/msdncompositedoc.xml`

   After you have downloaded it, double-click it to uncompress the files. Be sure to make note of where you've uncompressed them to. In a Command Prompt window, change to that directory and type

   ```
   xmlinst
   ```

   This will complete the installation.

Although I have yet to see it, Microsoft warns that some systems can become unstable after running `xmlinst.exe`, so run it only if you can't get the installation to pass the following test. To undo the effects of `xmlinst.exe`, navigate to the appropriate directory and type

```
xmlinst /u
```

Testing the Installation

To make sure the new software is being used, create the following two files in Listings 2.1 and 2.2 in the same directory. Don't worry about the content for now—we'll be looking at what it all means as soon as we know the software's working properly.

Listing 2.1—`test.xml`

```
<?xml version='1.0'?>
<?xml:stylesheet type="text/xsl" href="test.xsl"?>
<document>
    <message>
        It worked!
    </message>
</document>
```

Listing 2.2—`test.xsl`

```
<?xml version='1.0'?>
<xsl:stylesheet version="1.0"
    xmlns:xsl="http://www.w3.org/1999/XSL/Transform">

<xsl:template match="/">
    <html>
    <body>
        <h1><xsl:value-of select="//message" /></h1>
    </body>
    </html>
</xsl:template>

</xsl:stylesheet>
```

Using File, Open, open `test.xml` in Internet Explorer. You should see results similar to Figure 2.1.

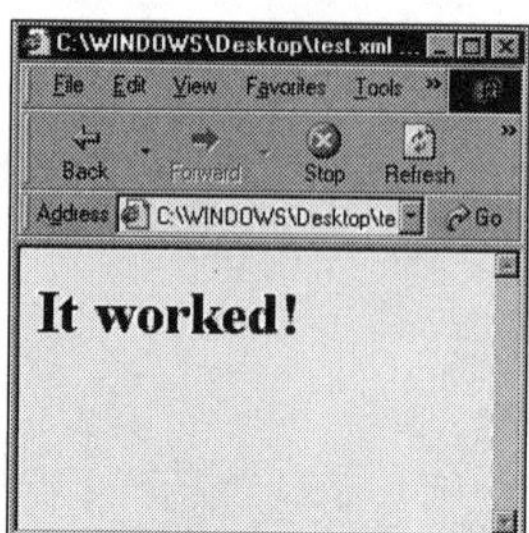

Figure 2.1

If MSXML3 has been installed properly, you will see results in the browser window.

If you don't see any results, make sure that you haven't omitted any steps in the installation. If all else fails, use the working draft. As we go along, we'll see how that works.

What We're Shooting For

Our ultimate goal is to take the complete XML file of vendors and products and turn it into a simple, one-page catalog like the one shown in Figure 2.2.

Figure 2.2

We'll use XSL to create a simple catalog page.

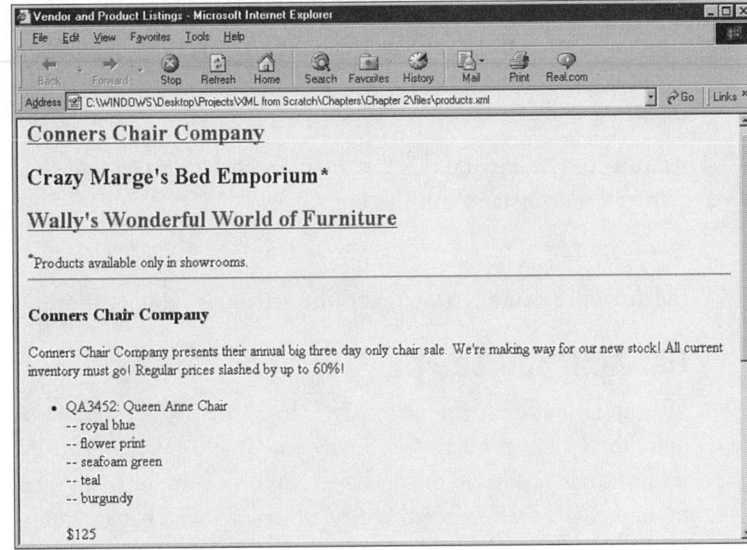

There's just one hitch: We can't use a normal CSS style sheet, as we did before.

Instead, we have to convert our raw XML data into XHTML. In addition, we have to find a way to attach style information to it.

It turns out that there's more than one way to use CSS2 properties. In addition to creating a style sheet, we can take the style information and put it directly into an HTML tag. For instance, the following XHTML text will look like Figure 2.3:

```
<p style="border: solid 1px red;font-weight:bold;">
This text should be bold, with a red border around it.</p>
```

Figure 2.3

Style information can be placed directly into an XHTML tag.

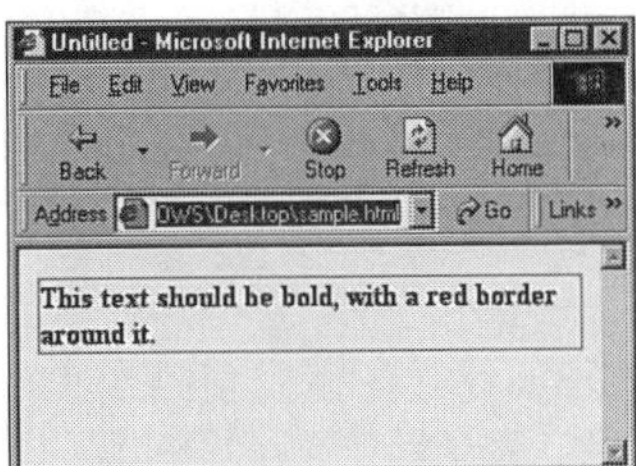

Placing style information directly into tags is definitely not recommended for sites of more than a few pages because it makes maintenance difficult. Use external style sheets instead.

In this case, the style information is contained in an attribute of the <p> tag. Other familiar information, such as the `href=` for an <a> tag or the `src=` for an <img> tag, are also attributes. An attribute gives useful information about the tag and its contents.

Attribute—An attribute is information about an element that's contained within its start tag. For instance, in the tag

```
<p align="left">
```

the attribute name is `align`, and the attribute value is `left`.

Our XML Source File

We can also add attributes to XML tags. In Listing 2.3, we've added two more vendors, the Conners Chair Company and Wally's Wonderful World of Furniture, as well as their products, to our basic XML document from Chapter 1, "Vendor Pages: Styling XML with Cascading Style Sheets." The basic structure is exactly the same as the one we used for Crazy Marge in Chapter 1, so it should look familiar. Crazy Marge herself is now at the end of the file. We've also changed some of the information in her listing slightly to accommodate the additional data we're storing.

Listing 2.3—`products.xml`: Our Source XML

```
<?xml version="1.0"?>

<products>
<vendor webvendor="full">
    <vendor_name>Conners Chair Company</vendor_name>
    <advertisement>
        <ad_sentence>
        Conners Chair Company presents their annual big three
        day only chair sale. We're making way for our new
        stock!  All current inventory must go!    Regular prices
        slashed by up to 60%!
        </ad_sentence>
    </advertisement>

    <product>
        <product_id>QA3452</product_id>
        <short_desc>Queen Anne Chair</short_desc>
        <price pricetype="cost">$85</price>
        <price pricetype="sale">$125</price>
        <price pricetype="retail">$195</price>
        <inventory color="royal blue" location="warehouse">
            12</inventory>
        <inventory color="royal blue" location="showroom">
            5</inventory>
        <inventory color="flower print" location="warehouse">
```

Listing 2.3—continued

```
            16</inventory>
        <inventory color="flower print" location="showroom">
            3</inventory>
        <inventory color="seafoam green" location="warehouse">
            20</inventory>
        <inventory color="teal" location="warehouse">
            14</inventory>
        <inventory color="burgundy" location="warehouse">
            34</inventory>
        <giveaway>
            <giveaway_item>
            Matching Ottoman included
            </giveaway_item>
            <giveaway_desc>
            while supplies last
            </giveaway_desc>
        </giveaway>
    </product>

    <product>
        <product_id>RC2342</product_id>
        <short_desc>Early American Rocking Chair</short_desc>
        <product_desc>
            with brown and tan plaid upholstery
        </product_desc>
        <price pricetype="cost">$75</price>
        <price pricetype="sale">$62</price>
        <price pricetype="retail">$120</price>
        <inventory location="warehouse">40</inventory>
        <inventory location="showroom">2</inventory>
    </product>

    <product>
        <product_id>BR3452</product_id>
        <short_desc>Bentwood Rocker</short_desc>
        <price pricetype="cost">$125</price>
        <price pricetype="sale">$160</price>
        <price pricetype="retail">$210</price>
        <inventory location="showroom">3</inventory>
    </product>

</vendor>

<vendor webvendor="partial">
    <vendor_name>
        Wally's Wonderful World of Furniture
    </vendor_name>
    <advertisement>
        <ad_sentence>
        Wally's Wonderful World of Furniture is closing its
        doors forever. Last chance to get great bargains.
```

Listing 2.3—continued

```
        Make us an offer. We can't refuse!
        </ad_sentence>
    </advertisement>

    <suite>
        <product_id>CDRS</product_id>
        <short_desc>Complete Dining Room Set</short_desc>
        <long_desc>
            This five piece dining set features swivel
            chairs with cushions in five exciting colors.
        </long_desc>
        <price pricetype="cost">$435</price>
        <price pricetype="sale">$699</price>
        <price pricetype="retail">$999</price>

        <product>
            <product_id>WWWdrt</product_id>
            <short_desc>Dining Room Table</short_desc>
            <price pricetype="cost">$105</price>
            <price pricetype="sale">$145</price>
            <price pricetype="retail">$195</price>
            <inventory location="warehouse">132</inventory>
        </product>
        <product>
            <product_id>WWWsc</product_id>
            <short_desc>Swivel Chair</short_desc>
            <price pricetype="cost">$50</price>
            <price pricetype="sale">$45</price>
            <price pricetype="retail">$99</price>
            <inventory location="warehouse">300</inventory>
        </product>
        <product>
            <product_id>WWWhch</product_id>
            <short_desc>Hutch</short_desc>
            <price pricetype="cost">$346</price>
            <price pricetype="sale">$425</price>
            <price pricetype="retail">$600</price>
            <inventory location="warehouse">232</inventory>
        </product>
    </suite>

    <product>
        <short_desc>Hall Bench</short_desc>
        <price pricetype="cost">$75</price>
        <price pricetype="sale">$62</price>
        <price pricetype="retail">$120</price>
        <inventory location="warehouse">143</inventory>
        <inventory location="showroom">5</inventory>
    </product>

    <product>
```

Listing 2.3—continued

```
        <short_desc>Sofa and Love Seat</short_desc>
        <price color="magnolia print" pricetype="cost">
             $125</price>
        <price color="nautical print" pricetype="cost">
             $145</price>
        <price pricetype="sale">$175</price>
        <price pricetype="retail">$250</price>
        <inventory color="magnolia print" location="showroom">
             3</inventory>
        <inventory color="magnolia print" location="warehouse">
             36</inventory>
        <inventory color="nautical print" location="warehouse">
             1</inventory>
        <inventory color="nautical print" location="showroom">
             432</inventory>
    </product>

</vendor>

<vendor webvendor="no">
    <vendor_name>Crazy Marge's Bed Emporium</vendor_name>
    <advertisement>
        <ad_sentence>
        We never have a sale because we've got the lowest
        prices in town!  Come in today and shop around. If
        you can find lower prices anywhere Crazy Marge will
        shave her husband's head!!!
        </ad_sentence>
        <ad_sentence>
        We have all kinds, all sizes. Don't see what you
        want?  Don't worry. We customize orders!
        </ad_sentence>
    </advertisement>

    <product>
        <product_id>3253435</product_id>
        <short_desc>Sleepeazy Mattresses</short_desc>
        <price pricetype="cost">$162</price>
        <price pricetype="retail">$300</price>
        <product_desc>per set, any size</product_desc>
        <giveaway>
            <giveaway_item>
            Free pillows
            </giveaway_item>
            <giveaway_desc>
            with every set
            </giveaway_desc>
        </giveaway>
        <inventory location="showroom">23</inventory>
        <inventory location="warehouse">15</inventory>
    </product>
```

Listing 2.3—continued

```
    <product>
        <product_id>5622345</product_id>
        <short_desc>CozyComfort Mattresses</short_desc>
        <price pricetype="starting">
            starting at only $99.99
        </price>
        <item>
            <product_desc>Queen</product_desc>
            <price pricetype="cost">$59.00</price>
            <price pricetype="sale">$69.00</price>
            <price pricetype="retail">$99.00</price>
        </item>
        <item>
            <product_desc>King</product_desc>
            <price pricetype="cost">$159.00</price>
            <price pricetype="sale">$209.00</price>
            <price pricetype="retail">$359.00</price>
        </item>
        <giveaway>
            <giveaway_item>
            Free sheets
            </giveaway_item>
            <giveaway_desc>
            with every set
            </giveaway_desc>
        </giveaway>
    </product>

    <product>
        <product_id>39981234</product_id>
        <short_desc>Floataway Waterbeds</short_desc>
        <giveaway>
            <giveaway_item>
            15 different styles to choose from
            </giveaway_item>
            <giveaway_desc>
            with free delivery -- we'll take your
            old mattress as a trade in!
            </giveaway_desc>
        </giveaway>
    </product>

    <special specialtype="weekly">
        This week only:  Round beds with rotating motors
        starting at a price that will make your head spin.
        Just talk to Crazy Marge, she'll tell you all about it!
    </special>
</vendor>

</products>
```

Attributes do more than just describe data. They can also allow us to have different values of data in a single element type and have it still make sense. For instance, notice that on lines 87 through 89, we have three different elements that apply to the Complete Dining Room Set. Because we have the `pricetype` attribute to tell us what each one of them is, we can call them all `price`. Later, we'll look at how to extract that attribute information.

Trees: The Basic Structure of XML

In Chapter 1, we talked about XML as a markup language and used it to display information on a page. In this capacity, it's little more than text—albeit specifically structured text. In actuality, there's much more to that structure than just neatness.

At its heart, XML is data. It might not be reader-friendly data, but it is data. And for data to be readable by something as simple-minded as a computer—as opposed to the human brain—it has to be organized logically.

In XML, we call this structure a *tree*. Each tree has a root, branches, and leaves, and each serves a specific purpose.

I can't stress enough how important it is to understand this. Just about every single thing we do from here on is going to involve the idea of an XML document as a tree, so let's take a few minutes to get our concepts and terminology straight.

To demonstrate, let's look at our XML document in Microsoft Internet Explorer 5. IE has a default style sheet that tells it to render an XML file as a collapsible tree of sorts. Choose File, Open and select an XML file. In our case, the result looks like Figure 2.3.

If you don't want to type all of Listing 2.3, you can download `products.xml` from the Que Web site at `http://www.quecorp.com`. (You can also download it from `http://www.nicholaschase.com/xmlfs/`.)

A minus sign before the text means that the element has been expanded, whereas a plus sign indicates that there's more data that's not being shown. To start, click the first minus sign to hide all the elements but the first one, as shown in Figure 2.4.

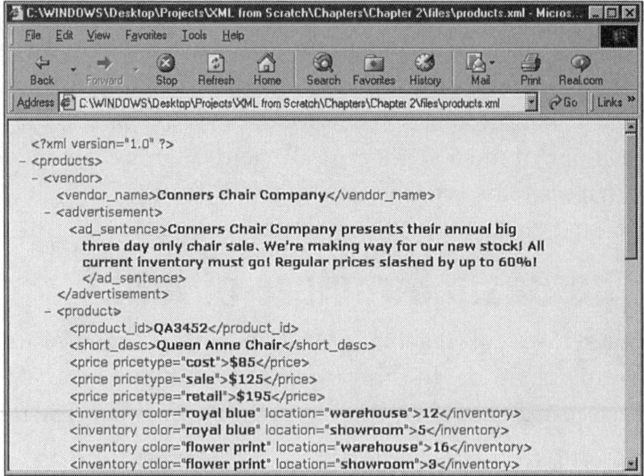

Figure 2.4

Internet Explorer automatically renders XML as a collapsible tree if no other style sheet is specified.

Figure 2.5

The root element of our document can be collapsed to hide the data.

Every XML tree has a root, although sometimes people get confused as to what that root represents. You see, there's the document root, which in this case is actually the document itself, and the root element, which is the `products` element contained in the document.

Document root—The document root is the actual document itself and is the parent of the root element.

Root element—The root element is the topmost element in a document. It is the child of the document itself and contains all the other elements in the document as descendants.

The root of a valid XML document must contain one and only one root element.

Now this element, `products`, may be called several things. It is, as mentioned, the root element. It is also a node and may be referred to as the root node.

EXCURSION

Hierarchical Versus Serialized Trees

The more experienced user might notice that we have been referring to nodes in an XML document, which, strictly speaking, isn't precisely accurate. The XML text file that we humans look at is known as a serialized version of the XML tree. It isn't until the serialized version is loaded into memory and becomes the in memory tree that nodes, parents, children, and so on are created.

Conceptually, however, it is useful to think of them that way from the start, even if it might not be semantically accurate.

There are several types of nodes. In this case, we're dealing with an element node because that's what it represents—an element.

An important thing to notice is that the root node has the document itself as its parent. It also has children, as shown in Figure 2.6.

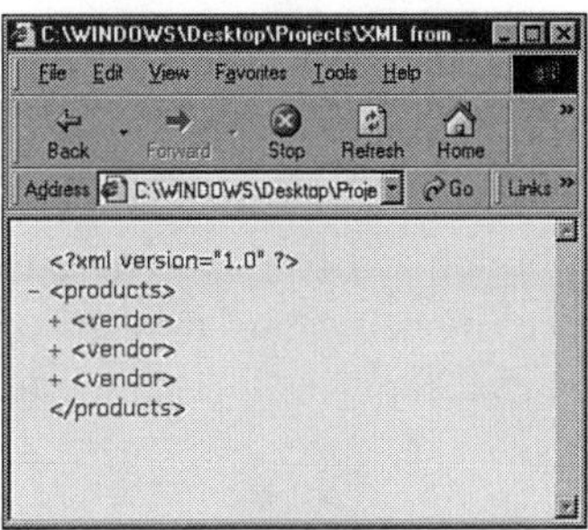

Figure 2.6

Expanding the root element shows its children.

Each of the `vendor` elements, as seen in Figure 2.6, is a child of the root element, `products`. Because they, too, have plus signs in front of them, we know that they also contain other elements. So we know the following about the `vendor` elements:

- They all share the same parent, the `products` node.
- Because they all share the same parent, they are siblings to each other.
- They contain other element nodes, and each of them is an element node, also known as a branch.
- Because they all contain other nodes, each of them has one or more child nodes.

If we go ahead and expand the first `vendor` element, we can get more information, as shown in Figure 2.7.

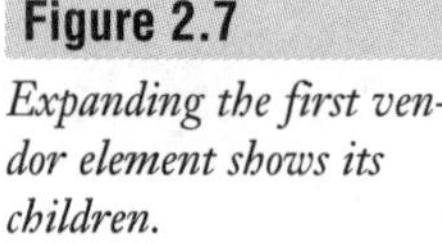

Figure 2.7

Expanding the first vendor element shows its children.

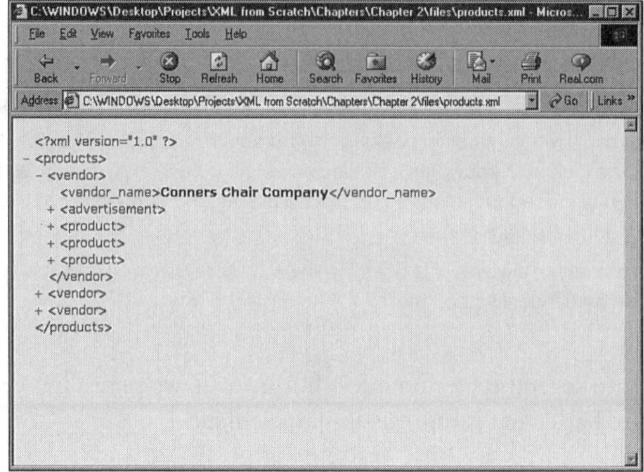

In this case, we've expanded the first `vendor` element but then closed all its child elements to make things a bit easier to read.

The `vendor` element actually has five child nodes: `vendor_name`, `advertisement`, and three `product` nodes. Not all of these are the same, however.

The `vendor_name` node does not contain any further elements. We can tell because there's no plus or minus sign before the name, and we can see the data right on the screen. Because of this, we can say that the `vendor_name` node, which is an element node, contains a text node (or leaf).

The rest of `vendor`'s children, however, also element nodes, contain children which are also element nodes.

Expanding the second `product` node shows even more information, all of it contained in elements with text node children.

To review, all those text nodes, such as `price` and `inventory`, are children of the `product` node, which is a child of the `vendor` node, which is a child of the `products` node. Overall, the structure of the document looks like Figure 2.8.

Applying the Structure to XSL

Why are we bothering to stress this? Because it's important to understand that when we build an XSL style sheet, we're not just creating a string of text.

On the contrary, we will be using the source tree (created from the original XML document) to create the result tree, which in this case just happens to look like an XHTML document. Later, when we start to do actual programming, the difference will become blindingly clear.

Figure 2.8

The structure of our XML document can change as we add more information.

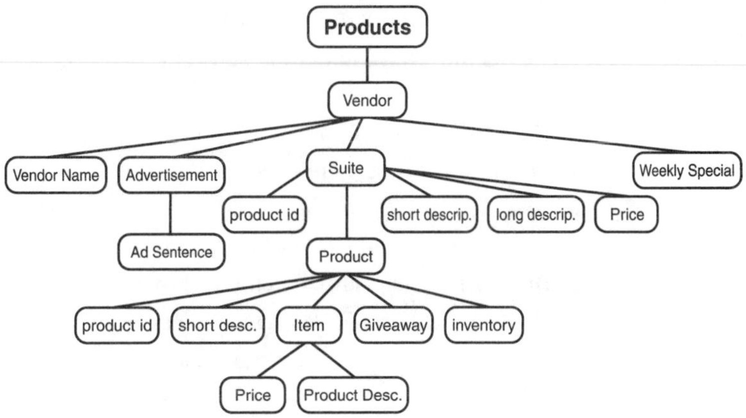

2

So, using the `product_id` as an example, let's look at the way in which a tree, in this case the source tree, is built (or grown, I suppose!).

First comes the document root, which, arguably, does not itself contain any information. To that we add the `products` node (also known as the root element because it's the one and only element which is a child of the document root) to the tree. To the `products` node, add a `vendor` node. To the `vendor` node, we add a `product` node, and then finally we add the `product_id` text node to its parent, the `product` node.

This will become more natural as we move into XSL, which is mostly the business of building a result tree using information from the source tree. The result tree can then be output, or serialized, similar to the way that we viewed the XML file in Chapter 1.

EXCURSION

Why Bother with Trees?

If all we were going to do was output text to a browser, it would be overkill to worry about nodes and result trees and the like.

As it happens, however, we're going to do a lot more with both the source tree and the result tree as we go along. Either can be processed by other applications, which will need the tree structure to interpret them.

Well-Formedness

One of the major differences between XML and traditional HTML is the need for XML to be well formed. This means that unlike an HTML 4.0 document, an XML document must meet the following criteria:

- It must have exactly one root element.
- All elements must have matching start and end tags. This includes case. <H1> and </H1> match, but <H1> and </h1> do not.
- All attributes must be in quotes. This is a common-sense rule, but HTML browsers often let authors get away without it.
- All elements must nest properly. This means that when we see a start tag for one element, we should never see anything but a completely nested subelement or an end tag for the original element. For instance,

  ```
  <B>This is my <I>tiger</I>. He is ferocious.</B>
  ```

  is well formed, but

  ```
  <B>This is my <I>tiger</B>. He is ferocious.</I>
  ```

  is not.

We've used HTML for many of these examples because it's familiar to many people, but HTML brings up a good point. What about the so-called empty elements, such as <br> or <hr>? They don't even have end tags, so how can we use them properly?

Well, that's not completely accurate. XHTML 1.0 is an XML version of the familiar HTML standard. Much of it remains the same, except for the preceding rules, of course, but one change is that elements such as <br> now have end tags. So, a line break is now actually
</br>.

Of course, it would be not just cumbersome but a little silly to worry about end tags for empty elements all the time, so XML has a solution. Empty elements actually have their own shorthand format. So,

```
<br></br>
```

becomes

```
<br/>
```

This way, the browser or other processor recognizes that the element has both started and ended.

Of course, this would seem to have limited application in XML itself outside of XHTML, but that's not actually true. Because of attributes, an empty element can carry quite a bit of information. For instance, we may have an empty XML tag that looks like this:

```
<saleitem permissible="yes"/>
```

We could then look for elements that contain this subelement to know what items we could put on sale.

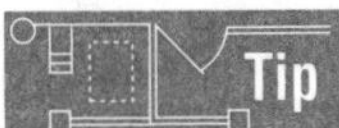

Because XML must be well formed, any application trying to read it should give an error if it's not. Because of this, we can use Internet Explorer to check the file for any incorrect tags, missing slashes, and so on by simply using it to open the document.

Building the Style Sheet

Now that we've got the basics down, let's start building our style sheet. The style sheet we'll use to process our XML document is actually an XML document itself, so let's start with the root element, as shown in Listing 2.2.

Listing 2.4—`catalog.xsl`: The Most Basic Style Sheet

```
1: <?xml version="1.0"?>
2: <xsl:stylesheet>
3: </xsl:stylesheet>
```

There's not a lot to this style sheet. In fact, it has only two items, really: the processing instruction on line 1 to tell the program (in this case, the browser) that this is an XML document, and the root element, `<xsl:stylesheet>`.

That root element, though, is something new. The `xsl:` part is to tell the browser that there's something special about this tag; it's not part of the normal XML. It is, in fact, an XSLT element.

Well, that's all well and good, but that's not enough information for the browser to know what to do with it, so we'd better provide some more.

In fact, this `<xsl:stylesheet>` syntax is part of an often misunderstood aspect of XML called XML Names, or namespaces. Namespaces are intended to help us separate out elements that either serve different purposes or come from different sources. This way, we can separate out the XSL commands from the other elements we're going to be using to format our text.

Of course, now that we've told the browser that we're using a namespace, we still have to tell it what namespace that is. The `xsl:` notation, you see, is an alias. It's used as shorthand for the actual namespace name. In this case, we want to use the namespace to indicate what particular version of XSL we're using.

This is more of an issue than it looks like. Although it would seem simple—XML is at version 1.0, HTML is at version 4.0, and so on—versioning for XSL is actually a bit more complicated.

As we mentioned earlier, when Microsoft was building Internet Explorer, the standard hadn't been completed, so they based it on an early working draft.

This means that IE's older implementation of XSL is a bit different from the W3C standard implementation, so because each one has its own designation, or namespace, we can use that to make clear which version—W3C XSLT or Microsoft "XSL"—we are using. For our style sheet to work, we need to tell the browser which version we want.

Now, the format for these version designations confuses people about namespaces. Deciding what version of XSL is only one of many uses for namespaces, so their names have to be descriptive enough to apply in any circumstance. What's more, they have to be unique. Because the whole point is to be able to sort out what elements belong to what, it would be a catastrophe if two namespaces had the same name.

This being the Internet, the answer was to identify namespaces using Uniform Resource Identifiers, or URIs—to be more specific, URLs.

This means that a namespace declaration looks like the latter part of line 2 in Listing 2.5.

Listing 2.5—Adding the Namespace

```
1: <?xml version="1.0"?>
2: <xsl:stylesheet xmlns:xsl="http://www.w3.org/1999/
➥XSL/Transform"  version="1.0">
3: </xsl:stylesheet>
```

For those using the working draft, or older version of MSXML, the namespace is `http://www.w3.org/TR/WD-xsl`.

Now, a common (mistaken) assumption is that there is some sort of information at that URL that identifies the namespace or provides information about it. Although that might be true, it is not the purpose of the namespace name at all. It is intended solely as a unique identifier for a particular purpose.

In this case, the purpose is to tell the browser (or other application) what implementation of XSL is being used.

We'll be discussing namespaces and their uses thoroughly in Chapter 6, "Adjusting Inventory: Using Namespaces and More About DOM." For now, this is all you need to know about them.

Associating the Style Sheet with the XML Document

The first thing that we're going to have to do is tell the XML document what style sheet we want to use to process it, as we're doing in Listing 2.6.

Listing 2.6—`products.xml`: Associating a Style Sheet to an XML Document

```
1: <?xml version="1.0"?>
2: <?xml-stylesheet href="catalog.xsl" type="text/xsl"?>
3: <products>
4: <vendor>
5:    <vendor_name>Conners Chair Company</vendor_name>
6:    <advertisement>
7:        <ad_sentence>
...
```

In this case, we took our XML file, `products.xml`, and added a processing instruction on line 2. This processing instruction tells the browser to go ahead and process the style sheet, which we've called `catalog.xsl` and which is located in the same directory as the XML file.

Notice also the type, which has changed from `text/css` to `text/xsl`.

So, now we've created a basic style sheet and associated it to an XML document. What happens when we try to view the document in our browser? Absolutely nothing happens, actually, as shown in Figure 2.9.

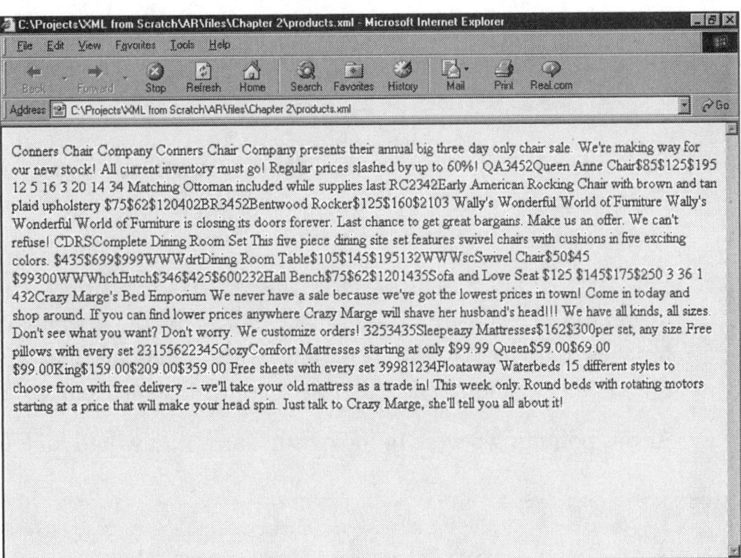

Figure 2.9

Without basic instructions, the browser simply won't know how to display the document.

Templates

Absolutely everything in XSLT is based on one element: the template. Templates are used to decide what elements should be output, and how. Although most applications have built-in templates, which makes it difficult to learn the basics, the Working Draft version of IE5 does not, which makes it easier for us to get a feel for what's happening. For the benefit of those using the older namespace, and because it won't hurt anything, we'll duplicate those built-in templates.

The most basic template is shown in Listing 2.7.

Listing 2.7—`catalog.xsl`: The Basic Template

```
0:<?xml version="1.0"?>
1:<xsl:stylesheet xmlns:xsl="http://www.w3.org/1999/
➥XSL/Transform" version="1.0">
2:
3:<xsl:template match="/">
4:      <xsl:value-of select="."/>
5:</xsl:template>
6:
7:</xsl:stylesheet>
```

Remember,

`<xsl:value-of select="."/>`

is just shorthand for

`<xsl:value-of select="."></xsl:value-of>`

Let's take a look at the anatomy of this element, or actually, these two elements. First, on lines 3 and 5, we have the opening and closing of a `template` element. On line 4, we have the instructions for that template.

Let's start on line 3. The `match` attribute tells the browser where to look for elements to add to the result tree. The / mark represents the document root, so we've told the browser to go back to the beginning. After it gets there, it will execute the instruction on line 4, and because there are no further instructions, it stops.

At this point, if we were to look at the output, it would look like Figure 2.10.

If your browser shows a blank page at this point, MSXML3 is not functioning properly. Try running `xmlinst.exe`, as described in "Installing MSXML3."

If it still doesn't work after restarting the browser, change the namespace to `http://www.w3.org/TR/WD-xsl` and keep in mind that you are seeing the earlier, working draft functionality.

Figure 2.10

Without formatting information, the browser treats the result tree as unformatted text.

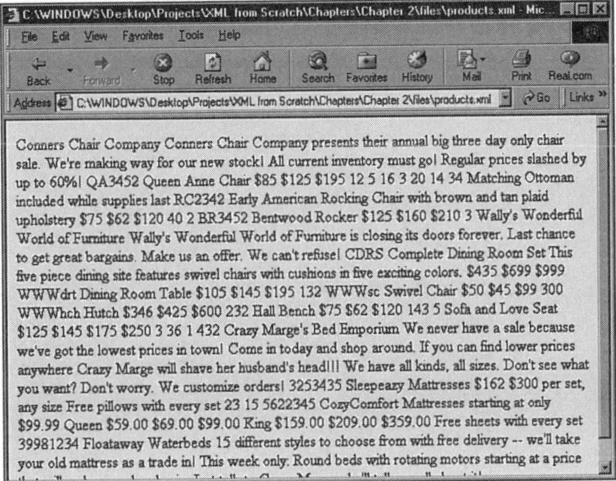

Looking at this, there's an interesting distinction to be made. The output is clearly all the content that we have in our XML document. But how did it get there? Was it added to the result tree all at once as part of the content of the root element, or did the browser move through each node of the tree and add it?

Fortunately, it's easy for us to find out. There's nothing to say that we can't add elements to the XSL document. In Listing 2.8, we're going to add a `<div>` element, which will encompass any element added to the result tree.

Listing 2.8—Adding HTML to the Template

```
<?xml version="1.0"?>
<xsl:stylesheet xmlns:xsl="http://www.w3.org/1999/XSL/Transform">

<xsl:template match="/">
    <div style="border: solid 3px; padding: 10px;">
        <xsl:value-of select="."/>
    </div>
</xsl:template>

</xsl:stylesheet>
```

If we then refresh the browser page, the results will look like Figure 2.11.

Notice that the browser behaves as though we'd given it a page where the content was surrounded by a `<div></div>` tag with the appropriate style information. If we were to choose View, Source from the browser, however, all we would see is the XML and a call to the style sheet. All the transformations are done in memory.

What we can see, however, is that the browser has added all the content at once, as part of the root element.

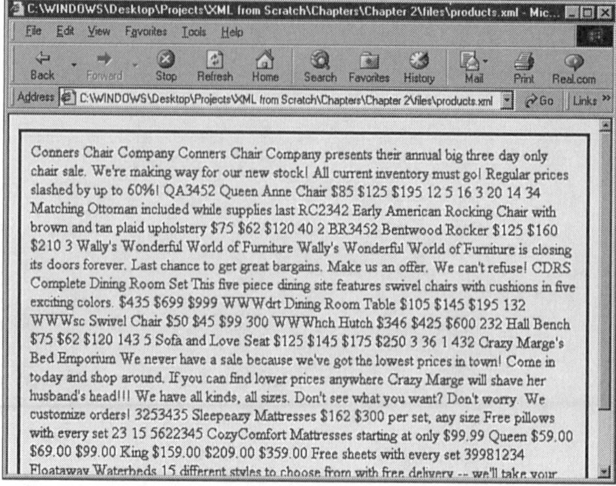

Figure 2.11

Adding a `<div>` *to the output shows that the results were added in one large chunk.*

Of course, because only the top-level element is being processed, this is of limited usefulness. Wouldn't it be nice if we could look at each element in turn and apply appropriate styles? Well, as I'm sure you've guessed, we can.

The first thing that we'll do is to look at the remaining built-in templates, as shown in Listing 2.9.

Listing 2.9—`catalog.xsl`: Adding Built-In Templates

```
<?xml version="1.0"?>
<xsl:stylesheet xmlns:xsl="http://www.w3.org/1999/
➥XSL/Transform" version="1.0">

<xsl:template match="*">
     <xsl:apply-templates/>
</xsl:template>

<xsl:template match="text()">
     <div style="border: solid 1px">
        <xsl:value-of select="."/>
    </div>
</xsl:template>

<xsl:template match="/">
     <div style="border: solid 3px red; padding: 10px;">
          <xsl:value-of select="."/>
    </div>
</xsl:template>

</xsl:stylesheet>
```

If we were to make these changes and refresh the page, we wouldn't see any change at all; we'd still see just the root element in one big box. To understand why, let's take a look at what's really happening.

Ideally, we would like for every text node to be processed by the XSLT processor in the browser individually, and if it ever makes it to the template on lines 7 through 11, that's just what will happen. Unfortunately, we're never getting that far.

On lines 3 through 5, we're using the wildcard again. The wildcard will match any node in the source tree, including, in this case, the root element. From there, it passes the node on for further processing by telling the processor to apply any other applicable templates.

At this point, the template on lines 7 through 11 does not apply yet. The `text()` function selects only text nodes, or nodes that don't contain subelements. Because the root element doesn't qualify, this template is not applied to it.

Finally, we get back down to our original template, on lines 13 through 17. The browser outputs the content of the root element to the browser in the `<div>` and then stops, giving us the same results we had before.

So, how can we get the browser to process the other nodes? We can do it by making a simple change, as shown in Listing 2.10.

Listing 2.10—`catalog.xsl`: Passing the Node On for Further Processing

```
0: <?xml version="1.0"?>
1: <xsl:stylesheet xmlns:xsl="http://www.w3.org/1999/
➥XSL/Transform" version="1.0">
2:
3: <xsl:template match="*">
4:      <xsl:apply-templates/>
5: </xsl:template>
6:
7:<xsl:template match="text()">
8:      <DIV style="border: solid 1px">
9:          <xsl:value-of select="."/>
10:     </DIV>
11:</xsl:template>
12:
13:<xsl:template match="/">
14:     <DIV style="border: solid 3px red; padding: 10px;">
15:         <xsl:apply-templates/>
16:     </DIV>
17:</xsl:template>
18:
19:</xsl:stylesheet>
```

By changing line 15 to `apply-templates`, we're telling the processor that after it's finished applying this template, it should go on and see whether there are any other templates that apply.

In doing that, the processor also looks down the tree to see what other elements and nodes are present. Eventually, it gets down to the leaf, or `text()` nodes, and applies the template on lines 7 through 11. The end result looks like Figure 2.12.

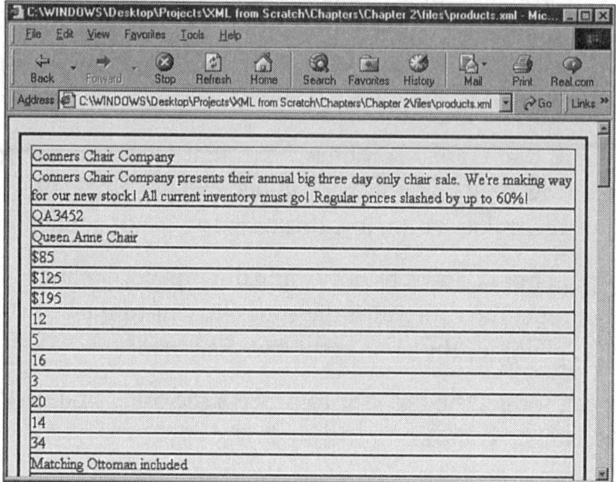

Figure 2.12

We can process each and every text node.

So, we can see clearly that every text node is being treated individually, but only after the original template is rendered.

Using `<xsl:apply-templates/>`, we can apply virtually any number of templates to a particular node, or to its ancestors or descendants.

Getting Specific—Using XPath

This is all well and good, but so far there's nothing that we couldn't have done with CSS, and with a lot less complication. One thing we can't do with CSS, however, is to actually select and transform the data before we display it. Let's start with selecting specific pieces of data. In Listing 2.11, we'll start by just listing the vendor names.

Listing 2.11—`catalog.xsl`: Selecting Specific Data

```
<?xml version="1.0"?>
<xsl:stylesheet xmlns:xsl="http://www.w3.org/1999/
➥XSL/Transform" version="1.0">

```

Listing 2.11—continued

```
3:<xsl:template match="/">
4:     <xsl:apply-templates/>
5:</xsl:template>
6:
7:<xsl:template match="*">
8:      <xsl:apply-templates/>
9:</xsl:template>
10:
11:<xsl:template match="text()">
12:     <xsl:apply-templates/>
13:</xsl:template>
14:
15:<xsl:template match="vendor_name">
16:     <p><xsl:value-of select="."/></p>
17:</xsl:template>
18:
19:</xsl:stylesheet>
```

Let's take a look at what's going on here. The root node is now processed by what is normally the default template on lines 3 through 5, which just tells it to move on to the other templates. This takes it to the template on lines 7 through 9, which sends each individual node looking for other templates that apply.

Let's take a further look at that statement. One at a time, each node on the tree becomes the context node. This means that at that moment, it is the point of reference for any directions. So, when the context node is a `vendor_name` node, it is processed by the template on lines 15 through 17. That's the significance of line 16. It tells the processor to output the value of the current node—in this case, the `vendor_name` node, as we see in Figure 2.13. This is called an XPath expression because it comes from the XPath specification. All the selectors we'll use in the chapter are XPath expressions.

Figure 2.13

Templates can select a single element type, such as the vendor name.

This idea of the context node will become increasingly important as we begin to navigate through the source tree, but for now we need to just keep in mind that if the context node had contained other nodes, they would have all been output, similar to what we saw when we were dealing with the root node.

We can also output the products for each vendor this way, as we're doing in Listing 2.12.

Listing 2.12—`catalog.xsl`: Outputting Other Nodes

```
0:<?xml version="1.0"?>
1:<xsl:stylesheet xmlns:xsl="http://www.w3.org/1999/
➥XSL/Transform" version="1.0">
2:
3:<xsl:template match="/">
4:     <xsl:apply-templates/>
5:</xsl:template>
6:
7:<xsl:template match="*">
8:      <xsl:apply-templates/>
9:</xsl:template>
10:
11:<xsl:template match="text()">
12:    <xsl:apply-templates/>
13:</xsl:template>
14:
15:<xsl:template match="product">
16:    <ul><li>
17:        <xsl:value-of select="product_id"/>:
18:        <xsl:value-of select="short_desc"/>
19:    </li></ul>
20:</xsl:template>
21:
22:<xsl:template match="vendor_name">
23:    <p><xsl:value-of select="."/></p>
24:</xsl:template>
25:
26:</xsl:stylesheet>
```

First, we've purposely put the `product` template before the `vendor_name` template to demonstrate that it doesn't indicate where the output will go, as shown in Figure 2.14.

Here the source tree is being processed in order, so the `vendor_name` node is reached before the `product` node and is displayed first. When the processor does get to the `product` node, it outputs the text on line 16. When it gets to line 17, however, it looks at the context node, which is that particular `product`, and instead of outputting the entire node, as we've done before, it outputs just the `product_id` node, a colon, and then the `short_desc`.

Figure 2.14

Product information is added to the page based on the template, not where the template is in the page.

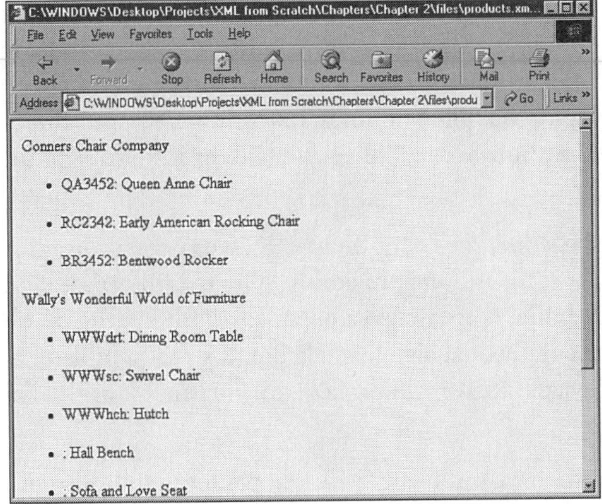

This can leave us with an additional issue, however, as shown in Figure 2.14. Notice that the last two lines of product don't actually have `product_ids`. Of course, in a real commerce situation we would need to deal with that issue, especially if the `product_id` were being used as an identifier elsewhere. But for now, let's look at how we can prevent the colon from coming up if there's no `product_id`.

In Listing 2.13, we change the way we're looking at our output.

Listing 2.13—`catalog.xsl`: Tweaking the Display

```
...

<xsl:template match="product">
    <ul><li>
        <xsl:apply-templates select="product_id"/>
        <xsl:value-of select="short_desc"/>
    </li></ul>
</xsl:template>

<xsl:template match="product/product_id">
    <xsl:value-of select="."/>:
</xsl:template>

<xsl:template match="vendor_name">
    <p><xsl:value-of select="."/></p>
</xsl:template>

</xsl:stylesheet>
```

Line 17 contains a slight modification to the usual `apply-templates` element. Normally, we tell it to pass the entire context node off to additional templates, but in this case we want only the `product_id`. The `product_id` node is passed on, and when it encounters the template on lines 22 through 24, both the value and the colon are output. The advantage here, of course, is that if there is no `product_id`, the colon won't appear.

You might be wondering why, on line 22, we specified `product/product_id` instead of just `product_id`, as done previously. The reason is that if we go back and check the original XML file, there is also a `product_id` for `suites`, and because we're processing every node, it would also be picked up by that template. So, instead, by using `product/product_id`, we will process only `product_ids` that have a `product` node as their parent.

Up to now, we have dealt only with the contents and existence of specific elements. Now let's look at attributes. Looking at the original XML file in Listing 2.3, we see that we have `inventory` notations that will give us `colors`. We'll take advantage of that in Listing 2.14.

Listing 2.14—`catalog.xsl`: Looking at Attributes

```
0:<?xml version="1.0"?>
1:<xsl:stylesheet xmlns:xsl="http://www.w3.org/1999/
➥XSL/Transform" version="1.0">
2:
3:<xsl:template match="/">
4:     <xsl:apply-templates/>
5:</xsl:template>
6:
7:<xsl:template match="*">
8:      <xsl:apply-templates/>
9:</xsl:template>
10:
11:<xsl:template match="text()">
12:     <xsl:apply-templates/>
13:</xsl:template>
14:
15:<xsl:template match="product">
16:     <ul><li>
17:         <xsl:apply-templates select="product_id"/>
18:         <xsl:value-of select="short_desc"/>
19:         <br/><xsl:apply-templates select="inventory[@color]"/>
20:     </li></ul>
21:</xsl:template>
22:
23:<xsl:template match="product/product_id">
24:     <xsl:value-of select="."/>:
25:</xsl:template>
26:
```

Listing 2.14—continued

```
27:<xsl:template match="inventory[@color]">
28:     -- <xsl:value-of select="@color"/><br/>
29:</xsl:template>
30:
31:<xsl:template match="vendor_name">
32:     <p><xsl:value-of select="."/></p>
33:</xsl:template>
34:
35:</xsl:stylesheet>
```

Because we might have more than one `color` for a particular `product`, we break the `colors` out into a different template, located on lines 27 through 29. What we're actually seeing in this example is two uses of an element's attribute. On lines 19 and 27, we're telling the processor to select only `inventory` elements that have a `color` attribute, as indicated by the `@`, or "at" sign. It doesn't matter what that `color` attribute is, as long as it exists. For instance, the Dining Room Table, Swivel Chair, and Hutch from Wally's Wonderful World of Furniture have `inventory` elements, but they don't have `color` attributes, so they don't get processed, as shown in Figure 2.15.

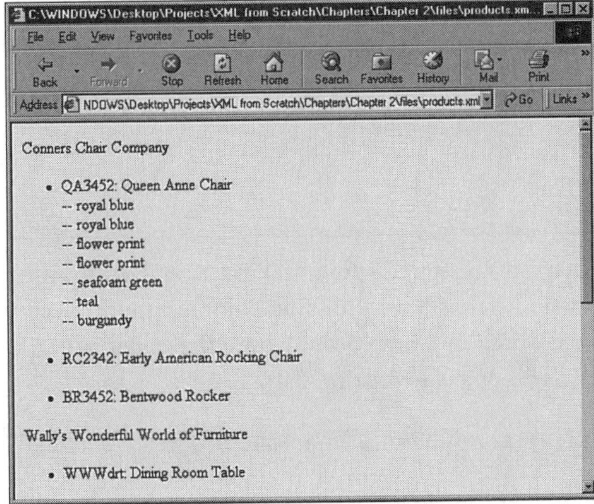

Figure 2.15

Only products with inventory elements that have color attributes are processed.

On line 28, we're telling the processor to actually go ahead and output the value of the attribute, as opposed to the element.

Of course, looking at the output shows another problem: Some colors are repeated. The reason for this becomes apparent if we look at the source document, as excerpted in Listing 2.15.

Listing 2.15—`products.xml`: An Excerpt of the Source Document

```
...
    <product>
        <product_id>QA3452</product_id>
        <short_desc>Queen Anne Chair</short_desc>
        <price pricetype="cost">$85</price>
        <price pricetype="sale">$125</price>
        <price pricetype="retail">$195</price>
        <inventory color="royal blue" location="warehouse">
            12</inventory>
        <inventory color="royal blue" location="showroom">
            5</inventory>
        <inventory color="flower print" location="warehouse">
            16</inventory>
        <inventory color="flower print" location="warehouse">
            3</inventory>
        <inventory color="seafoam green" location="warehouse">
            20</inventory>
        <inventory color="teal" location="warehouse">
            14</inventory>
        <inventory color="burgundy" location="warehouse">
            34</inventory>
        <giveaway>
            <giveaway_item>
            Matching Ottoman included
            </giveaway_item>
            <giveaway_desc>
            while supplies last
            </giveaway_desc>
        </giveaway>
    </product>
...
```

Because we have two different potential locations for inventory, we have two different inventory nodes that have the same color attribute. Because we're building a Web site, we'll probably want to show only the inventory in the warehouse, so we can set that condition, as in Listing 2.16.

Listing 2.16—`catalog.xsl`: Checking for a Specific Attribute Value

```
...
<xsl:template match="product">
    <ul><li>
        <xsl:apply-templates select="product_id"/>
        <xsl:value-of select="short_desc"/>
        <br/><xsl:apply-templates select="inventory[@color]"/>
    </li></ul>
</xsl:template>

<xsl:template match="product/product_id">
```

Listing 2.16—continued

```
24:    <xsl:value-of select="."/>:
25:</xsl:template>
26:
27:<xsl:template
28:      match="inventory[@color and @location='warehouse']">
29:    -- <xsl:value-of select="@color"/><br/>
30:</xsl:template>
31:
32:<xsl:template match="vendor_name">
33:    <p><xsl:value-of select="."/></p>
34:</xsl:template>
35:
36:</xsl:stylesheet>
```

In this case, we haven't changed the nodes that we're sending off to be processed on line 19, but when it comes to the actual template on lines 27 through 30 we're processing only the `inventory` elements that have a `location` attribute of `warehouse` in addition to any `color` attribute.

We can also use attribute values to display the proper `price`. Because this is a special, in Listing 2.17 we'll display any sale prices that we find.

Listing 2.17—`catalog.xsl`: Adding Sale Prices

```
...
15:<xsl:template match="product">
16:    <ul><li>
17:        <xsl:apply-templates select="product_id"/>
18:        <xsl:value-of select="short_desc"/>
19:        <br/><xsl:apply-templates select="inventory[@color]"/>
20:        <p><xsl:value-of select="price[@pricetype='sale']"/></p>
21:    </li></ul>
22:</xsl:template>
23:
24:<xsl:template match="product/product_id">
25:    <xsl:value-of select="."/>:
26:</xsl:template>
27:
...
```

This is fairly straightforward. We are telling the processor to output the value of the first `price` child of the `product` element that has a `pricetype` attribute of `sale`.

Here we run into a problem. Some `products` don't have sale prices. In that case, we want to output whatever `price` the product has listed—as long as it's not our cost! To do this, we're going to use a pipe. This is the vertical bar character that's normally the shift character for the backslash just above the Enter key.

Some keyboards, particularly in Europe and on UNIX systems, have the pipe key on the bottom left of the keyboard.

In Listing 2.18, we'll tell the processor that we want to display the sale `price` OR the first `price` that's not the cost.

Listing 2.18—`catalog.xsl`: Using the Pipe Notation for "or"

```
...
15:<xsl:template match="product">
16:    <ul><li>
17:        <xsl:apply-templates select="product_id"/>
18:        <xsl:value-of select="short_desc"/>
19:        <br/><xsl:apply-templates select="inventory[@color]"/>
20:        <p><xsl:value-of
21:                select="price[@pricetype='sale'] |
22:                        price[@pricetype != 'cost']"/></p>
23:    </li></ul>
24:</xsl:template>
...
```

Normally, we would put lines 20 through 22 on one line, but they wouldn't fit in the book that way, and the processor doesn't care. Also, that's not a typo on line 22. The `!=` symbol means "not equal to."

This takes care of most of the missing prices and even allows us some unexpected prices, such as the starting `price` we put into Crazy Marge's CozyComfort Mattresses, as shown in Figure 2.16.

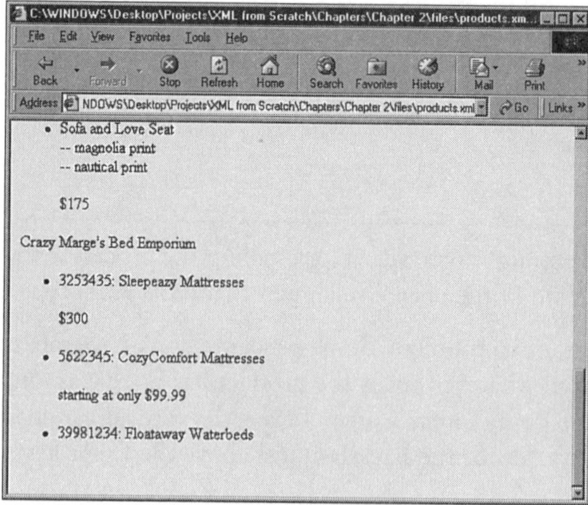

Figure 2.16

XSL allows us to take advantage of consistent naming conventions.

This is one advantage of attributes—they allow us to call things as they are. Yes, the starting `price` is a `price`. Using the sale `prices`, however, it's not really accurate. As you can see from line 188 of the excerpt in Listing 2.19, with the sale, there's actually a lower `price`.

Listing 2.19—`products.xml`: Excerpt from the Source Document

```
...
179:    <product>
180:        <product_id>5622345</product_id>
181:        <short_desc>CozyComfort Mattresses</short_desc>
182:        <price pricetype="starting">
183:            starting at only $99.99
184:        </price>
185:        <item>
186:            <product_desc>Queen</product_desc>
187:            <price pricetype="cost">$59.00</price>
188:            <price pricetype="sale">$69.00</price>
189:            <price pricetype="retail">$99.00</price>
190:        </item>
191:        <item>
192:            <product_desc>King</product_desc>
193:            <price pricetype="cost">$159.00</price>
194:            <price pricetype="sale">$209.00</price>
195:            <price pricetype="retail">$359.00</price>
196:        </item>
197:        <giveaway>
198:            <giveaway_item>
199:            Free sheets
200:            </giveaway_item>
201:            <giveaway_desc>
202:            with every set
203:            </giveaway_desc>
204:        </giveaway>
205:    </product>
...
```

So, this raises the question: If there was a sale `price` for this product, why didn't it come up instead of the starting `price`?

It all has to do with the structure. The product element actually has only one child that is a `price` element, and that's the starting `price` on lines 182 through 184. It does, however, have other descendants that are `price` elements, on lines 187 through 189 and lines 193 through 195. We just have to figure out how to make the style sheet tell the processor to look for them.

To do this, we need to take into consideration where we are. When we are in the template, this `product` node is the context node. We want to check any `price` descendants of this node, as opposed to children. Although a child can be only one level down, a descendant can be any number of levels. Let's take a look at the changes in Listing 2.20.

Listing 2.20—`catalog.xsl`: Looking for Descendants Instead of Children

```
...
15:<xsl:template match="product">
16:    <ul><li>
17:        <xsl:apply-templates select="product_id"/>
18:        <xsl:value-of select="short_desc"/>
19:        <br/><xsl:apply-templates select="inventory[@color]"/>
20:        <p><xsl:value-of
21:                select=".//price[@pricetype='sale'] |
22:                        .//price[@pricetype != 'cost']"/></p>
23:    </li></ul>
24:</xsl:template>
...
```

Here we use the `.//` notation to tell the processor that we were looking for any descendants of the context node. Unfortunately, this is still not going to do the trick.

The reason has to do with priority, and the way the tree is processed. Let's take it step by step.

The processor starts at the `product` level. When it gets to lines 21 and 22, it first checks all its children for a sale `price`. When it doesn't find one, it checks all its children for a `pricetype` other than `cost`. That it does find, with the starting `price`. Because it satisfied one of the two conditions, it's going to stop looking and just output the starting `price`.

To prevent this, we can change the condition for the `price`, as shown in Listing 2.21.

Listing 2.21—`catalog.xsl`: Looking for Retail Prices

```
...
15:<xsl:template match="product">
16:    <ul><li>
17:        <xsl:apply-templates select="product_id"/>
18:        <xsl:value-of select="short_desc"/>
19:        <br/><xsl:apply-templates select="inventory[@color]"/>
20:        <p><xsl:value-of
21:                select=".//price[@pricetype='sale'] |
22:                        .//price[@pricetype='retail']"/></p>
23:    </li></ul>
24:</xsl:template>
...
```

Now let's look at what the processor does. As before, it starts with the immediate children of the `product` node, looking for a sale `price`. When it doesn't find one, it looks for a retail `price` and doesn't find one of them, either. If we didn't have the descendant notation, the processor would stop there and not output anything. Because we do, however, it starts searching the children's children and finally finds the sale `price` in a grandchild of the `product` element.

Looping and Sorting

Until now, we've mostly gone along with the order of the XML document, although that might be difficult to see because we've been so selective about what we've output.

At this point, we're going to take a little more control over how things are done. Using the templates all by themselves, we can output the `vendor_name` only once (without jumping through some rather intricate hoops), but we want to have a list of vendor names at the top of the page with links to that vendor's offerings.

To do this, we need to keep in mind two things: how the document is actually processed and where we are in the source tree at all times.

We need to remember that the processor will do absolutely nothing until we tell it to start processing the root node. Even if we want a specific node much farther down the chain, we need to start at the top. So, it's the first template that's the key. Until now, it's just been

```
<xsl:template match="/">
      <xsl:apply-templates/>
</xsl:template>
```

Simple, but functional. All processing for this document started here, but all we were doing was sending the tree off to be processed by other templates. Now we're going to take control. The first thing that we want to do is display a list of `vendor_names` at the top of the page and then output a horizontal rule before we output the rest of our content. We do this in Listing 2.22.

Listing 2.22—`catalog.xsl`: Looping Through the Source Document

```
<?xml version="1.0"?>
<xsl:stylesheet xmlns:xsl="http://www.w3.org/1999/
➥XSL/Transform" version="1.0">

<xsl:template match="/">
    <xsl:for-each select="//vendor">
       <h2><xsl:value-of select="vendor_name"/></h2>
    </xsl:for-each>
```

Listing 2.22—continued

```
7:
8:      <hr/>
9:
10:      <xsl:apply-templates/>
11:</xsl:template>
12:
13:<xsl:template match="*">
14:       <xsl:apply-templates/>
15:</xsl:template>
...
41:<xsl:template match="vendor_name">
42:     <P><xsl:value-of select="."/></P>
43:</xsl:template>
44:
45:</xsl:stylesheet>
```

We haven't touched the rest of the style sheet, so everything that was output before will still be output, as shown in Figure 2.17. There's an important distinction, however, in how the document was created.

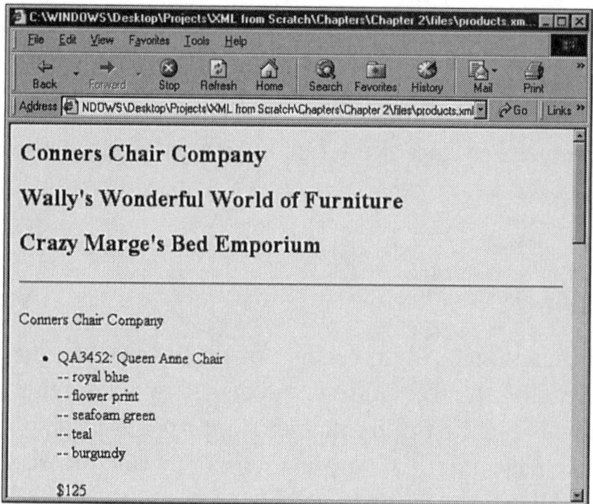

Figure 2.17

Adding a loop at the top of the page can be done without changing the rest of the output.

We start out on line 3 at the root element. From there, we are looking for any `vendors` in the document at all. Notice the distinction in the notation. On line 4, we're looking for `//vendor`, which means any descendants of the root element. We can use this anywhere, whereas `.//vendor` would mean any `vendors` that were descendants of the context node, whatever that happened to be.

After we reach a vendor node, we are outputting the vendor_name child of that particular vendor. We'll do this for each vendor element, and when we're done, we'll move on.

The next item in the style sheet is a horizontal rule. Just as a reminder, even though we would normally write <HR> in HTML, if we did that here we wouldn't have a well-formed XML document, so we have to use the empty-element notation of <hr/>.

We're then using the <xsl:apply-templates/> element again. Note that even though we've previously dipped down into the vendor elements, we're done now, and the context node is still the root element. So, all nodes will be processed just as if we'd never done the loop.

Sorting

Now that we've output their names, we want to sort them in alphabetical order, by vendor_name. This is a simple change, as shown in Listing 2.23.

Listing 2.23—catalog.xml: Looping Through the Source Document

```
<?xml version="1.0"?>
<xsl:stylesheet xmlns:xsl="http://www.w3.org/1999/
➥XSL/Transform" version="1.0">

<xsl:template match="/">
    <xsl:for-each select="//vendor">
        <xsl:sort select="vendor_name" />
       <h2><xsl:value-of select="vendor_name"/></h2>
    </xsl:for-each>

    <hr/>

     <xsl:apply-templates/>
</xsl:template>

<xsl:template match="*">
     <xsl:apply-templates/>
</xsl:template>
...
```

Adding the <xsl:sort> element as a child of the <xsl:for-each> element will force it to reorder the elements before it outputs them. Notice also that the context node for <xsl:sort> is the node that's actually being looped through. So, even though there is no vendor_name child to the root element, select="vendor_name" works because the vendor element does have a vendor_name child.

If you're using the older version of XSL, the code should actually read

```
<?xml version="1.0"?>
<xsl:stylesheet xmlns:xsl="http://www.w3.org/TR/WD-xsl"
➥version="1.0">

<xsl:template match="/">
     <xsl:for-each select="//vendor"
➥order-by="vendor_name">
         <h2><xsl:value-of select="vendor_name"/></h2>
     </xsl:for-each>

     <hr/>

     <xsl:apply-templates/>
</xsl:template>

<xsl:template match="*">
     <xsl:apply-templates/>
</xsl:template>
...
```

Of course, this leaves us with a situation in which the information on the bottom half of the page isn't in the same order as the information on the top half of the page. We can remedy that easily by adding another loop, as shown in Listing 2.24.

Listing 2.24—Sorting the Lower Content

```
<?xml version="1.0"?>
<xsl:stylesheet xmlns:xsl="http://www.w3.org/1999/
➥XSL/Transform" version="1.0">

<xsl:template match="/">
    <xsl:for-each select="//vendor">
        <xsl:sort select="vendor_name" />
        <H2><xsl:value-of select="vendor_name"/></H2>
    </xsl:for-each>

    <HR/>

    <xsl:for-each select="//vendor">
        <xsl:sort select="vendor_name" />
         <xsl:apply-templates/>
    </xsl:for-each>
</xsl:template>

```

Listing 2.24—continued

```
<xsl:template match="*">
      <xsl:apply-templates/>
</xsl:template>

<xsl:template match="text()">
    <xsl:apply-templates/>
</xsl:template>
...
```

Let's think about what's happening here. Previously in this template, we started out with the entire source tree because the context element is the root element. From there, we sent the nodes off to be processed by whatever templates they found that applied.

Now, however, we're letting this template narrow the field first, by processing only each `vendor` element. Granted, because that's all we were processing anyway, it doesn't make any difference to the output; it's still an important consideration. Unless we send a node off to be processed, it's not going to be touched.

The end result is that each vendor element is processed in alphabetical order according to name, so the entire document is sorted.

Adding Elements and Attributes

What we ultimately want to end up with at the top of the page is a series of XHTML links that bring us to the appropriate vendor's material. If this were HTML, the relevant parts of the page would look like Listing 2.25.

We've been leaving out a lot of the normal XHTML elements for the sake of clarity. When we're finished, we'll put them back in.

Listing 2.25—`catalog.xsl`: The XHTML We're Trying to Emulate

```
<a href="#Conners Chair Company"><H2>Conners Chair Company</H2></a>
<a href="#Crazy Marge's Bed Emporium">
          <h2>Crazy Marge's Bed Emporium</h2></a>
<a href="#Wally's Wonderful World of Furniture">
          <h2>Wally's Wonderful World of Furniture</h2></a>

<hr />

<a name="Conners Chair Company">Conners Chair Company</a>

```

Listing 2.25—continued

```
8: <ul><li>
9: QA3452: Queen Anne Chair <br />
10:-- royal blue<br />
11:-- flower print<br />
12:-- seafoam green<br />
...
25:
26:<a name="Crazy Marge's Bed Emporium">
26a:       Crazy Marge's Bed Emporium</a>
27:
28:<ul><li>
29:3253435: Sleepeazy Mattresses <br />
...
37:39981234: Floataway Waterbeds <br />
38:</li></ul>
39:
40:<a name="Wally's Wonderful World of Furniture">
40a:       Wally's Wonderful World of Furniture</a>
41:
42:<ul><li>
43:WWWdrt: Dining Room Table <br />
44:$145
45:</li></ul>
46:<ul><li>
```

Because we haven't dealt with most of this before, let's make sure that we understand the XHTML we're trying to emulate before we move on. In lines 0 through 2, we're turning the vendor names into links using the <a>, or anchor tag. Normally, the `href` attribute would be used to specify another Web site, such as `http://www.mcp.com`, or another page, such as `newcatalog.html`. In this case, however, we're actually pointing to a specific point in the page, which we've identified with the vendor name. We create those anchor points, or internal references, by creating <a> tags with name attributes, as we did on lines 6, 26, and 40.

In general, it's bad practice to use an identifier that can be so unpredictable, such as a vendor name. Many browsers can't handle the spaces and will not follow the link properly. Because we're using Internet Explorer for this exercise, however, we'll let it go for the sake of simplicity.

So, if we were to click on the top link for Wally's Wonderful World of Furniture, the browser would jump to the named anchor toward the bottom of the page.

In theory, this is just additional text for the page, so it should be pretty easy to add. In practice, however, it's not so simple. Let's take a look at what we would do to add the top links in Listing 2.26.

Listing 2.26—`catalog.xsl`: Adding Elements As Text

```
<?xml version="1.0"?>
<xsl:stylesheet xmlns:xsl="http://www.w3.org/1999/
➥XSL/Transform" version="1.0">

<xsl:template match="/">
    <xsl:for-each select="//vendor" >
        <xsl:sort select="vendor_name" />
        <a href="#<xsl:value-of select="vendor_name"/>">
            <h2><xsl:value-of select="vendor_name"/></h2>
        </a>
    </xsl:for-each>

     <hr/>

     <xsl:for-each select="//vendor" >
         <xsl:sort select="vendor_name" />
          <xsl:apply-templates/>
     </xsl:for-each>
</xsl:template>
...
```

All we're trying to do is add text to the page, using the vendor name as part of the `href`. If we try to run this, however, we'll see it's not that simple, as shown in Figure 2.18.

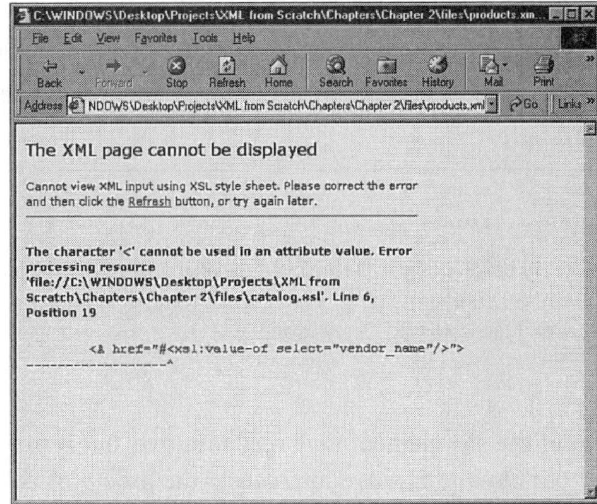

Figure 2.18

When adding text to the output, we have to remember we're building a result tree, not a stream of text, so this listing causes an error.

Remember, we're not just outputting text; we're creating a result tree. When the processor sees the opening for the <a> tag, it's going to treat it as any other tag, and it has to be created and nested properly.

Fortunately, there's an easy way around this. It takes into account the very nature of what we're doing. Although we think of it as outputting text, what we're actually doing is adding an <a> element to the result tree. So, we can use another XSL element called, not surprisingly, `<xsl:element>`, along with `<xsl:attribute>`, to do it. We'll add both sets of elements in Listing 2.27.

Listing 2.27—`catalog.xsl`: Adding Elements to the Result Tree

```
0: <?xml version="1.0"?>
1: <xsl:stylesheet xmlns:xsl="http://www.w3.org/1999/
➥XSL/Transform" version="1.0">
2:
3: <xsl:template match="/">
4:     <xsl:for-each select="//vendor">
5:        <xsl:sort select="vendor_name" />
6:         <xsl:element name="a">
7:             <xsl:attribute name="href">
8:                  #<xsl:value-of select="vendor_name"/>
9:             </xsl:attribute>
10:              <h2><xsl:value-of select="vendor_name"/></h2>
11:         </xsl:element>
12:     </xsl:for-each>
13:
14:     <hr/>
15:
...
48:
49:<xsl:template match="vendor_name">
50:<xsl:element name="a">
51:  <xsl:attribute name="name"><xsl:value-of select="."/></xsl:attribute>
52:  <p><xsl:value-of select="."/></p>
53:</xsl:element>
54:</xsl:template>
```

We haven't dealt with the issue of whitespace in XML, but if you try this exercise, make sure to put all of line 50 on one line, or spaces will be added to the anchor, and the links won't work properly.

The creation of the <a> element isn't very intuitive, but if we pick it apart, we can see what's going on. On line 5, we're instructing the processor to begin to create a new element, with the name of a. This is the equivalent of typing

```
<a
```

Then, on lines 6 through 8, we're instructing the processor to add an attribute to that element. This is the equivalent of typing, in the case of Conners Chair Company,

```
<a href="#Conners Chair Company"
```


Notice that the tag isn't closed yet. That happens when the processor gets to the first nonattribute item within the `<xsl:element>` element. So, when it evaluates line 9, the element becomes

```
<a href="#Conners Chair Company"><h2>Conners Chair Company</h2>
```

Finally, when it reaches the `</xsl:element>` tag, it knows to close the element, so we get

```
<a href="#Conners Chair Company"><h2>Conners Chair Company</h2></a>
```

The same process happens on lines 50 through 53. Note that because the processor is deciding what to do based on each item it comes across, we can't put any attributes after text for the element because the open tag will already be complete.

Conditionals

Now that we've begun to take control of the flow of our document by using looping, it's time to take even tighter control by adapting to the data itself.

We can output different data and differently formatted data based on the data itself. In this case, we're going to use the `webvendor` attribute of the `vendor` elements, displaying all information for `vendors` with a `webvendor` attribute of `full`, displaying only some information for those with a `webvendor` attribute of `partial`, and not displaying at all those with a `webvendor` attribute of `no`.

This last is easy. In Listing 2.28, we'll instruct the processor not to output any text unless the `webvendor` attribute is something other than "no."

Listing 2.28—`catalog.xsl`: A Simple Conditional

```
<?xml version="1.0"?>
<xsl:stylesheet xmlns:xsl="http://www.w3.org/1999/
➥XSL/Transform" version="1.0">

<xsl:template match="/">
    <xsl:for-each select="//vendor">
        <xsl:sort select="vendor_name" />
        <xsl:if test="@webvendor!='no'">
            <xsl:element name="a">
            <xsl:attribute name="href">
                #<xsl:value-of select="vendor_name"/>
```

Listing 2.28—continued

```
10:               </xsl:attribute>
11:               <h2><xsl:value-of select="vendor_name"/></h2>
12:           </xsl:element>
13:            </xsl:if>
14:       </xsl:for-each>
15:
16:       <hr/>
17:
18:       <xsl:for-each select="//vendor" >
19:            <xsl:sort select="vendor_name" />
20:           <xsl:if test="@webvendor!='no'">
21:                <xsl:apply-templates/>
22:           </xsl:if>
23:       </xsl:for-each>
24:</xsl:template>
...
61:</xsl:stylesheet>
```

This is a simple "yes or no" test. The context node in both cases is the `vendor` element, so if the `webvendor` attribute of the `vendor` element is not "no" (because we are using !=), the test comes out as `TRUE`. If the test comes out as `TRUE` then the processor goes ahead and does whatever's enclosed between `<xsl:if>` and `</xsl:if>`. So, on lines 6 through 12 it will display the link and the vendor's name, and on lines 20 through 22, it will send the `vendor` element on to be processed, but only for `vendor`s that pass the test, as shown in Figure 2.19.

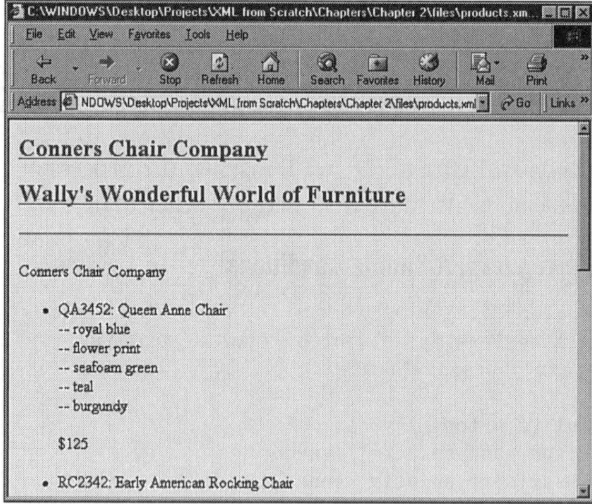

Figure 2.19

The `if` statement enables us to choose whether to output content.

This really is a little heavy handed, though. What if we still want to list our non-Web vendors but not display their information? There's no "else" to go with that "if."

There is, however, <xsl:choose>. This enables us to decide between multiple outcomes. In Listing 2.29, we'll display all the vendor names, but if a vendor shouldn't be displayed on the Web, we won't create a link.

Listing 2.29—catalog.xsl: Using <xsl:choose>

```
0:<?xml version="1.0"?>
1:<xsl:stylesheet xmlns:xsl="http://www.w3.org/1999/
➥XSL/Transform" version="1.0">
2:
3:<xsl:template match="/">
4:     <xsl:for-each select="//vendor">
5:          <xsl:sort select="vendor_name" />
6:       <xsl:choose>
7:         <xsl:when test="@webvendor!='no'">
8:            <xsl:element name="a">
9:               <xsl:attribute name="href">
10:                  #<xsl:value-of select="vendor_name"/>
11:               </xsl:attribute>
12:               <h2><xsl:value-of select="vendor_name"/></h2>
13:            </xsl:element>
14:         </xsl:when>
15:         <xsl:otherwise>
16:             <h2><xsl:value-of select="vendor_name"/>*</h2>
17:         </xsl:otherwise>
18:       </xsl:choose>
19:     </xsl:for-each>
20:
21:     <sup>*</sup>Products available only in showrooms.
22:     <hr/>
23:
...
```

If you're familiar with programming, this structure might look a bit strange to you, but we must maintain the well-formedness of our style sheet, even if we have several related items as we do here.

On line 6, we're opening an <xsl:choose> element. This tells the processor that we will have several possibilities. Each one of those possibilities will be contained in an <xsl:when> element, like the one on lines 7 through 14, or an <xsl:otherwise> element, like the one on lines 15 through 17.

The flow goes like this. The processor gets to the <xsl:choose> tag and looks for the first <xsl:when> tag. When it gets there, it evaluates the `test`, and if the `test` evaluates to `TRUE`, it processes the contents of the <xsl:when> element and skips down to the close of the `choose`, the </xsl:choose> tag. If the test for the <xsl:when> element evaluates to `FALSE`, it goes to each subsequent <xsl:when> element and repeats the process until it finds one that is `TRUE`. If it doesn't find one, as is the case for Crazy Marge, it executes whatever is in the <xsl:otherwise> element, as shown in Figure 2.20.

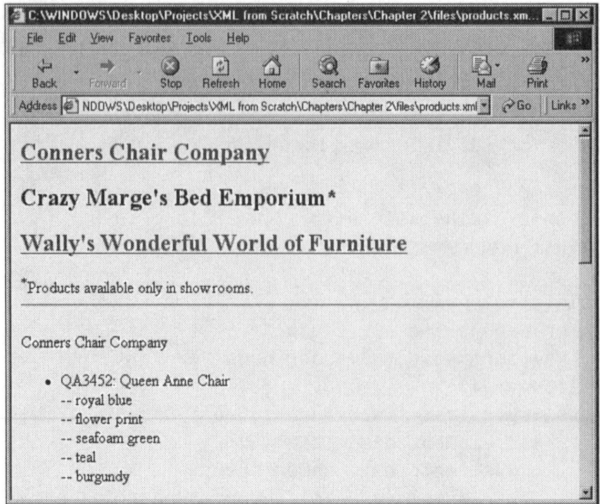

Figure 2.20

The `<xsl:choose>` element enables us to be more flexible in making decisions.

We can also apply this granularity to the lower part of the page. For instance, if a vendor is a full Web vendor, we want to display all its information, including a description, formatted nicely. If the vendor is only a partial Web vendor, we just want to display the description. If it's not a Web vendor at all, we don't want to display anything. We can make those changes in Listing 2.30.

Listing 2.30—`catalog.xsl`: Using `<xsl:choose>` to Format the Vendor/Product Information

```
<?xml version="1.0"?>
<xsl:stylesheet xmlns:xsl="http://www.w3.org/1999/
➥XSL/Transform" version="1.0">

<xsl:template match="/">
   <xsl:for-each select="//vendor">
        <xsl:sort select="vendor_name" />
     <xsl:choose>
       <xsl:when test="@webvendor!='no'">
             <xsl:element name="a">
             <xsl:attribute name="href">
                 #<xsl:value-of select="vendor_name"/>
              </xsl:attribute>
              <h2><xsl:value-of select="vendor_name"/></h2>
            </xsl:element>
        </xsl:when>
        <xsl:otherwise>
            <h2><xsl:value-of select="vendor_name"/>*</h2>
        </xsl:otherwise>
      </xsl:choose>
    </xsl:for-each>

    <sup>*</sup>Products available only in showrooms.
    <hr/>

```

Listing 2.30—continued

```
    <xsl:for-each select="//vendor">
         <xsl:sort select="vendor_name" />
        <xsl:apply-templates/>
    </xsl:for-each>
</xsl:template>

<xsl:template match="*">
      <xsl:apply-templates/>
</xsl:template>

<xsl:template match="text()">
    <xsl:apply-templates/>
</xsl:template>

<xsl:template match="product">
  <xsl:choose>
  <xsl:when test="parent::node()[@webvendor='full']">
    <ul><li>
          <xsl:apply-templates select="product_id"/>
        <xsl:value-of select="short_desc"/>
        <br/><xsl:apply-templates select="inventory[@color]"/>
        <p><xsl:value-of
                select=".//price[@pricetype='sale'] |
                        .//price[@pricetype='retail']"/></p>
    </li></ul>
  </xsl:when>
  <xsl:when test="parent::node()[@webvendor='partial']">
          <xsl:value-of select="short_desc"/><br/>
  </xsl:when>
  </xsl:choose>
</xsl:template>

<xsl:template match="product/product_id">
    <xsl:value-of select="."/>:
</xsl:template>

<xsl:template
     match="inventory[@color and @location='warehouse']">
    -- <xsl:value-of select="@color"/><br/>
</xsl:template>

<xsl:template match="vendor_name">
<xsl:if test="parent::node()[@webvendor!='no']">
<xsl:element name="a">
  <xsl:attribute name="name"><xsl:value-of select="."/></xsl:attribute>
  <h3><xsl:value-of select="."/></h3>
</xsl:element>
<P><xsl:value-of select="../advertisement"/></P>
</xsl:if>
</xsl:template>

</xsl:stylesheet>
```

We need to make sure that we've followed the path that each element is going to take so that nothing slips through the cracks. We start out in the root element template, and we make sure that the top links are output only if appropriate.

From there, the only elements that are getting passed on to the other templates are the `vendor` elements. They will first match against the template on lines 65 through 73. This template controls the display of the `vendor_name`. If the `vendor` is to be displayed, it should have a description, which we added on line 71. If it's not to be displayed, there is no command to display it, so that `vendor_name` element is done.

When the processor is done with the `vendor_name`, it moves on to `product`, the only other child of `vendor` that has a template to match it. From here, we have two choices. Either the `vendor` is a full Web vendor or a partial Web vendor. But remember, that information is stored at the `vendor` level, not the `product` level. Because it's actually the `product` node that's the context node on lines 40 and 50, we're checking the attribute of the parent node. That's what the notation `parent::node()` means.

If the `vendor` is a full Web vendor, we'll output all the information we've been displaying, including `colors` available and `price`. If the `vendor` is a partial Web vendor, we'll display only the product names. If the `vendor` is neither a full nor a partial Web vendor, it won't satisfy either of these two conditions. Because there's no `<xsl:otherwise>` catchall, the vendor simply won't be displayed, which is what we wanted.

Cleaning Up

Finally, we need to put in the standard HTML tags that we've been leaving out for the sake of clarity. Because the root element template is basically the page, that's where we'll put them, as shown in the complete listing, Listing 2.31.

Listing 2.31—The Complete Style Sheet

```
0:<?xml version="1.0"?>
1:<xsl:stylesheet xmlns:xsl="http://www.w3.org/1999/
➥XSL/Transform" version="1.0">
2:
3:<xsl:template match="/">
4:<html>
5:<head><title>Vendor and Product Listings</title></head>
6:<body>
7:    <xsl:for-each select="//vendor" >
25:         <xsl:sort select="vendor_name" />
8:      <xsl:choose>
9:        <xsl:when test="@webvendor!='no'">
10:            <xsl:element name="a">
11:              <xsl:attribute name="href">
12:                 #<xsl:value-of select="vendor_name"/>
13:              </xsl:attribute>
```

Listing 2.31—continued

```
       <h2><xsl:value-of select="vendor_name"/></h2>
      </xsl:element>
    </xsl:when>
    <xsl:otherwise>
      <h2><xsl:value-of select="vendor_name"/>*</h2>
    </xsl:otherwise>
   </xsl:choose>
  </xsl:for-each>

  <sup>*</sub>Products available only in showrooms.
  <hr/>

  <xsl:for-each select="//vendor">
     <xsl:sort select="vendor_name" />
    <xsl:apply-templates/>
  </xsl:for-each>

</body>
</html>
</xsl:template>

<xsl:template match="*">
   <xsl:apply-templates/>
</xsl:template>

<xsl:template match="text()">
  <xsl:apply-templates/>
</xsl:template>

<xsl:template match="product">
 <xsl:choose>
 <xsl:when test="parent::node()[@webvendor='full']">
  <ul><li>
    <xsl:apply-templates select="product_id"/>
    <xsl:value-of select="short_desc"/>
    <br/><xsl:apply-templates select="inventory[@color]"/>
    <p><xsl:value-of
        select=".//price[@pricetype='sale'] |
            .//price[@pricetype='retail']"/></p>
  </li></ul>
 </xsl:when>
 <xsl:when test="parent::node()[@webvendor='partial']">
     <xsl:value-of select="short_desc"/><br/>
 </xsl:when>
 </xsl:choose>
</xsl:template>

<xsl:template match="product/product_id">
  <xsl:value-of select="."/>:
</xsl:template>
```

Listing 2.31—continued

```
<xsl:template
     match="inventory[@color and @location='warehouse']">
    -- <xsl:value-of select="@color"/><br/>
</xsl:template>
<xsl:template match="vendor_name">
<xsl:if test="parent::node()[@webvendor!='no']">
<xsl:element name="a">
  <xsl:attribute name="name"><xsl:value-of select="."/></xsl:attribute>
  <h3><xsl:value-of select="."/></h3>
</xsl:element>
<p><xsl:value-of select="../advertisement"/></p>
</xsl:if>
</xsl:template>
</xsl:stylesheet>
```

Next Steps

In this chapter, we looked at the basics of Extensible Stylesheet Language Transformations by building a style sheet for Microsoft Internet Explorer.

We started with simple transformations, where we formatted specific content using HTML and a small amount of CSS. We moved on to more complex transformations, using looping and conditionals.

In Chapters 1 and 2, we've concentrated on working with XML in a way that would give immediate results, so we could become familiar with the language and how it works.

Transforming XML in one way or another is the basis for everything that we are going to do on the server side, which is why we took two chapters to get comfortable with it. From here, we move on to Chapter 3, "Defining the Data Structure: Document Type Definitions, XML Schema, and Parsers." It guides you through the process of installing and configuring the tools you'll need to process XML on the server side.

In this chapter

- *Introducing Java*
- *Installing the Java 2 Software Development Kit*
- *Installing the Xerces-J Parser*
- *Well-Formed Versus Valid Documents*
- *Document Type Definitions*
- *External DTDs*
- *Referential Integrity*
- *XML Schema*
- *Next Steps*

Chapter 3

Defining the Data Structure: Document Type Definitions, XML Schema, and Parsers

In the first two chapters of this book, we built some "placeholder" type pages—pages that will give our company a Web presence while we develop the real application.

Now it's time to get serious.

In this chapter, we'll start examining the actual structure of the data that we're going to use. We'll analyze it, model it, define it, and test it. This last will be accomplished with the help of a parser.

Parsers are applications that take long strings of information and make sense out of them. You're acting as a parser right now as you read this book, in fact. You look at each page and break it down into paragraphs, sentences, and words, and then you make sense out of the words. In this chapter, we're going to install a parser and use it to test the data structure we define.

The parser we're going to use, like the programs we're going to write, is built in Java, so the first thing we'll need to do is get our Java environment taken care of.

Introducing Java

You might have noticed that until now we haven't said much about what operating system you're using. That's because it doesn't matter. XML is just text and can be created on any operating system where you can create a text file.

Actually programming, however, is generally much more restrictive than that. After all, you can't just take a program written for, say, the Apple Macintosh and run it on Windows 98, right?

Well, of course, that used to be correct, and for good reason. The internal workings of each operating system and computer are different, so, of course, a program would have to know the right language to speak to them. This, as you might imagine, doesn't really fit well with the nature of the Web, where the same content can be accessed on virtually any type of system. So, it was only a matter of time before someone proposed a universal language of sorts.

That someone, in this case, was Sun Microsystems. Sun already had a decent foothold in the Internet space when it announced that it was working on Java, a programming language that would run in a variety environments, because at that time virtually all Internet servers ran on an operating system called UNIX, and a large percentage of those used Sun's flavor of UNIX, Solaris.

Of course, there weren't too many desktop machines using UNIX at the time, so the discrepancy between software that would run on the server and software that could run on the browser, or client, was huge.

Java would change all that.

The key to Java is the idea of the Java Virtual Machine, or JVM. The JVM sits between the code and the operating system, working as an interpreter, as illustrated in Figure 3.1.

Figure 3.1

A single Java program can run on any operating system, as long as a Java Virtual Machine is available.

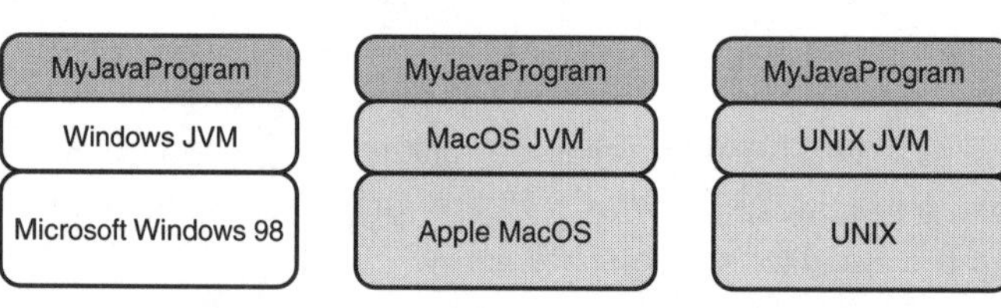

So, as long as there is a Java Virtual Machine for your operating system, be it Windows 98, UNIX, or even something you've written yourself, the same Java code will run on it. Hence the slogan, "Write Once, Run Anywhere."

Purists will note that in the late 1990s there was a bit of corporate ugliness over certain vendors producing versions of Java optimized for particular operating systems, leading to code that wouldn't necessarily run anywhere. This led to Sun's "100% Pure Java" and "Java Compatible" programs. For the purposes of this book, we won't be touching those discrepancies, and we'll rely only on Pure Java software.

The choice of words to describe the JVM as an interpreter was intentional. Programmers experienced in languages such as C++ will note that there are two types of languages: compiled and interpreted. A compiled language, such as C or C++, is written and then translated into the native language of the system on which it will run, which makes it fast. The downside is that because it's already been translated into that system's particular native language, it generally can't be used in a different environment. On the other hand, an interpreted language, such as BASIC or any scripting language, isn't translated into the native language until it's run, which makes it much more portable.

So, where does Java fall into that spectrum?

Somewhere in the middle, actually. A Java program is compiled into byte-code, which is then interpreted by the JVM when it's run. In the years since Java's introduction, Sun has also added a Just In Time, or JIT compiler, which compiles the code just before it's run, leading to improvements in performance. For the sake of portability, however, we'll think of Java as an interpreted language for now.

So, what does that all mean to us?

It means that Java, which is not tied to any particular operating system, is a natural choice for developing XML applications, which are not tied to any particular platform. The vast majority of XML tools and applications are produced in Java, and we're going to follow that trend.

If you don't have any Java experience, don't panic! We'll walk through each concept as it's needed, so you'll feel comfortable with what we're doing, and we won't pull any surprises.

Installing the Java 2 Software Development Kit

Before we can even think about running any Java applications, much less writing any, we need to install a few things. First, we need a Java Virtual Machine. We also need the base "classes," or programs that form the underlying structure of the language. Finally, we need the compiler that will turn our programs into byte-code that the JVM understands.

Locating the Java 2 SDK

Where to get all this depends on what operating system you're running. Sun Microsystems maintains versions for Microsoft Windows, Linux, and, of course, Solaris. There are Java Virtual Machines available from other companies, such as Apple, Microsoft, and IBM, as well. To download from Sun, point your browser to

```
http://java.sun.com/j2se/1.3/
```

We are going to use Java 2 SDK Version 1.3 for the examples in this book, but if this page shows a newer version, you should be fine using it. If your operating system isn't shown on this page, go to

```
http://java.sun.com/cgi-bin/java-ports.cgi
```

for a list of available versions. Make sure that you get the Software Development Kit, or SDK, and not just a runtime environment. For instance, if you're running MacOS and you follow the preceding link, you'll find a page that describes the necessary steps to get the Macintosh Runtime for Java, or MRJ 2.2.2. Although you will need this, if you want to actually build Java programs (as we will be doing throughout the rest of the book), you will also need the MRJ SDK. To get it, follow the links to

```
http://devworld.apple.com/java/text/download.html
```

and click the MRJ 2.2 SDK link in the sidebar. If you have trouble locating it, the direct download link is

```
ftp://ftp.apple.com/developer/Development_Kits/MRJ_SDK_2.2_Install.sit.bin
```

This version of the SDK is only Java 1.1.8, but this shouldn't be a problem for any of the coding that we're doing. The only potential problems stem from the applications that we'll be downloading, and all of them have instructions for those who are still using Java 1.1.8.

EXCURSION

What Do All These Acronyms Mean?

The programming world has been awash in acronyms since long before BASIC came into play. Unfortunately, now that marketing has entered into the picture, it's become even worse.

The software we need to build Java applications used to be known as the JDK, or Java Developer's Kit. (Some developers, in fact, still refer to it that way.) This included the JVM, or Java Virtual Machine, the compiler, `javac`, and several other tools. The first version was released as JDK 1.0.

Eventually, improvements were made, all the way up to JDK 1.1.8. At that time, Sun changed the focus of development (and the way many features were implemented) and decided to rename the platform as Java 2.

Unfortunately, Sun didn't change the version numbers. This means that Java 2 is actually what would have been called JDK 1.2, but is now Java 2 Software Developers Kit version 1.2. (Or, in our case, version 1.3.)

So, don't be alarmed if you can't find "the JDK." It's there; it's just been renamed.

Installation

Because the Java SDK is an application like any other, it normally comes in the form of an installer, with a wizard to guide you through your installation choices. Installation generally involves the following steps on Windows, with a similar set for other platforms:

1. Close any open applications.
2. Double-click the downloaded file (for example, `j2sdk1_3_0-win.exe`) to start the installer.
3. Read and accept the license agreement.
4. Choose a destination folder, as shown in Figure 3.2. You can choose whatever destination makes sense for you, but all instructions in this book will assume that you have installed the JDK in the root directory. This makes the destination folder `c:\jdk1.3`.

Figure 3.2

Install the JDK in the root directory.

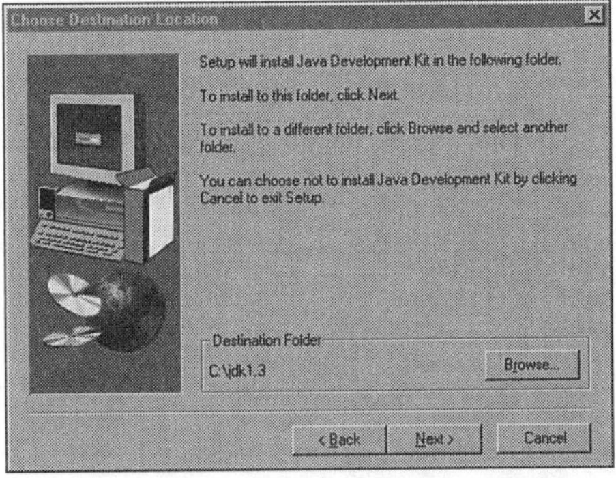

5. Determine what to install, as shown in Figure 3.3. To build and run Java applications, we'll need the program files but not the actual source files. If you're short on disk space, feel free to uncheck Java Sources.

   After the installer is complete, you can delete the downloaded file to recover disk space.

   The next two steps are actually optional right now but will save us a significant amount of typing. (We'll also need to set these two variables for future applications, so we might as well take care of it now.)

Figure 3.3

The actual Java source files are not necessary for this project.

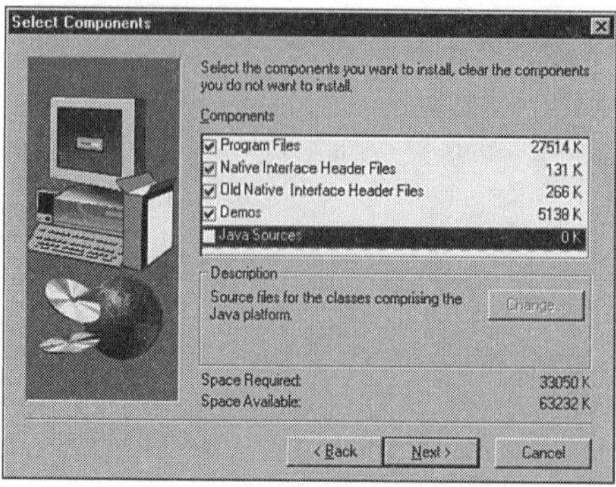

6. Set the PATH. Although we are striving for a browser-based environment, we will be doing some work from the command line. This means that we'll be typing instructions into a command prompt (or similar) window. If we wanted to use, say, javac, we would need to type

```
c:/jdk1.3/bin/javac myFile.java
```

Although there's nothing actually wrong with that, it can get tiresome in a hurry, and it is just that much more likely to cause typos. Fortunately, Windows provides a way to shortcut that process, using the `PATH` variable. If you type, instead,

```
javac myFile.java
```

Windows checks any directory listed in the `PATH` variable, looking for a program called `javac`. We'll want to add this to the `PATH` variable permanently (as opposed to every time we use it). The way to do this varies by operating system.

For Windows 95/98, we're going to put it into the `AUTOEXEC.bat` file, which runs every time the machine restarts.

MAKE A BACKUP OF THE AUTOEXEC.bat FILE BEFORE YOU CHANGE IT. Errors in this file can be a nightmare and can prevent the machine from operating properly, or even booting up. Please be careful!

After making a backup of `AUTOEXEC.bat`, open the file in Notepad (NOT WordPad!) and find the `PATH` statement. It typically looks something like this:

```
PATH C:\WINDOWS\COMMAND;C:\WINDOWS;
```

Add the `bin` directory, so that the statement looks something like this:

```
PATH C:\WINDOWS\COMMAND;C:\WINDOWS;c:\jdk1.3\bin;
```

Save the file.

To test the PATH (and make sure that you haven't introduced errors into AUTOEXEC.bat), open a command prompt window by choosing Start, Programs, MS-DOS Prompt (or the equivalent for your operating system). Type

```
autoexec
```

and press the Enter key. This runs the same script that runs when you start your computer. If there were errors, go back and fix them. If necessary, make a copy of the backup you made before you changed anything and start again.

3

If everything ran correctly, check the PATH by typing

```
path
```

at the prompt. You should see a string of directories that includes the one we added.

For Windows NT or Windows 2000, the process is much simpler. Choose Start, Control Panel, System, Environment. Under User Variables, look for PATH and highlight it. This gives you the opportunity to change the value. Add c:\jdk1.3\bin; (or the appropriate directory) to the end of the PATH variable. Do the same thing under System Variables.

For both Windows 9x and Windows NT/2000 users: If you have a previous version of the JDK installed, make sure that you either update or remove the reference to it, or at least make sure that the new reference comes first because only the first instance will be used.

Accept the changes and test them by opening a command prompt and typing PATH.

7. Set the CLASSPATH. Earlier versions of the Java SDK required users to add a variable called CLASSPATH, which told the application where to look for various code it needed. Java 2 actually works without a CLASSPATH being set, and there are other ways to pass that information into an application, if necessary. Other tools we'll be installing, however, require the CLASSPATH to work properly, so we'll go ahead and set it now.

   For Windows 95/98, we'll follow almost the same procedure as setting the path. Make a backup of the AUTOEXEC.bat file and open it in Notepad. If you don't have a CLASSPATH variable being set, add a line under the PATH declaration that looks like this:

   ```
   SET CLASSPATH=.;
   ```

Save the file and run it.

This will tell the application to start looking in the current directory for any code it needs. If you have an existing CLASSPATH setting with information needed by other applications, feel free to leave it, as long as you add the current directory as shown.

For Windows NT/2000, follow the same steps as for the PATH variable to make the preceding changes.

To test the CLASSPATH setting, type the following into a command prompt window:

```
set
```

This displays a list of all the current settings and what their values are. You should see a listing for the CLASSPATH.

8. Test the installation. At this point, we don't want to actually write any Java. We just want to be sure that it's installed correctly. To do that, type the following two lines at the command prompt:

```
cd c:\jdk1.3\demo\jfc\Stylepad
java -jar Stylepad.jar
```

After a few seconds, this should bring up a word-processor–like window with a page from Lewis Carroll's *Alice in Wonderland*.

If you downloaded a different version of the JDK, it might have different demos. Typically, they'll fall into two categories: Java foundation classes, or jfc, and applets. We will not be using applets at all, but if they are the only demos you have to test the installation, you'll need to use appletviewer for the test. For example, the standard JDK includes an applet called TicTacToe. To test the installation against this applet, type the following two lines:

```
cd c:\jdk1.3\demo\applets\TicTacToe
appletviewer example1.html
```

This should bring up a small game of Tic Tac Toe.

If you have difficulty with the installation, troubleshooting information can be found at

```
http://java.sun.com/j2se/1.3/install-windows.
html#troubleshooting
```

or on the site from which you downloaded the JDK itself.

Installing the Xerces-J Parser

Now that Java is installed and working, we need to install the actual parser that we'll use to check our data.

Development of applications, particularly those involving XML, revolves around the idea of an API, or Application Programming Interface. This is sort of like a minilanguage, in that it has a vocabulary where each command, or word, means something specific. Applications that use the same API can talk to each other more easily. Because of this, many XML-related programs are modular, in that different applications can be used for the same purpose, depending on the developer's preference.

API—An Application Programming Interface is a set of commands that programmers use to accomplish certain tasks. A program is said to implement an API if it can accomplish those tasks with those commands.

Modular—A modular program is one in which sections of code can be replaced without affecting the rest of the program.

This is especially true for parsers. Many parsers are available, but one of the most commonly used is Xerces, from the Apache Project.

The Apache Project is an open-source project that has produced the Apache Web Server and many other foundation products for the Web. Several corporations, including IBM, Sun, and Microsoft, have donated projects to Apache, making them freely available for the public use and to work on.

Xerces, and in particular its Java flavor, Xerces-J, is the base parser used with most of the more popular XML parsing applications, such as IBM's XML Parser for Java (XML4J, from which it actually originated) and Sun's Java API for XML Parsing (JAXP). We're going to use it directly to simplify installation issues, on the theory that every layer adds potential for problems that are out of the scope of this book to cover.

Installing Xerces-J

The Xerces-J parser can be found at

```
http://xml.apache.org/xerces-j/index.html
```

The current version as of this writing is 1.2.3, but we need to note a reality of XML development right now, and that is that things change. Specifically, the standards Xerces implements have not been finalized yet, so if there are changes, Xerces will have to keep up. Also, shortly before this writing, the group working on the Xerces-J project decided to change much of the focus of its work to add more simplicity and a new API, called JDOM. It is likely that by the time you read this, much of this new functionality will have been implemented, but for now we'll use the existing APIs.

Version numbers can change quickly in XML development. For instance, just during the writing of this book, Xerces has moved from version 1.1.3 through 1.2.0 to 1.2.3. Download the latest version of Xerces 1, but NOT Xerces 2. This refactoring is likely to be extremely different from version 1, and although you may eventually want to change over, it's better to learn the ropes on version 1, which is still an active project, first.

The important thing to remember is that although specific syntax may change, the concepts remain the same. If you're using a new version and something that looks right isn't working, check the documentation to see whether it's been changed.

To get the parser itself, click the Download button and look for the listings noted as "Latest Binaries," as shown in Figure 3.4. Download the zip file and put it in the same directory where you installed the Java SDK, but not in the Java itself. So, if the Java directory is `c:/jdk1.3`, put the zip file in `c:\`.

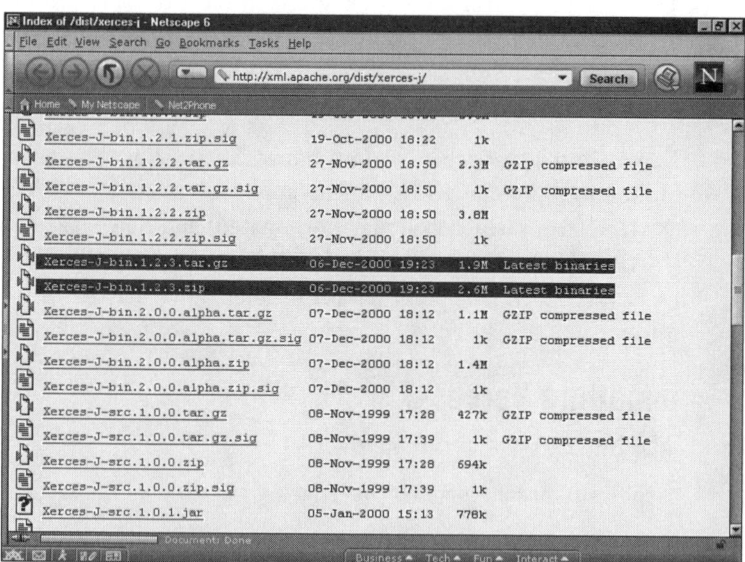

Figure 3.4

Download the latest binaries.

To unpack the files, we're going to use a Java tool called `jar`. Go to the directory where you've placed the zip file and type

```
jar xf Xerces-J-bin.1.2.3.zip
```

This takes a minute or so and creates a directory called `xerces-1_2_3` in that location.

Setting the CLASSPATH

Xerces requires that the `CLASSPATH` be set in order to function properly. (It also requires the `PATH`, but we set that already.) Add the following to your `CLASSPATH` the same way we added the current directory during the installation of the Java SDK:

```
c:\xerces-1_2_3\xerces.jar;c:\xerces-1_2_3\xercesSamples.jar;
```

For instance, in Windows 95/98, this line in the `AUTOEXEC.bat` file should now read

```
SET CLASSPATH=.;c:\xerces-1_2_3\xerces.jar;c:\xerces-1_2_3\xercesSamples.jar;
```

Remember, if you installed to a different location, make adjustments accordingly!

In Windows 95/98, this change won't take effect until you run `AUTOEXEC.bat`. If you run it manually, the changes will apply only to that window. After you restart, the changes will affect all windows.

If you are installing on UNIX, you need to change the ";" to ":" and the "\" to "/". You also need to remove the reference to drive `C:`, of course.

Testing the Installation

If all has gone well, you now have a functioning parser installed on your system. We're nowhere near ready to start programming to it, however, so, as we did with Java itself, we'll test the installation with one of the samples.

In this case, however, it's a sample that is actually useful. The SAXCount demo analyzes an XML file to determine certain things about it, such as how many elements or spaces it contains, and outputs it to the screen.

Although this is helpful, it also gives us a chance to validate our data, as we'll see in a little while. To test the installation, run the `AUTOEXEC.bat` file (or reboot), and then type the following two lines:

```
cd c:\xerces-1_2_3
java sax.SAXCount data/personal.xml -v
```

This command tells Java to run the `SAXCount` program to analyze the `personal.xml` file in the data directory and to check it against the defined structure while it's at it. You should see output similar to

```
data/personal.xml: 2250 ms (37 elems, 18 attrs, 150 spaces, 128 chars)
```

If you get an error telling you the class is not defined or can't be found, make sure that `CLASSPATH` for that window is referencing the Xerces files. If necessary, make the changes to `AUTOEXEC.bat` and restart your machine.

If the program appears to function properly but the XML file itself seems to come up with errors, the parser is not validating properly. This can be caused by old class files in your `CLASSPATH`. If you can't remove them, at least make sure that they appear after the new ones.

Well-Formed Versus Valid Documents

The first requirement of an XML document is that it must be well formed. Tags much be nested properly, attributes must be enclosed in quotation marks, it must have a single root element, and so on. We've dealt with all that in the first two chapters of this book.

But nothing that we've done says anything about requirements for the actual content of the data. This is a case where extensibility is a double-edged sword. We can put whatever we want into our XML document, as long as it's well formed. Unfortunately, so can anybody else.

For a single person working alone, this isn't an issue. When a second, or third, or three hundredth person enters the mix, however, slight (or even not-so-slight) differences in the way that data is represented can add up quickly. What's more, although they might be a nuisance in terms of displaying data, those differences are deadly when it comes to actually working with it.

To DTD or Not to DTD

For this reason, the XML 1.0 standard includes Document Type Definitions, or DTDs. A DTD can be either included in a document or associated with it (similar to the way we associated style sheets), allowing a validating parser to check the structure and content of the document.

valid document—A valid XML document conforms to the structure defined in a DTD or other definition.

validating parser—A validating parser checks an XML file not just for well-formedness, but for differences from a DTD or other definition.

DTDs were, and still are, essential to serious XML development, but they have a number of problems and limitations.

First, the syntax is different from XML syntax, making it a bit confusing for new users. Second, although DTDs can be powerful, there are still things developers need to do that simply can't be accomplished with a DTD.

For this reason, it wasn't long before other initiatives started to improve on the functionality of DTDs. Many of them have come and gone, but two that seem to have legs are XML Schema, which uses XML syntax and adds a great deal of functionality to the process, and a similar proposal, RELAX, out of Japan. It is likely that in the long run, one of these will take the place of DTDs for development moving forward.

None of these, however, has yet reached the status of "standard," so we are still going to need to take a look at DTDs. Although Xerces includes support for much of XML Schema, it's not yet complete or final. Besides, DTDs are used to describe XML vocabularies that can be used for data interchange within industries or for other purposes, so any serious XML developer is going to have to deal with them sooner, rather than later.

We'll look at the basics of DTDs, and when we come up against their limitations, we'll look at how XML Schema can help us overcome them.

EXCURSION

What Is a "Standard," Anyway?

In the world of the Internet, as in life, it's important for people to be able to understand one another. This is particularly important as people strive to interconnect diverse systems. Because of this, a standard way of communicating is crucial.

But although we throw the word around quite casually, it does actually have a real meaning. Technically, a standard is a document that has been approved by a national or international standards body, such as the International Organization for Standards (ISO) or the American National Standards Institute (ANSI).

The World Wide Web Consortium (W3C) is not a formal standards body.

"Wait a minute," you might be thinking. "How can the W3C not be a standards body when it publishes the standards for the Web and the Internet?"

Simple: It doesn't. The W3C publishes Recommendations, and it's very clear about that. Although, if desired, a W3C Recommendation could be submitted to a formal standards body such as ISO, they typically aren't, and with good reason.

That reason is also simple: It doesn't matter.

What makes a standard isn't the voting body that approves it, but rather the fact that everyone (or almost everyone) is using it. For instance, RELAX might be submitted for Fast Track approval by ISO and might be official before XML Schema gets through the process at W3C. But if nobody uses it, what difference does it make?

The W3C Recommendations are typically considered to be informal standards if they are what's in use, as in "the standard" way of doing something. Like most resources, we'll use "standard" and "recommendation" interchangeably, but it helps to keep the difference in mind.

Document Type Definitions

Eventually, we'll want to do an analysis of the different entities that we're relating together, but in beginning to build our DTD, we'll start off with an excerpt from our `products.xml` file.

Make a copy and save it in `C:\xerces-1_2_3\data` (or the appropriate directory on your system). Remove all but the first vendor, Conners Chair Company, as shown in Listing 3.1.

Listing 3.1—`products.xml`: The Data

```
<?xml version="1.0"?>
<products>
<vendor webvendor="full">
    <vendor_name>Conners Chair Company</vendor_name>
    <advertisement>
        <ad_sentence>
        Conners Chair Company presents their annual big three
        day only chair sale. We're making way for our new
        stock!  <b>All current inventory must go!</b>  Regular prices
        slashed by up to 60%!
        </ad_sentence>
    </advertisement>

    <product>
        <product_id>QA3452</product_id>
        <short_desc>Queen Anne Chair</short_desc>
        <price pricetype="cost">$85</price>
        <price pricetype="sale">$125</price>
        <price pricetype="retail">$195</price>
        <inventory color="royal blue" location="warehouse">
            12</inventory>
        <inventory color="royal blue" location="showroom">
            5</inventory>
        <inventory color="flower print" location="warehouse">
            16</inventory>
        <inventory color="flower print" location="showroom">
            3</inventory>
        <inventory color="seafoam green" location="warehouse">
            20</inventory>
        <inventory color="teal" location="warehouse">
            14</inventory>
        <inventory color="burgundy" location="warehouse">
            34</inventory>
        <giveaway>
            <giveaway_item>
            Matching Ottoman included
            </giveaway_item>
            <giveaway_desc>
            while supplies last
```

Listing 3.1—continued

```
39:             </giveaway_desc>
40:         </giveaway>
41:     </product>
42:
43:     <product>
44:         <product_id>RC2342</product_id>
45:         <short_desc>Early American Rocking Chair</short_desc>
46:         <product_desc>
47:             with brown and tan plaid upholstery
48:         </product_desc>
49:         <price pricetype="cost">$75</price>
50:         <price pricetype="sale">$62</price>
51:         <price pricetype="retail">$120</price>
52:         <inventory location="warehouse">40</inventory>
53:         <inventory location="showroom">2</inventory>
54:     </product>
55:
56:     <product>
57:         <product_id>BR3452</product_id>
58:         <short_desc>Bentwood Rocker</short_desc>
59:         <price pricetype="cost">$125</price>
60:         <price pricetype="sale">$160</price>
61:         <price pricetype="retail">$210</price>
62:         <inventory location="showroom">3</inventory>
63:     </product>
64:
65:</vendor>
66:
67:</products>
```


(Notice that we added a little bit of XHTML markup on line 8.)

In the spirit of testing as we go along, let's go ahead and parse the file to make sure that there's nothing wrong with it to start. To do this, open a command prompt window and type

```
cd c:\xerces-1_2_3
java sax.SAXCount data/products.xml
```

We should get a result similar to when we tested the Xerces installation, such as

```
data/products/xml: 330 ms (37 elems, 27 attrs, 0 spaces, 610 chars)
```

If you get an error saying that tags are missing or elements are not terminated properly, there is a problem with the `products.xml` file. You might have inadvertently removed or left an extra tag when you removed the extra two vendors.

If you get an error saying that the class or the file cannot be found, check for typing errors.

To save time and typing mistakes, commands can be placed in a batch file. For instance, we can take the command to parse this file

```
java sax.SAXCount data/products.xml
```

and place it in a text file called `val.bat`, which we place in the `c:\xerces-1_2_3` directory. Then, to check the file, we just go to that directory and type the following:

```
val
```

The script will handle it from there.

Notice that we left the `-v` switch off the command. The reason is that we're not ready to validate this file yet—we have no DTD to check against! Every single element would currently be an error because it's not defined.

Internal DTD Subsets

We'll start by embedding the DTD in the XML file, the same way we started with style sheets.

As we mentioned earlier, DTDs use a different syntax than XML itself does. To begin building one, we need to make a space for it in the document, as in Listing 3.2.

Listing 3.2—`products.xml`: Creating an Internal DTD

```
0: <?xml version="1.0"?>
1: <!DOCTYPE products [
2:
3:     <!-- Definition goes here -->
4:
5: ]>
6:
7: <products>
8: <vendor webvendor="full">
...
```

The `<!DOCTYPE>` notation on line 1 is called a Document Type Declaration and lets the processor know that this is the start of a Document Type Definition, or DTD. Line 1 also refers to products, which is the root element of the XML below it, starting on line 7. These two must match because the DTD can describe only specific structures. Notice also the brackets that start on line 1 end on line 5. They'll denote the start and the end of the definition itself. XML-style comments are allowed within the DTD, as you can see on line 3.

From here we can take a pretty literal, straightforward view. We want to define each element in terms of the other elements, attributes, or data it can contain. We'll start with the root element, `products`. In Listing 3.3, we add the only element that can be contained in `products`, the `vendor`.

Listing 3.3—`products.xml`: Defining the Root Element

```
0: <?xml version="1.0"?>
1: <!DOCTYPE products [
2:
3: <!ELEMENT products (vendor)+>
4:
5: ]>
6:
7: <products>
8: <vendor webvendor="full">
...
```

Line 3 tells the parser that we have an element named `products` and that all it can contain is `vendor` elements. The + sign tells the parser that we can have one or more `vendors`. Because this is the root element, we want to make sure that we have some data, so at least one is required. Now we need to define the `vendor` element, as in Listing 3.4.

Listing 3.4—Defining the Vendor Element

```
0: <?xml version="1.0"?>
1: <!DOCTYPE products [
2:
3: <!ELEMENT products (vendor)+>
4:
5: <!ELEMENT vendor (vendor_name, advertisement?, product*)>
6:
7: ]>
8:
9: <products>
10:<vendor webvendor="full">
...
```

Line 5 defines a `vendor` as an element that may contain a `vendor_name`, `advertisement`, and `products`. Actually, we're saying that it must contain exactly one `vendor_name`, it may contain one `advertisement` (using the `?`), and it may contain any number of `products`, including 0 (using the `*`).

We haven't completely defined the `vendor` element yet, however. Looking at the XML file, we see that vendor can have an attribute, `webvendor`. We need to put this into the DTD, as in Listing 3.5.

Listing 3.5—products.xml: Adding Attributes to the Vendor Element

```
0: <?xml version="1.0"?>
1: <!DOCTYPE products [
2:
3: <!ELEMENT products      (vendor)+>
4:
5: <!ELEMENT vendor     (vendor_name, advertisement?, product*)>
6: <!ATTLIST vendor     webvendor CDATA #REQUIRED>
7:
8: ]>
9:
10: <products>
11:<vendor webvendor="full">
...
```

Let's pick line 6 apart piece by piece. First, the <!ATTLIST> notation indicates that we're defining an attribute list for an element, as opposed to the element itself. Next, we note what element the attribute list is for—specifically, vendor. Then we list the name of the attribute, webvendor, and the type of data that can be contained in it, followed by the fact that the attribute is required.

So, the definition on line 6 means that the vendor element must have one attribute, which is called webvendor and can contain character data.

That's not really very helpful, though, because it doesn't specify anything about what that text should be. We need to make sure that it's one of our three choices, full, partial, or no. We can do that on line 6 of Listing 3.6.

Listing 3.6—products.xml: Specifying Content for the webvendor Attribute

```
0: <?xml version="1.0"?>
1: <!DOCTYPE products [
2:
3: <!ELEMENT products      (vendor)+>
4:
5: <!ELEMENT vendor     (vendor_name, advertisement?, product*)>
6: <!ATTLIST vendor     webvendor ( full | partial | no ) #REQUIRED>
7:
8: ]>
9:
10: <products>
11:<vendor webvendor="full">
...
```

We've seen the | connector before, when we were using XSLT. At that time it worked as a sort of "or" statement, and it still does. Only one of those three values is allowed. The value of webvendor must be full or partial or no.

Let's move on to our other elements. Listing 3.7 defines `vendor_name`, `advertisement`, and `product`.

Listing 3.7—`products.xml`: Specifying Content for the `vendor` Element

```
0: <?xml version="1.0"?>
1: <!DOCTYPE products [
2:
3: <!ELEMENT products     (vendor)+>
4:
5: <!ELEMENT vendor     (vendor_name, advertisement?, product*)>
6: <!ATTLIST vendor     webvendor ( full | partial | no ) #REQUIRED>
7:
8: <!ELEMENT vendor_name     (#PCDATA)>
9:
10:<!ELEMENT advertisement     (ad_sentence)+>
11:<!ELEMENT ad_sentence     (#PCDATA)>
12:
13:<!ELEMENT product (product_id, short_desc, product_desc?, price+,
➥inventory+, giveaway?)>
14:
15:<!ELEMENT product_id    (#PCDATA)>
16:<!ELEMENT short_desc    (#PCDATA)>
17:<!ELEMENT product_desc    (#PCDATA)>
18:
19:<!ELEMENT price       (#PCDATA)>
20:<!ATTLIST price        pricetype     (cost | sale | retail) 'retail'>
21:
22:<!ELEMENT inventory    (#PCDATA)>
23:<!ATTLIST inventory    color        CDATA #IMPLIED
24:                      location     (showroom | warehouse) 'warehouse'>
25:
26:<!ELEMENT giveaway    (giveaway_item, giveaway_desc)>
27:<!ELEMENT giveaway_item (#PCDATA)>
28:<!ELEMENT giveaway_desc (#PCDATA)>
29:
30:]>
31:
32:<products>
33:<vendor webvendor="full">
...
```

Let's take this one line at a time. `vendor_name`, on line 8, is a simple text element, as are `product_id`, `short_desc`, and `product_desc`. `#PCDATA` represents "Parsed Character Data." This means that it is normal text, but we're assuming that it has already been parsed—that is, there is no markup contained in it.

`advertisement` can contain one or more `ad_sentences`, and `giveaway` must contain one `giveaway_item` and one `giveaway_desc`.

The `product` element is a little more complicated but not much. It contains only elements: specifically, exactly one `product_id` and `short_desc`, one optional `product_desc`, one or more `prices`, one or more `inventory` elements, and then an optional `giveaway`.

It's important to note that the order matters. Subelements must appear in the order in which they're listed in the element's definition.

Now let's take some of the more interesting elements.

Attribute Definitions

On lines 19 and 20, we're defining the `price` element as having a single attribute, called `pricetype`, which may take the values of `cost`, `sale`, or `retail`. This is called an enumerated datatype, because we are choosing from a set of values. Although we do need to have this information for every `price` element, we have not made it required. Instead we've given it a default value. If a value isn't supplied, the default value of `'retail'` will be used when the data is processed.

This is one of the advantages of a DTD. We can add information to the document without even touching it!

Actually, all attributes need some way to handle default values. This can take one of four forms:

- `#REQUIRED`—As we saw with `webvendor`, we can force the XML file to provide a value for the attribute.
- `#IMPLIED`—If an attribute is `#IMPLIED`, it's not required. If a value isn't supplied, there is no default value, but it's not an error. For instance, we are not concerned if a color isn't specified.
- A literal default, such as `'retail'` or `'false'`—In this case, we provide a value that will be used if no value is provided for the attribute.
- `#FIXED 'literal'`—If an attribute is set as `#FIXED`, it must always have the literal value supplied. If it's not supplied, the parser will fill in the value. If it is supplied, it has to match.

Finally, on lines 22 through 24 we have the definition of the `inventory` element with two attributes, `color` and `location`, but we've taken advantage of the capability to include more than one attribute in a single declaration to make things easier to read. The color attribute is a string datatype, as we've indicated by setting it as CDATA, or character data.

At this point, we've defined all of our elements, so we're ready to go ahead and validate the document. To do that, we'll go to a command prompt and, after making sure that we're in the `xerces-1_2_3` directory, type

```
java sax.SAXCount data/products.xml -v
```

Mixed Content

At this point, if we haven't mistyped any of the elements in the DTD, we should see the results of parsing the document. The parser should return a message that says something like the following:

```
[Error] products.xml:40:14: Element type "b" must be declared.
[Error] products.xml:42:21: The content of element type "ad_sentence" must
➥match "(#PCDATA)".
data/products.xml: 3790 ms (38 elems, 27 attrs, 137 spaces, 473 chars)
```


Congratulations, you've validated your first document! But wait, what about those errors? Those errors mean that the parser is doing exactly what it's supposed to do. We specified `ad_sentence` as containing nothing but `#PCDATA`, or parsed character data. That means that no markup is allowed. Remember, however, that we went ahead and added a bit of markup to `ad_sentence` when we saved the file.

So, what can we do if we want to allow, say, some XHTML tags in the vendor's `advertisement`? We need to specifically tell the DTD that this element can contain both `#PCDATA` and elements. This is called Mixed Content. In Listing 3.8, we'll tell the DTD that `ad_sentence` can contain any number of the specified items.

Listing 3.8—Mixed Content

```
...
8: <!ELEMENT vendor_name     (#PCDATA)>
9:
10:<!ELEMENT advertisement (ad_sentence)+>
11:<!ELEMENT ad_sentence     (#PCDATA | b | i | p )*>
12:<!ELEMENT b (#PCDATA)>
13:<!ELEMENT i (#PCDATA)>
14:<!ELEMENT p (#PCDATA)>
15:
16:<!ELEMENT product     (product_id, short_desc, product_desc?, price+,
➥inventory+, giveaway?)>
...
```

Let's take a good hard look at what this means on line 11. First, because we're following the parentheses with the `*`, whatever is inside them can appear any number of times within the element. This means that it's acceptable for `ad_sentence` to be made up of `#PCDATA`, then a `b` element, then more `#PCDATA`, or any combination of `#PCDATA` and the elements listed.

Of course, we then have to go ahead and declare those elements, as we've done on lines 12 through 14. Even though you and I know they're just XHTML, the parser doesn't. To the parser, they are elements, just as `vendor` and `product` and `price` are elements.

Make the change to the DTD and revalidate the file. This time there should be no errors.

DTD Syntax Review

We've covered a lot of ground here, so let's take a moment and review the specific syntax for building DTDs. An element declaration consists of a name and a content model:

```
<!ELEMENT element-name (content)>
```

Content can be an element, a series of elements, a choice of elements, or `#PCDATA`. We can use the following special characters to add more information:

- `+`—At least one is required, but the element may repeat.
- `?`—The element is not required, and may appear only once.
- `*`—Not required, but may repeat.
- `|`—Indicates a choice between elements.

An attribute definition consists of information about the element, the type, and the default:

```
<!ATTLIST element-name attribute-name TYPE 'default'>
```

The type is typically either `CDATA`, which is just text, a series of choices (such as `(true | false)`), or `ID`, `IDREF`, and so on, which will be discussed later. Finally, we list the default, which can be `#IMPLIED`, `#REQUIRED`, `#FIXED 'somevalue'`, or just `'somevalue'`.

The First Limitation: Datatypes

One thing you might have noticed is that although we can (and must, in fact) get specific about the types of subelements an element can contain, we don't have a lot of control over the specific types of data after we get down to the text level. Elements can be `#PCDATA`, attributes are `CDATA`, and that's it. There's no way to indicate that, say, a `price` can be only a number, or `inventory` must be an integer.

This is one of the serious limitations of DTDs and was one of the first indications that a better system was needed. Datatypes will be covered by XML Schema.

External DTDs

Before the DTD gets any bigger, let's go ahead and move it out to its own document, as we did with the style sheets. First, we'll create the DTD file itself and call it `products.dtd`. We'll save it in the same directory as `products.xml`. As shown in

Listing 3.9, we're keeping the content the same, but this file doesn't include the `<!DOCTYPE>` declaration that was in the `products.xml` file.

Listing 3.9—Creating an External DTD

```
<!ELEMENT products     (vendor)+>

<!ELEMENT vendor     (vendor_name, advertisement?, product*)>
<!ATTLIST vendor     webvendor CDATA #REQUIRED>

<!ELEMENT vendor_name     (#PCDATA)>

<!ELEMENT advertisement (ad_sentence)+>
<!ELEMENT ad_sentence     (#PCDATA | b | i | p )*>
<!ELEMENT b (#PCDATA)>
<!ELEMENT i (#PCDATA)>
<!ELEMENT p (#PCDATA)>

<!ELEMENT product     (product_id, short_desc, product_desc?, price+, inventory+, giveaway?)>

<!ELEMENT product_id    (#PCDATA)>
<!ELEMENT short_desc    (#PCDATA)>
<!ELEMENT product_desc    (#PCDATA)>

<!ELEMENT price    (#PCDATA)>
<!ATTLIST price         pricetype     (cost | sale | retail) 'retail'>

<!ELEMENT inventory (#PCDATA)>
<!ATTLIST inventory   color        CDATA                    #IMPLIED
                      location     (showroom | warehouse) 'warehouse'>

<!ELEMENT giveaway    (giveaway_item, giveaway_desc)>
<!ELEMENT giveaway_item (#PCDATA)>
<!ELEMENT giveaway_desc (#PCDATA)>
```

Now we need to link this DTD to the `products.xml` file. We will do this using the `<!DOCTYPE>` declaration, which remains in that file, as shown in Listing 3.10.

Listing 3.10—Linking to an External DTD

```
<?xml version="1.0"?>
<!DOCTYPE products SYSTEM "products.dtd">

<products>
<vendor webvendor="full">
    <vendor_name>Conners Chair Company</vendor_name>
...
```

In this case, the `<!DOCTYPE>` declaration has just been changed to point to the file itself (which must be in the same directory as `products.xml`, in this case).

Just to be sure that we don't have any glitches or typos, go ahead and validate the document once more.

Let's take a look at this for a moment. In our case, we want to point to a specific file on our machine, so we use the keyword `SYSTEM` before we give it a location. There is, however, another use for the `DOCTYPE` declaration.

As mentioned earlier, one reason to learn the DTD syntax is because existing XML vocabularies have been written in it. For example, if the furniture industry decided on a particular DTD that would be used to describe its products, we might use a declaration like this:

```
<!DOCTYPE products PUBLIC "-//Furniture, Inc.//Furniture Catalog//EN"
"http://www.nicholaschase.com/dtds/furniture.dtd">
```

In this case, the keyword `PUBLIC` alerts the processor that it should check the public identifier, `"-//Furniture, Inc.//Furniture Catalog//EN"`, against its list of local DTD copies. If it's not found, it should go to `http://www.nicholaschase.com/dtds/furniture.dtd` and retrieve the DTD information.

Let's take a moment to examine the public identifier

```
-//Furniture, Inc.//Furniture Catalog//EN
```

The first item, `-`, indicates that this DTD is not registered with the ISO. If it were, this item would be a `+`. The second item, `Furniture, Inc.`, is the owner of the DTD. The third, `Furniture Catalog`, is a human-readable description of the DTD. Finally, the last item, `EN`, indicates the language of the DTD.

Adding the Rest of Our Vendors

Now that we think we've got the DTD pretty well finalized, we can put the rest of the data back into it.

Now we should be able to parse the document without a problem. When we do parse it, however, we see quite a few problems, which are shown in Listing 3.11.

Listing 3.11—Parsing Errors for `products.xml`

```
0: [Error] products.xml:81:13: Element type "suite" must be declared.
1: [Error] products.xml:84:21: Element type "long_desc" must be declared.
2: [Error] products.xml:125:16: The content of element type "product" must
➥match "(product_id,short_desc,product_desc?,price+,inventory+,giveaway?)".
3: [Error] products.xml:129:56: Attribute "color" must be declared for element
➥type "price".
4: [Error] products.xml:131:56: Attribute "color" must be declared for element
➥type "price".
5: [Error] products.xml:143:15: The content of element type "product" must
➥match "(product_id,short_desc,product_desc?,price+,inventory+,giveaway?)".
6: [Error] products.xml:145:11: The content of element type "vendor" must match
➥"(vendor_name,advertisement?,product*)".
```

Listing 3.11—continued

```
7: [Error] products.xml:178:16: The content of element type "product" must
➥match "(product_id,short_desc,product_desc?,price+,inventory+,giveaway?)".
8: [Error] products.xml:183:37: Attribute "pricetype" with value "starting"
➥must have a value from the list "(cost|sale|retail)".
9: [Error] products.xml:186:15: Element type "item" must be declared.
10:[Error] products.xml:192:15: Element type "item" must be declared.
11:[Error] products.xml:206:16: The content of element type "product" must
➥match "(product_id,short_desc,product_desc?,price+,inventory+,giveaway?)".
12:[Error] products.xml:220:16: The content of element type "product" must
➥match "(product_id,short_desc,product_desc?,price+,inventory+,giveaway?)".
13:[Error] products.xml:222:35: Element type "special" must be declared.
14:[Error] products.xml:222:35: Attribute "specialtype" must be declared for
➥element type "special".
15:[Error] products.xml:227:11: The content of element type "vendor" must match
➥"(vendor_name,advertisement?,product*)".
16:data/products.xml: 3740 ms (127 elems, 75 attrs, 1125 spaces, 2534 chars)
17:data/products.xml: 2920 ms (97 elems, 73 attrs, 353 spaces, 1641 chars)
```


This really isn't as bad as it looks. Although there are technically 16 errors, many of them are duplicates, in that the same problem causes several errors.

But wait a minute, if we took all this time to get the DTD right, why are we getting so many errors?

Because it's the nature of the business. This is the reason that a DTD must be tested against as much of the intended data as possible. Sometimes we'll change the data to match the DTD; sometimes we'll change the DTD to match the data. We need to do this now, during the design phase, so we don't find ourselves in a position later where we can't record the data we want because the structure won't allow it!

Let's take these errors one at a time. Lines 0 and 1 are easy; we never defined the suite in the DTD. We'll add the following to it:

```
<!ELEMENT vendor     (vendor_name, advertisement?, suite*, product*)>
<!ELEMENT suite (product_id, short_desc, long_desc, price+, product*)>
<!ELEMENT long_desc (#PCDATA)>
```

This also fixes line 6.

The error on line 2 tells us that we have a `product` that's not conforming to its content model, or definition. Fortunately, the error message tells us approximately where the problem is. In this case, it's somewhere around line 125, column 16. This works out to be the following product:

```
<product>
    <short_desc>Hall Bench</short_desc>
    <price pricetype="cost">$75</price>
    <price pricetype="sale">$62</price>
    <price pricetype="retail">$120</price>
```

```
        <inventory location="warehouse">143</inventory>
        <inventory location="showroom">5</inventory>
    </product>
```

Looking at the content model for product,

```
<!ELEMENT product (product_id, short_desc, product_desc?, price+, inventory+,
➥giveaway?)>
```

we see that this product is missing the mandatory product_id. In this case, the DTD did exactly what it was intended to—it enforced consistency in the data. We could alter the DTD to make the product_id optional, but that's probably not a good idea, so we'll go ahead and add a product_id for this product and any others that are missing one.

Lines 3 and 4 are both referring to the same problem. On lines 129 and 131 of products.xml, we've introduced color to the price element. Here we have a few choices:

- We can change the data so that each color item is its own product and then record the color in its own element. This won't take too much trouble, although we'll have to make sure to maintain both products.
- Because the sale and retail prices are the same for both colors, we can change the DTD to add a new element, cost, and change the pricing structure. This seems a bit of overkill, however, even in a small file like this.
- We can change the DTD to allow for a color attribute. This seems like the best solution because it also allows for different color items to be priced differently, if necessary. This is what we'll do:

```
<!ATTLIST price          pricetype      (cost | sale | retail)
'retail'
                                color CDATA #IMPLIED>
```

At first, line 5 doesn't seem to make any sense. The product in question is

```
    <product>
        <product_id>3253435</product_id>
        <short_desc>Sleepeazy Mattresses</short_desc>
        <price pricetype="cost">$162</price>
        <price pricetype="retail">$300</price>
        <product_desc>per set, any size</product_desc>
        <giveaway>
            <giveaway_item>
            Free pillows
            </giveaway_item>
            <giveaway_desc>
```

```
            with every set
            </giveaway_desc>
        </giveaway>
        <inventory location="showroom">23</inventory>
        <inventory location="warehouse">15</inventory>
    </product>
```

which seems to match the content model just fine. Or does it? Remember, order matters. To fix this error, we'll reorder the data.

Lines 6 through 10 are a little tougher and will probably involve changing the DTD. The product is

3

```
    <product>
        <product_id>5622345</product_id>
        <short_desc>CozyComfort Mattresses</short_desc>
        <price pricetype="starting">
            starting at only $99.99
        </price>
        <item>
            <product_desc>Queen</product_desc>
            <price pricetype="cost">$59.00</price>
            <price pricetype="sale">$69.00</price>
            <price pricetype="retail">$99.00</price>
        </item>
        <item>
            <product_desc>King</product_desc>
            <price pricetype="cost">$159.00</price>
            <price pricetype="sale">$209.00</price>
            <price pricetype="retail">$359.00</price>
        </item>
        <giveaway>
            <giveaway_item>
            Free sheets
            </giveaway_item>
            <giveaway_desc>
            with every set
            </giveaway_desc>
        </giveaway>
    </product>
```

For the `starting` price, we need to make a decision: Do we add this as a possible attribute value, or change the structure to allow for an infinite number of different pricing options?

If it looked like we'd have to deal with more of these, that'd be the way to go. This is probably the last one, though, so let's just add it to the definition of `price`.

```
<!ELEMENT price         (#PCDATA)>
<!ATTLIST price          pricetype   (cost | sale | retail | starting) 'retail'
                         color CDATA #IMPLIED>
```

This brings us to `item`. Unless we want to make significant changes to the data file (which we don't), we're going to need to change the DTD to accommodate it.

```
<!ELEMENT product      (product_id, short_desc, product_desc?, price+, item*,
➥inventory+, giveaway?)>
<!ELEMENT item (product_desc, price+)>
```

Finally, to conform to the content model for `product`, we'll have to add an `inventory` element. In doing this, we don't have any information, so the natural choice would be to leave the element completely blank, as in

```
<inventory />
```

This, however, makes no sense, and doesn't give us much to go on from a programming standpoint. Instead, we can make the inventory element optional, and use its absence as an indication that there's something wrong.

```
<!ELEMENT product      (product_id, short_desc, product_desc?, price+, item*,
➥inventory*, giveaway?)>
```

This is another advantage to checking against as much data as possible. You are likely to find problems that aren't directly causing us errors—yet.

We have a similar issue on line 11, where an item doesn't have a price. In this case, however, we don't want to make the price optional, so we need to add one. Because we don't have any information, however, we'll use the data to indicate that there's something wrong:

```
<product>
        <product_id>39981234</product_id>
        <short_desc>Floataway Waterbeds</short_desc>
        <price pricetype="cost">TBD</price>
        <giveaway>
            <giveaway_item>
            15 different styles to choose from
            </giveaway_item>
            <giveaway_desc>
            with free delivery -- we'll take your
            old mattress as a trade in!
            </giveaway_desc>
        </giveaway>
    </product>
```

Finally, lines 14 through 16 refer to the fact that we never defined the `special`. We can take care of that easily:

```
<!ELEMENT vendor     (vendor_name, advertisement?, suite*, product*, special?)>
<!ELEMENT special (#PCDATA)>
<!ATTLIST special specialtype CDATA #FIXED 'weekly'>
```

Right now we can accommodate only `weekly specials`, so we'll require that all `specials` be `weekly`.

We run the validation one more time and find that everything comes out clean. The final DTD and XML files are shown in Listings 3.12 and 3.13, respectively.

Listing 3.12—`products.dtd`: The Complete DTD

```
<!ELEMENT products   (vendor)+>
<!ELEMENT vendor     (vendor_name, advertisement?, suite*, product*,
➥special?)>
<!ATTLIST vendor     webvendor CDATA #REQUIRED>
<!ELEMENT special (#PCDATA)>
<!ATTLIST special specialtype CDATA #FIXED 'weekly'>
<!ELEMENT vendor_name   (#PCDATA)>
<!ELEMENT advertisement (ad_sentence)+>
<!ELEMENT ad_sentence   (#PCDATA | b | i | p )*>
<!ELEMENT b (#PCDATA)>
<!ELEMENT i (#PCDATA)>
<!ELEMENT p (#PCDATA)>
<!ELEMENT product (product_id, short_desc, product_desc?, price+, item*,
➥inventory*, giveaway?)>
<!ELEMENT product_id    (#PCDATA)>
<!ELEMENT short_desc    (#PCDATA)>
<!ELEMENT product_desc    (#PCDATA)>
<!ELEMENT price (#PCDATA)>
<!ATTLIST price pricetype  (cost | sale | retail | starting) 'retail'
                color      CDATA #IMPLIED>
<!ELEMENT item (product_desc, price+)>
<!ELEMENT inventory   (#PCDATA)>
<!ATTLIST inventory   color    CDATA                      #IMPLIED
                      location (showroom | warehouse) 'warehouse'>
<!ELEMENT giveaway    (giveaway_item, giveaway_desc)>
<!ELEMENT giveaway_item (#PCDATA)>
<!ELEMENT giveaway_desc (#PCDATA)>
<!ELEMENT suite (product_id, short_desc, long_desc, price+, product*)>
<!ELEMENT long_desc (#PCDATA)>
```

Listing 3.13—`products.xml`: The Complete, Updated XML File

```
<?xml version="1.0"?>
<!DOCTYPE products SYSTEM "products.dtd">

<products>

<vendor webvendor="full">
   <vendor_name>Conners Chair Company</vendor_name>
   <advertisement>
       <ad_sentence>
       Conners Chair Company presents their annual big three
       day only chair sale. We're making way for our new
       stock!  <b>All current inventory must go!</b>  Regular prices
       slashed by up to 60%!
        </ad_sentence>
    </advertisement>

    <product>
        <product_id>QA3452</product_id>
        <short_desc>Queen Anne Chair</short_desc>
        <price pricetype="cost">$85</price>
        <price pricetype="sale">$125</price>
        <price pricetype="retail">$195</price>
        <inventory color="royal blue" location="warehouse">
            12</inventory>
        <inventory color="royal blue" location="showroom">
            5</inventory>
        <inventory color="flower print" location="warehouse">
            16</inventory>
        <inventory color="flower print" location="showroom">
            3</inventory>
        <inventory color="seafoam green" location="warehouse">
            20</inventory>
        <inventory color="teal" location="warehouse">
            14</inventory>
        <inventory color="burgundy" location="warehouse">
            34</inventory>
        <giveaway>
            <giveaway_item>
            Matching Ottoman included
            </giveaway_item>
            <giveaway_desc>
            while supplies last
            </giveaway_desc>
        </giveaway>
    </product>

    <product>
        <product_id>RC2342</product_id>
        <short_desc>Early American Rocking Chair</short_desc>
        <product_desc>
```

Listing 3.13—continued

```
            with brown and tan plaid upholstery
        </product_desc>
        <price pricetype="cost">$75</price>
        <price pricetype="sale">$62</price>
        <price pricetype="retail">$120</price>
        <inventory location="warehouse">40</inventory>
        <inventory location="showroom">2</inventory>
    </product>

    <product>
        <product_id>BR3452</product_id>
        <short_desc>Bentwood Rocker</short_desc>
        <price pricetype="cost">$125</price>
        <price pricetype="sale">$160</price>
        <price pricetype="retail">$210</price>
        <inventory location="showroom">3</inventory>
    </product>

</vendor>

 <vendor webvendor="partial">
    <vendor_name>
        Wally's Wonderful World of Furniture
    </vendor_name>
    <advertisement>
        <ad_sentence>
        Wally's Wonderful World of Furniture is closing its
        doors forever. Last chance to get great bargains.
        Make us an offer. We can't refuse!
        </ad_sentence>
    </advertisement>

    <suite>
        <product_id>CDRS</product_id>
        <short_desc>Complete Dining Room Set</short_desc>
        <long_desc>
            This five piece dining site set features swivel
            chairs with cushions in five exciting colors.
        </long_desc>
        <price pricetype="cost">$435</price>
        <price pricetype="sale">$699</price>
        <price pricetype="retail">$999</price>

        <product>
            <product_id>WWWdrt</product_id>
            <short_desc>Dining Room Table</short_desc>
            <price pricetype="cost">$105</price>
            <price pricetype="sale">$145</price>
            <price pricetype="retail">$195</price>
            <inventory location="warehouse">132</inventory>
        </product>
```

Listing 3.13—continued

```
            <product>
              <product_id>WWWsc</product_id>
               <short_desc>Swivel Chair</short_desc>
               <price pricetype="cost">$50</price>
               <price pricetype="sale">$45</price>
               <price pricetype="retail">$99</price>
               <inventory location="warehouse">300</inventory>
          </product>
           <product>
               <product_id>WWWhch</product_id>
              <short_desc>Hutch</short_desc>
               <price pricetype="cost">$346</price>
              <price pricetype="sale">$425</price>
               <price pricetype="retail">$600</price>
               <inventory location="warehouse">232</inventory>
           </product>
       </suite>

       <product>
           <product_id>HallBench</product_id>
           <short_desc>Hall Bench</short_desc>
           <price pricetype="cost">$75</price>
           <price pricetype="sale">$62</price>
           <price pricetype="retail">$120</price>
           <inventory location="warehouse">143</inventory>
          <inventory location="showroom">5</inventory>
       </product>

       <product>
           <product_id>SofaLoveSeat</product_id>
           <short_desc>Sofa and Love Seat</short_desc>
           <price color="magnolia print" pricetype="cost">
                $125</price>
           <price color="nautical print" pricetype="cost">
                $145</price>
           <price pricetype="sale">$175</price>
           <price pricetype="retail">$250</price>
           <inventory color="magnolia print" location="showroom">
               3</inventory>
           <inventory color="magnolia print" location="warehouse">
                36</inventory>
           <inventory color="nautical print" location="warehouse">
                1</inventory>
           <inventory color="nautical print" location="showroom">
                432</inventory>
      </product>

</vendor>

<vendor webvendor="no">
      <vendor_name>Crazy Marge's Bed Emporium</vendor_name>
```

Listing 3.13—continued

```
<advertisement>
    <ad_sentence>
    We never have a sale because we've got the lowest
    prices in town!  Come in today and shop around. If
    you can find lower prices anywhere Crazy Marge will
    shave her husband's head!!!
    </ad_sentence>
    <ad_sentence>
    We have all kinds, all sizes. Don't see what you
    want?  Don't worry. We customize orders!
    </ad_sentence>
</advertisement>

<product>
    <product_id>3253435</product_id>
    <short_desc>Sleepeazy Mattresses</short_desc>
    <product_desc>per set, any size</product_desc>
    <price pricetype="cost">$162</price>
    <price pricetype="retail">$300</price>
    <inventory location="showroom">23</inventory>
    <inventory location="warehouse">15</inventory>
    <giveaway>
        <giveaway_item>
        Free pillows
        </giveaway_item>
        <giveaway_desc>
        with every set
        </giveaway_desc>
    </giveaway>
</product>

<product>
    <product_id>5622345</product_id>
    <short_desc>CozyComfort Mattresses</short_desc>
    <price pricetype="starting">
        starting at only $99.99
    </price>
    <item>
        <product_desc>Queen</product_desc>
        <price pricetype="cost">$59.00</price>
        <price pricetype="sale">$69.00</price>
        <price pricetype="retail">$99.00</price>
    </item>
    <item>
        <product_desc>King</product_desc>
        <price pricetype="cost">$159.00</price>
        <price pricetype="sale">$209.00</price>
        <price pricetype="retail">$359.00</price>
    </item>
    <giveaway>
```

Listing 3.13—continued

```
            <giveaway_item>
            Free sheets
            </giveaway_item>
            <giveaway_desc>
            with every set
            </giveaway_desc>
        </giveaway>
    </product>

    <product>
        <product_id>39981234</product_id>
        <short_desc>Floataway Waterbeds</short_desc>
       <price pricetype="cost">TBD</price>
        <giveaway>
            <giveaway_item>
            15 different styles to choose from
            </giveaway_item>
            <giveaway_desc>
            with free delivery -- we'll take your
            old mattress as a trade in!
            </giveaway_desc>
        </giveaway>
    </product>

    <special specialtype="weekly">
        This week only:  Round beds with rotating motors
        starting at a price that will make your head spin.
        Just talk to Crazy Marge, she'll tell you all about it!
    </special>
</vendor>

</products>
```

Referential Integrity

Now that we know we can accommodate all our data, let's look at whether this is really the best way to do it.

Anyone who works with relational databases is probably screaming "Finally!" This structure makes a lot of sense from an XML standpoint, where products are embedded within vendors, and so on, but in a typical enterprise application, this is not the way it's done.

We'll be dealing with traditional databases in Chapter 8, "Updating Inventory: SQL Databases and SAX," but let's take a moment to look at the implications or this comment method of data storage.

In a relational database, types of information are stored together, with keys that link them together. For instance, vendors and products would probably be stored in a structure similar to Figure 3.5.

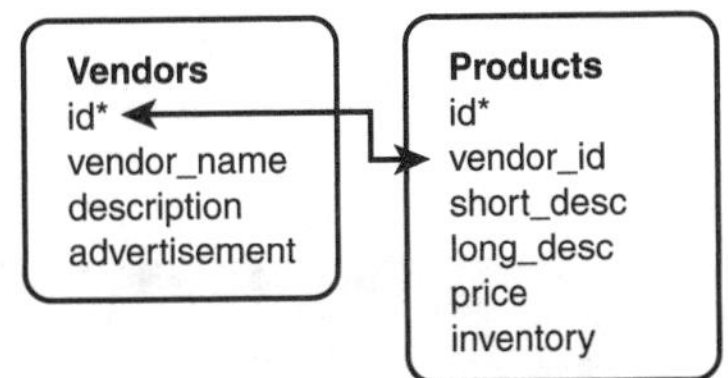

Figure 3.5

A typical relational database structure links data in one table to data in another.

In this case, `vendors` and `products` are separate database tables holding information on `vendors` and `products`, respectively. Each record, or item, is noted by a unique identifier, the ID. We can also tie the two tables together by requiring the `vendor_id` to match an `id` in the `vendor` table. This way, we know that each `product` belongs to a legitimate `vendor`.

But why bother doing this, when we can just put everything in one place, as we've done here? That is the basic question behind relational databases.

Previously, databases have been, essentially, flat files—meaning the data was stored together, as we have it here. There were several problems with this. For one thing, information was repeated more often than it needed to be. For instance, a flat file database table of Crazy Marge's data would look like Figure 3.6.

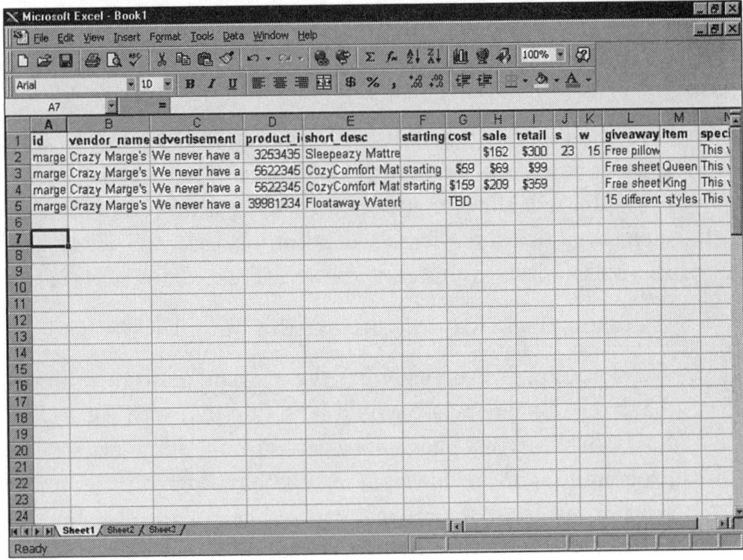

id	vendor_name	advertisement	product_i	short_desc	starting	cost	sale	retail	s	w	giveaway	item	speci
marge	Crazy Marge's	We never have a	3253435	Sleepeazy Mattre			$162	$300	23	15	Free pillow		This v
marge	Crazy Marge's	We never have a	5622345	CozyComfort Mat	starting	$59	$69	$99			Free sheet	Queen	This v
marge	Crazy Marge's	We never have a	5622345	CozyComfort Mat	starting	$159	$209	$359			Free sheet	King	This v
marge	Crazy Marge's	We never have a	39981234	Floataway Watert		TBD					15 different styles		This v

Figure 3.6

A flat file of Crazy Marge's data would include a lot of duplicated information.

Notice that a lot of information, such as the `vendor_name` and `advertisement`, is listed on every line, even though it's exactly the same. Also, if we wanted to add a new `pricetype`, we would need to add it to every single row, even if it didn't apply to that particular `product`.

By separating out information, we can eliminate a lot of these problems, as illustrated in Figure 3.7.

Figure 3.7

Breaking information into several tables makes it much easier to manage.

	A	B	C
1	**Vendors:**		
2			
3	**id**	**vendor_name**	**advertisement**
4	marge	Crazy Marge's Bed Emporium	We never have a sale because we've got the lowest...
5			
6	**Products:**		
7			
8	**vendor_id**	**product_id**	**short_desc**
9	marge	3253435	Sleepeazy Mattresses
10	marge	5622345	CozyComfort Mattresses
11	marge	5622345	CozyComfort Mattresses
12	marge	39981234	Floataway Waterbeds
13			
14	**Prices:**		
15			
16	**product_id**	**pricetype**	**price**
17	3253435	sale	162
18	3253435	retail	300
19	5622345	starting	99
20	5622345	cost	59
21	5622345	sale	69
22	5622345	retail	99
23	5622345	starting	99
24	5622345	cost	159

This way, the information becomes much cleaner and easier to manage. A change to a vendor's advertisement has to be made just once, not once for every product.

The key is to make sure that information is never lost because of bad data. If, perhaps, we specified a `product`'s `vendor_id` of `marge`, that product would be lost to us, because it would never appear with an existing vendor. The idea is to implement it in such a way that the referring data (in this case, the `vendor_id`) always matches the appropriate key (in this case, the `id`). This is known as referential integrity.

We can implement a structure like this using DTDs.

We're not going to actually use the `product` to do this, however. Although it is likely that a relational database would be set up that way, we are, in fact, dealing with XML. In short, just because we can do something, doesn't mean that we should. Programming for databases is very different from programming for XML. Moving `product` out from under `vendor` would be a nightmare for us later, so, instead we'll examine this issue by moving the `specials`.

In Listings 3.14 and 3.15, we're pulling the `special` out from under `vendors` and dropping it into the root element but linking it back to its `vendor` using IDs.

Listing 3.14—`products.xml`: Moving Specials Out to the Root Element

```
<?xml version="1.0"?>
<!DOCTYPE products SYSTEM "products.dtd">

<products>

<vendor webvendor="full" id="conners">
   <vendor_name>Conners Chair Company</vendor_name>
...
</vendor>

 <vendor webvendor="partial" id="wally">
     <vendor_name>
         Wally's Wonderful World of Furniture
     </vendor_name>
...
</vendor>

<vendor webvendor="no" id="marge">
    <vendor_name>Crazy Marge's Bed Emporium</vendor_name>
    <advertisement>
        <ad_sentence>
...
                </giveaway_item>
                <giveaway_desc>
                with free delivery -- we'll take your
                old mattress as a trade in!
                </giveaway_desc>
        </giveaway>
    </product>

</vendor>

<special specialtype="weekly" vendor_id="marge">
    This week only:  Round beds with rotating motors
    starting at a price that will make your head spin.
    Just talk to Crazy Marge, she'll tell you all about it!
</special>

</products>
```

Listing 3.15—`products.dtd`: Accommodating the Changes in the DTD

```
<!ELEMENT products   (vendor | special)+>

<!ELEMENT vendor     (vendor_name, advertisement?, suite?, product*)>
<!ATTLIST vendor     webvendor CDATA #REQUIRED>

```

Listing 3.15—continued

```
5:<!ELEMENT special (#PCDATA)>
6:<!ATTLIST special specialtype CDATA #FIXED 'weekly'>
7:
8:<!ELEMENT vendor_name   (#PCDATA)>
...
```

Considering the magnitude of the structural change we just made, we really didn't have to change the DTD all that much. The first thing we did, on line 0, was to accommodate the changes to the root element. Note that syntax is important here. The way we have it written, we can have one or more `vendors` or `specials`, in any order. We could have written this definition as follows:

```
<!ELEMENT products     (vendor+, special+)>
```

This would have required us to list all the `vendors` first, and then all the `specials`. Although this is probably closer to what would happen in this situation, we don't want to require it.

Now that we've got the files reorganized, we need to tell the DTD that we want to enforce the referential integrity. This means that any value in `vendor_id` must match an existing `vendor id` attribute. We do this using two new datatypes, `ID` and `IDREF`, as in Listing 3.16.

Listing 3.16—`products.dtd`: Adding IDs and IDREFs

```
<!ELEMENT products   (vendor | special)+>

<!ELEMENT vendor     (vendor_name, advertisement?, suite?, product*)>
<!ATTLIST vendor     webvendor CDATA #REQUIRED
                     id        ID    #REQUIRED>

<!ELEMENT special (#PCDATA)>
<!ATTLIST special specialtype CDATA #FIXED 'weekly'
                  vendor_id   IDREF #REQUIRED>
...
```

We're actually doing two things with this listing. First, we're creating a primary key on `vendor` called `id` by setting it to type `ID`. A primary key is a value that must be present and must be unique. No two vendors may have the same value for `id`. Second, we're creating an attribute of type `IDREF`. This means that its values will have to match an existing value of an `ID` attribute (in this case, the `vendor id` attribute).

The Second Limitation: Keys

Now, this is extremely handy and goes a long way toward emulating the relational database structure, but it doesn't go quite far enough.

For instance, it would be natural (and in fact, expected) to put a primary key on the `id` attributes for `product` and `suite`, but this causes two problems.

First, whereas primary keys are most commonly numeric, `ID`s in XML must be Names—they must start with a letter. There's no particular reason for this except that it's what's specified in the Recommendation.

Second, you'll notice that there's no way to tell an `IDREF` which `ID` it's supposed to be referencing. In fact, each document has only one "pool" of `ID`s. For instance, if we specified that the `id` attribute for `products` was an `ID`, we'd find that a `product` and a `vendor` can't have the same `ID` because they would no longer be unique (even though they're different elements). What's more, a `special` could have a `vendor_id` that matches the `product` but not a `vendor`, and the processor will not see it as a problem.

3

The Third Limitation: Same Name, Different Element

Another limitation of DTDs stems from the fact that each element is declared in a vacuum, so to speak, without reference to the elements that contain it. For instance, we have `products` that are part of the root element, and we have `products` that are part of a `suite`. It is not inconceivable that these two products might have different requirements, but within the structure of DTDs, the only way to define them differently would be to give them different names.

Fortunately, all three of these limitations can be overcome using XML Schema.

XML Schema

XML Schema is an initiative from the W3C that attempts to eliminate the problems with DTDs by replacing them with something better. XML Schemas are more flexible than DTDs, more powerful, and more familiar, as they use XML syntax.

As of this writing, the XML Schema has advanced to "Candidate Recommendation" status at W3C, but Xerces version 1.2.3 uses the April 7, 2000 draft, located at

`http://www.w3.org/TR/2000/WD-xmlschema-1-20000407/`

`http://www.w3.org/TR/2000/WD-xmlschema-2-20000407/`

and

`http://www.w3.org/TR/2000/WD-xmlschema-3-20000407/`

To begin converting our DTD to a schema, we'll create a third text file called `products.xsd` (for XML Schema Document) and save it in the same directory as `products.xml`. The file should contain the text in Listing 3.17.

Listing 3.17—`products.xsd`: The Basic Schema Document

```
<?xml version="1.0" ?>
<schema>

</schema>
```

Notice that this is just an XML document, same as all the others we've used so far. All definitions we create will be part of the `schema` element. This file is called our schema document. The file we're validating—our XML file—is called our instance document, because it's an instance of the data that we're defining.

Now, you may remember that an XSL style sheet was also an XML document, and that we separated the XSL commands from the output using namespaces—specifically, the `xsl:` namespace. We're going to do the same with our schema document, but namespaces allow us to do something else: We can exclude elements from validation, if we want to.

To do this, we'll create a namespace that points to schema validation, and then tell the parser that any elements that are not part of that namespace need to be processed according to our schema document. We'll do this by making the changes in Listing 3.18 to `products.xml`.

Listing 3.18—`products.xml`: Associating Our XML with a Schema Document

```
<?xml version="1.0"?>
<products  xmlns:xsi="http://www.w3.org/1999/XMLSchema-instance"
           xsi:noNamespaceSchemaLocation='products.xsd'>

<vendor webvendor="full" id="conners">
...
```

Now we're ready to start converting our DTD to a Schema.

Datatypes

The concept behind XML Schema is that we start with simple datatypes (such as a string of text or a number) and build them into more complex structures, known as complex datatypes. This in and of itself is an improvement over DTDs, where we couldn't specify that, say, a `price` had to be a number. Some of the simple types built into XML Schema include the following:

- `string`—This is simple text.
- numeric types—These include `float`, `double`, `decimal`, `integer`, `nonPositiveInteger`, `negativeInteger`, `long`, `int`, `short`, `byte`, `nonNegativeInteger`, `unsignedLong`, `unsignedInt`, `unsignedShort`, `unsignedByte`, and `positiveInteger`.
- time-related types—These include `timeInstant`, `timeperiod`, `month`, `year`, `century`, `recurringDate`, `recurringDay`, `timeDuration`, `recurringDuration`, `date`, and `time`.
- XML 1.0 tokenized types—These are type names that have special meanings, such as `ID`, `IDREF`, `ENTITY`, and `NMTOKEN`.

Let's start by creating the elements that use simple datatypes in Listing 3.19.

Listing 3.19—Our Simple Elements

```
<?xml version="1.0">
<schema>

<element name="vendor_name" type="string"/>
<element name="b" type="string"/>
<element name="i" type="string"/>
<element name="p" type="string"/>
<element name="short_desc" type="string"/>
<element name="product_desc" type="string"/>
<element name="giveaway_item" type="string"/>
<element name="giveaway_desc" type="string"/>
<element name="long_desc" type="string"/>
<element name="product_id" type="string"/>

</schema>
```

Now, it just so happens that all the simple types we had originally defined as `#PCDATA` really were strings, but if we had any that needed to be, say, numbers or dates, we would define them here.

Next, we'll start to build up the elements that use these simple elements into complex datatypes. The simplest way of doing this is shown in Listing 3.20.

Listing 3.20—`products.xsd`: Creating an Element of Elements

```
<?xml version="1.0"?>
<schema>

<element name="vendor_name" type="string"/>
<element name="b" type="string"/>
<element name="i" type="string"/>
<element name="p" type="string"/>
<element name="short_desc" type="string"/>
```

Listing 3.20—continued

```
8: <element name="product_desc" type="string"/>
9: <element name="giveaway_item" type="string"/>
10:<element name="giveaway_desc" type="string"/>
11:<element name="long_desc" type="string"/>
12:<element name="product_id" type="string"/>
13:
14:<element name="giveaway">
15:     <element name="giveaway_item" type="string"/>
16:     <element name="giveaway_desc" type="string"/>
17:</element>
18:
19:</schema>
```

On lines 14 through 17, we're building the definition of the giveaway element the same way that we'll build the element itself: by nesting the elements inside it. A `giveaway` consists of a `giveaway_item` and a `giveaway_desc`, so we include them as part of this definition on lines 15 and 16. We also add attributes to an element this way, as shown in Listing 3.21.

Listing 3.21—`products.xsd`: Creating Attributes

```
...
16:     <element name="giveaway_desc" type="string"/>
17:</element>
18:
19:<element name="special" type="string">
20:   <attribute name="specialtype" type="string" use="fixed" value="weekly" />
21:</element>
22:
23:</schema>
```

Here, on lines 19 through 21 we're adding attributes much the same way we added them under XSL. We do, however, have two new values to look at on line 20. The `use` value (in this case `"fixed"`) tells the processor whether this attribute is `implied`, `required`, and so on. If there is a default to be specified, it will be found as the value, as we did here with `"weekly"`.

Next we'll construct some of the more complex elements. So far we've looked at elements that will contain text. In Listing 3.22, we will look at elements that are made up of other elements.

Listing 3.22—Specifying Element Occurrences

```
...
19:<element name="special" type="string">
20:  <attribute name="specialtype" type="string" use="fixed" value="weekly" />
21:</element>
22:
```

Listing 3.22—continued

```
23:<element name="item" content="elementOnly">
24:      <element ref="product_desc" />
25:      <element ref="price" minOccurs="0" maxOccurs="unbounded"/>
26:</element>
27:
28:<element name="suite" content="elementOnly">
29:      <element ref="product_id" />
30:      <element ref="short_desc" />
31:      <element ref="long_desc" />
32:      <element ref="price" />
33:      <element ref="product" minOccurs="0" maxOccurs="unbounded" />
34:</element>
35:
36:<element name="product" content="elementOnly">
37:      <element ref="product_id" />
38:      <element ref="short_desc" />
39:      <element ref="product_desc" minOccurs="0" maxOccurs="1" />
40:      <element ref="price" minOccurs="1" maxOccurs="unbounded" />
41:      <element ref="item" minOccurs="0" maxOccurs="unbounded" />
42:      <element ref="inventory" minOccurs="0" maxOccurs="unbounded" />
43:      <element ref="giveaway" minOccurs="0" maxOccurs="1" />
44:</element>
45:
46:<element name="vendor" content="elementOnly">
47:      <element ref="vendor_name" />
48:      <element ref="advertisement" minOccurs="0" maxOccurs="1" />
49:      <element ref="suite" minOccurs="0" maxOccurs="unbounded" />
50:      <element ref="product" minOccurs="0" maxOccurs="unbounded" />
51:      <attribute name="webvendor" type="string" use="required" />
52:      <attribute name="id" type="ID" use="required" />
53:</element>
54:
55:</schema>
```

There's a lot of new material here, but most of it is along the same lines, so let's start with `items` on lines 23 through 26. First of all, an item element can contain only other elements, which is what `content="elementOnly"` means on line 23. The actual elements themselves are specified on lines 24 and 25, but because both `product_desc` and `price` appear elsewhere, rather than defining them here, we'll simply refer to the datatypes we've already created.

On line 25, we see the first of the attributes that limit how many times an element can occur. When we created the DTD, we specified a price element within an item element with `*`, meaning that it could occur 0 or more times. Now we're duplicating this requirement with `minOccurs` and `maxOccurs`. The advantage here over a DTD is that if we wanted to, we could set these values to specific integers, as opposed to just `0`, `1`, or `unbounded`.

We've used the same information to describe the `suite` element on lines 28 through 34, `product` on lines 36 through 44, and `vendor` on lines 46 through 53.

That leaves us with `price`, `inventory`, `advertisement`, and our root element, `products`. We'll look at `advertisement` and `products` in a moment, but `price` and `inventory` have a special complication to them: enumerated values. In Listing 3.23, we see how to specify enumerated values for an attribute.

Listing 3.23—`products.xsd`: Enumerated Values

```
...
52:     <attribute name="id" type="ID" use="required" />
53:</element>
54:
55:<element name="price" type="decimal">
56: <attribute name="pricetype" type="NMTOKEN" use="default" value="retail">
57:         <simpleType base="string">
58:             <enumeration value="cost"/>
59:             <enumeration value="sale"/>
60:             <enumeration value="retail"/>
61:             <enumeration value="starting"/>
62:         </simpleType>
63: </attribute>
64: <attribute name="color" type="string" use="implied" />
65:</element>
66:
67:<element name="inventory" type="integer">
68: <attribute name="location" type="NMTOKEN" use="default" value="warehouse">
69:         <simpleType base="string">
70:             <enumeration value="warehouse"/>
71:             <enumeration value="showroom"/>
72:         </simpleType>
73: </attribute>
74:    <attribute name="color" type="string" use="implied" />
75:</element>
76:
77:</schema>
```

On lines 55 through 65, we're specifying the `price` element. The first thing to notice is that on line 55 we specified the type as `decimal`, which we certainly couldn't have done with a DTD. On lines 56 through 63, we're defining the `pricetype` attribute. This attribute is a new datatype, `NMTOKEN`. That means that we can use only certain defined values, or tokens. On lines 57 through 62, we're defining those values. The `simpleType` element tells the processor that ultimately, we're going to wind up with a string. The elements on lines 58 through 61 place further conditions on the value. In this case, we're specifying certain values, but other restrictions are possible.

Line 64 is just a straight attribute definition, as we've already seen, and we're repeating the process for the inventory element on lines 67 through 75.

We'll create the `products` element in Listing 3.24.

Listing 3.24—`products.xsd`: Creating the Root Element

```
...
    <attribute name="color" type="string" use="implied" />
</element>

<element name="products" content="elementOnly">
     <choice maxOccurs="unbounded">
        <element ref="vendor" />
        <element ref="special" />
     </choice>
</element>

</schema>
```

Our DTD specified that the `products` element could have any number of `vendors` or `specials`, in no particular order. To achieve this same result in the schema, we can use the `choice` element. Alone, it allows one of those elements to be present. After we add `maxOccurs="unbounded"`, any number of them is allowed.

Finally, we're down to our problem child, `advertisement`. It's our problem child because it has both text and elements. This is known as mixed content. We'll take care of it in Listing 3.25.

Listing 3.25—Specifying Mixed Content

```
...
</element>

<element name="advertisement" content="mixed">
     <element name="ad_sentence" content="mixed">
           <element ref="b" minOccurs="0"/>
           <element ref="i" minOccurs="0"/>/>
           <element ref="p" minOccurs="0"/>/>
     </element>
</element>

</schema>
```

I've included this example here even though it's not really what we want. When we defined mixed content with the DTD, we were not able to control the order of content, or even whether items appeared. With schemas, we can, by specifying the content as it is in Listing 3.25. In this case, however, we don't care about the order, so it's better to use a `choose` element as we did in Listing 3.24.

Features Still to Come

Two of the most promising features of XML Schema, uniqueness and referential integrity, have not been implemented in the version of Xerces that we are using. It is, however, worth taking a few moments to discuss how they work.

Uniqueness, as the name implies, is the ability to specify that every value of a particular element or attribute must be different; there can be no duplicates. Referential integrity, as we discussed earlier, is when we specify that one value, such as a `special`'s `vendor_id` attribute, must match a value elsewhere, such as the `vendor`'s `id` attribute.

For both uniqueness and referential integrity, we need to create keys. These keys involve the element that the key is attached to and the field or attribute that is being checked. For instance, to specify that we want the `id` to be unique for a `vendor`, we would add the following to the schema:

```
<unique>
        <selector>/products/vendor</selector>
        <field>vendor[@id]</field>
</unique>
```

If that selector looks familiar, it should. It's an XPath expression, just like the ones that we used with XSL. This way, we can distinguish between a `product_id`, and a `vendor id`.

To create referential integrity, we first create the `vendor_id` as a key:

```
<key name="vendor_key">
<selector>/products/vendor</selector>
<field>vendor[@id]</field>
</key>
```

We then create a `keyref` type:

```
<keyref refer="vendor_key">
<selector>/products/special</selector>
<field>special[@vendor_id]</field>
</keyref>
```

This forces any `vendor_id` attribute to match the `vendor_key`.

Next Steps

In this chapter, we've covered a lot of ground. We started out by installing Java, so we could use a parser to check our documents. We then created a Document Type Definition for our data, analyzed it, tweaked it, and converted it to a basic XML Schema.

All of this was designed to allow us to make sure our data was exactly as we expect it, because next we'll be writing programs to analyze it.

In the next chapter, "Getting Serious: XSL Processors and Server-Side Processing," we'll start doing some basic Java programming, as well as using server-side scripts to perform XSL transformations on our data. We will be taking our data and writing programs that will create product pages in preparation for taking orders.

Chapter 4

In this chapter

- *XSL Processors*
- *Xalan*
- *Advanced XSLT: Includes and Imports*
- *Java Basics*
- *Advanced XSLT: Parameters*
- *Our First DOM: Stepping Through Our XML*
- *Installing and Configuring Tomcat*
- *Next Steps*

Getting Serious: XSL Processors and Server-Side Processing

Ready to get serious? In Chapter 3, "Defining the Data Structure: Document Type Definitions, XML Schema, and Parsers," we just used a Java program that came to use already written and ready to run. In this chapter, we're going to take a program called an XSL processor and integrate it into a Java program we write ourselves. Never worked with Java before? That's okay; we'll go over everything you need to know.

We're going to take an XSL processor and use it to transform our XML files into HTML, the same way the processor behind Internet Explorer did in Chapter 2, "Product Pages: Transforming XML in the Browser Using XSL." First, we'll do that without any custom programming. Then, we'll take a look at what it takes to build our own Java programs to use those transformations, and even add to them.

We'll also learn how to write Java servlets, small server-side applications in which we'll be doing all our programming. For those who are familiar with CGI scripts, servlets are used in a similar way.

XSL Processors

Before we actually download any software, let's talk about what we're getting.

In Chapter 2, we talked a lot about how the browser was transforming the XML. Strictly speaking, that's not true. What actually did the transforming was an XSL processor that worked with the browser to translate the XML code into something the browser could understand.

We did this with a style sheet, and it's important to understand that this gives us an enormous amount of flexibility. For one thing, we can transform our XML into virtually anything, not just HTML. We can transform it into HTML, Scalable Vector Graphics, plain text, or even a different set of XML tags! The trick is to know what we're trying to turn it into at any given moment.

Xalan

It's common for XML parsers and XSL processors to come in pairs, so to speak. Most programmers using the Xerces XML parser use the Xalan XSL processor, which also comes from the Apache project. To download Xalan, go to

```
http://xml.apache.org/xalan-j/index.html
```

This page contains a link to the latest version of Xalan-Java 2.

Make sure that you are downloading version 2 of Xalan-Java, and not version 1. The API is completely different, and most of what we're doing here won't work with version 1.

Installing Xalan

After you download the appropriate `*.zip` or `*.tar` file (depending on your platform), unzip or uncompress it. If you extract it to the root directory, you'll wind up with a directory something like

```
C:\xalan-j_2_0_D05
```

For convenience, let's change it to

```
C:\xalan
```

After the files themselves have been installed, we'll need to update the system `CLASSPATH`. Using the instructions from Chapter 3, set the `CLASSPATH` as follows:

```
CLASSPATH=.;c:\xalan\bin\xerces.jar;c:\xalan\bin\xalan.jar
```

That's all there is to it.

If you installed the files to a different directory, be sure to make the appropriate changes to the `CLASSPATH` shown previously.

Notice that we've actually replaced the `CLASSPATH` that we created in Chapter 3, rather than just adding to it, and that we're now pointing to a version of Xerces that's in the `Xalan` directory. There's a good reason for this. In general, it's better not to have more than one version of a particular program on your machine, because it can lead to confusion over which one is being called. For instance, if Xalan were using a newer or older version of Xerces than the one we downloaded in Chapter 3, there could be problems. To prevent those problems, we're listing the version that comes with Xalan in the `CLASSPATH`. Java will always check locations in the order in which they appear in the `CLASSPATH`, so it won't matter if we have a different version elsewhere on our machine.

Don't forget the run the `AUTOEXEC.bat` file, so the new `CLASSPATH` takes effect.

Testing the Installation

As we did with Xerces, we'll use a sample provided with Xalan to test the installation. The Java class `SimpleTransform` simply takes the file `birds.xml` and transforms it using the style sheet `birds.xsl`. The resulting text is sent to the file `birds.out`.

Finally, we're ready to test. First, we need to compile `SimpleTransform.java`. We'll look at that process in more depth when we write our own programs, but for now just open a command prompt window and type the following:

```
cd c:\xalan\samples\SimpleTransform
javac SimpleTransform.java
java SimpleTransform
```

The output should be as follows:

```
************* The result is in birds.out *************
```

You can open `birds.out` with any text file. You should see a list of bird classes and species.

If you get an error telling you a class can't be found, make sure that you've set the `CLASSPATH` correctly. If you get an error telling you the program can't read `birds.xml`, make sure that both `birds.xml` and `birds.xsl` are in the same directory as `SimpleTransform`.

If there are no errors, you have a working XSL processor installed!

Converting a File from the Command Line

In Chapters 1 and 2, we built placeholder pages to live on our site until we were ready with real content. Now it's time to build that content.

When people come to the ChaseWeb Furniture site, the first thing they will see is the home page. That home page will contain various links, including company information, phone numbers and addresses, and so on. All that information will be plain XHTML pages such as those we built in previous chapters. If you're looking for something more ornate, you can also build your page with any Web page editor such as Macromedia Dreamweaver or Microsoft FrontPage. (Or, if you prefer, you can always build it by hand, as we have done so far.)

The meat of the page, however, will be a list of vendors and their products. This page will be similar to the page we built in Chapter 2, with one important difference: Because the end result will be HTML (or more specifically, XHTML), we don't have to worry about whether the browser will support XML, XSL style sheets, and so on.

Although we won't have to worry about browser support for XSL style sheets, it's always a good idea to make sure that the target browser for your audience can handle the XHTML pages you're building. The latest features can cause unpredictable results in older browsers. Always test your site using the oldest browser you're expected to support.

Input and Output Files

To start, of course, we're going to need an XML source document. In our case, that will be `products.xml`, the file we wound up with at the end of Chapter 3. This file has all the information we need, and it's been standardized during the process of developing the DTD and Schema.

To get started, we'll move `products.xml` from the Xerces data directory to our files directory. (You can overwrite the old version.) Because the data has already been validated, we can remove the XML Schema namespace so that the top of the file reads as in Listing 4.1.

Listing 4.1—`products.xml`: Removing the Schema Information

```
<?xml version="1.0"?>
<products>

<vendor webvendor="full" id="conners">
    <vendor_name>Conners Chair Company</vendor_name>
    <advertisement>
        <ad_sentence>
...
```

Ultimately, we'll want our page to look something like Figure 4.1.

Looking at this page, we see that it has three basic sections:

- The top of the page, including the header graphic and the links to other sections of the site. This information should be on every page of the site.
- The descriptive paragraph above the vendor names. This text belongs only here.

- The vendor names. These come directly from the `products.xml` document we've been working on all along. If that information changes, we want to be able to have the change reflected on this page.

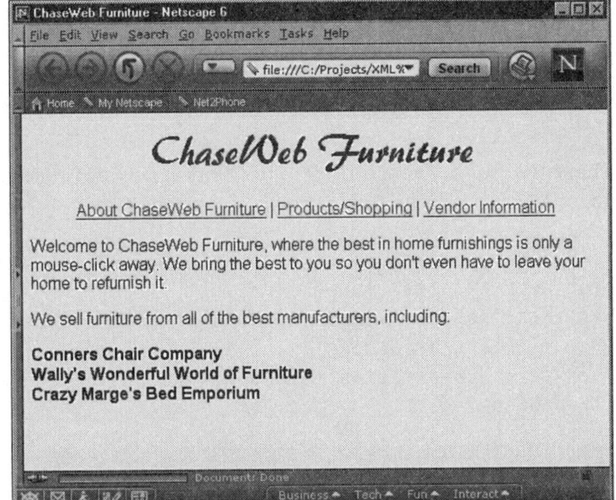

Figure 4.1

The home page includes some basic elements.

4

Because we want the vendor information from `products.xml`, we'll naturally want to create a style sheet that extracts that information and creates the rest of the page. This style sheet is shown in Listing 4.2.

Listing 4.2—`index.xsl`: The Home Page Style Sheet

```
<?xml version="1.0"?>
<xsl:stylesheet
    xmlns:xsl="http://www.w3.org/1999/XSL/Transform"
    version="1.0">

<xsl:template match="/">
<html>
<head>
   <title>ChaseWeb Furniture</title>
</head>
<body style="background-color: F6F6F6;font-family: Arial">

    <center>
    <img src="chasewebfurniture.gif" alt="ChaseWeb Furniture"/>
    </center>

    <p align="center">
        <a href="index.html">About ChaseWeb Furniture</a>
        |
        <a href="products.html">Products/Shopping</a>
        |
        <a href="vendors.html">Vendor Information</a>
    </p>
```

Listing 4.2—continued

```
23:
24:     <p>
25:     Welcome to ChaseWeb Furniture, where the best in home
26:     furnishings is only a mouse-click away. We bring the
27:     best to you so you don't even have to leave your home
28:     to refurnish it.
29:     </p>
30:
31:     <p>
32:     We sell furniture from all of the best manufacturers,
33:     including:
34:     </p>
35:
36:     <xsl:for-each select=".//vendor">
37:         <xsl:sort select="vendor_name" case-order="upper-first"
38:                order="ascending"/>
39:         <b><xsl:value-of select="vendor_name"/></b><br />
40:     </xsl:for-each>
41:
42:</body>
43:</html>
44:</xsl:template>
45:
46:</xsl:stylesheet>
```

On line 5, as usual, we tell the processor to start with the document root and begin the transformation. Lines 6 through 34 are just the XHTML to display the top of the page. Finally, lines 36 through 40 search for all vendor elements in the document and display them.

Call this file `index.xsl` and save it to the same directory as `products.xml`. We'll also need to create a graphic—any graphic—called `chasewebfurniture.gif`, and save it to the same directory.

Processing the Document

Now that we have our input documents ready, we can go ahead and process them. Because we have Xalan installed, this is simple. Open a command prompt window and change to the directory where both files are located. Type the following and press the Enter key:

```
java org.apache.xalan.xslt.Process -in products.xml -xsl index.xsl
➥-out index.html
```

Let's break this up and see what each of the pieces means.

The first, `java`, is the Java interpreter, which runs all Java programs, or classes, we'll work with.

Next is the class itself. In this case, we're using the `Process` class, which belongs to a group of classes called the `org.apache.xalan.xslt` package.

Class—Java is an object-oriented language, which means that instead of procedural programs doing the requested work, it's done by objects created in memory. Strictly speaking, a class is the definition, or template, for an object, but for now you can just think of a class as a program.

Package—A package is a group of classes, normally related to one another in terms of what they do. For instance, if we were to distribute a "Java program," what we're really distributing is a package (or several packages) of classes. This helps to avoid name conflicts with other people's classes and also has security implications.

The pieces of information that we provide on the command line are called the arguments. The program takes this information and acts on it. The `-in` argument represents the XML source document. The `-xsl` argument represents the style sheet we're using to process the XML document. Finally, the `-out` document represents the filename where we want our output.

This is a change from our earlier XSL work. Whereas before we were only seeing a representation of the transformation in the browser, we can now see the actual XHTML. If we were to open the `index.html` document with our browser, we would see the same document that was in Figure 4.1. If we then were to look at the XHTML source of that document (using View, Source or View, Page Source), we would see plain old XHTML, instead of the XML we saw before. More importantly, we could now open the `index.html` document with any HTML browser, not just those that understand XML. Later, we'll use this to create pages that can be displayed on a whole range of devices, right down to cell phones and other nontraditional Web devices.

Advanced XSLT: Includes and Imports

What we've done here is useful for one file, but we can make it even more useful. The top part of the file, including any header graphics and the links to other sections of the site, really belong on every page of the site. What would be helpful is the capability to take that information and separate it out into a page that we can use in many different places.

Includes

One way that XSLT provides for us to do that is by allowing us to include one style sheet within another. All we need to do is separate out our reusable information into a style sheet of its own and then call it from whatever page we want. The actual reusable style sheet looks like Listing 4.3.

Listing 4.3—topinclude.xsl: Our Reusable Style Sheet

```
<?xml version="1.0"?>
<xsl:stylesheet version="1.0"
    xmlns:xsl="http://www.w3.org/1999/XSL/Transform">

<xsl:template match="/">
<html>
<head>
    <title>ChaseWeb Furniture</title>
</head>
<body style="background-color: F6F6F6;font-family: Arial">

    <center>
    <img src="chasewebfurniture.gif" alt="ChaseWeb Furniture"/>
    </center>

    <p align="center">
        <a href="index.html">About ChaseWeb Furniture</a>
        |
        <a href="products.html">Products/Shopping</a>
        |
        <a href="vendors.html">Vendor Information</a>
    </p>

    <xsl:apply-templates />

</body>
</html>
</xsl:template>
</xsl:stylesheet>
```

In this case, we have a fully functional style sheet, but one that really performs only one task: It processes the document root, adding our top text and then sending the rest of the document off to be processed.

This leaves us with the descriptive text and the vendor information, which we'll process in `index.xsl` itself. We'll start by pulling out the information that's in the include, as in Listing 4.4.

Listing 4.4—index.xsl: Stripping Down to the Basics

```
<?xml version="1.0"?>
<xsl:stylesheet
    xmlns:xsl="http://www.w3.org/1999/XSL/Transform"
    version="1.0">

<xsl:include href="topinclude.xsl"/>

<xsl:template match="/">

  <p>
   Welcome to ChaseWeb Furniture, where the best in home
```

Listing 4.4—continued

```
11:     furnishings is only a mouse-click away. We bring the
12:     best to you so you don't even have to leave your home
13:     to refurnish it.
14:     </p>
15:
16:     <p>
17:     We sell furniture from all of the best manufacturers,
18:     including:
19:     </p>
20:
21:     <xsl:for-each select="//vendor">
22:         <xsl:sort select="vendor_name" case-order="upper-first"
23:                 order="ascending"/>
24:         <b><xsl:value-of select="vendor_name"/></b><br />
25:     </xsl:for-each>
26:
27:</xsl:template>
28:
29:</xsl:stylesheet>
```

4

This seems fairly straightforward. We include the general information in the `topinclude.xsl` style sheet on line 5; then, we process the rest of the style sheet. If we process the files using

```
java org.apache.xalan.xslt.Process -in products.xml -xsl index.xsl
➥-out index.html
```

however, we find that something is amiss, as shown in Figure 4.2.

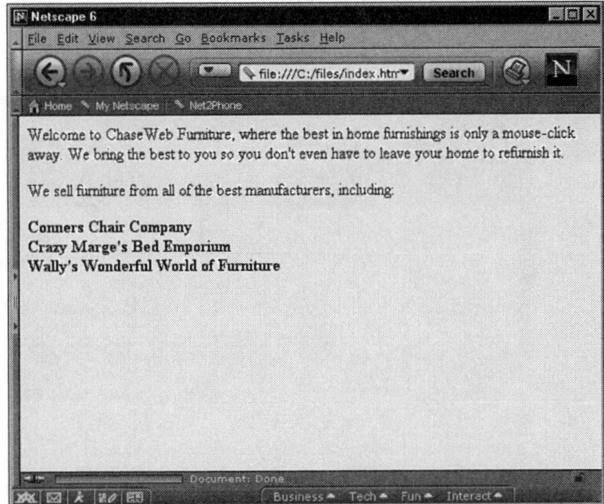

Figure 4.2

Something about our include is not processing properly, as evidenced by the fact that the top of the page is gone.

So, what happened? Well, let's think about what the import actually does. It takes all the instructions included in `topinclude.xsl` and makes them part of the `index.xsl` style sheet. So far so good, but if we look, we'll see that there are two templates for the document root, "/"!

What we have here is a case of priorities. Simply put, the template with the highest priority is going to be applied, and the others aren't. Because we didn't explicitly set the priority for these templates, the second one, which comes later and is part of the original in the style sheet, has a higher priority. We could explicitly set the priorities using the priority attribute, as shown in Listings 4.5 and 4.6.

Listing 4.5—Setting Priority in `index.xsl`

```
...
<xsl:include href="topinclude.xsl"/>

<xsl:template match="/"

    <P>
...
```

Listing 4.6—Setting Priority in `topinclude.xsl`

```
...

<xsl:template match="/" priority="10">
<HTML>
...
```

Now if we process the document again, the included style sheet will take precedence, as shown in Figure 4.3.

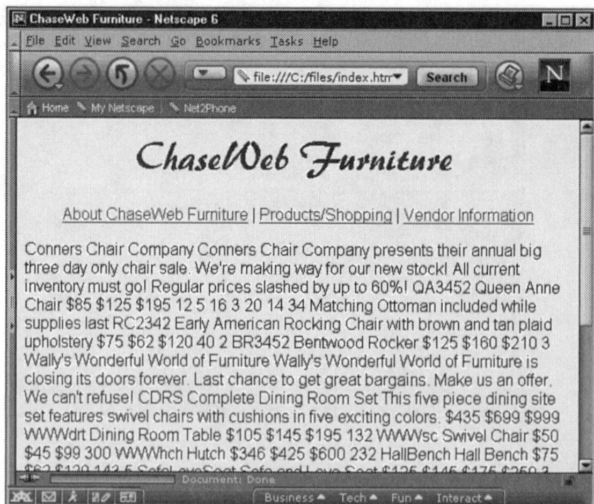

Figure 4.3

We can specify that the included style sheet should take precedence.

Well, that's not right either! Of course, it isn't. We simply have to deal with the fact that we can run only one template for "/". So, how can we include our descriptive text? We don't want it to appear for each vendor, so we can't include it in that template. We need an element that will appear only once.

Fortunately, every well-formed XML document has one: the root element. In our case, the root element is the products element, so let's go ahead and change our style sheet accordingly, as in Listing 4.7.

Listing 4.7—`index.xsl`: The Complete File

```
0:<?xml version="1.0"?>
1:<xsl:stylesheet
2:    xmlns:xsl="http://www.w3.org/1999/XSL/Transform"
3:    version="1.0">
4:
5:<xsl:include href="topinclude.xsl"/>
6:
7:<xsl:template  match="products">
8:
9:    <p>
10:    Welcome to ChaseWeb Furniture, where the best in home
11:    furnishings is only a mouse-click away. We bring the
12:    best to you so you don't even have to leave your home
13:    to refurnish it.
14:    </p>
15:
16:    <p>
17:    We sell furniture from all of the best manufacturers,
18:    including:
19:    </p>
20:
21:    <xsl:apply-templates />
22:
23:</xsl:template>
24:
25:<xsl:template match="vendor">
26:
27:        <b><xsl:value-of select="vendor_name"/></b><br />
28:
29:</xsl:template>
30:
31:<xsl:template match="special">
32:</xsl:template>
33:
34:</xsl:stylesheet>
```

On line 7, we change the first template so that instead of looking at the document root, it is looking at the actual root element `products`. The `<xsl:apply-templates>` element on line 21 means that the processor will try to process each of the elements in products. In this case, there are only two types: `vendor` and `special`. We'll break out the vendor logic into its own template on lines 21 through 35, removing the sort because we're dealing with only one vendor at a time now. Lines 31 and 32 are an empty template to trap the specials element and prevent it from appearing on the page.

In fact, because we'll probably want to trap the specials on all pages, we can put that template in topinclude.xsl. If we want to actually see the specials, a template in the main style sheet will override it. It's the best of both worlds!

Imports

There is also a second way that we could have combined topinclude.xsl with index.xsl, and that's by importing it instead of including it. Imports are indicated using

```
<xsl:import href="topinclude.xsl"/>
```

instead of the include element we used previously.

Importing works exactly the same as including, except that the base style sheet (in this case, index.xsl) takes precedence over the imported style sheet (in this case, topinclude.xsl).

We can, however, "force" our imports to be applied by using

```
<xsl:apply-imports/>
```

instead of

```
<xsl:apply-templates/>
```

Java Basics

Theoretically, we could create style sheets that create a product page for each of our products, but it would be a time-consuming and ultimately unmaintainable nightmare. So, we have reached the point where we'll actually need to start writing programs instead of simply using programs that other people have written.

Diving Right In: Hello World!

It is tradition that the first program new programmers write is to announce their presence to the world. We'll keep up that tradition, starting with a program that simply outputs the text "Hello World!"

Before we write anything, however, let's review the structure of Java and how it affects what we'll need to do.

Java programs are made up of plain text compiled into byte-code, or machine-readable files that the Java Virtual Machine on the target computer can interpret to actually run the program. So, we'll complete the following steps:

1. Write the program and save it to a file that ends in `.java`.
2. Compile the program using the `javac` utility that comes with the Java Software Development Kit.
3. If the program doesn't compile because of errors, correct the `.java` file and go back to step 2.
4. After the program is compiled, run it using the java command.
5. If the program doesn't run because of errors, correct the `.java` file and go back to step 2.

So, the first thing we'll need to do is create the `.java` file.

Writing `HelloWorld`

First, open your trusty text editor and create a new file, saving it as `HelloWorld.java`. It doesn't matter where you save it, although for consistency, the files directory is probably a good choice. Just keep track of where it is.

EXCURSION

Don't I Need Special Tools for Writing Java?

Several products on the market right now, such as Jbuilder, Forte for Java, CodeWarrior, and others, are designed to help programmers build Java programs faster and more efficiently. These programs, called Integrated Development Environments, or IDEs, typically include functionality that verifies code, suggests code the programmer might need, aids in debugging code, and so on.

Such tools can definitely make your life easier and more productive, but they are in no way absolutely necessary for writing Java code. Everything you need to do that is included with the Java 2 Software Development Kit, and we will assume in all our instructions that that is what you're using.

If you are interested in looking at IDEs, however, Sun has a list of some downloadable IDEs at

`http://java.sun.com/j2se/1.3/download-windows.html`

The text for our `HelloWorld` class looks like Listing 4.8.

Listing 4.8—`HelloWorld.java`

```
public class HelloWorld extends Object {

    public static void main (String args[]) {
        System.out.print("Hello World!");
```

Listing 4.8—continued

```
    }

}
```

As with our XML and XSL pages, the line numbers are just there for illustration and are not part of the code.

Compiling `HelloWorld`

Before we start analyzing, let's compile and run our program. In a command prompt window, change to the directory where `HelloWorld.java` is located and type

```
javac HelloWorld.java
```

If all goes well, it should compile without incident, leaving a file called `HelloWorld.class` in the same directory.

If you weren't able to compile `HelloWorld`, here are some suggestions:

- If your system wasn't able to find `javac`, make sure that the bin directory (that is, `c:\jdk1.3\bin`) is in your path, or type the full path to it on the command line.
- If you get an error similar to

  ```
  helloWorld.java:1: class helloWorld is public, should be declared in
  ➥a file named helloWorld.java
  public class helloWorld extends Object {
         ^
  
  1 error
  ```

  you need to make sure that the class name and the name of the file are exactly the same, including case. Java is a case-sensitive language, so `helloWorld` and `HelloWorld` are different.
- If you get an error similar to

  ```
  HelloWorld.java:4: cannot resolve symbol
  ```

  something has been mistyped. Make sure that your file matches the listing exactly, including case, and that you haven't left out any punctuation, such as) or ;.

After the program is compiled, we're ready to run it.

Executing `HelloWorld`

To actually run the program, make sure that you're in the same directory as the new `HelloWorld.class` file and type

```
java HelloWorld
```

The output should be

```
Hello World!
```

That's it. You've built your first Java program!

What It All Means

Now that we've actually created a Java program and run it, let's go back and take a look at what we've done.

Early programming languages were procedural, which means that the computer would start at the beginning and work its way down to the end, and that's it. Each command would be evaluated and executed, pretty much in the order in which it appeared. As you might imagine, a complex program can get fairly difficult to read and maintain, much less change!

A variation on this was the capability to create subprocedures and functions, which were modules of code that could be called from other locations, so they could be reused. This also helped with maintainability somewhat, but programs can still get complex.

Another school of thought is that programming should be object-oriented, which means that instead of having a single program that does all the work, we create objects to do it.

For instance, to use an offline example, we could create a television object. This object would have things we can do with it, called methods, such as turn it on, set the channel, or change the volume. It would also have properties, such as the channel it was currently set to, or whether or not it was on.

So, if my life were a computer program and I wanted to watch a particular television program, I would do the following:

1. Create a television object, called, say, `myTV`.
2. Use the `turnOn` method to turn on the `myTV` object.
3. Check the `getChannel` property to see whether it's turned to the right channel.
4. If it's not, use the `setChannel` method to change the channel.

Java objects work the same way. We create a class, such as the `Television` class in the preceding example, and then we create an object, or instance of that class, such as myTV. In this case, Television is just a template that explains what myTV should do and tells it how to do it.

Inheritance

One advantage of objects is that they can be used as building blocks, so we don't have to constantly reinvent the wheel. For instance, take the preceding example of the television. Let's say that I like the television, but I want one with a remote control. All the other aspects of the television, such as the need to turn it on and off, the capability to change the channel, and so on, are the same; it's just that now I want to be able to change the channel and turn it on with a remote control instead of by walking over to the set.

I'd rather not have to build this new television from scratch, so instead I can create a new class called, say, RemoteTelevision, which extends Television. (This process is also called subclassing.) I can then take RemoteTelevision and change the setChannel method to look for a signal from the remote, or I can add a browseChannels method. These changes wouldn't affect myTV because that's just a Television object, but if I created a new RemoteTelevision object called myRemoteTV, it would have the new features.

Looking at HelloWorld

Now let's look at how all that applies to our HelloWorld program, shown again here in Listing 4.9.

Listing 4.9—HelloWorld.java

```
0: public class HelloWorld extends Object {
1:
2:     public static void main (String args[]) {
3:         System.out.print("Hello World!");
4:     }
5:
6: }
```

Let's start with line 0, which states just what we're creating here.

First, we see that this thing we're creating is public. That means that any program anywhere, including the command line, can call it. This is not always true with Java code. In some cases, we'll want to hide what we're doing from other programs, usually using private instead of public.

Next, we see that we're creating a class called HelloWorld. All Java programs start with a class because we need an object to do any work! That object might call other objects, but we've got to start with one and go from there. In this case, our class is called HelloWorld.

Next, we're stating what kind of class it is. We don't want to go through the trouble of explaining the whole idea of an object just to get to the point where we can write our program, so instead we'll just extend `Object`, the class that is the basic template for all objects. That means that whatever an `Object` can do, `HelloWorld` can do. Later, we'll see that classes can extend classes other than `Object`. (There is also another way to gain from an existing definition, but we'll deal with that later.)

So, now we have our class, which is enclosed in `{}`. These brackets are not optional. Like a well-formed XML document, the structure needs to be correct, or the class won't compile, much less run.

Of course, we also have to give our class of objects something to do. `main()` is a special method because it's the method called when a program is run from the command line. If we're not going to run the program from the command line, we can leave out the `main()` method, but in this case, we need it.

So, let's take a look at line 3, where we begin to define the `main()` method.

First, because it needs to be called from the command line, `main()` has to be `public`.

Next, we have the keyword `static`. This means that as soon as we call the `HelloWorld` program, this method exists. If it weren't `static`, we would have to explicitly create an instance of `HelloWorld` to execute it.

Just before the name of the method is the type of data that it will return. Because this is the `main()` method and will be called from the command line, we don't want it to return anything, so we'll designate that the return type is `void`.

Finally, we have the name of the method, `main()`, and following that the types of parameters it is expecting. `main()` always expects any number of `Strings`, or text data. The designation `String args[]` defines an Array, or list, that can be filled up with `String` data. For instance, we can change our `HelloWorld` class as shown in Listing 4.10.

Listing 4.10—`HelloWorld.java`: Displaying an Argument

```
0: public class HelloWorld extends Object {
1:
2:     public static void main (String args[]) {
3:         System.out.print("Hello, " + args[0] + "!");
4:     }
5:
6: }
```

Save the file and recompile the class using

```
javac HelloWorld.java
```

On line 3, we've told the program to go ahead and display the first argument—Java arrays start with 0—on the command line; so, if we were to type

```
java HelloWorld Nick
```

we would see output of

```
Hello, Nick!
```

The + signs tell the Java interpreter to combine all three `Strings` into one before displaying it.

Reading a File from a Java Application

Now that we've got the basics, we're ready to start looking at our files. We'll start with something simple, like reading the XML file and displaying it on the screen. But first, let's look at the way that Java handles variables because there are similarities in how it handles objects.

Declaring Variables

Variable—A variable is simply a place in memory that holds information. If we assign a value of "Nick" to the variable `name`, we can use `name` throughout the program, and Java will substitute "Nick." That way, we can change the value in one place, and it will take effect everywhere. The most common use for variables is to hold a place for information we need but don't have yet.

Java is a strongly typed language, which means that we must declare all variables and their types before we use them. One advantage of a strongly typed language is that it's much less likely for typos to go unnoticed because the misspelled variable won't have been declared. It also makes it easier to avoid reusing a variable unintentionally. For instance, if we declare the variable `vProduct_ID` as a number, future programmers can't put text in it, causing all kinds of problems, unless they explicitly dedefine it.

Java has eight primitive datatypes and one special type. Let's look at how they are used in Listing 4.11. Create the file `Variables.java` and type the following:

Listing 4.11—`Variables.java`: Declaring and Using Variables

```
public class Variables {
    public static void main (String args[]) {

        //char and String are TEXTUAL data types
        char c;
        c = 'X';
        System.out.println(c);

        String s;
        s = "XML";
        System.out.println(s);

        //byte, short, int and long are INTEGRAL data types
```

Listing 4.11—continued

```
13:         byte b;
14:         b = 100;
15:         System.out.println(b);
16:
17:         int i;
18:         i = 37;
19:         System.out.println(i);
20:
21:         //float and double are FLOATING POINT data types
22:         float f;
23:         f = 3.14F;
24:         System.out.println(f);
25:
26:     }
27:}
```


Compile the program using

```
javac Variables.java
```

and run it using

```
java Variables
```

The program should output the following:

```
X
XML
100
37
3.14
```

Let's take a look at what we've got here. Lines 0 and 1 are similar to our `HelloWorld` application, where we define the class and then create a `main()` method so we can call it from the command line. Lines 3, 12, and 21 are comments. They don't affect the program, but they make it easier to see what's going on. Together, they describe the three categories of primitive data.

On line 4, we declare a variable called `c` and define it as a `char` variable. That means that whatever else we do, we can only put one character in it, and it must be surrounded by single quotes. That's what we do on line 5, when we actually assign a value to the variable. Finally, on line 6 we print the value out to the screen, as we did with `HelloWorld`. In this case, we'll use `println()`, which adds a line feed after the output, instead of `print()`, which doesn't.

Lines 8 through 10 go through the same process for a `String` variable. Strictly speaking, a `String` is not a primitive data type, but an object. It's so commonly used, however, that Java's designers made it possible to use `String` like a primitive type. (Of course, we still have the advantages of its status as an object!) Notice that because it is a `String`, we set it off with double quotes, and not single quotes.

Lines 13 through 15 look at a `byte` variable. A `byte` is similar to a `char`, except that it's actually the numeric representation of the character, as opposed to the character itself. Typically, when data is moving within a system, it moves as a stream of bytes, as we'll see shortly.

Lines 17 through 19 show a simple integer, which is a number with zero decimal places, such as 3, 12, or 17,304.

Lines 22 through 24 show a `float` variable. `float` is one of two floating point data types. These are numbers that can have one or more decimal places. The difference between them is principally size. A `float` variable is 32 bits, whereas a double is 64 bits. Because a smaller number can be either a float or a double, we can add an F or a D to the number to signify which, as on line 23.

Now that we've talked about data types, let's talk about syntax. With each set of commands, we were performing the same sequence of events. First, we declared the variable and type; then, we assigned a value, and then displayed it. There is a shortcut that we can take, however, as shown in Listing 4.12.

Listing 4.12—`VariableShort.java`: A Cleaner Way to Define Variables

```
0: public class VariablesShort {
1:     public static void main (String args[]) {
2:         char c = 'X';
3:         System.out.println(c);
4:
5:         String s = "XML";
6:         System.out.println(s);
7:
8:         byte b = 100;
9:         System.out.println(b);
10:
11:        int i = 37;
12:        System.out.println(i);
13:
14:        float f = 3.14F;
15:        System.out.println(f);
16:    }
17:}
```

As we can see on lines 2, 5, 8, 11, and 14, we can declare a variable and assign it a value all at one time. This is a common way of doing things, so it's important to understand that all we're doing is what we did in Listing 4.11: declaring a variable to have a certain type and then assigning a value to it.

Now that we understand the syntax, let's look at something more useful.

Displaying the Contents of a File

Before we go too far into trying to code this, let's take a look at the actual process of getting information out of a file.

First, we can't just "read" a file. We have to create an object that represents the file itself and then we have to create a stream of data coming from it, like digging a ditch to drain the water out of a pond. Let's begin the process in Listing 4.13.

Listing 4.13—`FileClass.java`: Creating the File and the Input Stream

```
0: import java.io.*;
1:
2: public class FileClass extends Object {
3:
4:    public static void main (String args[]) {
5:
6:          String filename = args[0];
7:
8:          // Create the file object using the actual file
9:          File XMLFile = new File(filename);
10:
11:         // Create an input stream to read the file
12:         FileInputStream XMLStream = new FileInputStream(XMLFile);
13:
14:    }
15:
16:}
```

Let's start in the middle with the slightly familiar and work our way out to the new material.

On line 6, we extract the name of the file, which should be entered on the command line, just as we did when we modified `HelloWorld` to display a name. We'll use that name to create the File object on line 9.

On line 9, we do exactly what we did with our variables in Listing 4.12, but we do it with an object instead of a primitive data type. A `File` is a type of object, and we create a variable called `XMLFile` that has `File` as its type. Then, after we have our `File` variable, we give it a value by telling Java to create a new `File` object using our filename and assign it to the `XMLFile` variable.

Anytime you see the word "new," you know you're dealing with objects. The keyword new tells Java to execute a special set of commands called a constructor. A constructor has all the instructions Java needs to set up the object properly, such as executing specific commands or creating variables and assigning values to them.

So, on line 9, we create a `File` object that represents the file that we want to read. Now we have to get the information out of it. We do that with an object called a `FileInputStream`. A `FileInputStream` does exactly what it says. It takes data from the underlying file and allows us to do something with it. But before we can actually use the `FileInputStream`, we have to create one.

That's what we do on line 12. First, we declare a variable named `XMLStream` and tell Java that it's a `FileInputStream`. Then, we create the actual `FileInputStream` and tell it that it will be reading our `File` object, `XMLFile`. We aren't actually reading the file yet, however.

Before we move on, let's take a look at the new addition on line 0. The `import` statement tells the compiler that we will be pulling classes from the `java.io` package, or group of classes. We could have left it out, but we would have had to specify the location of those classes explicitly. Lines 9 and 12, for example,

```
File XMLFile = new File(filename);
FileInputStream XMLStream = new FileInputStream(XMLFile);
```

would have become

```
java.io.File XMLFile = new java.io.File(filename);
java.io.FileInputStream XMLStream = new java.io.FileInputStream(XMLFile);
```

There's nothing wrong with doing it this way—it's just a little harder to read.

Now let's move on to actually reading the file, as in Listing 4.14.

Listing 4.14—`FileClass.java`: Reading the File

```
...
11:         // Create an input stream to read the file
12:         FileInputStream XMLStream = new FileInputStream(XMLFile);
13:
14:         // Read all the bytes in the stream
15:         int num_bytes = XMLStream.available();
16:         byte fileBytes[] = new byte[num_bytes];
17:         XMLStream.read(fileBytes);
18:
19:         String outString = new String(fileBytes);
20:         System.out.print(outString);
21:     }
22:
23:}
```

First, we need to find out just how much data is in the stream waiting for us. On line 15, we declare an integer variable called `num_bytes` and assign it the number of bytes available.

Let's take a closer look at that. `XMLStream` is a `FileInputStream` object, and all `FileInputStream` objects have a certain group of methods, or functions. One of those methods is `available()`, which returns the number of bytes currently in the stream. We'll assign that number to the `num_bytes` variable so we have it for later.

Of course, it would be tiresome (and slow!) to read the stream of bytes one-by-one, so instead, we need to create somewhere to put a whole bunch of them when we read them from the stream. That's what we do on line 16. We create an array of bytes called `fileBytes`. That's what the `[]` signifies. For instance, because the first member of an array is always 0, if we later wanted the third item on the list, we'd ask for `fileBytes[2]`. We need to set the size on an array, however, so we'll set it to the number of bytes we have available using new `byte[num_bytes]`.

Array—An array is a group of similar objects which are numbered uniquely. An array is usually declared to be a certain length.

Now that we have the array ready, on line 17 we read the file into it, or more specifically, we read the stream into it. `read()` is another method of a `FileInputStream`, and the argument that it takes is the place where we want to put the data—in this case, our `fileBytes` array.

4

After we have the data, we need to do something with it, but we can't output it while it's still an array. Instead, we need to change it into a `String`, which we do on line 19. We create a `String` variable called `outString` and then create the new `String` to go inside it, so to speak. Remember, when we use the `new` keyword, we're actually calling a constructor. When the `String` constructor sees that array, it knows that it needs to turn those individual bytes into one long string.

When that's done, all we have to do is output the `String` on line 20.

That's all we need to do from a functionality standpoint, but we still have one more problem to take care of before we can run this program.

Exceptions

If we were to try to compile the class just like this, we'd get a rather strange error, something like this:

```
FileClass.java:13: unreported exception java.io.FileNotFoundException; must be
➥caught or declared to be thrown
        FileInputStream XMLStream = new FileInputStream(XMLFile);
                                    ^

FileClass.java:16: unreported exception java.io.IOException; must be caught or
➥declared to be thrown
        int num_bytes = XMLStream.available();
                                 ^

FileClass.java:18: unreported exception java.io.IOException; must be caught or
➥declared to be thrown
        XMLStream.read(fileBytes);
                 ^

3 errors
```

Does this mean that we typed something wrong? No. It means that we left something out.

Problems are inevitable when programming. Someone moves a file, a distant server becomes unavailable, someone mistypes an address, and so on. In the real world of programming, all these possibilities should be accounted for. Unfortunately, that doesn't always happen. The architects of Java, recognizing this, decided they'd "encourage" more robust programming by requiring developers to at least acknowledge the fact that a problem is possible, or better yet, to allow for it within the program.

There are actually two types of problems: errors and exceptions.

An error is something you generally can't recover from, such as running out of memory. An exception, on the other hand, is something that throws a monkey wrench into the works, but if it's handled properly, the program can continue. This is known as catching an exception.

All exceptions are subclasses, or descendants, of the general `Exception` class. Because different operations can cause different kinds of problems, there are lots of specific exceptions, such as the `FileNotFoundException` and `IOException`, mentioned previously. We can even create our own exceptions and raise them when certain conditions arise. For instance, we could create a `NoSuchVendorException` and raise it if someone tried to create a product with an invalid vendor ID.

It's generally preferable to catch and handle exceptions, and we'll do that a little later, but for now we can instead declare that our `main()` method has the potential to throw an exception. We can list them specifically, but to keep things simple, we can just use the general `Exception` class. Because both of the specific exceptions are descendants of that class, they are both exceptions, so they'll both be covered in Listing 4.15.

Listing 4.15—`FileClass.java`: Declaring an Exception to Be Thrown

```
import java.io.*;

public class FileClass extends Object {

   public static void main (String args[]) throws Exception {

         String filename = args[0];
...
```

So, even though we haven't handled the exception, we've at least acknowledged the possibility that problems could arise.

Save the file and recompile it; then run it using

```
java FileClass index.html
```

The actual file mentioned isn't important, but we need to either choose a file in the same directory as `FileClass.class` or specify the full path. Also, because we're outputting the contents of the file to the screen, it's probably better to choose a text file.

Transforming an XML File from Within a Java Program

Now that we're getting more comfortable with Java, let's do something really useful: create our product pages. We'll start by using a Java program to create XHTML files that traditional browsers can read even if they don't understand XML.

Creating the Style Sheet

The first thing that we need to do is to create the style sheet that we'll use for transforming the product page. Let's start by getting the basic formatting down, as in Listing 4.16.

Listing 4.16—`productpage.xsl`: The Overall Style Sheet

```
<?xml version="1.0"?>
<xsl:stylesheet version="1.0"
    xmlns:xsl="http://www.w3.org/1999/XSL/Transform">

<xsl:include href="topinclude.xsl"/>

<xsl:template match="//product">

  Product Number: <xsl:value-of select="product_id"/><br />
  <p><xsl:value-of select="short_desc"/></p>
  <p>Price <xsl:value-of select="price"/></p>

  <xsl:if test="inventory[@location='warehouse' and @color]">
    Available in these great colors:
    <ul>
        <xsl:for-each
           select="inventory[@location='warehouse' and @color]">

            <li><xsl:value-of select="@color"/></li>

        </xsl:for-each>
    </ul>
  </xsl:if>

  <xsl:if test="inventory[@location='showroom']">
    <p>Also available in our stores!</p>
  </xsl:if>
  <hr />

</xsl:template>

```

Listing 4.16—continued

```
31:<xsl:template match="vendor">
32:    <xsl:apply-templates select="product"/>
33:</xsl:template>
34:
35:</xsl:stylesheet>
```

Earlier, we created the `topinclude.xsl` file to allow us to reuse the style sheet that creates that top of the page, and now it's beginning to pay off as we use it again on line 4. The rest of the style sheet is similar to what we did in Chapter 2, when we created the style sheet for the browser. All products will actually appear on this page, as shown in Figure 4.4, similar to the page we wound up with at the end of Chapter 2. The difference is that now we can finally do something about it.

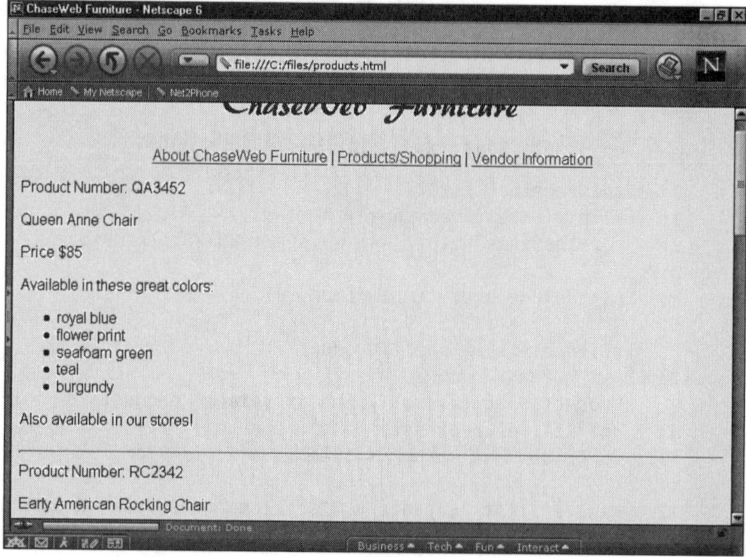

Figure 4.4

The general style sheet puts all products on the same page.

We could run the transformation from the command line, as we did previously, but we're going to make our new Java class do more for us, so let's get it started with this transformation in Listing 4.17.

Listing 4.17—`TransformProd.java`: The Basic Transformation

```
import javax.xml.transform.TransformerFactory;
import javax.xml.transform.Transformer;
import javax.xml.transform.stream.StreamSource;
import javax.xml.transform.stream.StreamResult;
import java.io.FileOutputStream;

public class TransformProd extends Object {

public static void main (String args[]) throws Exception
```

Listing 4.17—continued

```
9:  {
10:     String XMLFileName = "products.xml";
11:     String XSLSheetName = "productpage.xsl";
12:     String outputURL = "products.html";
13:
14:     TransformerFactory transFactory = TransformerFactory.newInstance();
15:     Transformer transformer =
16:               transFactory.newTransformer(new StreamSource(XSLSheetName));
17:
18:     transformer.transform(new StreamSource(XMLFileName),
19:                          new StreamResult(new FileOutputStream(outputURL)));
20:  }
21:
22:}
```


Overall, this program should do exactly what the command line did, except that it has the potential to be used in many different ways as we go along.

On lines 0 through 4, we have the `import` statements that cover all our new objects. We could have just written

```
import javax.xml.transform.*;
import javax.xml.transform.stream.*;
import java .io.*;
```

but then we would be importing much more than we needed. In general, it's better to be more specific.

On lines 6 through 9, we simply create the class and the new `main()` so that we can call it from the command line.

Now let's talk about what we actually need to transform an XML file. In all cases, we need the following:

- An XML source—In this case, we're dealing with an XML file. Later, we'll talk about using generated XML source. On line 10, we designate the name of the file that we want to use.
- An XSL style sheet—Again, this is a file, in this case, specified on line 11. Style sheets can also be dynamically generated, although we're not doing that here.
- Somewhere for the transformed data to go—Here again we specify a file on line 12, but later in this chapter we'll look at how to send the data directly to the browser without creating a file first.
- An XSL processor, called a `Transformer`, to do the actual transformation—Earlier in this chapter, we called a processor directly from the command line. Here, we declare and create the Transformer on lines 14 through 16. A `TransformerFactory` is a class that has a special method for creating those objects, called `newTransformer()`.

When the `Transformer` is created, it is based on a specific style sheet, which was specified on line 16. This style sheet can be a stream, as it is here, a DOM object, or a SAX stream. (We'll deal with the latter two in later chapters.)

After the `Transformer` is created, we can use it to transform our XML. On line 18, we are feeding the `Transformer` the source, as a stream created from `products.xml`, and specifying where we want the result to go—in this case, to a `FileOutputStream` pointing to `products.html`.

We can compile this class in the same directory as our XML and XSL files, and then run it to create the `products.html` file. After we've run the program, we can use any HTML browser to open the `products.html` file and take a look at the results.

Advanced XSLT: Parameters

Like the variables we've been discussing, a parameter holds information for use later. One great application for this is when we want to create an XHTML page for a single product, as opposed to every product that we have. We can do that by setting a parameter and then checking each product against it to see whether we should add its information to the page. Let's do that in Listing 4.18.

Listing 4.18—`productpage.xsl`: Adding a Parameter

```
<?xml version="1.0"?>
<xsl:stylesheet version="1.0"
   xmlns:xsl="http://www.w3.org/1999/XSL/Transform">

<xsl:include href="topinclude.xsl"/>

<xsl:param name="vProduct_id"> </xsl:param>

<xsl:template match="//product">

<xsl:if test="product_id=$vProduct_id">

  Product Number: <xsl:value-of select="product_id"/><BR/>
  <p><xsl:value-of select="short_desc"/></p>
...
  <xsl:if test="inventory[@location='showroom']">
    <p>Also available in our stores!</p>
  </xsl:if>

</xsl:if>

</xsl:template>

</xsl:stylesheet>
```

A parameter, such as the one we included on line 6, can either be placed at the top level of the file, as we have it here, or it can be specifically included in a template. We create it with a specific name, such as `vProduct_id`, and a value, such as `QA3452`.

We've then modified the style sheet to check each `product_id` against the value of `vProduct_id` on line 10. The `$` indicates that the style sheet is looking for a parameter or a style sheet variable, which is similar. If the `product_id` matches, the information is added to the page. If not, it isn't.

The main advantage of a style sheet parameter is the fact that when we call the spreadsheet, we can specify the value, so it can be different every time without ever touching the style sheet. We'll see how to do this in Listing 4.19.

Listing 4.19—`TransformProd.java`: Adding a Parameter Value

```
...

    TransformerFactory transFactory = TransformerFactory.newInstance();
    Transformer transformer =
              transFactory.newTransformer(new StreamSource(XSLSheetName));

    transformer.setParameter("vProduct_id", "QA3452");

    transformer.transform(new StreamSource(XMLFileName),
                        new StreamResult(new FileOutputStream(outputURL)));
  }

}
```

Notice that we're actually setting this value in the processor and not the style sheet itself. It's the processor that needs to manage this information, so we give it the name of the parameter and the value.

Compile this class and run it; then check `products.html` again. This time, only product `QA3452` is displayed.

Our First DOM: Stepping Through Our XML

It's great that we can set a parameter for the style sheet, but if we have to run each product page separately, what have we gained? It would certainly be more convenient if we could find a way to run all our pages at once. What we need to do is find a way to create a product page for every product in our XML file.

Fortunately, we can use Java to step through our XML and process the style sheet for each `product_id` it finds.

The first thing we need to do is parse the document and find out just how many `product_ids` there are, as in Listing 4.20.

Listing 4.20—`TransformProd.java`: Parsing the Document

```
0 :import javax.xml.transform.TransformerFactory;
1 :import javax.xml.transform.Transformer;
2 :import javax.xml.transform.stream.StreamSource;
3 :import javax.xml.transform.stream.StreamResult;
4 :import java.io.FileOutputStream;
5 :import org.apache.xerces.parsers.DOMParser;
6 :import org.w3c.dom.Document;
7 :import org.w3c.dom.NodeList;
8:
9: public class TransformProd extends Object {
10:
11:public static void main (String args[]) throws Exception
12:{
13:     String XMLFileName = "products.xml";
14:     String XSLSheetName = "productpage.xsl";
15:     String outputURL = "products.html";
16:
17:     TransformerFactory transFactory = TransformerFactory.newInstance();
18:     Transformer transformer =
19:              transFactory.newTransformer(new StreamSource(XSLSheetName));
20:
21:     DOMParser parser = new DOMParser();
22:     parser.parse(XMLFileName);
23:     Document document = parser.getDocument();
24:
25:     NodeList products =
26:              document.getElementsByTagName("product_id");
27:     int num_products = products.getLength();
28:
29:     System.out.println("There are "+num_products+" products.");
30:
31:
32:     transformer.setParameter("vProduct_id", "QA3452");
33:
34:     transformer.transform(new StreamSource(XMLFileName),
35:                      new StreamResult(new FileOutputStream(outputURL)));
36:  }
37:
38:}
```

Now, if you're one of those people who started Java only a few pages ago, this might look a little intimidating. Don't worry, all we're doing is creating objects and looking at them, and we're going to go through it line by line.

Let's start by looking at the new `import` statements on lines 5 through 7. The first one is the Xerces parser, which will be doing the work, in this case. The next two statements refer to classes from the Document Object Model, or DOM. DOM is an API, or Application Programming Interface, for handling XML data. An API defines a set of commands and functions that can be used for various purposes. Several APIs are available for XML, but DOM is the earliest.

The Document Object Model is based on the idea of XML as a tree structure. It requires the entire XML tree to be in memory for it to be read, but because of that, we can read any element after the DOM tree is built.

There are several alternatives to DOM, some of which we'll examine later in the book.

In our case, we want to read `product_ids`. Let's take the new section of actual code, starting on line 21. As before, we start by telling Java what type of object we want. In this case, we want a `DOMParser`, part of the Xerces package, so on line 21, we create a new `DOMParser` object and call it `parser`. We can then use the `parser` object to do any of the methods that have been defined for a `DOMParser` object.

The primary purpose of a parser, of course, is to parse, so on line 22, we tell the `parser` object to go ahead and parse our `products.xml` file.

When a `DOMParser` parses a file, it does more than just read through it. It creates the XML tree in memory, waiting for us to do something with it.

After we have the tree in memory, we have to find a way to use it. We do that by creating a `Document` object out of it. On line 19, we use the `getDocument()` method of the `DOMParser` class to create that `Document` object, which we'll go on to manipulate. `document` now contains all of the XML tree that was in memory.

Our ultimate goal is to run through all the `product_ids` and use each of them to create an XHTML page. We start by checking to see just how many of them we have. To do that, we want to get a list of all our products. On lines 25 and 26, we use the `getElementsByTagName()` method of the document object to create a `NodeList` called `products`.

A `NodeList` is a type of object that is exactly what it sounds like: a list of nodes that exist in various places in the document. Like any list, a `NodeList` has a certain number of items in it, and we extract that number using the `getLength()` method on line 27, assigning it to the `num_products` variable.

Finally, we print the number of products to the command line window, just as we printed "`Hello World!`". Compile and run this program to see how many `product_id` elements are in `products.xml`.

So, now we know how many nodes are on the list, but what are they? We can find out by looping through the list, as in Listing 4.21.

Listing 4.21—`TransformProd.java`: Looping Through the `Nodelist`

```
...
27:     int num_products = products.getLength();
28:
29:     System.out.println("There are "+num_products+" products.  They are:");
30:
31:     String product_id;
32:     for (int i = 0; i < num_products; i++) {
33:         product_id = products.item(i).getNodeValue();
34:         System.out.println(product_id);
35:     }
36:
37:     transformer.setParameter("vProduct_id", "QA3452");
38:...
```

Line 31 should be easy by now; we just declare a `String` variable called `product_id`.

Lines 32 through 35 are what's known as a `for-loop`, or a `for-next` loop. A `for-next` loop takes a variable, such as `i`, and uses it to keep track of how many times the loop code has run. We can dissect line 32 this way:

- `int i =0`—This declares the integer variable `i` and gives it an initial value of `0`.
- `i < num_products`—This is the test condition. As long as `i` is less than (<) `num_products`, the loop will continue.
- `i++`—This is a shortcut, really, specifying what should happen each time the loop is complete. It's short for `i=i+1`.

So, `i` starts out with a value of `0`, and each time the loop is executed, `i` is incremented by 1 until it's no longer less than `num_products`.

The purpose of the loop is to look at each node in `products` and output its value, but if we were to compile and run this program, the output would look like this:

```
There are 12 products. They are:
null
null
null
null
null
null
null
null
null
null
```

That doesn't make any sense. We must have done something wrong. But how can we tell? The first place to start is, of course, the documentation.

Because we installed Xerces in a previous chapter, we have all the documentation locally, but it is also available on the Web at

```
http://xml.apache.org/apiDocs/index.html
```

If you were to point your browser to that address, you would find a page that looks like Figure 4.5.

Figure 4.5

This is the opening page for the Xerces Javadoc.

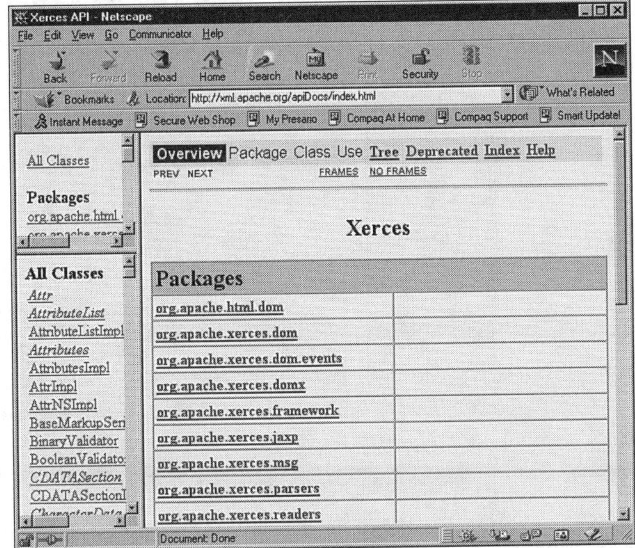

In this case, we know we started with `document.getElementsByTagName()`, so we'll start by seeing what information we can gather on what it's returning. In the lower-left frame, we'll click on the Document link (because document is a `Document` object), which brings up the documentation for a `Document` in the main frame. We can scroll down to the information on `getElementsByTagName()` method, as shown in Figure 4.6.

We see that we did call it correctly and that it did return a `NodeList` (which we already knew). Maybe we can get more information by looking at `NodeList`. Click the `NodeList` link. Here we see information on the two methods for a `NodeList`, `getLength()` and `item()`.

So, `products` is a list of items, each of which is callable by using `products.item(`*`n`*`)` where *n* is the number of the item, in order. We see from the definition on this page that `products.item()` is a `Node`. Maybe we can get some clues from the documentation on `Node`.

If we click `Node`, we find that the documentation offers some interesting clues. For instance, we see the `Field Summary`, which is a list of different types of `Nodes` (see Figure 4.7). Two of those types are `ELEMENT_NODE` and `TEXT_NODE`. If the `Node` object considers them different, maybe we're not looking at what we think we're looking at. We can also see, in the `Method Summary`, a method called `getNodeType()`.

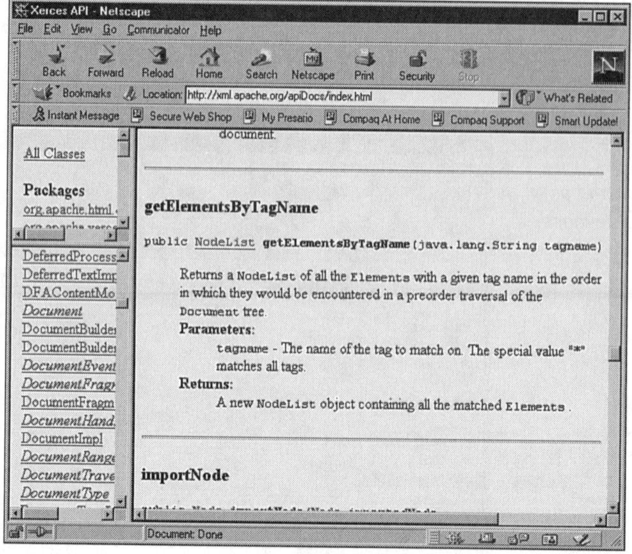

Figure 4.6

`Javadoc` provides information on how to call a method, what it returns, and what it's used for.

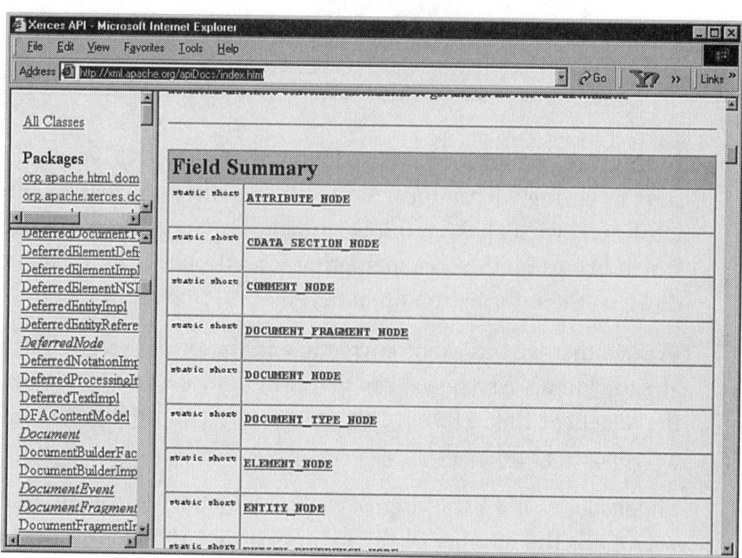

Figure 4.7

The documentation shows the different values that may be stored in a `Node` object.

With these two pieces of information, we can start to debug our code. Add the statements in Listing 4.22 to `TransformProd.java` and compile and run the program.

Listing 4.22—`TransformProd.java`: A Little Debugging

```
...
34:         System.out.println(product_id);
35:     }
36:
37:     System.out.println("ELEMENT_NODE="+products.item(0).ELEMENT_NODE);
38:     System.out.println("TEXT_NODE="+products.item(0).TEXT_NODE);
39:     System.out.println("This element="+products.item(0).getNodeType());
40:
41:     transformer.setParameter("vProduct_id", "QA3452");
...
```

The new lines print out the values represented by the two types and then print the actual type for our first `item()`. The output looks like this:


```
ELEMENT_NODE=1
TEXT_NODE=3
This element=1
```

Arrays in Java are zero based. That means that the first element has an index of 0, and the tenth element has an index of 9. So, the largest element in an array always has an index of `num_items -1`.

So, it would seem that the reason we're not getting the value of our products is that there aren't any! What we have here are specifically element nodes. So, it would seem logical that the text must be a child of the element.

Checking the `Method Summary`, we see that there is a `getChildNodes()` method for every `Node`, and that it returns a `NodeList`, just like `getElementsByTagName()` did. If we were to write it all out longhand, getting to the value we want might look like this:

```
Node productNode = products.item(0);
NodeList productNodeChildren = productNode.getChildNodes();
Node productTextNode = productNodeChildren.item(0);
String productTextValue = productTextNode.getValue();
```

That would be cumbersome, though, so Java lets us shorten all that code to

```
String productTextValue =
➥products.item(0).getChildNodes().item(0).getNodeValue();
```

Each object builds on the last to form the chain.

We can use this in our program to see the actual values of the `product_ids`. Take out the debugging statements and change the line 33 as shown in Listing 4.23.

Listing 4.23—TransformProd.java: Outputting the Actual Value

```
...
NodeList products =
        document.getElementsByTagName("product_id");
int num_products = products.getLength();

System.out.println("There are "+num_products+" products.  They are:");

String product_id;
for (int i = 0; i < num_products; i++) {
  product_id = products.item(i).getChildNodes().item(0).getNodeValue();
  System.out.println(product_id);
}

transformer.setParameter("vProduct_id", "QA3452");
...
```

Now if we compile and run the program, the output should be as follows:

```
There are 10 products. They are:
QA3452
RC2342
BR3452
CDRS
WWWdrt
WWWsc
WWWhch
3253435
5622345
39981234
```

Now that we have the values, let's put them to work. We want to create different files, so they'll all have to have different names. The most logical choice would be to use the product number as the filename. We'll also have to process our files from within the loop because we need one for each `product_id`, as in Listing 4.24.

Listing 4.24—TransformProd.java: Transforming Each File

```
...

public class TransformProd extends Object {

public static void main (String args[]) throws Exception
{
    String XMLFileName = "products.xml";
    String XSLSheetName = "productpage.xsl";

    TransformerFactory transFactory = TransformerFactory.newInstance();
    Transformer transformer =
...

    System.out.println("There are "+num_products+" products.  They are:");

```

Listing 4.24—continued

```
30:     String product_id;
31:     for (int i = 0; i < num_products; i++) {
32:       product_id = products.item(i).getChildNodes().item(0).getNodeValue();
33:       System.out.println(product_id);
34:
35:       String outputURL = product_id+".html";
36:       transformer.setParameter("vProduct_id", product_id);
37:
38:       transformer.transform(new StreamSource(XMLFileName),
39:                             new StreamResult(new FileOutputStream(outputURL)));
40:
41:     }
42:
43:   }
44:
45:}
```

We didn't add much that was new, but we did have to move a few things around.

Each file needs to have its own name, so inside the loop, on line 35, we set the value of `outputURL` to a filename made up of the product ID and `.html`. Then, still in the loop, on line 37, we set `vProduct_id` to be the current `product_id` and process this version of the style sheet on lines 38 and 39.

After we compile and run the program, we can see that we now have 12 new files in the directory, each named for a product. We can open any one of those files with the browser and see the page for that product.

From here it doesn't matter whether our XML file has 12 products or 12,000. The program will simply run through each of them, creating the appropriate files.

Automating Further: Adding Next and Previous Links

Being able to create all our files at once was handy, but the resulting pages don't have any navigation on them that lets the user go to another product. Ideally, we want our users to be able to go from one product to the next, or go back, if they want. We can do that by adding a few lines to our program to look forward and backward at the list of products.

We already have one parameter for the `product_id` being processed. Now, because we'll also be feeding this information to the style sheet, we need parameters for the next and previous products, as in Listing 4.25. We'll also add the links themselves.

Listing 4.25—`productpage.xsl`: Adding Next and Previous Links

```
<?xml version="1.0"?>
<xsl:stylesheet version="1.0"
    xmlns:xsl="http://www.w3.org/1999/XSL/Transform">
```

Listing 4.25—continued

```
3:
4:<xsl:include href="topinclude.xsl"/>
5:
6:<xsl:param name="vProduct_id"> </xsl:param>
7:<xsl:param name="vPrev_id"> </xsl:param>
8:<xsl:param name="vNext_id"> </xsl:param>
9:
10:<xsl:template match="//product">
11:
12:<xsl:if test="product_id=$vProduct_id">
13:
14:  Product Number: <xsl:value-of select="product_id"/><br />
15:  <p><xsl:value-of select="short_desc"/></p>
16:  <p>Price<xsl:value-of select="price"/></p>
17:
18:  <xsl:if test="inventory[@location='warehouse' and @color]">
19:    Available in these great colors:<br />
20:    <ul>
21:      <xsl:for-each
22:           select="inventory[@location='warehouse' and @color]">
23:
24:           <li><xsl:value-of select="@color"/></li>
25:
26:      </xsl:for-each>
27:    </ul>
28:  </xsl:if>
29:  <br />
30:  <xsl:if test="inventory[@location='showroom']">
31:    <p>Also available in our stores!</p>
32:  </xsl:if>
33:  <hr />
34:  <xsl:element name="a">
35:       <xsl:attribute name="href">
36:            <xsl:value-of select="$vPrev_id"/>.html
37:       </xsl:attribute>
38:       Previous Product
39:   </xsl:element>
40:   <br/>
41:   <xsl:element name="a">
42:       <xsl:attribute name="href">
43:            <xsl:value-of select="$vNext_id"/>.html
44:       </xsl:attribute>
45:       Next Product
46:   </xsl:element>
47:</xsl:if>
48:</xsl:template>
49:
50:</xsl:stylesheet>
```

On lines 7 and 8, we simply add two more parameters, which will be set by our Java program. On lines 34 through 46, we actually create the links that use those values.

Now we'll add the code to actually calculate and set those parameters, in Listing 4.26.

Listing 4.26—Adding the Next and Previous Parameters

```
...
24:    NodeList products =
25:             document.getElementsByTagName("product_id");
26:    int num_products = products.getLength();
27:
28:    System.out.println("There are "+num_products+" products.  They are:");
29:
30:    String product_id;
31:    String prev_id;
32:    String next_id;
33:
34:    for (int i = 0; i < num_products; i++) {
35:      product_id = products.item(i)
36:                             .getChildNodes().item(0).getNodeValue();
37:      System.out.println(product_id);
38:
39:      if (i != 0) {
40:          prev_id = products.item(i-1)
41:                             .getChildNodes().item(0).getNodeValue();
42:      } else {
43:          prev_id = products.item(num_products-1)
44:                             .getChildNodes().item(0).getNodeValue();
45:      }
46:
47:      if (i != (num_products-1)) {
48:          next_id =
49:             products.item(i+1).getChildNodes().item(0).getNodeValue();
50:      } else {
51:          next_id =
52:             products.item(0).getChildNodes().item(0).getNodeValue();
53:      }
54:
55:      String outputURL = product_id+".html";
56:      transformer.setParameter("vProduct_id", product_id);
57:      transformer.setParameter("vPrev_id", prev_id);
58:      transformer.setParameter("vNext_id", next_id);
59:
60:      transformer.transform(new StreamSource(XMLFileName),
61:                  new StreamResult(new FileOutputStream(outputURL)));
62:
63:     }
64:
65:   }
66:
67:}
```

The first thing we need to do is declare our variables, on lines 31 and 32.

We want this to be a circle. When the user gets to the last product, he should be able to click Next and get the first product. Similarly, if the user is looking at the first product, he should be able to click Previous and get the last product.

Several things are going on on lines 39 through 45. First, on line 39, we check to see whether we're on the first product. Remember, arrays in Java are zero based. The first product will have an index of 0, and the last product will have an index of (`num_products -1`).

This is an `if` statement. If the condition in parentheses (in this case, `i!=0`, or "i is not equal to zero") is true, the commands in the first set of brackets will be executed. If it's false, the commands in the second set of brackets will be executed. So, if we're on the first product, `prev_id` will be set to the last `product_id`. If not, it will be set to the `product_id` just before.

If we compile and run the program, we'll see that previous and next links are added to our pages, as in Figure 4.8.

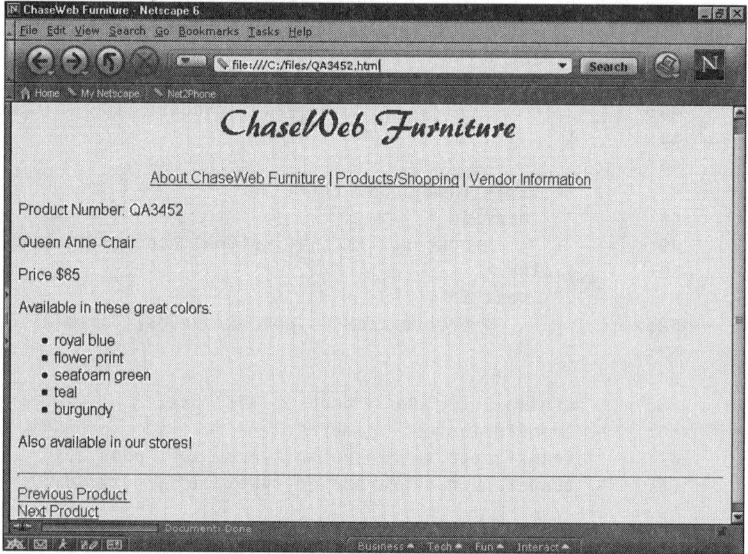

Figure 4.8

Next and previous links are added to our product pages.

If we run through those links, however, we'll see a problem. Everything is fine until we get to product CDRS. That page has no content, as you see in Figure 4.9!

Why should this be? It's probably not the Java program because the other pages are fine. The same reasoning would seem to apply to the style sheet. Maybe it's something about the data. Is there something different about it?

Figure 4.9

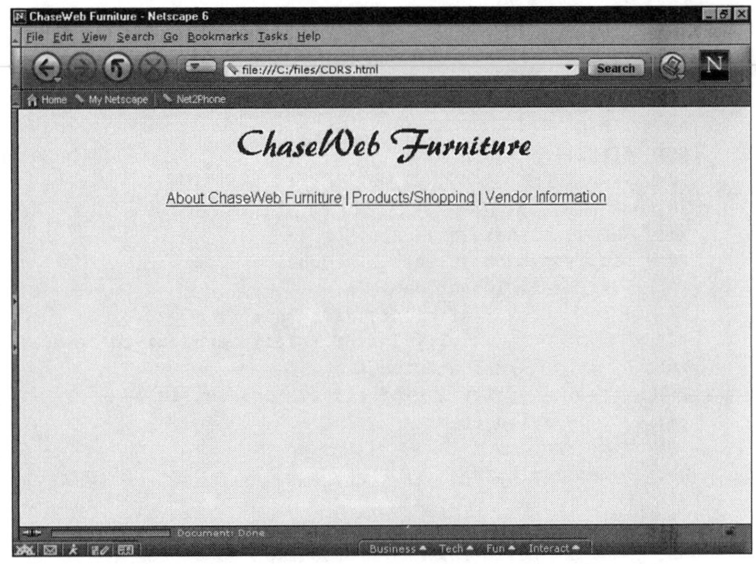

Product CDRS has no content.

In fact, there is. CDRS is a suite, not a product, even though it has a `product_id`, and the style sheet is set to process only products. If we want the suites to be processed too, we'll have to make a change to the style sheet.

We could just go ahead and add suites to the template match for products, but consider that if we did, the products that are children of the suite would never get processed. Instead, we want to create a slightly modified template just for the suites, as in Listing 4.27.

Listing 4.27—`productpage.xsl`: Adding Suites

```
...
</xsl:if>
</xsl:template>

<xsl:template match="suite">

<xsl:if test="product_id=$vProduct_id">

  Product Number: <xsl:value-of select="product_id"/><br />
  <p><xsl:value-of select="short_desc"/></p>
  <p>Price<xsl:value-of select="price"/></p>

  <xsl:if test="inventory[@location='warehouse' and @color]">
    Available in these great colors:<br />
    <ul>
      <xsl:for-each
            select="inventory[@location='warehouse' and @color]">

            <li><xsl:value-of select="@color"/></li>
```

Listing 4.27—continued

```
65:
66:       </xsl:for-each>
67:     </ul>
68:  </xsl:if>
69:
70:
71:  See also these products:<br />
72:  <xsl:for-each select="./product">
73:       <xsl:element name="a">
74:           <xsl:attribute name="href">
75:               <xsl:value-of select="product_id"/>.html
76:           </xsl:attribute>
77:           <xsl:value-of select="product_id"/>
78:       </xsl:element>
79:       <br />
80:  </xsl:for-each>
81:
82:  <br />
83:  <xsl:if test="inventory[@location='showroom']">
84:    <p>Also available in our stores!</p>
85:  </xsl:if>
86:  <hr />
87:  <xsl:element name="a">
88:       <xsl:attribute name="href">
89:            <xsl:value-of select="$vPrev_id"/>.html
90:       </xsl:attribute>
91:       Previous Product
92:   </xsl:element>
93:   <br />
94:   <xsl:element name="a">
95:       <xsl:attribute name="href">
96:            <xsl:value-of select="$vNext_id"/>.html
97:       </xsl:attribute>
98:       Next Product
99:   </xsl:element>
100:</xsl:if>
101:
102:</xsl:template>
103:
104:</xsl:stylesheet>
```

The templates are the same except for the sections highlighted. On lines 71 through 80, we added links to the products that are part of the suite.

If we compile and run the program, we'll see that we now have full pages for all the products and suites.

Well, almost full pages.

The pages look pretty empty, so let's go ahead and add some vendor information to the top of the page. As we did earlier, we'll use the products node because we know it appears only once.

Add the vendor information to `productPage.xsl`, as in Listing 4.28.

Listing 4.28—`productpage.xsl`: Adding Vendor Information

```
<?xml version="1.0"?>
<xsl:stylesheet version="1.0"
    xmlns:xsl="http://www.w3.org/1999/XSL/Transform">

<xsl:include href="topinclude.xsl"/>

<xsl:param name="vProduct_id">QA3452</xsl:param>
<xsl:param name="vPrev_id"> </xsl:param>
<xsl:param name="vNext_id"> </xsl:param>

<xsl:template match="vendor[product/product_id=$vProduct_id]
➥| vendor[suite/product_id=$vProduct_id]">
    <h1 align="center">
        <xsl:value-of select="vendor_name"/>
    </h1>
    <xsl:value-of select="advertisement"/>
    <hr />
    <xsl:apply-templates select="product | suite"/>
</xsl:template>

<xsl:template match="//product">

<xsl:if test="product_id=$vProduct_id">

...
```

We don't have to compile our Java program again, but if we run it, we'll see that the vendor information is added to the tops of all our product pages.

This is one of the beautiful things about XML. We can change entire sites just by changing a style sheet. But what if we know that the data will be changing on a regular basis? Do we really want to have to regenerate the entire site just because we changed one or two prices? Of course not. That's what servlets are for.

Adding a Web Server to the Mix

Although we know we're building a Web site, we haven't, so far, discussed one of the most important aspects: the Web server itself. In some ways, that is how it should be. A Web server should sit in the background, unnoticed, quietly doing its job.

But until now we've been building static Web pages that we could test with a browser and just place on the Web server, wherever it was. Now we're going to need to use the Web server itself to create the content.

The actual process of sending and receiving a Web request has a few more steps, but that's not important right now.

Let's stop for a moment and look at what a Web server does. When we enter a URL into our browser, our computer, the client, makes a request to the Web server, which assembles a request and sends it back to the client. The type of information the client was looking for (for example, an image, or the results of a script) determines what the Web server has to do to assemble that request. If it is just an image or a plain HTML file, the server finds it and sends it back.

In our case, however, we want the server to actually DO something and then send those results back to the client. For much of the Web's history, this was called using the CGI, or Common Gateway Interface, and the scripts were, more than likely, Perl or C programs.

With the advent of Java, however, the idea of servlets arrived on the scene. A servlet is a small Java application that runs on the Web server and returns a result to the client.

Not all Web servers can run servlets, although most can, with the addition of a server plug-in called a servlet engine. Some of those servlet engines can also be used as the Web server itself, as is the case with Tomcat.

Installing and Configuring Tomcat

Tomcat is also from the Apache Software Foundation, as part of the Jakarta project. Virtually identical to Sun's Java Server Web Development Kit, from which it was originally derived, Tomcat can be downloaded from

```
http://jakarta.apache.org/downloads/binindex.html
```

or

```
http://java.sun.com/products/jsp/tomcat/
```

Download the latest release build (as opposed to the milestone builds) and uncompress it into the directory you want to use. If you want to match the instructions here, uncompress the files into your root directory and then rename the resulting `jakarta-tomcat` directory to be simply `tomcat`.

Completing the Installation

That's all there is to installing Tomcat, but we will need to do a bit of configuring. Specifically, we need to add two new environment variables, similar to `CLASSPATH`. They are `JAVA_HOME`, and `TOMCAT_HOME`. We also need to add some new files to `CLASSPATH`. For instance, to add these variables to `AUTOEXEC.bat`, we would edit it to look like the following:

```
SET CLASSPATH=.;c:\xalan\bin\xerces.jar;c:\xalan\bin\xalan.jar;
SET CLASSPATH=%CLASSPATH%c:\tomcat\lib\webserver.jar;c:\tomcat\lib\jasper.jar;
SET CLASSPATH=%CLASSPATH%c:\tomcat\lib\xml.jar;c:\tomcat\lib\servlet.jar;
➥c:\tomcat\lib\tools.jar;

SET TOMCAT_HOME=c:\tomcat
SET JAVA_HOME=c:\jdk1.3
PATH=%PATH%;%JAVA_HOME%\bin;
```

4

Finally, edit line 38 of `tomcat\bin\tomcat.bat` so that it reads

```
set CLASSPATH=%cp%;%CLASSPATH%;
```

Testing the Installation

After setting the new environment variables (and executing `AUTOEXEC.bat`, if necessary), open a command prompt window and type the following:

```
cd c:\tomcat\bin
startup
```

This should start `Tomcat` in a separate window. To make sure that it's running, open a browser and point it to

```
http://localhost:8080
```

`Localhost` is a generic name that refers to your machine, and `8080` is the port number that the server is running on. This page gives general information about the installation and also contains a link to the servlet examples.

Port number—A port is like a telephone in a large office building. It has a number attached to it so that people can "call" it, but if there's no one there listening, the request will go unanswered.

To make sure that everything is working properly, click the Servlet Examples link and then click one of the examples themselves, such as Hello World. If you don't see an error, Tomcat is installed properly.

If the example doesn't work, try the following:

1. Make sure that your environment variables (`CLASSPATH`, `JAVA_HOME`, and so on) are set properly. You may need to reboot your machine after making the changes to `AUTOEXEC.bat`.

2. Make sure you are pointing to the proper URL.
3. Visit the troubleshooting areas on the Apache Web site, at `http://www.apache.org`. If Tomcat doesn't install quickly, there is usually an obscure reason that can be ferreted out on the site.

We still need a place to run our own programs from, however. Make a copy of the `webapps/examples` directory and call it `book` (so that you have a `webapps/book` directory). This will copy all the structure of the directory, including the subdirectories underneath it.

The last step is to add our new Web application to the server's configuration file. This is actually an XML file in the `conf` directory called `server.xml`. It's a wonderful example of how XML can be used to configure programs.

The section we're interested in is at the end. We want to add a new Web application called book, as shown in Listing 4.29.

Listing 4.29—`server.xml`: Adding a New Web Application

```
<?xml version="1.0" encoding="ISO-8859-1"?>

<Server>
    <!-- Debug low-level events in XmlMapper startup -->
    <xmlmapper:debug level="0" />

    <!-- This is quite flexible; we can either have a log file per
         module in Tomcat (example: ContextManager) or we can have
         one for Servlets and one for Jasper, or we can just have
        one tomcat.log for both Servlet and Jasper.

     If you omit "path" there, then stderr should be used.

     verbosityLevel values can be:
        FATAL
        ERROR
        WARNING
            INFORMATION
            DEBUG
         -->

    <Logger name="tc_log"
            path="logs/tomcat.log"
            customOutput="yes" />

    <Logger name="servlet_log"
            path="logs/servlet.log"
            customOutput="yes" />

    <Logger name="JASPER_LOG"
        path="logs/jasper.log"
            verbosityLevel = "INFORMATION" />
```

Listing 4.29—continued

```

    <!-- Add "home" attribute if you want tomcat to be based on a
➥different directory
         "home" is used to create work and to read webapps, but not for
➥libs or CLASSPATH.
         Note that TOMCAT_HOME is where tomcat is installed, while
➥ContextManager home is the
         base directory for contexts, webapps/ and work/
      -->
    <ContextManager debug="0" workDir="work" >
        <!-- ContextInterceptor
➥className="org.apache.tomcat.context.LogEvents" / -->
        <ContextInterceptor
➥className="org.apache.tomcat.context.AutoSetup" />
        <ContextInterceptor
➥className="org.apache.tomcat.context.DefaultCMSetter" />
        <ContextInterceptor
➥className="org.apache.tomcat.context.WorkDirInterceptor" />
        <ContextInterceptor
➥className="org.apache.tomcat.context.WebXmlReader" />
        <ContextInterceptor
➥className="org.apache.tomcat.context.LoadOnStartupInterceptor" />
        <!-- Request processing -->
        <RequestInterceptor
➥className="org.apache.tomcat.request.SimpleMapper" debug="0" />
        <RequestInterceptor
➥className="org.apache.tomcat.request.SessionInterceptor" />
        <RequestInterceptor
➥className="org.apache.tomcat.request.SecurityCheck" />
        <RequestInterceptor
➥className="org.apache.tomcat.request.FixHeaders" />

        <Connector className="org.apache.tomcat.service.SimpleTcpConnector">
            <Parameter name="handler"
➥value="org.apache.tomcat.service.http.HttpConnectionHandler"/>
            <Parameter name="port" value="8080"/>
        </Connector>

        <Connector className="org.apache.tomcat.service.SimpleTcpConnector">
            <Parameter name="handler"
➥value="org.apache.tomcat.service.connector.Ajp12ConnectionHandler"/>
            <Parameter name="port" value="8007"/>
        </Connector>

        <!-- example - how to override AutoSetup actions -->
        <Context path="/examples" docBase="webapps/examples" debug="0"
➥reloadable="true" >
        </Context>

   <Context path="/book" docBase="webapps/book" debug="0" reloadable="true" >
        </Context>

```

Listing 4.29—continued

```
68:         <!-- example - how to override AutoSetup actions -->
69:        <Context path="" docBase="webapps/ROOT" debug="0" reloadable="true" >
70:         </Context>
71:
72:  <Context path="/test" docBase="webapps/test" debug="0" reloadable="true" >
73:         </Context>
74:
75:     </ContextManager>
76:</Server>
```

Our new Web application is on lines 65 and 66. The path attribute is what appears as part of the URL. The `docBase` is the main directory for this application. We're not debugging, so we want to set debug equal to zero so we don't generate that information. Finally, `reloadable="true"` is a new feature of Tomcat that allows us to see changes to our servlets without having to stop and start the Web server.

We do, however, need to stop and start the server after we've made this change. The best way is to go back to the window where we typed startup and type

```
shutdown
startup
```

This causes the Web serve to stop and then start, forcing it to read the changes in the `server.xml` file.

To test our new application, point your browser to

```
http://localhost:8080/book/servlet/HelloWorldExample
```

and make sure that it's displayed properly.

The First Servlet

Create the file `HelloWorldServlet.java` in the `tomcat/webapps/book/WEB-INF/classes` directory and give it the text in Listing 4.30.

Listing 4.30—`HelloWorldexample.java`

```
import java.io.*;
import javax.servlet.*;
import javax.servlet.http.*;

public class HelloWorldServlet extends HttpServlet {

    public void doGet(HttpServletRequest request,
                      HttpServletResponse response)
        throws IOException, ServletException

    {
        response.setContentType("text/html");
```

Listing 4.30—continued

```
12:
13:        PrintWriter out = response.getWriter();
14:
15:        out.println("<html><body>");
16:        out.println("<h1>Hello World!</h1>");
17:        out.println("</body></html>");
18:    }
19:}
```

Although what we're doing might seem completely new, there's really very little here that is different from what's come before.

Lines 0 through 2 are just the imported classes, saving us the time of typing the full package name for each class we use.

On line 4, we create the class, the same way we did before. Only this time, instead of just extending `Object`, we extend `HttpServlet`. The `HttpServlet` class already has many of the methods we would need to make this servlet work.

The same way that all the applications we have built so far have had a `main()` method so we could call them from the command line, we need a method that the Web server can call. There are several different ways to send a request to a Web server, such as `GET` and `POST`. Those are covered in Chapter 5, "Taking Orders: Manipulating Data with JDOM," but for now just keep in mind that all the requests that we are going to send from the browser are "get" requests, so the Web server will automatically try to execute the `doGet()` method.

The `doGet()` method takes two arguments: a `Request` object, `HttpServletRequest`, and a `Response` object `HttpServletResponse`. These are exactly what they sound like. The request is the information coming from the browser, and the response is the information that will be sent back to it.

On line 7, we explicitly declare the exceptions that we might throw in the course of executing this servlet instead of just using the general Exception, as we've done previously.

The actual code for this servlet is just five lines long. The first line, line 11, sets the content type for the response. The content type, such as `text/html` or `images/gif`, is sent back to the browser before the actual page, so the browser knows what it needs to do with it.

Line 13 creates an object that we can use to add information to the response. Because we're not writing to the console window anymore, we can't just use `System.out.println`. Instead, we need to use a `PrintWriter` object that's attached to the response.

Finally, lines 15 through 17 actually print the message on the page.

Before we can actually call up the Web page, however, we need to compile the servlet into a class, just as we've done before. Change to the `tomcat/webapps/book/WEB-INF/classes` directory and type

```
javac HelloWorldServlet.java
```

This should compile without incident. If the compiler tells you that it can't find the classes you're trying to import, chances are that the `CLASSPATH` isn't set yet. If you've made your changes to `AUTOEXEC.bat`, run the file in the window where you want to compile the class.

After the class is compiled, we can call it up in the browser. Point your browser to

```
http://localhost:8080/book/servlet/HelloWorldServlet
```

You've written your first servlet. (Today is a day for firsts, isn't it!)

Extracting Request Information

The Web is certainly a more interesting place when we can interact with it, and that means telling a Web site just what we want. Normally, this is done through forms, which we'll cover in Chapter 5, but we're going to get a small taste of it now.

We want to be able to have our servlet display a single product page requested by the user, so we have to have a way to know which product page the user wants. One way to do that is to embed information directly into the URL.

Before we go back to `TransformProd`, let's take a look at extracting that information using `HelloWorldServlet`. Add the information shown in Listing 4.31 and recompile.

Listing 4.31—Extracting Information from the URL

```
import java.io.*;
import javax.servlet.*;
import javax.servlet.http.*;

public class HelloWorldServlet extends HttpServlet {

    public void doGet(HttpServletRequest request,
                      HttpServletResponse response)
        throws IOException, ServletException

    {
        response.setContentType("text/html");

        PrintWriter out = response.getWriter();

        out.println("<html><body>");
        out.println("<h1>Hello World!</h1>");

        String product_id = request.getParameter("product_id");
```

Listing 4.31—continued

```
19:        out.println("You have asked for product_id "+product_id);
20:
21:        out.println("</body></html>");
22:    }
23:}
```

Line 18 uses the `getParameter()` method to retrieve the information, and line 16 outputs it. To test this, point your browser to the following URL:

`http://localhost:8080/book/servlet/HelloWorldServlet?product_id=QA3452`

The `?` tells the server that the resource, such as a page or servlet name, is done, and what follows is data. Data normally comes in name-value pairs. So, in this case, `product_id` is the name, and `QA3452` is the value. The output should look something like Figure 4.10.

4

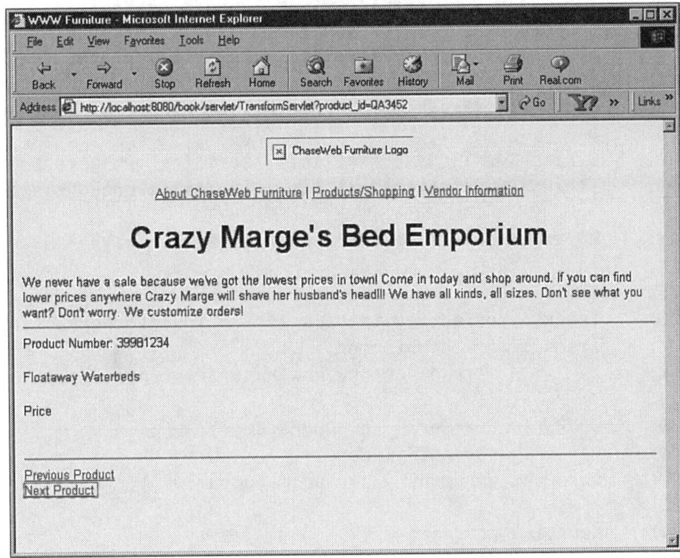

Figure 4.10

We can interact with the server by extracting information from the URL.

Now we're ready to incorporate this into `TransformProd`. To adapt this application for use as a servlet, we need to do several things:

- Add import statements for servlet-specific classes
- Extend `HttpServlet` instead of `Object`
- Change the `main()` method to the `doGet()` method, with the proper arguments and exceptions
- Change the output from `System.out.println` to a `PrintWriter` object

None of this is new. We'll put it all together in Listing 4.32 and rename it `TransformServlet`, making sure to save it to the classes directory.

Listing 4.32—`TransformServlet.java`: Putting It All Together

```
import javax.xml.transform.TransformerFactory;
import javax.xml.transform.Transformer;
import javax.xml.transform.stream.StreamSource;
import javax.xml.transform.stream.StreamResult;
import java.io.FileOutputStream;
import org.apache.xerces.parsers.DOMParser;
import org.w3c.dom.Document;
import org.w3c.dom.NodeList;
import java.io.*;
import javax.servlet.*;
import javax.servlet.http.*;

public class TransformServlet extends HttpServlet  {

    public void doGet(HttpServletRequest request,
                      HttpServletResponse response)
            throws IOException, ServletException
    {
    String thisProduct_id = request.getParameter("product_id");

    String XMLFileName = "file:///C:/files/products.xml";
    String XSLSheetName = "file:///C:/files/productpage.xsl";

    PrintWriter output = response.getWriter();

    try {
    TransformerFactory transFactory = TransformerFactory.newInstance();
    Transformer transformer =
             transFactory.newTransformer(new StreamSource(XSLSheetName));

    DOMParser parser = new DOMParser();
    parser.parse(XMLFileName);
    Document document = parser.getDocument();

    NodeList products =
           document.getElementsByTagName("product_id");
    int num_products = products.getLength();

    String product_id;
    String prev_id;
    String next_id;

    for (int i = 0; i < num_products; i++) {
      product_id = products.item(i)
                         .getChildNodes().item(0).getNodeValue();

      if (thisProduct_id.equals(product_id)) {

          if (i != 0) {
```

Listing 4.32—continued

```
49:                 prev_id = products.item(i-1)
50:                            .getChildNodes().item(0).getNodeValue();
51:             } else {
52:                 prev_id = products.item(num_products-1)
53:                             .getChildNodes().item(0).getNodeValue();
54:             }
55:
56:             if (i != (num_products-1)) {
57:                 next_id =
58:                products.item(i+1).getChildNodes().item(0).getNodeValue();
59:             } else {
60:                 next_id =
61:                products.item(0).getChildNodes().item(0).getNodeValue();
62:             }
63:
64:             transformer.setParameter("vProduct_id", product_id);
65:             transformer.setParameter("vPrev_id", prev_id);
66:             transformer.setParameter("vNext_id", next_id);
67:
68:             transformer.transform(new StreamSource(XMLFileName),
69:                            new StreamResult(output));
70:          }
71:
72:        }
73:       } catch (Exception e) {
74:             output.print("Problem transforming the file.");
75:       }
76:
77:    }
78:
79:}
```


In addition to the changes mentioned previously, we made a few other significant changes. On lines 20 and 21, we give the complete path to the XML and XSL files, so that the Web server can find them now that we're in a separate directory.

Lines 25 and 73 through 75 are extremely important. Earlier, we talked about exceptions, and how we either had to throw them or catch them. We got around worrying about catching them by just throwing the generic `Exception` on the `main()` method, but we can't do that this time.

The reason is the `doGet()` method for an `HttpServlet` is already defined, so we can't change what it throws. But because it has a specific list of exceptions that it throws, we have to catch any others.

All our parsing and transformations have the potential to throw exceptions, so we enclose them in a try-catch block. If any exceptions occur, the catch block—the error message on line 74, in this case—will be executed.

Finally, we check for `next_id` and `prev_id` by comparing the values of `thisProduct_id` and `product_id`. Notice that we can't just say `thisProduct_id == product_id` because these are `Strings`, and although it doesn't matter most of the time, they are objects, and comparisons work a little differently than we might expect, as we'll discuss in Chapter 5.

After the servlet is compiled at the command line, we point our browser to

```
http://localhost:8080/book/servlet/TransformServlet?product_id=QA3452
```

and see that the product page comes up in the browser. As shown previously in Figure 4.10, however, we do have a slight problem, in that the image is missing. This is because the relative reference that we were using before (meaning that the image and the style sheet were in the same directory) won't work from the Web page. So, instead, we'll need to make a slight fix to the style sheet, as in Listing 4.33.

Listing 4.33—`topinclude.xsl`: Fixing the Image

```
...
    <center>
    <img src="file:///c:/files/chasewebfurniture.gif"
➥alt="ChaseWeb Furniture Logo"/>
    </center>
...
```

After we save the style sheet, we can recheck the page without having to recompile the servlet. As before, now that we have everything set up, if we want to make any changes, we just have to change the XML or XSL files.

Getting It Together

At this point, we have all the makings of a basic Web site, but we need to put them together.

The first thing we need to do is update the style sheet so that instead of the Next and Previous links pointing to the HTML files, they're pointing to the servlet, as in Listing 4.34.

Listing 4.34—`productpage.xsl`: Pointing to the Servlet

```
...
    <xsl:if test="inventory[@location='showroom']">
        <p>Also available in our stores!</p>
    </xsl:if>
    <hr />
    <xsl:element name="a">
      <xsl:attribute name="href">/book/servlet/TransformServlet?product_id=
➥<xsl:value-of select="$vPrev_id"/></xsl:attribute>
      Previous Product
```

Listing 4.34—continued

```
37:    </xsl:element>
38:    <br />
39:    <xsl:element name="a">
40:      <xsl:attribute name="href">/book/servlet/TransformServlet?product_id=
➥<xsl:value-of select="$vNext_id"/></xsl:attribute>
41:        Next Product
42:   </xsl:element>
43:
44:</xsl:if>
45:
46:</xsl:template>
...
80:     <br />
81:     </xsl:for-each>
82:     <br />
83:     <xsl:if test="inventory[@location='showroom']">
84:         <p>Also available in our stores!</p>
85:      </xsl:if>
86:      <hr />
87:      <xsl:element name="a">
88:        <xsl:attribute name="href">/book/servlet/TransformServlet?product_id=
➥<xsl:value-of select="$vPrev_id"/></xsl:attribute>
89:        Previous Product
90:    </xsl:element>
91:    <br />
92:    <xsl:element name="a">
93:        <xsl:attribute name="href">/book/servlet/TransformServlet?product_id=
➥<xsl:value-of select="$vNext_id"/></xsl:attribute>
94:        Next Product
95:   </xsl:element>
96:</xsl:if>
97:</xsl:template>
...
```

All we've done on lines 35, 40, 88, and 93 is change the link so it's pointing to the servlet instead of the XHTML file. This way, all of our pages are updated when `products.xml` is updated, or when changes are made to the style sheet.

Next Steps

In this chapter, we installed and used the Xalan XSL processor, both from the command line and from within a Java application. We also learned the basics of writing Java applications and wrote one that stepped through a list of elements from our products file. We installed the Tomcat Web server and learned the basics of using servlets. Finally, we built a servlet that takes in a `product_id` and returns the proper product page via a servlet.

All of this leaves us with the beginning pieces of a Web site. In Chapter 5, we'll knit these pages together a little more neatly and then create an order page using XHTML forms. Whereas, in this chapter we used the DOM API to step through the XML document, in the next chapter we'll examine a new API, JDOM. JDOM is designed to be easier to learn and to use than other XML APIs, and we'll use a servlet to create and edit XML itself, which allows us to create an order system for our Web site.

Chapter 5

In this chapter

- *What Is JDOM?*
- *Installing JDOM*
- *Developing an Algorithm*
- *Creating the Shopping Cart—AddToOrder.java*
- *Manipulating an XSL Style Sheet*
- *Next Steps*

Taking Orders: Manipulating Data with JDOM

In the last chapter, we talked briefly about Application Programming Interfaces (APIs). Simply put, an *API* is a set of commands that a program understands. If you try speaking English to someone who understands only French, you're not going to get anywhere. Similarly, if you try to use commands that are outside a program's API, you're not going to accomplish anything.

In the XML world, a number of APIs are vying for attention, all of which are in various stages of acceptance and best suited for different purposes.

The first XML-related API was the Document Object Model (DOM). DOM, which actually preceded XML, started as a way for client-side JavaScript and VBScript programmers to identify specific parts of a Web page. Now informally called called DOM Level 0, this API broke HTML documents down into the now familiar tree structure. For instance, the `<body>` tag was considered the child of the `<html>` tag.

DOM Level 0 was never an actual W3C Recommendation, but rather represents the functionality that existed in Netscape Navigator 3 and Microsoft Internet Explorer 3 browser. Since being taken up by the W3C, DOM has been expanded and enhanced. DOM Level 1 was the first official version of DOM, and DOM Levels 2 and 3 contain much, much more functionality.

DOM is handy because it provides that tree structure, which enables users to move around within the data and change it, but it also requires that the entire structure be read into memory before any of it can be worked with. Not only is this inefficient if you're just reading the data, but it can also lead to huge memory requirements.

DOM Level 2 is a W3C Recommendation (with the exception of one module, which at the time of this writing had moved back to Working Draft status) and Level 3 is at the working draft stage, which means it has been through the W3C process; however, that's not the only way a de facto standard can come into being.

David Megginson and members of the XML-DEV mailing list, in fact, created the Simple API for XML (SAX). SAX takes an entirely different view of XML. Instead of the object-based perspective of DOM, SAX comes at a document from an event-based perspective.

What this means is that SAX sees an XML document as a series of events, such as "start an element" and "end an element." For instance, say we had the following document:

```
<html>
<head><title>Page Title</title></head>
<body>This is the body content.</body>
</html>
```

DOM's conceptual view of this document would look like Figure 5.1, with an `html` root element that contains `head` and `body` children, and `title` as the child of `head`.

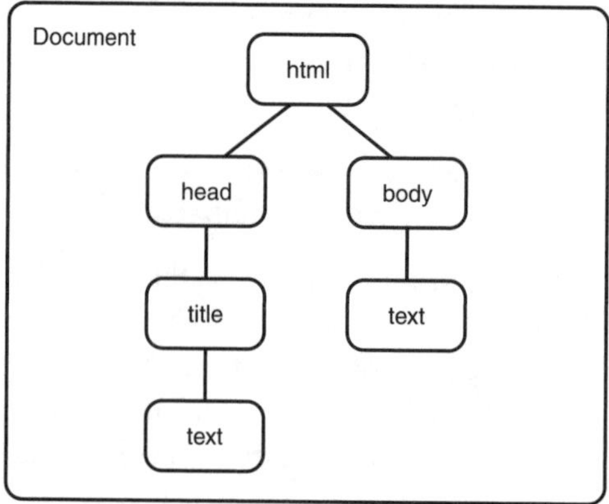

Figure 5.1
The Document Object Model's view of the document is shown here.

SAX, on the other hand, would look at this as a series of events, specifically:

```
Start document
Characters: newline
Start element: html
Start element: head
Start element: title
Characters: Page title
End element: title
End element: head
Characters: newline
Start element: body
Characters: This is the body content.
End element: body
```

```
Characters: newline
End element: html
End document
```

Now, if all we wanted was the text in the body element, this might be more efficient than building the DOM tree and then traversing it to get to that element. What's more, we don't need to store the entire document in memory. If we wanted to make changes, however, this would not help us very much. SAX is a one-pass system. After it's gone, it's gone, unless we read the document all over again.

That's not to say that we can't build DOM trees out of SAX events, and vice versa. This is quite common, and in fact, it's customary to use a SAX parser to build a DOM tree because of its inherent speed.

So, both of these APIs have their uses, but they also have one drawback: They're not as easy to use as they could be.

Part of the problem stems from the nature of the beast: They were both designed to be language independent, so they could be implemented in C++, Perl, VBScript, and so on, as well as Java. Therefore, they're not necessarily tuned to the way Java programmers tend to think. They're also capable of doing just about anything you'd like to do with them, but this functionality comes at the cost of ease of use.

It's like buying a camera. That top-of-the-line professional rig that lets you take pictures in the dark while simultaneously adding your own special effects is great, but if all you want to do is take snapshots at the beach, the point-and-shoot all-in-one from the drugstore is all you really need—and if you're just starting out in photography, you'll probably get better pictures out of it.

That's the theory behind one of the many other contenders out there, JDOM.

What Is JDOM?

JDOM is an API that is currently being designed by a group of programmers led by Brett McLaughlin and Jason Hunter. As it says at `jdom.org`, "JDOM should solve 80% (or more) of Java/XML problems with 20% (or less) of the effort." What this means is that JDOM is a simplified way of dealing with XML. It doesn't do everything, but what it does do is a lot easier than with DOM or SAX. (It also does it in such a way that we can move our data to and from the DOM and SAX APIs without much of a problem.)

JDOM is also quickly gaining acceptance in the XML community. In fact, JDOM will reportedly be included in the Xerces Refactoring Initiative, which will be rewriting the Xerces parser from the ground up. (At the time of this writing, Xerces 2 was still in alpha.)

For all these reasons, we're going to start out with JDOM. This will allow us to get used to manipulating XML through Java without getting bogged down in some of the less intuitive ways of the other APIs. Then, after our feet are good and wet, we'll take another look at DOM and SAX as we move beyond that 80% into the areas JDOM isn't designed for.

Installing JDOM

Originally, version 1.0 of JDOM was supposed to be ready sometime during the summer of 2000, but at the time of this writing (January, 2001), final preparations for release are still being made. Although it is unlikely, some of the commands or method names we use in our listings here might have changed slightly. If changes do occur, they will be posted on the book's Web site at `www.quecorp.com`. I'll also keep a current list at `http://www.nicholaschase.com`.

The method of installation depends on which version of JDOM is available and which version you choose to install. In general, three options are available:

- **Binaries**—In this case, you can download a compressed file with all the compiled code for JDOM, and all you need to do is uncompress it into the appropriate directory. At the time of this writing, no binaries were available at `www.jdom.org`.
- **Source Drop**—A source drop could be a milestone (such as Beta 5) or a nightly source drop. These have varying degrees of reliability, but they are typically all the source in one compressed file. Fortunately, building, or compiling, the source is very straightforward; we'll be discussing that in a moment.
- **CVS**—For the truly hard-core (and adventurous!) programmer, there is the CVS tree. CVS is an open source version control system called the Concurrent Versions System. CVS provides a way for multiple people to work on the same project without stepping on each other. The most up-to-date version of JDOM will always be found in the CVS tree, and it's always advisable to check these files before reporting or fixing bugs. Because it requires yet another software download and installation, however, we'll be sticking with option two for this book.

Visit `http://www.jdom.org` and follow the Downloads link. If binaries are available, simply download the compressed file and unzip it into the `jdom` directory; then, skip ahead to "Setting the `CLASSPATH`," later in this chapter.

If no binary version is available (which is normally the case), or if you simply want a later version, source drops are located at

```
http://www.jdom.org/dist/source/
```

For instance, Beta 5 can be found at

```
http://www.jdom.org/dist/source/jdom-b5.zip (or jdom-b5.tar.gz)
```

Daily snapshots of the code can be found at `http://cvs.jdom.org/source/jdom-complete.zip` (or `jdom-complete.tgz`). Finally, links to all downloads can be found at `http://www.jdom.org/downloads/source.html`.

The examples in this book use the JDOM Beta 5 source drop.

Installing JDOM

Installing JDOM from source code involves the following steps:

1. After you've downloaded the source files, uncompress them into the root directory. This process should put all the files into a directory called `jdom-b5`. For convenience, we'll rename that directory `jdom`.
2. After the source files are extracted, you must build them to create the binaries. Fortunately, this process is very simple because a build script is included with the download. Open a command prompt and change to the `jdom` directory.
3. Set `JAVA_HOME`. The build script needs to find the Java executable, so this environment variable must be set to the main Java directory. This variable can be set the same way you set the `CLASSPATH`, as in

   ```
   set JAVA_HOME=c:\jdk1.3
   ```

   (If you've been following along with previous chapters, this should already be in your `AUTOEXEC.bat`.)
4. Build JDOM. From the `jdom` directory, type

   ```
   build
   ```

   This executes `build.bat` or `build.sh`, whichever is appropriate.
5. Build the samples. Type the following:

   ```
   build samples
   ```

   This compiles the samples you'll use to test the installation.
6. Build the documentation. Type

   ```
   build javadoc
   ```

   This is especially important because of the possibility of changes to the JDOM API. `Javadoc` automatically generates up-to-date documentation based on the actual code.

At the time of this writing, the build script for Windows packaged with the daily source drop gave an error. If you experience difficulties running the build script, open `build.bat` in Notepad—not WordPad—and replace the black boxes with returns. Save the file and it will work.

Setting the CLASSPATH

For Tomcat to be capable of finding our JDOM classes, we need to ensure that `JDOM.jar` is on the `CLASSPATH`. Using the instructions in Chapter 3, "Defining the Data Structure: Document Type Definitions, XML Schema, and Parsers," add the following to your `CLASSPATH`:

```
set CLASSPATH=%CLASSPATH%c:\jdom\build\jdom.jar;
```

If you added it to the `AUTOEXEC.bat`, don't forget to run it so the new settings will take effect.

Running the Samples

Just to make sure our installation is all right, let's run one of the samples we built. In the command prompt window, type the following:

```
cd \jdom\build\classes
java WarReader web.xml
```

This executes a JDOM program to read and analyze a Tomcat configuration file. The output should look like this:

```
This WAR has 2 registered servlets:
        snoop for SnoopServlet (it has 0 init params)
        file for ViewFile (it has 1 init params)
This WAR contains 3 roles:
        manager
        director
        president
This WAR is distributed
```

Developing an Algorithm

Until now, the coding we've done has been fairly straightforward, and we've just plowed ahead without too much forward planning. Now, however, we're getting into territory where a little planning can save us a lot of time later.

An *algorithm* is simply a way of doing things. For instance, if I were to plan out my workday morning, it might look like this:

```
Turn off alarm clock
Get out of bed
Shower
Shave
Get dressed
Eat breakfast
Kiss wife goodbye
Get into car
Start car
Drive to work
```

The handy thing about doing this is that I can review it before I've committed a whole lot of time to it. This way, if anything doesn't make sense, it can be fixed before I commit to it. For instance, if I left out "get dressed," I'd certainly like to realize it before I "drive to work."

Granted, I'm not likely to forget something like that (no matter how tired I am), but it's just as important (and perhaps even more so!) to do the planning beforehand when we're programming. It's easy to spend a lot of time coding something that simply isn't necessary because there's a better way of doing things.

The Overall Algorithm

In this chapter, we know we want to do one thing: build an order system. In actuality, however, this encompasses several steps:

```
Add items to order
Review order for completeness/correctness
Check and adjust inventory
Finalize order (gather user and payment information)
```


Even at this very high level, we can make decisions about what we want the algorithm to look like. For instance, do we want to check the inventory levels after we've finalized the order and while we're adjusting it, or would it make more sense to check it before the order is finalized, or even before we allow the customer to place an order in the first place?

At first glance, it appears that this is the most logical way to do it, but what if we adjust the inventory and the user decides not to purchase it after all? Could we even check it afterward?

We could, as long as a problem wouldn't occur in the event that the user bought an item that just went out of stock. That's a business decision. If we made the decision that, if that happened, we would just backorder the item, that wouldn't be a problem. Also, either way, we should probably let the user know her order status. So, the actual algorithm might be

```
Add items to order
Review order for completeness/correctness
Finalize order (gather user and payment information)
Check and adjust inventory
Display order status
```

That's certainly easier to fix BEFORE we program it!

Creating the Shopping Cart—`AddToOrder.java`

We can take each of these items individually, because that's how they'll be experienced by the user. In this chapter, we'll add an item to the user's shopping cart. To do that, we need him or her to click a link that includes the `product_id`, so we know which product to add. (We'll take care of the rest of the order process in Chapter 6, "Adjusting Inventory: Using Namespaces and More About DOM.") Let's add an "Add To Order" link to the product page, as in Listing 5.1.

Listing 5.1—`productpage.xsl`: The Add To Order Link

```
...
<br />
<xsl:if test="inventory[@location='showroom']">
  <p>Also available in our stores!</p>
</xsl:if>
<hr />
<xsl:element name="a">
   <xsl:attribute name="href">AddToOrder?addProduct_id=<xsl:value-of
➥select="product_id"/></xsl:attribute>Add To Order
</xsl:element>
<hr />
<xsl:element name="a">
     <xsl:attribute name="href">
          <xsl:value-of select="$vPrev_id"/>.html
     </xsl:attribute>
     Previous Product
 </xsl:element>
...
```

All we've done is add a new section of the page with a link to our new servlet, `AddToOrder`, as in Figure 5.2. Note that the link is all on one line to prevent spaces from being added.

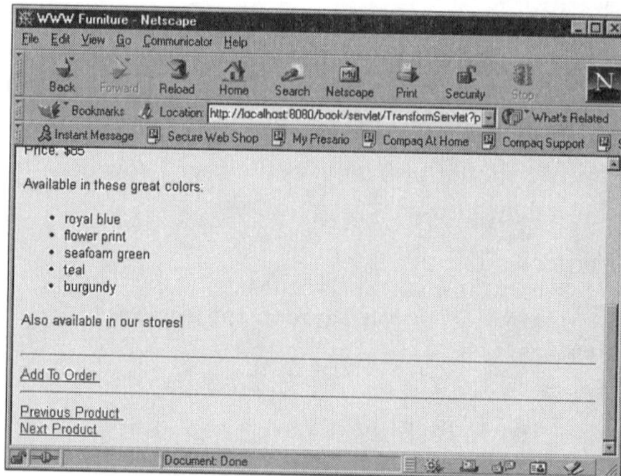

Figure 5.2
The Add To Order link is shown here.

Now, let's look at the algorithm for our first task, adding an item to an order. Our first stab at it might look like this:

```
Get existing orders from orders.xml
Does this order exist?
```

```
If this order does not exist:
    Create this order
Add this item to this order
Save orders.xml
```

That seems pretty reasonable. Let's think about what might go wrong. For one thing, what if `orders.xml` doesn't exist yet? We'll need to create it. Let's add that to our algorithm:

```
Does orders.xml exist?
If orders.xml doesn't exist:
    Create orders.xml
    Save orders.xml
Get existing orders from orders.xml
Does this order exist?
If this order does not exist:
    Create this order
Add this item to this order
Save orders.xml
```


Looking further, we need to deal with the fact that the user might try to add the same product more than once. Again, how to handle this is a business decision. Do we want to reject the second addition, ignore it, or increment the quantity ordered? Let's increment the quantity. This makes our algorithm look like this:

```
Does orders.xml exist?
If orders.xml doesn't exist:
    Create orders.xml
    Save orders.xml
Get existing orders from orders.xml
Does this order exist?
If this order does not exist:
    Create this order
If this item is already part of this order:
    Increment the quantity
Else
    Add this item to this order
Save orders.xml
```

That should do it for our algorithm. Now, we just have to decide on the structure of the `orders.xml` file itself. We know that each order will have some sort of identifier, and that it will store the items the user wants to buy. We also know that we'll eventually want to add payment and status information to it. Initially, the order itself might look like Listing 5.2.

Listing 5.2—`orders.xml`: The Basic Structure of the Orders File

```
<?xml version="1.0" encoding="UTF-8">
<orders>
<order>
        <order_id>1234</order_id>
        <order_status>in progress</order_status>
        <items>
```

Listing 5.2—continued

```
            <item>
                <product_id>abc</product_id>
                <quantity>1</quantity>
            </item>
            <item>
                <product_id>def</product_id>
                <color>blue</color>
                <quantity>2</quantity>
            </item>
        </items>
    </order>
    <order>
        <order_id>1234</order_id>
        <order_status>in progress</order_status>
        <items>
            <item>
                <product_id>abc</product_id>
                <color>red</color>
                <quantity>1</quantity>
            </item>
        </items>
    </order>
</orders>
```

Here's where we see another benefit of building the algorithm first. Although Listing 5.2 is a perfectly acceptable way of putting together the order information, it is certainly not the only way. The question is: Is it the best way?

Looking at the algorithm, we see that before we add an item to the order, we will be checking to see whether it already exists. Looking at our sample `orders.xml` file, we see that the `product_id` is four levels down on the tree. That's going to make it awkward to retrieve by walking the tree, so to speak. Let's try and move it up somewhat. We'll do the same for the `order_id`. The second version is in Listing 5.3.

Listing 5.3—`orders.xml`: Streamlining the File

```
<?xml version="1.0" encoding="UTF-8">
<orders>
    <order order_id="1234">
        <order_status>open</order_status>
        <item product_id="abc">
            <quantity>1</quantity>
        </item>
        <item product_id="def" color="blue">
            <quantity>2</quantity>
        </item>
    </order>
    <order order_id="1235">
        <order_status>open</order_status>
        <item product_id="abc" color="red">
```

Listing 5.3—continued

```
            <quantity>1</quantity>
        </item>
    </order>
</orders>
```

In this case, we've eliminated the entire `items` level of the tree, and made `item` the child of `order`. We've also made the `product_id` and `order_id` attributes of their various elements, instead of making them child elements themselves. That should simplify our lives somewhat. Imagine if we'd tried to do that after we'd already started coding!

What about payment information? Theoretically, we could put it into this file, but from a security standpoint, that's probably not the best way to handle it. If we put it into a separate file, we have the option to put in additional security measures so that the payment information file is better protected. After all, the `orders.xml` file is going to be accessed pretty frequently (we hope!) and not very securely. So, let's leave the payment information out until we need it. When we create the payment information, we'll link it to the order via the `order_id`.

Of course, all this planning doesn't mean that everything is carved in stone. Inevitably, we'll discover things we hadn't considered and we'll need to change them. But by taking into account as much as possible beforehand, we'll certainly streamline the process.

In addition, another advantage to writing out algorithms exists: They can be used as part of the documentation nobody ever seems to have time to write, as we can see as we begin to build `AddToOrder.java` in Listing 5.4.

Listing 5.4—`AddToOrder.java`: The Skeleton

```
import java.io.*;
import javax.servlet.*;
import javax.servlet.http.*;

public class AddToOrder extends HttpServlet {

public void doGet(HttpServletRequest request,
                        HttpServletResponse response)
                throws IOException, ServletException
{
  // Retrieve item to be added
  String thisProduct_id =
              request.getParameter("addProduct_id");

  response.setContentType("text/html");
  PrintWriter out = response.getWriter();
  out.print("Adding item "+thisProduct_id+" ...");

  // Does orders.xml exist?
  // If orders.xml doesn't exist:
  //      Create orders.xml
```

Listing 5.4—continued

```
//     Save orders.xml

// Get existing orders from orders.xml
// Does this order exist?
// If this order does not exist:
//     Create this order

// If this item is already part of this order:
//     Increment the quantity
// Else
//     Add this item to this order

// Save orders.xml

}
}
```

We've started with our basic servlet. All we're actually doing is retrieving the `product_id` we want to add to the order, printing it to the page, and then leaving comments about what we've still got to add.

Before we move on, let's make sure we've got the structure right. Save `AddToOrder.java` in the classes directory (`tomcat\webapps\book\web-inf\classes\`) of the Web server and compile it. If no errors occur, we can click the Add To Order link we created in Listing 5.1. This should give us a message that we're adding the correct `product_id`, as in Figure 5.3.

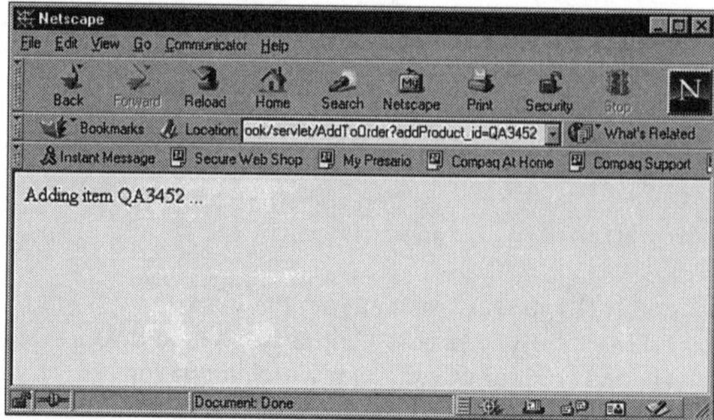

Figure 5.3

Here we check our basic servlet.

If all is well, we should get a message telling us which product we're adding. Now that we know the structure of the servlet is sound, let's move on and start filling in some of these sections (see Listing 5.5).

Listing 5.5—`AddToOrder.java`: Checking for the Existence of a File

```
...

 response.setContentType("text/html");
```

Listing 5.5—continued

```
15: PrintWriter out = response.getWriter();
16: out.print("Adding item "+thisProduct_id+" ...");
17:
18: // Does orders.xml exist?
19: File orderFile = new File ("/files/orders.xml");
20:
21: // If orders.xml doesn't exist:
22: if (!orderFile.exists()) {
23:    out.print ("Orders File Doesn't Exist.");
24:    //     Create orders.xml
25:    //     Save orders.xml
26: } else {
27:    out.print ("Orders File Exists.");
28:    // Do Nothing
29: }
30:
31: // Get existing orders from orders.xml
...
```


Taking our algorithm from the top, we need to find out whether the `orders.xml` file exists. We can do that by creating a `File` object on line 19. Creating a `File` object doesn't actually create a file, just an `Object` that has the means to manipulate one. We feed it the location of the file in question, and Java tries to read it.

The `File` object has a number of useful methods we can call. Some of them provide us with information, such as `getPath()`, `lastModified()`, and `length()`. On the other hand, some of them enable us to actually do things, such as `renameTo()` or `delete()`. Sometimes a `File` object doesn't actually refer to a file at all, but a directory. We can test that using `isFile()` or `isDirectory()`, and if it is a directory, we can use `mkdir()` to create it, or `list()` to get the names of the directories and files it contains.

In our case, we just want to know whether the file exists yet, so on line 22, we'll get the value returned by the `exists()` method. Using the `!` symbol before it is like saying "not." So, on line 22, we want this statement to be true if the file does not exist, in which case we'll output some text to let us know. On lines 26 through 29, we have the servlet output some text if the file does exist, even though we won't be doing anything. After we're sure this section is working properly, we can take out this debugging statement.

Compile the servlet and reload the page to ensure that it's working.

Now, we're ready to create the file. First, we must create the content; then we must create the file itself, as in Listing 5.6.

Listing 5.6—`AddToOrder.java`: Adding `orders.xml`

```
import java.io.*;
import javax.servlet.*;
```

Listing 5.6—continued

```
import javax.servlet.http.*;
import org.jdom.Element;
import org.jdom.Document;
import org.jdom.output.XMLOutputter;

public class AddToOrder extends HttpServlet {

  public void doGet(HttpServletRequest request,
                    HttpServletResponse response)
             throws IOException, ServletException
{
  // Retrieve item to be added
...

  // Does orders.xml exist?
  File orderFile = new File ("/files/orders.xml");

  // If orders.xml doesn't exist:
  if (!orderFile.exists()) {
     out.print ("Creating Orders...<br />");
     //     Create orders.xml
     Element root = new Element("orders");
     root.addContent(" ");
     Document document = new Document(root);

     //     Save orders.xml
     try {

          FileOutputStream outStream =
                   new FileOutputStream(orderFile);

          XMLOutputter outToFile = new XMLOutputter();
          outToFile.output(document, outStream);

          outStream.flush();
          outStream.close();

     } catch (IOException e) {

          out.print("Can't save orders.xml: "
                         + e.getMessage()+"<br />");

     }

  } else {
     out.print ("Orders File Exists.");
     // Do Nothing
  }

  // Get existing orders from orders.xml
...
```

We're doing only two things in Listing 5.6: creating a basic structure of information and saving it to a file. First, because we'll be using classes from JDOM, on lines 3, 3a, and 4 we'll go ahead and import them—as we did in the last chapter with the Xalan methods.

We actually create the content on lines 27 through 29. On line 27, we create an `Element`. We call the element itself `root`, because it will be the root element of our document, but the name of the tag will be `orders`, as we decided earlier.

Because we don't have any actual content to add to it yet, we just give it a single space as content on line 28. (Otherwise, there will be no content at all in the document, so it will be blank.)

At this point, we just have a freeform `Element` floating around in the information universe. Therefore, on line 29 we create a new `Document` and assign `root` to be its root element.

Now that we've created a JDOM tree, we need to save it to a file. JDOM provides several output methods. They are `DOMOutputter`, to create a traditional DOM tree in memory; `SAXOutputter`, to create a stream of SAX events to be read by another object; and `XMLOutputter`, to output an actual XML stream. This is what we'll use to create `orders.xml`.

`XMLOutputter` takes two arguments. One is the `Document`, which we created on line 29, and the other is an `OutputStream`.

`OutputStream` is an abstract class. An *abstract* class is one that has all its methods defined, but not all of them are *implemented*. This means that some of the methods actually have no instructions in them. An abstract class generally exists as a template for other classes to extend. We can't instantiate, or create, an instance of them. Instead, we create a `FileOutputStream`—which extends `OutputStream`—and connect it to our `File`. We do that on lines 34 and 35. This way, when the `XMLOutputter` streams the data, it winds up in `orders.xml`.

Implementation—Actual code that does some work. A method or section of our algorithm can be defined, but if we haven't written the code yet, it's not implemented.

Abstract class—An abstract class is a Java class that has some methods with no implementations. These methods are called *abstract methods*. We can extend an abstract class, but we would need to provide implementations (code) for all its abstract methods.

Interface—An interface is a class that has all abstract methods. Interfaces are used to get around Java's restrictions, allowing classes to extend only one other class. A class can implement (as opposed to extending) as many interfaces as the programmer wants. Similar to an abstract class, if we implement an interface, we need to provide implementations (code) for all its methods.

On line 37, we create the `XMLOutputter` object, and on line 38, we use it to output `document` to our file.

After we've done that, on line 40, we `flush()` the stream to make sure all our data gets to the file before we `close()` it on line 41. If we don't `close()` the file, we won't be able to move or delete it, because it will still be in use by the Web server, even though the servlet has completed.

Now, all that activity has the potential to run into input/output (IO) problems, so we enclose it in a `try-catch` block. If any problems occur—such as a nonexistent directory or other file-access issues—we get not only our message, but also information as to what the actual problem is, which we output on lines 45 and 46.

After we compile the servlet, we can call it by refreshing the page in the browser. The first time we run it, if no `orders.xml` file exists in the `files` directory, we see the message we're creating it. If we try to run it again, we should see the message that the orders file already exists.

Let's take a look at the file. As we have it now, the file should look like this:

```
<?xml version="1.0" encoding="UTF-8"?><orders> </orders>
```

Now that's just fine for a machine to read it, but after we start inserting order information, this is going to look downright ugly to the human eye. Let's tell `XMLOutputter` that we want to include newlines between elements, and that we want to indent items in the tree, as in Listing 5.7.

Listing 5.7—`AddToOrder.java`: Formatting `orders.xml` for Human Readability

```
...
34:         FileOutputStream outStream =
35:                   new FileOutputStream(orderFile);
36:
37:         XMLOutputter outToFile = new XMLOutputter("  ", true);
38:         outToFile.output(document, outStream);
39:
40:         outStream.flush();
41:         outStream.close();
...
```

On line 37, we're still creating an `XMLOutputter`. Checking the Javadoc shows that there is a second version of `XMLOutputter`, which accepts two parameters: `indent` and `newlines`. `indent` is a string that is used to format the XML nicely, so if we set `indent` as two spaces, each level of the tree will be indented by two spaces. `newlines` is a Boolean value, so if it's `true`, each element will be on its own line, and if `false`, it won't.

EXCURSION

Whitespace and Mixed Content

The previous code makes the orders file a bit more readable for humans, but it also brings up some other issues. Without indenting, newlines, and so on, the `orders.xml` file (with an order in it) starts out looking something like this:

```
<?xml version="1.0" encoding="UTF-8"?><orders><order
order_id="To1010mC24980190282174342At"><order_status>open</order_status><item
product_id="RC2342"><quantity>1</quantity></item></order></orders>
```

With indenting and newlines, the first time `AddToOrder` runs, it looks something like this:

```
<?xml version="1.0" encoding="UTF-8"?>
<orders>
    <order order_id="To1010mC24980190282174342At">
        <order_status>open</order_status>
            <item product_id="RC2342">
                <quantity>1</quantity>
            </item>
        </order>
</orders>
```

That seems a lot nicer, but this gets a little funny if you are repeatedly reading the file and writing it back out again, as we are. The second time `AddToOrder` is run, it looks like this:

```
<?xml version="1.0" encoding="UTF-8"?>
<orders>

        <order order_id="To1010mC24980190282174342At">

                <order_status>open</order_status>

                <item product_id="RC2342">

                        <quantity>1</quantity>

                </item>

        </order>

</orders>
```

The reason is that the first time we ran it, we had nothing but the actual elements we had added to the document. When we read it back in, however, we were getting not just the elements, but also text nodes containing the newlines. When we output the document again, those text nodes got their own lines. It is as if the document looked like this:

```
<?xml version="1.0" encoding="UTF-8"?>
<orders>
    (whitespace text node)
        <order order_id="To1010mC24980190282174342At">
            (whitespacetext node)
                <order_status>open</order_status>
                (whitespacetext node)
                <item product_id="RC2342">
```

```
                        (whitespacetext node)
                            <quantity>2</quantity>
                        (whitespacetext node)
                    </item>
                (whitespacetext node)
            </order>
        (whitespacetext node)
    </orders>
```

The moral of the story? If your files aren't going to be read by humans, it's probably better to leave out the line breaks and indents.

This combination of elements and text nodes is known as *mixed content* and is often overlooked by programmers who think they don't have any text nodes because it's just white-space.

Now that we have the `orders.xml` file, it's time to start working with it. The next tasks in our algorithm are to read in existing orders and see whether ours is among them. Of course, because we haven't actually added any orders yet, we KNOW this one won't be there, so let's start by adding it.

The first decision we must make is how we will distinguish this order from all the others in the system. There are plenty of values we could use for an `order_id`, such as the current date and time or the user's name and a sequential number, but whatever we use, it must fulfill two criteria:

- It must be absolutely unique from session to session.
- It must be consistent throughout a single session.

We could generate a random number and then use *cookies* to access it from page to page, but an easier way exists. The designers of the servlet API created the `sessionID`, which we'll use to track our orders.

Cookie—A cookie is a small text file written to the user's hard drive for retrieval later by the site that put it there. These are often used to store information that enables a site to identify a specific individual who has previously visited, so a personalized experience can be provided or just to track user behavior.

In Listing 5.8, we load the tree, and then add our new order to it.

Listing 5.8—`AddToOrder.java`: Adding an Order to `orders.xml`

```
import java.io.*;
import javax.servlet.*;
import javax.servlet.http.*;
import org.jdom.Element;
import org.jdom.Document;
import org.jdom.output.XMLOutputter;
import org.jdom.input.SAXBuilder;

public class AddToOrder extends HttpServlet {
```

Listing 5.8—continued

```

  public void doGet(HttpServletRequest request,
                       HttpServletResponse response)
              throws IOException, ServletException
{
 // Retrieve item to be added
 String thisProduct_id =
              request.getParameter("addProduct_id");
...
 } else {
    out.print ("Orders File Exists.");
    // Do Nothing
 }

 // Get existing orders from orders.xml
 try {

   SAXBuilder builder = new SAXBuilder();
   Document document = builder.build(orderFile);

 } catch (JDOMException e) {

   out.print("There was a problem building the document: "
             +e.getMessage()+"<br />");

 }

 // Does this order exist?
 // If this order does not exist:
 //     Create this order

 HttpSession session = request.getSession(true);
 String session_id = session.getId();

 Element order = new Element("order");
 order.addAttribute("order_id", session_id);

 Element root = document.getRootElement();
 root.addContent(order);

 // If this item is already part of this order:
 //     Increment the quantity
 // Else
 //     Add this item to this order

 // Save orders.xml

}
}
```

On line 60, we want to build the `document` in memory from the file, but we need a builder to do it. That builder is created on line 59. Notice, though, that even though we're creating a DOM-like structure, we're using a `SAXBuilder` to do it. This is because, unlike the `DOMOutputter` and `SAXOutputter`, the "DOM" and "SAX" in `DOMBuilder` and `SAXBuilder` refer to the method used to build the document, and not to what comes out. Because SAX is faster, we'll use that to build our `document`.

At this point, we have the `document`, and we're ready to add our order to it. First, on line 73, we tell the servlet to go ahead and create a new session if one doesn't already exist, and then return an `HttpSession` object. We can use the `session` object to get the `session_id` on line 74.

After we have that, on lines 76 and 77 we can create an `order` element, and then add the `order_id` attribute to it. Finally, on lines 79 and 80, we get the root element from the `document` and add the new `order` to it.

Now, all this is perfectly good code, except for one problem. If we try to compile it, we get this error:

```
C:\tomcat\webapps\book\WEB-INF\classes>javac AddToOrder.java
AddToOrder.java:80: cannot resolve symbol
symbol  : variable document
location: class AddToOrder
  Element root = document.getRootElement();
                 ^
1 error
```

Why won't Java recognize the `Document` object? After all, we did create it properly on line 60.

Well, yes, we did, but the trouble is where we did it. Situated as it is in that `try-catch` block, there's no guarantee that line 60 is ever going to be executed. If it isn't, we're referring to a nondeclared variable.

We have a couple of options. The first is to enclose the rest of the servlet in the `try-catch` block, but that's not going to be terribly readable. Instead, let's look at breaking some of this servlet out into separate methods.

We're already using a method, actually—the `doGet()` method. Fortunately, there's nothing that says we can't call one method from inside another. Let's start by breaking out the creation of the `Document` in Listing 5.9.

Listing 5.9—`AddToOrder.java`: Breaking Out `getDocument()`

```
...
4: import org.jdom.output.XMLOutputter;
5: import org.jdom.input.SAXBuilder;
6:
7: public class AddToOrder extends HttpServlet {
8:
```

Listing 5.9—continued

```
9:  public Document getDocument() {
10:  try {
11:
12:    SAXBuilder builder = new SAXBuilder();
13:    Document document = builder.build(orderFile);
14:    return document;
15:
16:  } catch (JDOMException e) {
17:
18:    out.print("There was a problem building the document: "
19:               +e.getMessage()+"<br />");
20:
21:  }
22:} // End getDocument()
23:
24: public void doGet(HttpServletRequest request,
25:                       HttpServletResponse response)
26:             throws IOException, ServletException
27:{
...
36:  // Does orders.xml exist?
37:  File orderFile = new File ("/files/orders.xml");
38:
...
70:
71:  // Get existing orders from orders.xml
72:  Document document = getDocument();
73:
74:  // Does this order exist?
75:  // If this order does not exist:
76:  //     Create this order
77:
78:  HttpSession session = request.getSession(true);
79:  String session_id = session.getId();
...
```


On lines 9–22, we create a new method called `getDocument()`. Let's start by analyzing line 9:

```
9:  public Document getDocument() {
```

This line tells us several things. First of all, this is a public method, so we can call it from anywhere, including another class. We don't have to make this method public, but let's leave it that way for now. Next, we see that this method returns a `Document` object. This is important, because that's what we want to get out of it. Next is the actual name of the method, `getDocument`, and the fact that it doesn't take any arguments.

Line 72, where we had previously been building the `Document` object, is where we make a call to the method. Theoretically, we should be able to call this method and get back the `Document`.

However, if we try to compile it like this, we get a new set of errors:

```
AddToOrder.java:14: cannot resolve symbol
symbol  : variable orderFile
location: class AddToOrder
    Document document = builder.build(orderFile);
                                      ^
AddToOrder.java:19: cannot resolve symbol
symbol  : variable out
location: class AddToOrder
    out.print("There was a problem building the document: "
    ^
2 errors
```

Oh, no! This is even worse than before!

Well, actually, it's not. What we're running up against here is an issue of scope. Scope is the area of a program where a particular variable or object exists. Both our `orderFile` object and `out` object exist only in the `doGet()` method. Therefore, when we try to call them from `getDocument()`, the compiler doesn't know what to do with them.

As usual, we have a couple of options.

We could change the scope of `orderFile`, making it a member variable. A *member variable* is an object or variable that exists in the class but not in any particular method, so it's available to all methods. We can't do that with `out`, however, because we can't create `out` without `response`, which has to be part of the `doGet()` method.

Another drawback of going the member variable route is that we can use this method to build from only one file. Instead, let's pass as arguments the `File` object to build from and the `OutputStream` to send errors to, as in Listing 5.10.

Listing 5.10—`AddToOrder.java`: Passing Objects As Arguments

```
...
public class AddToOrder extends HttpServlet {
 public Document getDocument(File sourceFile,
                             PrintWriter errorsOut) {
  try {
    SAXBuilder builder = new SAXBuilder();
    Document document = builder.build(sourceFile);
    return document;
  } catch (JDOMException e) {
    errorsOut.print("There was a problem building the document: "
              +e.getMessage()+"<br />"+
              "Returning blank document.");
    return new Document(new Element("blank"));
```

Listing 5.10—continued

```
23:
24:  }
25:}
26:
27: public void doGet(HttpServletRequest request,
28:                     HttpServletResponse response)
29:           throws IOException, ServletException
30:{
31:  // Retrieve item to be added
32:  String thisProduct_id =
33:           request.getParameter("addProduct_id");
34:
35:  response.setContentType("text/html");
36:  PrintWriter out = response.getWriter();
37:  out.print("Adding item "+thisProduct_id+" ...<br />");
38:
39:  // Does orders.xml exist?
40:  File orderFile = new File ("/files/orders.xml");
41:
...
73:
74:  // Get existing orders from orders.xml
75:  Document document = getDocument(orderFile, out);
76:
77:  // Does this order exist?
78:  // If this order does not exist:
...
```


On lines 9 and 10, we've added our two arguments by listing the types of objects they are (such as `File` or `PrintWriter`) and the names we'll call them by in the method (such as `sourceFile` or `errorsOut`). Strictly speaking, we could have called them `orderFile` and `out`—because they're in a different scope, no conflict exists. To avoid confusion, however, let's call them something different.

We did make a couple of changes to the method itself. In addition to the obvious name change on lines 14 and 19, we had to make sure that whether or not the `try-catch` block succeeds, this method returns a `Document` object. This is non-negotiable, because we've already declared that that's what the method will return on line 9.

Let's take a look at the shorthand on line 22:

```
return new Document(new Element("blank"));
```

It's really nothing new; it's just that we haven't put things together like this before. This is equivalent to saying

```
Element blank = new Element("blank");
Document returnDoc = new Document(blank);
return returnDoc;
```

We've just put all the steps together on one line. This is a common practice, as we've seen in earlier examples.

Finally, on line 75, we call the new method with the arguments. As was mentioned before, we now have a method we can use to build a document from an arbitrary file.

As long as we're breaking functionality out into methods, you might have noticed that there are actually two places in this servlet where we need to save the XML document to `orders.xml`: once when the file is first created, and again after we've added more information to it. Let's break that out into a method as well, and then we can just call it whenever we need to, as in Listing 5.11.

Listing 5.11—`AddToOrder.java`: Adding `saveDocument` to `AddToOrder.java`

```
0:  import.java.io.*;
1: import javax.servlet.*;
2: import javax.servlet.http.*;
3: import org.jdom.Element;
3a:import org.jdom.Document;
4: import org.jdom.output.XMLOutputter;
5: import org.jdom.input.SAXBuilder;
6:
7:  public class AddToOrder extends HttpServlet {
8:
9:    //*******BEGIN getDocument() *********
10:   public Document getDocument(File sourceFile,
11:                                  PrintWriter errorsOut) {
...
26:   }
27:    //*******END getDocument() *********
28:
29:    //*******BEGIN saveDocument() *********
30:    public void saveDocument (Document saveDoc,
31:                                 File saveFile,
32:                                 PrintWriter errorsOut) {
33:       try {
34:            FileOutputStream outStream =
35:                       new FileOutputStream(saveFile);
36:
37:            XMLOutputter outToFile =
38:                       new XMLOutputter("    ", true);
39:            outToFile.output(saveDoc, outStream);
40:
41:            outStream.flush();
42:            outStream.close();
43:       } catch (IOException e) {
44:            errorsOut.print("Can't save orders.xml: "
45:                            + e.getMessage()+"<br />");
46:       }
47:   }
48:    //*******END saveDocument() *********
49:
50:    //*******BEGIN doGet() *********
```

Listing 5.11—continued

```
public void doGet(HttpServletRequest request,
                   HttpServletResponse response)
           throws IOException, ServletException
{
// Retrieve item to be added
String thisProduct_id =
           request.getParameter("addProduct_id");

response.setContentType("text/html");
PrintWriter out = response.getWriter();
out.print("Adding item "+thisProduct_id+" ...<br />");

// Does orders.xml exist?
File orderFile = new File ("/files/orders.xml");

// If orders.xml doesn't exist:
if (!orderFile.exists()) {
   out.print ("Creating Orders...<br />");
   //     Create orders.xml
   Element root = new Element("orders");
   root.addContent(" ");
   Document document = new Document(root);

   //     Save orders.xml
   saveDocument (document, orderFile, out);

} else {
   out.print ("Orders File Exists.");
   // Do Nothing
}

// Get existing orders from orders.xml
Document document = getDocument(orderFile, out);

// Does this order exist?
// If this order does not exist:
//     Create this order

HttpSession session = request.getSession(true);
String session_id = session.getId();

Element order = new Element("order");
order.addAttribute("order_id", session_id);

Element root = document.getRootElement();
root.addContent(order);

// If this item is already part of this order:
//     Increment the quantity
// Else
//     Add this item to this order

```

Listing 5.11—continued

```
103:  // Save orders.xml
104:  saveDocument (document, orderFile, out);
105:
106:}
107: //*******END doGet() *********
108:
109:}
```

In this case, we just moved the code that was within `doGet()` to lines 29 through 48. (Lines 29 and 48, as well as those similar to them, are just comments to help us sort out what part of the growing servlet is what!) We made the same minor changes that we made to `getDocument()`, and voilà! We have a method we can call from lines 75 and 104. This is certainly easier and more maintainable than copying and pasting the code!

One note about `saveDocument()`: Although `getDocument()` was intended to return something, specifically the `Document` object, `saveDocument()` is just intended to do something and will not return anything. For that reason, we place the keyword `void` on line 30 to indicate that it returns nothing.

If we compile this code and run it now, we find that `orders.xml` looks something like this:

```
<?xml version="1.0" encoding="UTF-8"?>
<orders>
     <order order_id="To1011mC41271515992654706At" />
</orders>
```

We've successfully added an order to `orders.xml`.

Now, the next time we run this servlet, we know that our order will already exist, so we'd better take care of checking for it now. In Listing 5.12, we look at all the orders, checking for one that matches the current `session_id`. If we don't find one, we'll create one.

Listing 5.12—`AddToOrder.java`: Checking for an Existing Order

```
0: import.java.io.*;
1: import javax.servlet.*;
2: import javax.servlet.http.*;
3: import org.jdom.Element;
3a:import org.jdom.Document;
4: import org.jdom.output.XMLOutputter;
5: import org.jdom.input.SAXBuilder;
6: import java.util.List;
7:
8: public class AddToOrder extends HttpServlet {
9:
...
51:   //*******BEGIN doGet() *********
52:   public void doGet(HttpServletRequest request,
```

Listing 5.12—continued

```
53:                          HttpServletResponse response)
54:                throws IOException, ServletException
55:    {
...
82:
83:    // Get existing orders from orders.xml
84:    Document document = getDocument(orderFile, out);
85:
86:    // Does this order exist?
87:    HttpSession session = request.getSession(true);
88:    String session_id = session.getId();
89:
90:    Element root = document.getRootElement();
91:    List orders = root.getChildren();
92:    int num_orders = orders.size();
93:    boolean orderExists = false;
94:    for (int i=0; i < num_orders; i++) {
95:       Element iOrder = (Element)orders.get(i);
96:       String iOrder_id = iOrder.getAttributeValue("order_id");
97:       if (iOrder_id.equals(session_id)) {
98:          orderExists = true;
99:          break;
100:      }
101:   }
102:   // If this order does not exist:
103:   //      Create this order
104:   if (!orderExists) {
105:      Element order = new Element("order");
106:      order.addAttribute("order_id", session_id);
107:     Element status = new Element("order_status");
108:     status.setText("in progress");
109:     order.addContent(status);
110:      root.addContent(order);
111:   }
112:
113:   // If this item is already part of this order:
114:   //      Increment the quantity
115:   // Else
116:   //      Add this item to this order
117:
118:   // Save orders.xml
119:   saveDocument (document, orderFile, out);
120:
121: }
122:  //*******END doGet() *********
123:
124: }
```

First, on line 6, we use some new classes we haven't seen before, such as `java.util.List`, so we'll go ahead and import it.

Lines 87 through 90 aren't really new, but we've moved them around a bit because we need them well before we actually create the order.

Line 91 is the first new material. `root` is the `orders` element, and we know that all our `order` elements are children of `orders`. By using the `getChildren()` method, we get a `List` of all the children of `order`. This `List` is more than just a notation of what the children are. It's a set of references to the actual objects. If we change a value for an element in the `List`, it's changed for the actual element. If we remove an element from the list, it's gone from the tree itself.

Remember, we're talking about the in-memory tree here. No changes will affect the file until we save the in-memory document back out to the file.

Using the `List`, we can see how many `orders` exist, as we do on line 92. After we know that, we can use a `for` loop as we did in Chapter 4, "Getting Serious: XSL Processors and Server-Side Processing," looping through all our child elements on lines 94 through 101.

On line 93, we set a flag. The `orderExists` flag tells us whether or not the loop has found our current session among the orders already in the file. It starts out as `false`. As long as nothing happens to change that, it tells us the order doesn't exist.

One thing that could happen to change that is the `for` loop finding our `session_id` in the existing `orders`. For each element in the list, we check the `order_id` attribute against the `session_id`.

On line 95, we pull out the `i`th `Object` on the list to look at it. Notice that I said `Object`, and not `Element`. `List`s can be collections of any type of `Object`, so the `get()` method is very general. The trouble is that we don't want just any `Object`—we want an `Element`. That's what we mean by the following:

```
(Element)orders.get(i)
```

Putting it into words, it means "Get me the `Object` at position `i`, but show it to me as an `Element`." This is called *casting*.

Casting—Casting in Java is the act of taking an object or variable of one type and turning it into an object or variable of another type. This is usually done between classes and subclasses. There is, of course, a limit to this sort of thing. For instance, we can't turn the word "hello" into a number.

After we have the element, on line 96 we can get the value of the `order_id` attribute. From there, it's just a matter of comparing them, using `equals()`, as before. If they're equal, we set our `orderExists` flag on line 98 and then tell the servlet we don't need to complete the loop on line 99. After all, `orderExists` isn't going to get any more `true`!

One way or the other, we exit the loop. Either we break out of it because we've established that the order already exists, or we loop through all the values and determine that it doesn't. On line 104, we take that information and decide whether or not to create the order anew. If we do create the order anew, we'll set its status on lines 107 through 109.

Next, we compile the servlet and test it by reloading the page in our browser. We should see no effect in the `orders.xml` file because we're still in the same order we created a little while ago. If we close all browser windows and then open a new one, however, we have a new session. If we go to any of the product pages and choose Add To Order, we should see a new order in the `orders.xml` file.

We also might be assigned a new session if it has been a very long time since we reloaded the page. This is because sessions time out—they are discarded if they haven't been used in a certain period of time. In our case, it will just result in a new order number. In a live site, however, this could conceivably be a problem, and many sites overcome it by using cookies instead of server sessions.

5

That takes care of adding orders. Now we need to do the same thing with the specific item, as shown in Listing 5.13.

Listing 5.13—`AddToOrder.java`: Adding a Specific Item

```
0:  import.java.io.*;
1:  import javax.servlet.*;
2:  import javax.servlet.http.*;
3:  import org.jdom.Element;
3a: import org.jdom.Document;
4:  import org.jdom.output.XMLOutputter;
5:  import org.jdom.input.SAXBuilder;
6:  import java.util.List;
7:
8:
9:  public class AddToOrder extends HttpServlet {
10:
...
52:   //******BEGIN addItem() *********
53:   public void addItem(Element orderElement, String product_id) {
54:
55:       Element newItem = new Element("item");
56:       newItem.addAttribute("product_id", product_id);
57:       Element quantity = new Element("quantity");
58:       quantity.addContent("1");
59:       newItem.addContent(quantity);
60:       orderElement.addContent(newItem);
61:
```

Listing 5.13—continued

```
} //*******End  addItem() *********

//*******BEGIN doGet() *********
public void doGet(HttpServletRequest request,
                        HttpServletResponse response)
             throws IOException, ServletException
{
// Retrieve item to be added
String thisProduct_id =
             request.getParameter("addProduct_id");

response.setContentType("text/html");
PrintWriter out = response.getWriter();
out.print("Adding item "+thisProduct_id+" ...<BR />");

// Does orders.xml exist?
File orderFile = new File ("/files/orders.xml");

...
// Get existing orders from orders.xml
Document document = getDocument(orderFile, out);

// Does this order exist?
 HttpSession session = request.getSession(true);
 String session_id = session.getId();

 Element root = document.getRootElement();
 List orders = root.getChildren();
 int num_orders = orders.size();
 boolean orderExists = false;
 int orderIndex = 0;
 for (int i=0; i < num_orders; i++) {
    Element iOrder = (Element)orders.get(i);
    String iOrder_id = iOrder.getAttributeValue("order_id");
    if (iOrder_id.equals(session_id)) {
       orderExists = true;
       orderIndex = i;
       break;
    }
 }
// If this order does not exist:
//     Create this order
if (!orderExists) {
   Element order = new Element("order");
   order.addAttribute("order_id", session_id);
   Element status = new Element("order_status");
   status.setText("open");
   order.addContent(status);

   // If the order didn't exist, the item certainly
   // wasn't part of it.
   addItem(order, thisProduct_id);
```

Listing 5.13—continued

```
129:
130:      root.addContent(order);
131:   } else {
132:
133:     // Is this item part of the order?
134:     Element thisOrder = (Element)orders.get(orderIndex);
135:     boolean itemExists = false;
136:     int itemIndex = 0;
137:     List items = thisOrder.getChildren("item");
138:     int num_items = items.size();
139:     for (int i=0; i < num_items; i++) {
140:        Element iItem = (Element)items.get(i);
141:        String iProduct_id =
142:                    iItem.getAttribute("product_id").getValue();
143:        if (iProduct_id.equals(thisProduct_id)) {
144:           itemExists = true;
145:           itemIndex = i;
146:           break;
147:        }
148:     }
149:
150:     // If this item is already part of this order:
151:     if (itemExists) {
152:       //     Increment the quantity
153:       Element thisItem = (Element)items.get(itemIndex);
154:       String currentQuantity =
155:                             thisItem.getChildText("quantity");
156:       int newQuantity = Integer.parseInt(currentQuantity) + 1;
157:       String strQuantity = new String().valueOf(newQuantity);
158:       thisItem.getChild("quantity").setText(strQuantity);
159:     } else {
160:     // Else
161:     //     Add this item to this order
162:       addItem(thisOrder, thisProduct_id);
163:     }
164:   }
165:   // Save orders.xml
166:   saveDocument (document, orderFile, out);
167:
168:}
169: //*******END doGet() *********
170:
171:}
```

In this case, there are two situations in which we might have to add an item to the order. The first is when we have a newly created `order`. In that case, we're not even going to look for existing `items`, because we know none exist, so we can add our `item` when we create the order. We do that on line 128. We'll also have to add the `item` if it's not a part of the current order, as we do on line 162.

Whenever we're doing the same thing more than once, we should make a method we can call rather than duplicate code, so we've done that on lines 52 through 62.

First, on line 53, we start by declaring that the method is public and that it doesn't return anything. We also provide, as arguments, the actual `order` element to add this `item` to and the `product_id` we want to add. This way, we can call this method in a variety of circumstances and it will still be useful.

On line 55, we create the new `item` element, which gets its `product_id` attribute on line 56. Because we're just adding this item now, we know the quantity is 1, so we create the `quantity` element and set its content on lines 57 and 58. Finally, we add the `quantity` element to the new `item` and add the `item` to the supplied `order`.

EXCURSION

Modularization

How do you decide whether it's worth making a method? My personal rule of thumb is that if I'm tempted to copy and paste more than two lines of code, it's worth my time to create a method.

I'll also create a method for actions that are based on business rules. This enables my code to be insulated from the decision changes of those who will actually use the software.

The name of the game here is modularization. We want to be able to make changes to one section of a program without affecting everything else.

For instance, we've created a method called `addItem()` that enables us to add an item to the supplied order element. This could be useful under a variety of circumstances. Perhaps we want to add a special gift to all orders placed on certain dates. Or perhaps we want to ensure that an item is never added to an order without checking for export restrictions first.

By modularizing this code, it's easier for a single programmer to manage these changes. It's also easier to work in a multiprogrammer environment. One person can be working on code to add an item to an order, and another can just use it without worrying about the mechanics of how that's accomplished. This also has applications in ensuring the security of various sections of code.

If the `order` did exist, we would want to find out whether we need to add the `item` or just update the `quantity`. However, before we can do that, we need to know which order we're looking at.

When we were just adding the `order`, that was easy. If it's an existing order, however, that's a little tougher. We can get a specific `order` out of the `orders List`, but we have to know which one. So, while we're looping through the list on lines 108 through 115, we can make a note of the index when we find it. We create that variable on line 107, and then save the value on line 113.

This way, on line 134, we can pull out the specific `order` element we need and assign it to `thisOrder`. The process of searching for our `item` is virtually identical to that of searching for our `order`, except that now we're looking at the children of `thisOrder` instead of the `orders` element. In addition, we're comparing the value we want to an attribute (on lines 141 and 142) instead of to the content of an element.

If the `item` is part of the `order`, we want to update the `quantity` on lines 152 through 158. To do that, however, we have to deal with some different data types.

First, on line 153, we get the appropriate `item` element. Now, for a human, it would make perfect sense to simply retrieve the `quantity`, add 1 to it, and save it back out as a `quantity`. Unfortunately, it's not so simple for a computer.

First off, we indeed retrieve the `quantity`. Using `getChildText()` on lines 154 and 155, we get the value, but we get it as a `String`. To be able to use it in addition, we need to have it as the primitive `int`.

The first thing that comes to mind is that we can cast the `String` to an `int`, but unfortunately, we can cast only to other object classes—not primitive data types. To change our `String` into the primitive `int`, on line 156 we use the `Integer` class. Similar to the `String` object, `Integer` is a class that has a number of methods that enable us to perform various operations. Fortunately, one of them is `parseInt()`, which enables us to change a `String` into an `int`. On that same line, we perform the addition, although we could easily have spread it out over two lines.

But now we have the opposite problem. We want to take our `int` value, `newQuantity`, and save it as the value of our element—but to do that, we need it as a `String`! So, on line 157, we create a new `String` object and assign it a value of `newQuantity`. We can then assign that value to the `quantity` element on line 158.

Finally, on line 162, if the `item` doesn't exist in this `order`, we add it using our new method.

At this point, we have a working shopping cart, but it's not very elegant. For one thing, the output is downright ugly and doesn't make a lot of sense. For another, if a user wants to buy more than one of something, he shouldn't have to just add one repeatedly.

We'll take care of the formatting of the results page in a minute, but first let's take care of the `quantity` issue.

Right now, we just have a link on the product page. Ideally, though, we would have a text box that enables the user to decide how many of this product he or she wants, as in Figure 5.4.

This is called an *XHTML form*. Forms are used to collect information from users directly. This information can be as simple as a term to search for in a search engine or as complicated as a mortgage application. We're going to create a fairly simple form on the product page.

Figure 5.4

We can allow the user to decide the `quantity` *of* `items` *added to his or her order.*

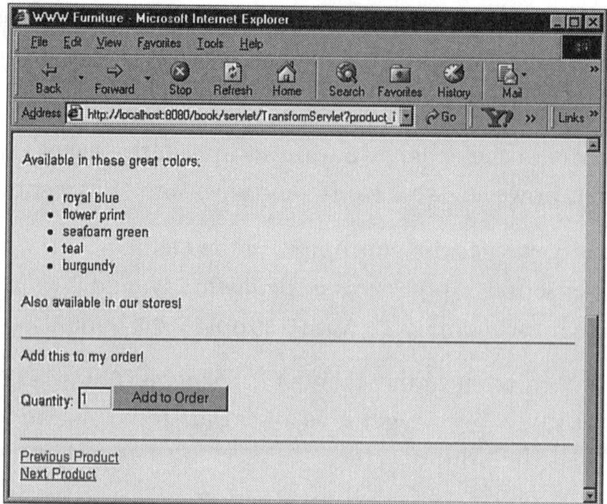

The XHTML for the form is pretty straightforward. The relevant fragment of it looks similar to Listing 5.14.

Listing 5.14—The Basic Quantity Form

```
0: Add this to my order!<br />
1: <form action="AddToOrder" method="get">
2:     <input value="QA3452" type="hidden" name="addProduct_id">
3:     Quantity:  <input type="text" name="addQuantity" value="1" size="3">
4:     <input value="Add to Order" type="submit">
5: </form>
```

The form—which we create on lines 1 and 5—is intended to send information to be processed by a particular location, or action, which we've specified as an attribute of the form. A form also needs to have its method specified. Forms generally can be submitted via either a `get` method or a `post` method.

The `get` method is great for debugging because all values show up on the URL line of the resulting page, but that's about all it's good for. `get` methods can carry a limited amount of information, and they expose all our internal information to anyone looking over the user's shoulder. These methods can also encourage users to play with the values being submitted, with unpredictable, even dangerous, results.

The `post` method, on the other hand, is a bit more secure because the information is being sent as a part of the request the user can't easily get to. That's not to say it's foolproof, of course. The user can always write her own `post`ed form, after all. But there's no limit to the amount of information that can be submitted, and `post`ed forms are generally a better option to use whenever possible.

Having said that, using `post` with a servlet requires us to do a little extra work, so we'll just use `get` for now and come back to it.

One of the pieces of information that must be sent to `AddToOrder` is, of course, the `product_id`. You might notice, however, that nowhere in Figure 5.4 is that information displayed. Instead, on line 2, we send it as a `hidden` value, keeping the name of `addProduct_id` that the servlet is already expecting. The name attribute is what determines the name of the value the action receives. For instance, our hidden form element of

```
<input value="QA3452" type="hidden" name="addProduct_id">
```

is the same as adding

```
addProduct_id=QA3452
```

to our earlier link.

A number of `input` types are available, such as `hidden`, which is used in the previous code. `text` and `submit`, which we'll see in a moment, are two more types you can use, and `checkboxes` and `select` lists are two that we'll see later.

On line 3, we create the `text` box that will hold the `quantity` value. For the convenience of our users, we set the initial `value` to `1`. The user can always change it if he or she wants more than one. We also set the name as `addQuantity`, to make it consistent with our first parameter, and limit the width of the box to three characters. If a user wants to type more than that in the box, he or she can, but the text will scroll to the left to allow it.

Finally, on line 4, we add a submit button so the user can send the form.

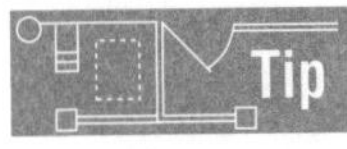

If we were to add a name attribute to the `submit` button, its value, Add To Order, would be submitted with the rest of the form. This can come in handy when we have multiple buttons on a form and we want the user to be able to perform various functions with them.

Adding this form to the style sheet isn't too bad, although we need to dynamically generate the hidden field, which can make it a little cumbersome. The changes to `productpage.xsl` are shown in Listing 5.15.

Listing 5.15—`productpage.xsl`: Adding the Form

```
...
<xsl:if test="inventory[@location='showroom']">
  <p>Also available in our stores!</p>
</xsl:if>
<he/>
Add this to my order!<br />
<form method="get" action="AddToOrder">
   <xsl:element name="input">
```

Listing 5.15—continued

```
45:        <xsl:attribute name="value"><xsl:value-of
select="product_id"/></xsl:attribute>
46:        <xsl:attribute name="type">hidden</xsl:attribute>
47:        <xsl:attribute name="name">addProduct_id</xsl:attribute>
48:      </xsl:element>
49:      Quantity:  <input type="text" name="addQuantity" value="1" size="3" />
50:      <input type="submit" value="Add to Order" />
51:   </form>
52:   <hr />
...
```

Most of the form will remain constant from product to product, so we can simply embed it into the style sheet, as we do on lines 42, 43, and 49 through 51. The hidden element, however, needs to be dynamic, and we generate it on lines 44 through 48. Remember, whitespace is preserved in these attributes, so if we want our `product_id` attribute to be accurate, it must be all on one line, with no spaces.

After we have the form, adding support for it to `AddToOrder` is easy, as we see in Listing 5.16.

Listing 5.16—`AddToOrder.java`: Adding Quantities from the Product Page

```
...
   //******BEGIN addItem() *********
   public void addItem(Element orderElement,
                       String product_id,
                       String quant) {

      Element newItem = new Element("item");
      newItem.addAttribute("product_id", product_id);
      Element quantity = new Element("quantity");
      quantity.addContent(quant);
      newItem.addContent(quantity);
      orderElement.addContent(newItem);

   } //*******End  addItem() *********

   //*******BEGIN doGet() *********
   public void doGet(HttpServletRequest request,
                       HttpServletResponse response)
             throws IOException, ServletException
   {
   // Retrieve item to be added
   String thisProduct_id =
             request.getParameter("addProduct_id");
   String thisQuantity =
             request.getParameter("addQuantity");

   response.setContentType("text/html");
   PrintWriter out = response.getWriter();
   out.print("Adding "+thisQuantity+" of item "
```

Listing 5.16—continued

```
80:                     +thisProduct_id+" ...<br />");
81:
...
130:
131:      // If the order didn't exist, the item certainly
132:      // wasn't part of it.
133:      addItem(order, thisProduct_id, thisQuantity);
134:
135:      root.addContent(order);
136:    } else {
137:
138:      // Is this item part of the order?
...
155:      // If this item is already part of this order:
156:      if (itemExists) {
157:        //     Increment the quantity
158:        Element thisItem = (Element)items.get(itemIndex);
159:        String currentQuantity =
160:                      thisItem.getChildText("quantity");
161:        int newQuantity = Integer.parseInt(currentQuantity)
162:                             + Integer.parseInt(thisQuantity);
163:        String strQuantity = new String().valueOf(newQuantity);
164:        thisItem.getChild("quantity").setText(strQuantity);
165:      } else {
166:      // Else
167:      //     Add this item to this order
168:        addItem(thisOrder, thisProduct_id, thisQuantity);
169:      }
170:    }
171:    // Save orders.xml
172:    saveDocument (document, orderFile, out);
173:
174: }
175:  //*******END doGet() *********
176:
177: }
```


We haven't really had to do much to the servlet to record the new `quantity`. We collect it on lines 74 and 75, and from there it's just a matter of making sure the value carries through when we add or update an element.

On line 55, we add the quantity as an argument for `addItem()`, and then have the method add the `quantity` itself instead of just `1` on line 60. We then add `thisQuantity` to the method call on lines 133 and 168.

Finally, on line 162, we have the servlet add the `int` value of `thisQuantity` to the current `quantity`, instead of `1`, as we were doing before.

Experiment with adding different quantities of different products and check the `orders.xml` file to make sure it's working properly.

Adding post to the Servlet

Now that we have our form working, let's revisit the form method. As was mentioned earlier, using `get` is not the preferable way to do things. If we try to change the form to use `post`, however, we see an error similar to Figure 5.5.

Figure 5.5

Using `post` causes an error unless we're prepared for it.

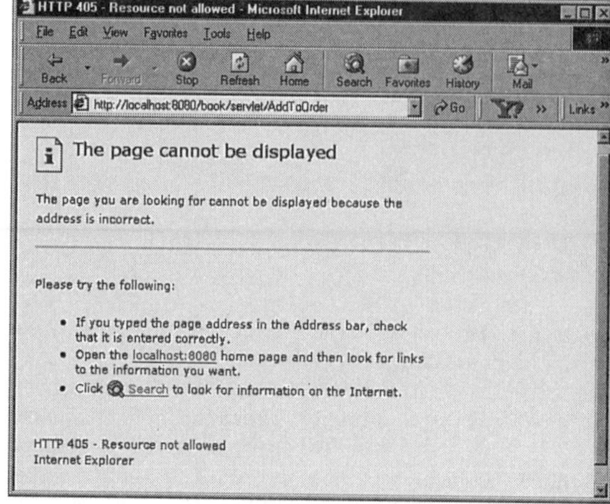

So, why does the form work perfectly using `get`, but not at all using `post`? Is this a configuration issue?

No, it's not. If we look at the servlet, what method are we executing? It's `doGet()`. Because no `doPost()` exists, the servlet engine doesn't know what to do with a `post` request.

The simplest way to solve this problem is to change `doGet()` to `doPost()`. Aside from the fact that this is a very easy change, it also has the advantage of the fact that users couldn't fake a `get` request by building a URL manually. On the other hand, this prevents us from calling `AddToOrder` using a plain URL, as we did when we were starting out.

The most flexible solution, therefore, is to have a `doPost()` method that does exactly the same thing as the `doGet()` method. Of course, it would be horrible if we had to copy and paste, because we'd have to maintain both copies. Instead, we can create a `doPost()` that simply calls `doGet()` and passes along the information, as we see in Listing 5.17.

Listing 5.17—`AddToOrder.java`: Adding `doPost()`

```
...
saveDocument (document, orderFile, out);

```

Listing 5.17—continued

```
174:}
175: //*******END doGet() *********
176:
177: //*******BEGIN doPost() *********
178: public void doPost(HttpServletRequest request,
179:                          HttpServletResponse response)
180:                throws IOException, ServletException
181:  {
182:         doGet(request, response);
183:  }
184: //*******END doPost() *********
185:}
```

All we need to do is create the method, which we do on lines 178 through 180, and call `doGet()`, which we do on 182. Let's look at what happens when we do that.

The servlet engine calls `doPost()`, feeding it the `HttpServletRequest` (our form submission) and the `HttpServletResponse` (the stream of XHTML back to our browser). `doPost()` then takes those objects and feeds them to `doGet()`. This way, when `doGet()` is doing its thing, it's acting on the same `request` and `response` that `doPost()` would have worked on, so we see the correct results no matter how the form is submitted.

To actually send the results via `post`, we need to update the style sheet, as in Listing 5.18.

Listing 5.18—`productpage.xsl`: Sending Results via `post`

```
...
Add this to my order!<br />
<form method="post" action="AddToOrder">
   <xsl:element name="input">
...
```

Manipulating an XSL Style Sheet

Finally, we need to output a message to our users to let them know the product was successfully added to their orders. When we do this, however, we want to ensure that we use the same format as the rest of the site.

We've gone to great lengths to modularize our style sheets. We've even pulled our main interface elements out into a separate style sheet, `topinclude.xsl`. What we want to do now is use `topinclude.xsl`, but change it slightly so the result looks similar to Figure 5.6. `topinclude.xsl`, you might remember, looks similar to Listing 5.19.

Figure 5.6

The final results page is displayed.

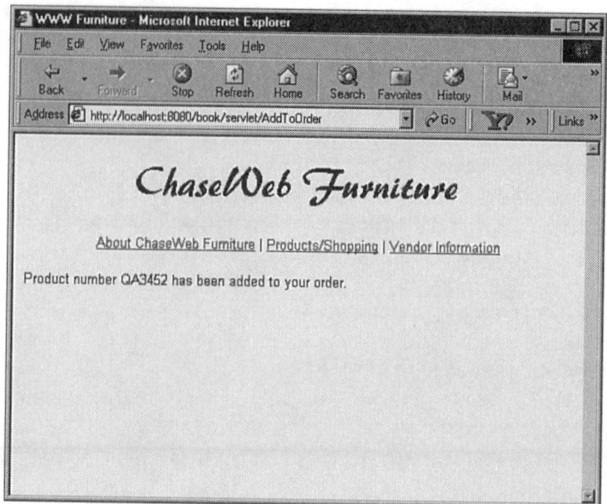

Listing 5.19—topinclude.xsl

```
<?xml version="1.0"?>
<xsl:stylesheet version="1.0"
   xmlns:xsl="http://www.w3.org/1999/XSL/Transform">

<xsl:template match="/" priority="10">
<html>
<head>
    <title>ChaseWeb Furniture</title>
</head>
<body style="background-color: F6F6F6;font-family: Arial">

    <center>
    <img src="file:///c:/files/chasewebfurniture.gif"
➥alt="ChaseWeb Furniture"/>
    </center>

    <p align="center">
        <a href="index.html">About ChaseWeb Furniture</a>
        |
        <a href="products.html">Products/Shopping</a>
        |
        <a href="vendors.html">Vendor Information</a>
    </p>

    <xsl:apply-templates />

</body>
</html>
</xsl:template>

<xsl:template match="special">
```

Listing 5.19—continued

```
30:</xsl:template>
31:
32:</xsl:stylesheet>
```

Normally, our content would appear at line 23, and that's exactly where we want to add it.

The first thing we need is the resulting text. Because we want this to be maintainable, we pull it into its own XML file, `resultText.xml`. This enables nontechnical staff to change the content without help from us. `resultText.xml` is shown in Listing 5.20.

Listing 5.20—`resultText.xml`

```
<resultText>
<!-- DO NOT REMOVE productIdHere tag! -->
    Product number <productIdHere></productIdHere> has
    been added to your order.
</resultText>
```


Because we want this to be a well-formed XML document, we need a root element, which in this case is `resultText`. We also have a child element, `productIdHere`, that we can use to insert the `product_id` that has been added to the `order`.

`resultText` has what's known as *mixed content*—it has some text, an element or two, some comments, and so on.

So, the goal, in this case, is to put the `product_id` in `productIdHere`, and then embed the entire `resultText` element inside `topinclude.xsl`. This way, if the design crew changes `topinclude.xsl`, the order results page is still correct.

Because `resultText.xml` is going to be included in another XML document, we must leave out the XML declaration; the including document will have one of its own.

Let's first look at `resultText`, which is shown in Listing 5.21.

Listing 5.21—`AddToOrder.java`: Preparing the Result Text

```
...
public class AddToOrder extends HttpServlet {

  //*******BEGIN returnResult()*********
  public void returnResult( String product_id,
                            PrintWriter out )
```

Listing 5.21—continued

```
14:  {
15:     File resultFile = new File("/files/resultText.xml");
16:     Document resultDoc = getDocument(resultFile, out);
17:     Element resultText = resultDoc.getRootElement();
18:     Element productIdHere = resultText.getChild("productIdHere");
19:     productIdHere.addContent(product_id);
20:  }
21:  //*******END returnResult()*********
22:
23:  //*******BEGIN getDocument() *********
24:  public Document getDocument(File sourceFile,
...
```

We didn't have to break `returnResult()` out into its method, but it can't hurt. In fact, on line 16, we see, once again, our `getDocument()` method. This time we call it with a completely different file—`resultText.xml`—to get a `Document` we can manipulate. The first thing we do is get the `root` element.

Next, we must insert our `product_id`. We left a blank element for it, so all we have to do is locate that element on line 18 and add `product_id` as its content on line 19.

What we just did was pretty simple and straightforward. We located an element, and we changed the content. We're going to do the same thing with `topinclude.xsl`, but we must go about it in a slightly less straightforward way. What we want is to use the `List`, so we can replace `apply-templates` with our `resultText`, as in Listing 5.22.

Listing 5.22—`AddToOrder.java`: Replacing `apply-templates`

```
...
//*******BEGIN returnResult()*********
public void returnResult( String product_id,
                          PrintWriter out )
{
   File resultFile = new File("/files/resultText.xml");
   Document resultDoc = getDocument(resultFile, out);
   Element resultText = resultDoc.getRootElement();
   Element productIdHere = resultText.getChild("productIdHere");
   productIdHere.addContent(product_id);

   File includeFile = new File("/files/topinclude.xsl");
   Document includeDoc = getDocument(includeFile, out);
   Element styleSheetRoot = includeDoc.getRootElement();

   List templates = styleSheetRoot.getChildren();
   for (int i=0; i < templates.size(); i++) {
       Element thisTemplate = (Element)templates.get(i);
       String thisMatch = thisTemplate.getAttributeValue("match");
       if (thisMatch.equals("/")) {
           Element htmlElement = thisTemplate.getChild("html");
           Element bodyElement = htmlElement.getChild("body");
```

Listing 5.22—continued

```
32:             Namespace xslns = Namespace.getNamespace("xsl",
33:                           "http://www.w3.org/1999/XSL/Transform");
34:             List allContent =
35:                  bodyElement.getChildren("apply-templates", xslns);
36:             allContent.set(0, resultText);
37:             break;
38:         }
39:     }
40: }
41: //*******END returnResult()*********
42:
43: //*******BEGIN getDocument() *********
44: public Document getDocument(File sourceFile,
...
```


Before we can do anything with the `Document`, of course, we need to build it in memory. We do this on lines 21 and 22, and we get the `root` element on line 23.

From there, we should loop through the children until we find the node that corresponds to our main template, `match="/"`. Here's where we see that a style sheet is just another XML document. `match="/"` is just an attribute of the `xsl:template` element, so we can get the attribute on line 28 and see whether it's what we're looking for on line 29.

If it is, we need to work our way down the tree to the `apply-templates` element. Looking at the structure, we know that it's a child of the `body` element, which is a child of the `html` element, which is a child of the `template` element. Because this is the way a final page should be constructed, it's reasonable to require any design changes to `topinclude.xsl` to maintain this structure, so we can use it to get to this element.

On lines 30 and 31, we work our way down into the `body` element, where we can get a list of children. Now, we do have the option of getting a `List` of all the children and looping through it, but the fact is, we know exactly what it is that we want: the `apply-templates` element.

The difficulty here lies in the fact that, although we will talk more extensively about them in the next chapter, we are dealing with two different namespaces here. `body` has no namespace, whereas `apply-templates` is in the namespace aliased by `xsl`. If we just did

```
BodyElement.getChildren("apply-templates");
```

it wouldn't be found.

Instead, we need to specify the namespace in which we're looking. To do that, we must create a `Namespace` object.

So far, all the objects we've seen either have been created using `new` (as in `new Element()`), or have been created out of other objects (as in `includeDoc.getRootElement()`). Here, however, we will do something a little different.

When a class is created, it has constructors. A *constructor* is code that is called when we try to get a new object or instantiate it. Most methods of an object can be called only after the object is instantiated, but exceptions do exist. If we define a method as `static`, we can call it without actually having an object of that class. For instance, the `getNamespace()` method is declared as

```
public static Namespace getNamespace(String prefix, String uri)
```

Therefore, we can call it from anywhere (`public`) without instantiating the object (`static`), and it returns a `Namespace` object. That's what we do on lines 32 and 33.

After we have it, we can use it to specify the `Namespace` of the child we're looking for on lines 34 and 35. This gives us a `List` of all the children of `body`, in the `xsl` namespace, with the name `apply-templates`. If we weren't certain that only one existed, we might want to loop through this list. But because we do, we can access it directly.

On line 36, we replace the `apply-templates` element with our `resultText` element. Finally, on line 37, we've completed our mission, so we can break out of the loop.

At this point, we have a style sheet in memory that displays what we want, but we need to get it back out to the page. The Xalan processor we used earlier can do it, but we have some type issues. It's not that the processor can't take an in-memory object; it can. But it can't take a JDOM object. Before we can use it, we have to turn our JDOM tree into a DOM tree, as in Listing 5.23.

Listing 5.23—`AddToOrder.java`: Converting to a DOM Tree and Processing

```
...
3: import org.jdom.Element;
4: import org.jdom.Document;
5: import org.jdom.JDOMException;
6: import org.jdom.Namespace;
7: import org.jdom.output.XMLOutputter;
8: import org.jdom.input.SAXBuilder;
9: import java.util.List;
10:import org.jdom.output.DOMOutputter;
11:import javax.xml.transform.TransformerFactory;
12:import javax.xml.transform.Transformer;
13:import javax.xml.transform.dom.DOMSource;
14:import javax.xml.transform.stream.StreamResult;
15:
16:public class AddToOrder extends HttpServlet {
17:
18:   //*******BEGIN returnResult()*********
19:   public void returnResult( String product_id,
20:                             PrintWriter out )
```

Listing 5.23—continued

```
21:  {
...
40:                List allContent =
41:                     bodyElement.getChildren("apply-templates", xslns);
42:                allContent.set(0, resultText);
43:                break;
44:            }
45:        }
46:
47:        try {
48:            org.w3c.dom.Document DOMDoc;
49:            DOMOutputter DomOut = new DOMOutputter();
50:            DOMDoc = DomOut.output(includeDoc);
51:
52:            TransformerFactory transFactory =
53:                 TransformerFactory.newInstance();
54:            Transformer transformer =
55:                 transFactory.newTransformer(new DOMSource(DOMDoc));
56:            transformer.transform(new DOMSource(DOMDoc),
57:                                  new StreamResult(out));
58:        } catch (Exception e) {
59:            out.print("There was a problem with the transformation. ")
60:        }
61:  }
62:  //*******END returnResult()*********
63:
64://*******BEGIN getDocument() *********
65: public Document getDocument(File sourceFile,
66:                             PrintWriter errorsOut)
...
```


The first thing to note is that we now have two different `Documents` to deal with. The first, `org.jdom.Document`, is imported through the `import org.jdom.Document` statement on line 4. This is the `Document` we've been using until now. The second is the DOM version of `Document`, `org.w3c.dom.Document`. Because of this conflict, we name it explicitly on line 41, creating a DOM `Document` object.

Next, on line 49, we create the `DOMOutputter` object. As we mentioned earlier, this object enables us to take a JDOM tree (`includeDoc`) and output it as a DOM object on line 43.

After we have `DOMDoc`, we can apply the style sheet to … what? We're not trying to include any outside information; we just want to output the (now completely static) text of the style sheet. So, it doesn't really matter what we feed the transformer as a source XML file, because none of the information is going to appear.

The code on lines 52 through 57 has been pretty much lifted wholesale from `TransformServlet`, with the exception of the fact that what had been a StreamSource is now a DOMSource on lines 55 and 56.

All we have to do now is remove our debugging statements and make a call to `returnResult()` and we've got a working shopping cart! The complete code is shown in Listing 5.24.

Listing 5.24—The Complete `AddToOrder.java`

```
import java.io.*;
import javax.servlet.*;
import javax.servlet.http.*;
import org.jdom.Element;
import org.jdom.Document;
import org.jdom.JDOMException;
import org.jdom.Namespace;
import org.jdom.output.XMLOutputter;
import org.jdom.input.SAXBuilder;
import java.util.List;
import org.jdom.output.DOMOutputter;
import javax.xml.transform.TransformerFactory;
import javax.xml.transform.Transformer;
import javax.xml.transform.dom.DOMSource;
import javax.xml.transform.stream.StreamResult;

public class AddToOrder extends HttpServlet {

   //*******BEGIN returnResult()*********
   public void returnResult( String product_id,
                             PrintWriter out )
   {
       File resultFile = new File("/files/resultText.xml");
       Document resultDoc = getDocument(resultFile, out);
       Element resultText = resultDoc.getRootElement();
       Element productIdHere = resultText.getChild("productIdHere");
       productIdHere.addContent(product_id);
       File includeFile = new File("/files/topinclude.xsl");
       Document includeDoc = getDocument(includeFile, out);
       Element styleSheetRoot = includeDoc.getRootElement();

       List templates = styleSheetRoot.getChildren();
       for (int i=0; i < templates.size(); i++) {
           Element thisTemplate = (Element)templates.get(i);
           String thisMatch = thisTemplate.getAttributeValue("match");
           if (thisMatch.equals("/")) {
               Element htmlElement = thisTemplate.getChild("html");
               Element bodyElement = htmlElement.getChild("body");
               Namespace xslns = Namespace.getNamespace("xsl",
                            "http://www.w3.org/1999/XSL/Transform");
               List allContent =
                    bodyElement.getChildren("apply-templates", xslns);
               allContent.set(0, resultText);
               break;
           }
       }

```

Listing 5.24—continued

```
    try {
        org.w3c.dom.Document DOMDoc;
        DOMOutputter DomOut = new DOMOutputter();
        DOMDoc = DomOut.output(includeDoc);

        TransformerFactory transFactory =
             TransformerFactory.newInstance();
        Transformer transformer =
             transFactory.newTransformer(new DOMSource(DOMDoc));
        transformer.transform(new DOMSource(DOMDoc),
                              new StreamResult(out));
    } catch (Exception e) {
        out.print("There was a problem with the transformation. ");
    }
}
//*******END returnResult()*********

//*******BEGIN getDocument() *********
public Document getDocument(File sourceFile,
                            PrintWriter errorsOut)
{
  try {

      SAXBuilder builder = new SAXBuilder();
      Document document = builder.build(sourceFile);
      return document;

  } catch (JDOMException e) {
      errorsOut.print("There was a problem building the document: "
             +e.getMessage()+"<br />"+
             "Returning blank document.");
      return new Document(new Element("blank"));
  }
}
//*******END getDocument() *********

//*******BEGIN saveDocument() *********
public void saveDocument (Document saveDoc,
                          File saveFile,
                          PrintWriter errorsOut) {
    try {
        FileOutputStream outStream =
                new FileOutputStream(saveFile);

        XMLOutputter outToFile =
                new XMLOutputter("    ", true);
        outToFile.output(saveDoc, outStream);

        outStream.flush();
        outStream.close();
    } catch (IOException e) {
        errorsOut.print("Can't save orders.xml: "
```

Listing 5.24—continued

```
                        + e.getMessage()+"<br />");
    }
}
//*******END saveDocument() *********

//******BEGIN addItem() *********
public void addItem(Element orderElement,
                    String product_id,
                    String quant) {

    Element newItem = new Element("item");
    newItem.addAttribute("product_id", product_id);
    Element quantity = new Element("quantity");
    quantity.addContent(quant);
    newItem.addContent(quantity);
    orderElement.addContent(newItem);

}
//*******END  addItem() *********

public void doGet(HttpServletRequest request,
                  HttpServletResponse response)
          throws IOException, ServletException
{
  // Retrieve item to be added
  String thisProduct_id =
           request.getParameter("addProduct_id");
  String thisQuantity =
           request.getParameter("addQuantity");

  response.setContentType("text/html");
  PrintWriter out = response.getWriter();

  // Does orders.xml exist?
  File orderFile = new File ("/files/orders.xml");

  // If orders.xml doesn't exist:
  if (!orderFile.exists()) {
      //     Create orders.xml
      Element root = new Element("orders");
      root.addContent(" ");
      Document document = new Document(root);

      //     Save orders.xml
      saveDocument (document, orderFile, out);
  } else {
      // Do Nothing
  }

  // Get existing orders from orders.xml
  Document document = getDocument(orderFile, out);

```

Listing 5.24—continued

```
// Does this order exist?
HttpSession session = request.getSession(true);
String session_id = session.getId();

Element root = document.getRootElement();
List orders = root.getChildren();
int num_orders = orders.size();
boolean orderExists = false;
int orderIndex = 0;
for (int i=0; i < num_orders; i++) {
    Element iOrder = (Element)orders.get(i);
    String iOrder_id = iOrder.getAttributeValue("order_id");
    if (iOrder_id.equals(session_id)) {
        orderExists = true;
        orderIndex = i;
        break;
    }
}

// If this order does not exist:
if (!orderExists) {
    //     Create this order

    Element order = new Element("order");
    order.addAttribute("order_id", session_id);
    Element status = new Element("order_status");
    status.setText("in progress");
    order.addContent(status);

    // If the order didn't exist, the item certainly
    // wasn't part of it.
    addItem(order, thisProduct_id, thisQuantity);
    root.addContent(order);
}

Element thisOrder = (Element)orders.get(orderIndex);
boolean itemExists = false;
int itemIndex = 0;
List items = thisOrder.getChildren("item");
int num_items = items.size();
for (int i=0; i < num_items; i++) {
    Element iItem = (Element)items.get(i);
    String iProduct_id =
                 iItem.getAttribute("product_id").getValue();
    if (iProduct_id.equals(thisProduct_id)) {
      itemExists = true;
      itemIndex = i;
      break;
    }
}

// If this item is already part of this order:
```

Listing 5.24—continued

```
    if (itemExists) {
        //      Increment the quantity
        Element thisItem = (Element)items.get(itemIndex);
        String currentQuantity =
                            thisItem.getChildText("quantity");
        int newQuantity = Integer.parseInt(currentQuantity)
                            + Integer.parseInt(thisQuantity);

        String strQuantity = new String().valueOf(newQuantity);
        thisItem.getChild("quantity").setText(strQuantity);
    } else {
        //      Add this item to this order
        addItem(thisOrder, thisProduct_id, thisQuantity);
    }

    // Save orders.xml
    saveDocument (document, orderFile, out);

    returnResult (thisProduct_id, out);

  }
  //*******END doGet() *********

  //*******BEGIN doPost() *********
  public void doPost(HttpServletRequest request,
                          HttpServletResponse response)
             throws IOException, ServletException
  {
      doGet(request, response);
  }
 //*******END doPost() *********
}
```

Next Steps

In this chapter, we've created the beginnings of a shopping cart using the JDOM API. We've also talked about various programming issues, such as creating methods, casting objects between types, and scope.

In Chapter 6, we complete the shopping cart, allowing users to review their orders and check out. Also, we look at checking and adjusting inventory. In doing that, we delve more deeply into namespaces and how to use them as we further manipulate style sheets via Java programming. We also look at other uses for namespaces, such as integrating vendor data.

Chapter 6

In this chapter

- *Manipulating In-Memory Documents*
- *The Structure of a DOM Document*
- *Adding Namespaces*
- *Creating the Review Page*
- *The Final Style Sheet*
- *Collecting Payment Information*
- *Accepting Payment Information*
- *Next Steps*

Adjusting Inventory: Using Namespaces and More About DOM

In the last chapter, we built the beginnings of a shopping cart, allowing the user to add items to an order. In this chapter, we complete the order process, allowing him or her to review the shopping cart and check out, as well as adjusting the inventory on hand.

To do this, we will begin to look at segregating data into various namespaces, such as products and orders.

Almost from the beginning, we have talked about namespaces, but until now, we haven't said much about them.

In XML, *namespaces* actually have a number of uses. The first, which we talked about in Chapter 2, "Product Pages: Transforming XML in the Browser Using XSL," is to distinguish between various implementations of a standard. For instance, the namespace we use to define the `xsl:` prefix determines how Internet Explorer handles the XSL transformation.

This, however, is really more of a side effect than the original intention for their use, and we'll discuss it further in a moment.

Namespaces in XML were intended to fulfill much of the same use as they do in programming. There, they are similar to scope, in that they define the area where a particular name means something. If two objects have the same name, there's no clash unless they are in the same namespace.

For instance, I'm the only Nick who works in my office, so when somebody says, "Hey, Nick," we all know whom they're talking to. If we had more than one Nick, they'd have to ask for Nick Chase, or Nick C., or some name that makes it clear. But because we don't, just "Nick" is a sufficient identifier. We can think of the office as one namespace.

On the other hand, we also have a client company whose contact is named Nick. That company is its own namespace, so if the receptionist announces that there's a client call for Nick from Nick, we still know what's going on. The client Nick is calling for the employee Nick. Both namespaces are identified.

If I'm not in the office and the receptionist tells Chuck that Nick is on the phone, however, we have a potential conflict. Which Nick is it? In all likelihood, Chuck will assume it's me, because the office is the default namespace. If the call had come from the client namespace, the receptionist would have said so.

It's not always that easy, however. If I'm at home and I get a call from someone named Nick, I can't make any assumptions; there is no namespace to reference.

The same thing happens with XML namespaces. Not only do we need to distinguish between namespaces when we have different elements with the same name, but we also need to know how to treat items in each namespace. When he picks up the phone, Chuck needs to know whether he has to be serious because this is a client (and even how serious, depending on which client), or whether he can joke with me about the fact that I'm not in the office.

We saw a prime example of this when we were working with XSL style sheets. Elements that began with `xsl:` were involved in the transformation logic and had to be treated accordingly. We also saw the fact that different namespaces could be treated differently, such as when we discussed how changing our style sheet namespace determines how Internet Explorer would treat the document.

In this chapter, we start out by combining product and order information into a single document to process it conveniently, using namespaces to help us sort out what's what. In doing that, we'll also get a much closer look at DOM, as well as using style sheets to help us manipulate data.

Manipulating In-Memory Documents

Now that we've created an order, we need to give the user a way to review the items that have been added to it. Our algorithm for doing that might look something like this:

```
Check for an existing order
If the order exists, display information on each item:
    Get the order item
    Retrieve information on the item from products.xml
```

```
    Display the information on that item
Else
    Display a message that there is no current order
```

Let's think about how we want to do this. Looking at the `orders.xml` file, a typical order might look similar to this:

```
<order order_id="To1010mC7161452772864825At">
  <order_status>open</order_status>
    <item product_id="RC2342">
      <quantity>3</quantity>
    </item>
    <item product_id="QA3452">
      <quantity>1</quantity>
    </item>
  </order>
```

Technically, we have all the information we need to produce a final order page, in that the `product_id` attribute for each item will lead us to the full information from the product. If you remember the structure of the `products.xml` file, however, products can be at any level (such as within suites), and searching for them by looping through the file can be a real hassle. Fortunately for us, the XPath techniques we learned for style sheets can come in handy here.

6

What we should do is create a style sheet that combines the data from the order with the product information from the `products.xml` file. What we'll get back is actually a new XML document we can process to add totals and other information.

The first thing we need is a single XML document that contains all the product information, as well as the user's order information.

Creating the New Document

In Chapter 5, "Taking Orders: Manipulating Data with JDOM," we took a look at JDOM, a simplified way of looking at XML data. This enabled us to become familiar with the concepts behind building servlets and working with XML using Java. In this chapter, we examine the Document Object Model (DOM) itself in more detail, using it instead of JDOM to do our work.

Let's start by creating our algorithm for building the new document out of the products and orders. We'll have to do the following:

```
Create an empty Document
Read the first source Document
Set the first namespace
Copy the data into the new Document
Read the second source Document
Set the new namespace
Copy the data into the new Document
```

Let's start with the basics: creating the empty document.

First, let's create a new servlet called `ReviewOrder` and use it to parse our `orders.xml` file, as in Listing 6.1.

Listing 6.1—`ReviewOrder.java`: The Skeleton

```
0: import java.io.*;
1: import javax.servlet.*;
2: import javax.servlet.http.*;
3: import org.apache.xerces.parsers.DOMParser;
4: import org.w3c.dom.Document;
4a:import org.apache.xerces.dom.DocumentImpl;
5: import org.w3c.dom.Element;
6:
7: public class ReviewOrder extends HttpServlet {
8:
9:   public void doGet(HttpServletRequest request,
10:                     HttpServletResponse response)
11:              throws IOException, ServletException
12:    {
13:    response.setContentType("text/html");
14:    PrintWriter out = response.getWriter();
15:
16:    try {
17:
18:        DOMParser parser = new DOMParser();
19:        parser.parse("/files/orders.xml");
20:        Document orders = parser.getDocument();
21:
22:    } catch (org.xml.sax.SAXException SAXe) {
23:        out.print("There was a problem with the source"
24:            + " document.");
25:    } catch (IOException IOe) {
26:        out.print("There was an IO error. Make sure the file"
27:            + " exists and is readable.");
28:    } catch (Exception e) {
29:        out.print("There was an error: "+e.getMessage());
30:    }
31:
32:    out.print("Done.");
33:
34:  }
35:
36:}
```

As we have done in the last couple of chapters, we start out with a basic servlet that implements the `doGet()` method to do our work. Lines 0 through 5 perform the relevant imports, with 3 through 5 being specific to the DOM work we're about to perform. Lines 13 and 14 are our standard preparations for sending information back to the browser.

Now that we have the basics out of the way, let's start by looking at lines 18 through 20, where we actually retrieve the document. On line 18, we create a `DOMParser`. Unlike with JDOM, if we want a DOM document, we must use a DOM parser. This gives us an object we can then use to parse as many files as we want.

Line 19 is where we actually do the parsing, after supplying the parser with the location of our `orders.xml` file. This doesn't, however, give us the `Document` with which to work.

It's not until we specifically request the `Document` on line 20 that the application creates it for us, returning it to our `orders Document`. `getDocument()` returns the last parsed document, whatever it happens to be. So, later, when we want to get the `products` information, we can just parse the file and return the `Document` without having to create the `DOMParser` all over again.

Of course, in doing all this, a few things can go wrong, causing exceptions to be thrown. If we check the `Javadocs`, we can see which exceptions can be thrown and then look for them specifically. To do this, we can use the browser to locate the file

```
C:\xerces-1_2_3\docs\apiDocs\index.html
```

because Xerces is the product we use to do the parsing.

6

If you installed Xerces in a different location, adjust the address for the documentation accordingly.

From here, we can choose `DOMParser` in the left frame, which pulls up all the information for `DOMParser`. If we look at the list of methods for `DOMParser`, however, we don't see `parse()`!

This is because `DOMParser` is a subclass of `org.apache.xerces.framework.XMLParser`, which is the class that actually implements `parse()`. Whenever we don't see a method we know is accessible from a particular class, we should look at the inherited methods, as shown in Figure 6.1.

We can then click `parse()` and see what kinds of exceptions it throws, as shown in Figure 6.2.

Java requires us to either check for these exceptions or throw them. As we saw earlier, we can't change the definition of `doGet()` to throw these exceptions, so we need to check for them. (It makes more sense from a programming standpoint, as well!)

Because both of these exceptions are subclasses of `java.lang.Exception`, we could just check for that, because any exception falls into that category. But by checking for each individual type on lines 22 through 30, we can give the user much more information about what has gone wrong with the application. It might take us a bit more time to do this, but it's generally worth it from a usability standpoint.

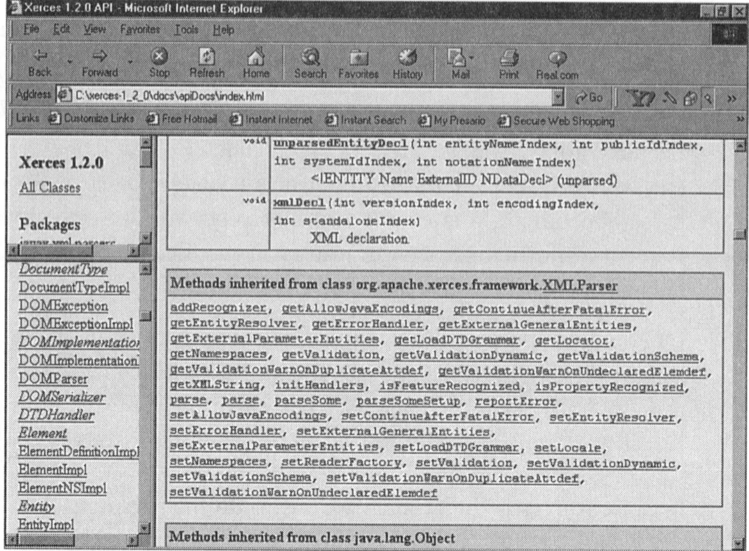

Figure 6.1

Methods we're using often come from the parents of classes we're using.

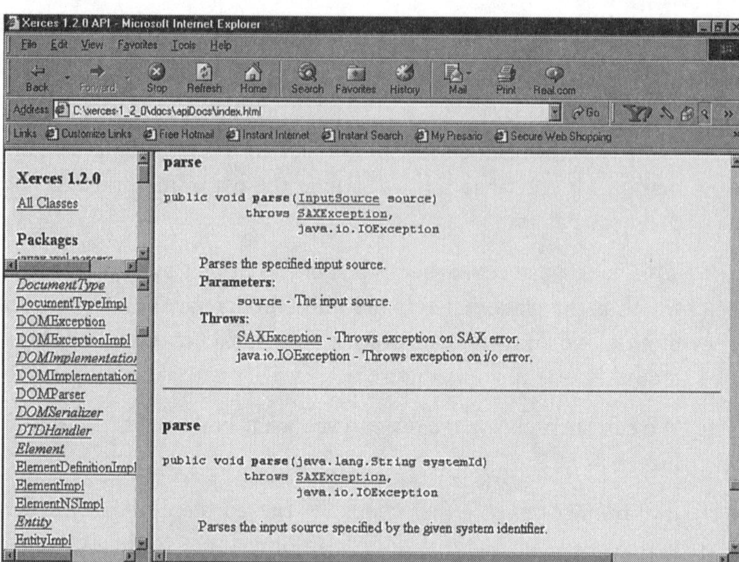

Figure 6.2

The `Javadocs` *show what a method does and also which kinds of exceptions it throws.*

Finally, on line 32, we just print out a message to let the user know that everything has completed successfully. Eventually, this is where we'll be outputting our order for review; but for now, we'll leave it at that.

Now we can go ahead and create the document to which we're going to copy this data. If we just copied our data directly into an empty document, it would look something like this:

```
<orders>
    <order>
    ...
    </order>
    <order>
    ...
    </order>
</orders>
<products>
    <vendor>
    ...
    </vendor>
    <vendor>
    ...
    </vendor>
</products>
```

Unfortunately, this isn't a well-formed document, because it has no root node. Instead, we want something like this:

```
<orderSystem>
    <orders>
    <order>
    ...
    </order>
    <order>
    ...
    </order>
    </orders>
    <products>
    <vendor>
    ...
    </vendor>
    <vendor>
    ...
    </vendor>
    </products>
</orderSystem>
```

To begin to create this, we need to get the empty document and add the root element.

Creating DOM Objects

When we were working with JDOM, we were able to create objects directly, by using `new`, as in `new Element()`. This is because the classes with which we wanted to work, such as `Element`, `Document`, and so on, were objects. So, to create a new `Document` with JDOM, we did the following:

```
Create a new Element
Create a new Document with the Element as its root
```

6

Working with DOM is, in many respects, just the opposite. The DOM objects we have been talking conceptually about all this time, such as `Document`, `Element`, `Node`, and so on, are interfaces. This means they are abstract, and we can't instantiate them directly using `new`.

That's not to say we can't work with them at all. The Xerces implementation of the DOM API has implementation classes, such as `DocumentImpl`, `ElementImpl`, and so on, that we can use to create the objects we want. So, to create a new `Document` with DOM and assign it a root element, we would do the following:

```
Create the new Document using its implementation
Use that Document object to create a new Element
Append that Element to the Document
```

We can see these steps in action in Listing 6.2.

Listing 6.2—`ReviewOrder.java`: Creating the Blank `Document`

```
...
17:     try {
18:
19:         DOMParser parser = new DOMParser();
20:         parser.parse("/files/orders.xml");
21:         Document products = parser.getDocument();
22:
23:         Document newDoc = new DocumentImpl();
24:         Element orderSystem = newDoc.createElement("orderSystem");
25:         newDoc.appendChild(orderSystem);
26:
27:     } catch (org.xml.sax.SAXException SAXe) {
28:         out.print("There was a problem with the source"
29:             + " document.");
...
```

On line 23, we create the `Document` object by instantiating its implementation class. We could just as easily have said

```
DocumentImpl newDoc = new DocumentImpl();
```

Because `Document` is a parent of `DocumentImpl`—`DocumentImpl` is said to implement `Document`, instead of extending it, because `Document` is an interface—we can use `DocumentImpl` to create a `Document`.

After we have the `Document` object, `newDoc`, we can use it to create any number of other objects, such as our root `Element`, `orderSystem`. That's what we do on line 24. Similar to creating a `new Element()` in JDOM, however, `orderSystem` is just an `Element` floating out there until we add it to the document on line 25.

The Structure of a DOM Document

Until now, we've been using the terms *element* and *node* almost as though they are synonymous. In some cases they are; all elements are nodes. But not all nodes are elements. In fact, `Element` is a subclass of `Node`, and just one of many types.

Twelve types of nodes exist. They are as follows:

- **Attributes**—The usual attributes of an element that we've already seen, such as `order_id`:

  ```
  <order order_id="123ABC"></order>
  ```

- **CData sections**—A section of text that the processor should not attempt to parse. In an XHTML page, scripts are often CData sections because they contain markup and other text we don't want processed. CData sections are set off with special characters that tell the processor to ignore them, as in

  ```
  The time is:
  <script language="JavaScript">
  <![CDATA[
       var today = new Date();
      document.write( today.getHours()+':'+today.getMinutes() );
  ]]>
  </script>
  ```

- **Comments**—Normal comments within the page, such as

  ```
  <!-- Each order has a unique order_id attribute -->
  ```

- **Document fragments**—A document fragment is a part of a document that might or might not be well formed. For instance, it can be a group of elements with no root element, such as the following:

  ```
  <order order_id="1234">
      <status>open</status>
  </order>
  <order order_id="2134">
      <status>closed</status>
  </order>
  ```

- **Documents**—A complete document, including the XML declaration:

  ```
  <?xml version="1.0" encoding="UTF-8"?>
  <orders>
  <order order_id="1234">
          <status>open</status>
  </order>
  <order order_id="2134">
  ```

6

```
        <status>closed</status>
</order>
</orders>
```

- **Document types**—Also known as the Doctype declaration, this is the information that lets the processor know what the document is. We saw this when we discussed valid documents in Chapter 3, "Defining the Data Structure: Document Type Definitions, XML Schema, and Parsers."

  ```
  <!DOCTYPE HTML PUBLIC "-//W3C//DTD HTML 4.0//EN">
  ```

- **Text**—This is any text that is within another node. For example, in

  ```
  <status>in progress</status>
  ```

  the characters `in progress` are a text node.
- **Elements**—An element node is essentially a set of tags. For instance, in this example

  ```
  <order order_id="1234"><status>open</status></order>
  ```

  `order` is an element node, because it contains only the `status` node. We'll take a closer look at element and text nodes shortly.
- **Entities, entity references, and notations**—These are some of the more advanced features of DTDs.
- **Processing instructions**—This is a way for the XML author to provide instructions to the processor that don't necessarily have to do with the data itself. For example,

  ```
  <?xml-stylesheet href="catalog.xsl" type="text/xsl" version="1.0" ?>
  ```

  is a processing instruction that lets the processor know which style sheet to use. Processing instructions are always in the form of

  ```
  <? instruction name="value" name="value"... ?>
  ```

Even though it is in the form `<? ?>`, the XML declaration `<?xml version="1.0" encoding="UTF-8"?>` is not considered a processing instruction.

To make things a little easier, every `Node` object has these types assigned to constants that are member variables. That means that if we had a `Node` called `orderSystem`, as we do in the previous example, we could actually test for the value of

```
OrderSystem.ELEMENT_NODE
```

and get an integer back. This makes it possible for us to write code that can distinguish between the various types and still be understandable to human eyes. To get a better look at how these different node types fit together (and in preparation for adding them to `newDoc`), let's take a look at the various types of nodes in our `orders.xml` file. Listing 6.3 shows the contents of my `orders.xml` file, whereas Listing 6.4 takes the orders document and loops through the first level of children, displaying the type and value for each.

Listing 6.3—`orders.xml`

```
<?xml version="1.0" encoding="UTF-8"?>
<orders>
    <order order_id="To1010mC24980190282174342At">
        <order_status>in progress</order_status>
        <item product_id="RC2342">
            <quantity>5</quantity>
        </item>
    </order>
    <order order_id="To1010mC7161452772864825At">
        <order_status>in progress</order_status>
        <item product_id="RC2342">
            <quantity>3</quantity>
        </item>
        <item product_id="QA3452">
            <quantity>1</quantity>
        </item>
    </order>
</orders>
```

Listing 6.4—`ReviewOrder.java`: Displaying Node Types

```
import java.io.*;
import javax.servlet.*;
import javax.servlet.http.*;
import org.apache.xerces.parsers.DOMParser;
import org.w3c.dom.Document;
import org.apache.xerces.dom.DocumentImpl;
import org.w3c.dom.Element;
import org.w3c.dom.Node;
import org.w3c.dom.NodeList;

public class ReviewOrder extends HttpServlet {

  public String getNodeTypeName(int type) {

      String[] nodeTypeNames = { "No node type 0",
                                 "ELEMENT_NODE",
                                 "ATTRIBUTE_NODE",
                                 "TEXT_NODE",
                                 "CDATA_SECTION_NODE",
                                 "ENTITY_REFERENCE_NODE",
                                 "ENTITY_NODE",
                                 "PROCESSING_INSTRUCTION_NODE",
                                 "COMMENT_NODE",
                                 "DOCUMENT_NODE",
```

Listing 6.4—continued

```
22:                                    "DOCUMENT_TYPE_NODE",
23:                                    "DOCUMENT_FRAGMENT_NODE",
24:                                    "NOTATION_NODE" };
25:     return nodeTypeNames[type];
26: }
27:
28: public void doGet(HttpServletRequest request,
29:                   HttpServletResponse response)
30:           throws IOException, ServletException
31:   {
32:   response.setContentType("text/html");
33:   PrintWriter out = response.getWriter();
34:
35:   try {
36:
37:       DOMParser parser = new DOMParser();
38:       parser.parse("/files/orders.xml");
39:       Document orders = parser.getDocument();
40:
41:       Document newDoc = new DocumentImpl();
42:       Element orderSystem = newDoc.createElement("orderSystem");
43:       newDoc.appendChild(orderSystem);
44:
45:       Node orderRoot = orders.getFirstChild();
46:       NodeList orderChildren = orderRoot.getChildNodes();
47:       for (int i=0; i < orderChildren.getLength(); i++) {
48:           Node thisChild = orderChildren.item(i);
49:           out.print("Child number: "+i+"<br />");
50:           out.print("Node Name: "+thisChild.getNodeName());
51:           out.print("<br />");
52:           out.print("Node Value: "+thisChild.getNodeValue());
53:           out.print("<br />");
54:           out.print("Node Type: "
55:                  +getNodeTypeName(thisChild.getNodeType()));
56:           out.print("<br />");
57:           out.print("<br />");
58:       }
59:
60:   } catch (org.xml.sax.SAXException SAXe) {
61:       out.print("There was a problem with the source"
...
```

Let's start on line 45. `orders` is the document, but if we want to start looking at the data, we need the root element. In this case, the root element is the first child node of the document itself, so we can retrieve it with `getFirstChild()`.

Next, on line 46, we get all the direct children of orders using `getChildNodes()`. This returns a `NodeList`, similar to the way that `getChildren()` returned a list in JDOM. Because it's a `NodeList`, however, when we retrieve the item on line 48, it actually comes back as a `Node`, and we don't have to cast it the way we did with the objects returned by `List`.

So, on lines 47 through 58, we loop through each of the children of `orders`. For each one, we note which one it is, and then display a set of information about it. The `name` and `value` on lines 50 and 52 are fairly straightforward. Line 55 is where it gets interesting.

`ThisChild.getNodeType()` returns an `int` value, as we mentioned before. This value will correspond to the list of node types. We could have just output that integer, but instead, we've created a method—`getNodeTypeName()`—to convert that integer into an actual name.

`getNodeTypeName()` is on lines 10 through 26 of the listing. On line 12, we define an array of `Strings` called `nodeTypeNames`; on lines 12 through 24, we initialize it with a set of values. An *array* is a structure that has a value accessed through an index. For instance, if we were looking for `nodeTypeNames[3]`, the value would be `TEXT_NODE`. Because the values we're looking for start at `1`, we've put a placeholder in the 0th spot. Otherwise, we'd have to change line 25 to

```
return nodeTypeNames[type-1]
```

to make up for the offset.

So, on line 55, `getNodeType()` returns an `int` value, which we then feed to `getNodeTypeName()` to get the actual text information.

Running this program with the `orders.xml` file, as it is in Listing 6.3, gives the following results:

```
Child number: 0
Node Type: TEXT_NODE
Node Name: #text
Node Value:

Child number: 1
Node Type: ELEMENT_NODE
Node Name: order
Node Value: null

Child number: 2
Node Type: TEXT_NODE
Node Name: #text
Node Value:

Child number: 3
Node Type: ELEMENT_NODE
Node Name: order
Node Value: null

Child number: 4
Node Type: TEXT_NODE
Node Name: #text
Node Value:

Done.
```

At first glance, this doesn't seem to make any sense. Where did those three text nodes come from? And why does the value of `order` come up as `null`, when we know that there is information in it?

First of all, three text nodes are in the `orders` element. They are the line feeds and spaces between lines 1 and 2, lines 7 and 8, and lines 16 and 17.

Second, no value exists for the `order` elements exactly because they themselves are element nodes. An element node contains other nodes, not a value itself. Even the `order_status` node doesn't contain a value; it contains a text node that contains a value. We can see that as we start to move down the tree.

Recursion

To move down the tree, we use a process called recursion. *Recursion* is when a method calls itself, as we can see in Listing 6.5.

Listing 6.5—Using Recursion to Examine Node Types

```
...
      return nodeTypeNames[type];
  }

  public void processNode(Node thisNode,
                          PrintWriter out,
                          String spacer) {

    if (thisNode.getNodeType() == thisNode.ELEMENT_NODE) {

        out.print(spacer+" Element: "
                        + thisNode.getNodeName() + "<br />");

        NodeList thisKids = thisNode.getChildNodes();
        for (int i=0; i < thisKids.getLength(); i++) {
            processNode(thisKids.item(i), out, spacer+"--");
        }

        } else if (thisNode.getNodeType() == thisNode.TEXT_NODE) {
            out.print(spacer+" Text: "
                        + thisNode.getNodeValue() + "<br />");
    }

  }

  public void doGet(HttpServletRequest request,
                    HttpServletResponse response)
          throws IOException, ServletException
    {
...

        Node orderRoot = orders.getFirstChild();
        processNode(orderRoot, out, "--");
```

Listing 6.5—continued

```
68:
69:     } catch (org.xml.sax.SAXException SAXe) {
70:         out.print("There was a problem with the source"
71:             + " document.");
...
```

Line 67 replaces all the looping we were doing previously, as we tell the servlet to process just one node—the root node. It is the method, `processNode()`, on lines 28 through 47 that actually does the work of digging down into the tree.

On line 32, we check to see whether this is an element node. If it is, the numeric `getNodeType()` matches the numeric `ELEMENT_NODE`. In that case, we print out the name of the element, and then select all this element's children. Each one of those children is processed by this very same method on line 39. For each one, the `spacer` `String` gets longer, showing us how deep into the document we are.

On the other hand, if the node is a text node, on lines 43 and 44 we print the actual value. When we run this servlet, we get results similar to the following:


```
-- Element: orders
---- Text:
---- Element: order
------ Text:
------ Element: order_status
-------- Text: open
------ Text:
------ Element: item
-------- Text:
-------- Element: quantity
---------- Text: 5
-------- Text:
------ Text:
---- Text:
---- Element: order
------ Text:
------ Element: order_status
-------- Text: open
------ Text:
------ Element: item
-------- Text:
-------- Element: quantity
---------- Text: 3
-------- Text:
------ Text:
------ Element: item
-------- Text:
-------- Element: quantity
---------- Text: 1
-------- Text:
---- Text:
Done.
```

The spacers enable us to see how deep each level of recursion is. We start out on line 0 in just the first level of recursion, but when we get there, we are processing the five nodes under `orders`. Each of these nodes (which start with four dashes) sends the servlet processing its own children and then comes back out to its own level.

So, we see that where we think there are just elements, there are actually text nodes and elements nodes—because of the line feeds between elements. If we were to clean up the `orders.xml` file so that no line breaks existed, such as

```
<?xml version="1.0" encoding="UTF-8"?><orders><order
order_id="To1010mC24980190282174342At"><order_status>open</order_status><item
product_id="RC2342"><quantity>5</quantity></item></order><order
order_id="To1010mC7161452772864825At"><order_status>open</order_status><item
product_id="RC2342"><quantity>3</quantity></item><item
product_id="QA3452"><quantity>1</quantity></item></order></orders>
```

we would find that the output adjusts accordingly, to the following:

```
-- Element: orders
---- Element: order
------ Element: order_status
-------- Text: open
------ Element: item
-------- Element: quantity
---------- Text: 5
---- Element: order
------ Element: order_status
-------- Text: open
------ Element: item
-------- Element: quantity
---------- Text: 3
------ Element: item
-------- Element: quantity
---------- Text: 1
Done.
```

This is more in line with what we were expecting when we originally looked at the file!

The astute might notice that some information is still missing from this display. What happened to our attributes?

In DOM, attributes are not children of an element, but they are attached to it, as we can see in Listing 6.6.

Listing 6.6—ReviewOrder.java: Retrieving Attributes

```
import org.w3c.dom.NodeList;
import org.w3c.dom.NamedNodeMap;
...
  public void processNode(Node thisNode,
                          PrintWriter out,
                          String spacer) {

```

Listing 6.6—continued

```
32:     if (thisNode.getNodeType() == thisNode.ELEMENT_NODE) {
33:
34:         out.print(spacer+" Element: "
35:                         + thisNode.getNodeName());
36:
37:         NamedNodeMap attributes = thisNode.getAttributes();
38:         if (attributes.getLength() > 0) {
39:                   out.print(" has attributes ");
40:             for (int i=0; i < attributes.getLength(); i++) {
41:                 Node thisAttr = attributes.item(i);
42:                     out.print(thisAttr.getNodeName() + " = " +
43:                               thisAttr.getNodeValue());
44:                 }
45:         }
46:
47:             out.print("<br />");
48:
49:         NodeList thisKids = thisNode.getChildNodes();
50:         for (int i=0; i < thisKids.getLength(); i++) {
51:             processNode(thisKids.item(i), out, spacer+"--");
52:         }
53:
54:         } else if (thisNode.getNodeType() == thisNode.TEXT_NODE) {
55:             out.print(spacer+" Text: "
56:                         + thisNode.getNodeValue() + "<br />");
57:     }
58:
59:   }
...
```


Elements are the only type of node we are looking at right now that can have attributes, so that's where we'll try to find them. On line 37, we get a `NamedNodeMap` called `attributes` and populate it with any attributes the element might have.

A `NamedNodeMap` is a structure that enables us to retrieve or set a value based on its name. For instance, if we wanted the value of the `order_id`, we could ask for the following:

```
attributes.getNamedItem("order_id")
```

This is especially handy for attributes, where we know the name of the value we want, so that's what's returned by a call to `getAttributes()`.

On line 38, we check to see whether any attributes actually exist. If any do, we display each attribute node individually on lines 40 through 44.

Running this code gives us this result:

```
-- Element: orders
---- Element: order has attributes order_id = To1010mC24980190282174342At
------ Element: order_status
```

```
-------- Text: open
------ Element: item has attributes product_id = RC2342
-------- Element: quantity
---------- Text: 5
---- Element: order has attributes order_id = To1010mC7161452772864825At
------ Element: order_status
-------- Text: open
------ Element: item has attributes product_id = RC2342
-------- Element: quantity
---------- Text: 3
------ Element: item has attributes product_id = QA3452
-------- Element: quantity
---------- Text: 1
Done.
```

Adding Nodes to a Document

Now that we know we're accessing all the information in our document, it's time to start adding it to the new document. To do that, we need to make changes to our `processNode()` method. But what sort of changes? Let's think about what we want to do each time the method processes a node.

Aside from just printing out its progress, for each node of the old document, we must create a new node with the same information. To do that, we need a `Document` object, to enable us to have access to the creation methods we talked about earlier. We also will need to know which node to add this new node to!

In Listing 6.7, we start by adding these new nodes to `processNode()`.

Listing 6.7—`ReviewOrder.java`: Adding Nodes to a Document

```
...
public void processNode(Node thisNode,
                        PrintWriter out,
                        Node newParent,
                        Document newDoc,
                        String spacer) {

    if (thisNode.getNodeType() == thisNode.ELEMENT_NODE) {

        out.print(spacer+" Element: " + thisNode.getNodeName());

        Element newElement =
                newDoc.createElement(thisNode.getNodeName());
        newParent.appendChild(newElement);

        NamedNodeMap attributes = thisNode.getAttributes();
        if (attributes.getLength() > 0) {
            out.print(" has attributes ");
            for (int i=0; i < attributes.getLength(); i++) {
            Node thisAttr = attributes.item(i);
```

Listing 6.7—continued

```
47:                  out.print(thisAttr.getNodeName() + " = " +
48:                                  thisAttr.getNodeValue());
49:              }
50:          }
51:
52:          out.print("<br />");
53:
54:          NodeList thisKids = thisNode.getChildNodes();
55:          for (int i=0; i < thisKids.getLength(); i++) {
56:              processNode(thisKids.item(i), out, newElement,
57:                                           newDoc, spacer+"--");
58:          }
59:
60:      } else if (thisNode.getNodeType() == thisNode.TEXT_NODE) {
61:          out.print(spacer+" Text: "
62:                        + thisNode.getNodeValue() + "<br />");
63:      }
64:
65:  }
66:
67:  public void doGet(HttpServletRequest request,
68:                    HttpServletResponse response)
69:             throws IOException, ServletException
70:    {
71:    response.setContentType("text/html");
72:    PrintWriter out = response.getWriter();
73:
74:    try {
75:
76:        DOMParser parser = new DOMParser();
77:        parser.parse("/files/orders.xml");
78:        Document orders = parser.getDocument();
79:
80:        Document newDoc = new DocumentImpl();
81:        Element orderSystem = newDoc.createElement("orderSystem");
82:        newDoc.appendChild(orderSystem);
83:
84:        Node orderRoot = orders.getFirstChild();
85:        processNode(orderRoot, out, orderSystem, newDoc, "--");
86:
87:    } catch (org.xml.sax.SAXException SAXe) {
...
```


We start by actually creating the new `Document` on line 80. After we have it, we can create a new soon-to-be root element, which we'll call `orderSystem`. At this point, it's just floating out there in the ether, so on line 82 we add it to our new `Document`.

Now we have the new `Document` we're going to create and the first node we're going to add elements to. We know we will need to feed this information to `processNode()`, so on lines 30 and 31 we add it to the signature of `processNode()`. In addition, on line 85 we add it to the call to `processNode()`.

Signature—The signature of a function or method is the number and types of parameters it takes and the type of value (if any) it returns. Java uses the signature of a method to determine which one to use, in the case of method overloading.

Method overloading—Method overloading occurs when two or more methods have the same name, but can be distinguished based on the types of parameters they accept.

We didn't change too much in `processNode()` itself. First, we realize that for every element we encounter in the old `Document`, we want to create a new element in the new `Document`. We also want it to have the same name as the element in the old `Document`. That's what we do on line 28.

`newDoc` will always be the `Document` we create in the main body of the program. `newParent`, on the other hand, changes every time this routine is called. To start off, `newParent` is the `orderSystem` root node. For the first node in the old `Document`, we add `newElement` to that, on line 40.

In this case, what we're calling the "main body" is actually the `doGet()` method. A lot is happening before `doGet()` is actually called, but for our purposes, that's where the action is.

Let's think about what happens as we move down the chain, however. After we execute line 40, we have the two structures shown in Table 6.1.

Table 6.1—Comparing the Two Documents

Document 1	*Document 2*
<orders> <order order_id="To1010mC24980190282174342At"> <order_status>open</order_status> <item product_id="RC2342"> <quantity>5</quantity> </item> </order> <order order_id="To1010mC7161452772864825At"> <order_status>open</order_status> <item product_id="RC2342"> <quantity>3</quantity> </item> <item product_id="QA3452"> <quantity>1</quantity> </item> </order> </orders>	<orderSystem> <orders></orders> </orderSystem>

The next time we run through `processNode()`, we'll want to add an element, such as the first `order_status` in `orders.xml` to the first `orders` element in the new document. Therefore, `orders`, which is `newElement`, becomes the `newParent`. We can see this in the call to `processNode()`on lines 56 and 57.

At this point, we should have all our elements created, even if they are completely empty. It would probably be useful to be able to look at the document in progress to ensure that we're on the right track.

Serializing the Document

In Java, the notion of serializing was first used in references to objects. In *serializing* an object, we essentially save it to a file so it can be re-created (or unserialized) later.

We do the same with XML documents. In fact, the XML files we've been dealing with all this time are serialized versions of XML documents. It's the in-memory documents that really deserve the name.

When we were saving our `orders.xml` file in Chapter 5, what we were really doing was serializing the JDOM document and saving it to a file—even though we called it *outputting*. Now, when we're dealing with straight DOM, we'll use the proper name: serialization.

In Listing 6.8, we change the output of the servlet from descriptions of the original document to the serialized representation of our new document.

Listing 6.8—Serializing the New Document

```
0: import java.io.*;
1: import javax.servlet.*;
2: import javax.servlet.http.*;
3: import javax.xml.parsers.*;
4: import org.apache.xerces.parsers.*;
5: import org.w3c.dom.*;
6: import org.apache.xerces.dom .*;
7: import org.apache.xml.serialize.XMLSerializer;
7a:import org.apache.xml.serialize.OutputFormat;
8:
9: public class ReviewOrder extends HttpServlet {
...
60:  public void doGet(HttpServletRequest request,
61:                    HttpServletResponse response)
62:               throws IOException, ServletException
63:    {
64:    response.setContentType("text/html");
65:    PrintWriter out = response.getWriter();
66:
67:    try {
68:
...
```

Listing 6.8—continued

```
76:
77:         Node orderRoot = orders.getFirstChild();
78:         processNode(orderRoot, out, orderSystem, newDoc, "--");
79:
80:         OutputFormat format = new OutputFormat();
81:         XMLSerializer output = new XMLSerializer(out, format);
82:         output.serialize(newDoc);
83:
84:     } catch (org.xml.sax.SAXException SAXe) {
...
```

On line 7, we import the package that contains `XMLSerializer`. This package also contains some other useful classes, such as `XHTMLSerializer` and `TextSerializer`. It also includes the `OutputFormat` class, which enables us to specify how we want our document to be formatted.

On line 80, we create an `OutputFormat`, but we just use the default values for now. On line 81, we actually create the `XMLSerializer`, telling it that we want the output to go to the browser and that we want to use our new format. We also can send the results to a file, but for now, we'll send them to the screen. Finally, on line 82, we serialize the document.

One thing to note here: We could compile and run the servlet just like this, but the results we get will depend on which browser we use. The reason is this: The browser is receiving an XML document, complete with XML declaration. It doesn't care that the document didn't come from a file. All it knows is that it's to treat it like XML.

Now, if we call the servlet from a browser such as Netscape Navigator 4.x, we see the text of the elements (of which there isn't any yet). In addition, if we looked at the source, we'd see the tags. On the other hand, if we were to try to call the servlet from Microsoft Internet Explorer 5.x, the browser would complain (loudly) that the XML document is not well formed, because of all the other debugging statements we also printed.

For that reason, we've also removed our previous `out.print()` statements, so the only output (unless an exception is thrown) is from the serializer.

If we compile and run the servlet, we get one of two results. In Netscape, we see nothing, and in IE, we see a neat and orderly document. In either case, the source looks like this:

```
<?xml version="1.0" encoding="UTF-8"?>
<orderSystem><orders><order><order_status/><item><quantity/></item></order>
➥<order><order_status/><item><quantity/></item><item><quantity/>
➥</item></order></orders></orderSystem>
```

To make it look at bit neater, we can tweak the `OutputFormat` we created. Specifically, if we change line 80 to

```
OutputFormat format = new OutputFormat(newDoc, "UTF-8", true);
```

the source will be "pretty printed," which means it will have indenting and generally be easier to interpret.

Adding Data

At this point, our serialized document looks like this:

```
<?xml version="1.0" encoding="UTF-8"?>
<orderSystem>
    <orders>
        <order>
            <order_status/>
            <item>
                <quantity/>
            </item>
        </order>
        <order>
            <order_status/>
            <item>
                <quantity/>
            </item>
            <item>
                <quantity/>
            </item>
        </order>
    </orders>
</orderSystem>
```

It's nice to see the structure beginning to take shape, but we still have no data. We've added the elements already, so now we just have to add the text and attribute nodes, as in Listing 6.9.

Listing 6.9—Adding Data to the New Document

```
...
public void processNode(Node thisNode,
                        PrintWriter out,
                        Node newParent,
                        Document newDoc,
                        String spacer) {

    if (thisNode.getNodeType() == thisNode.ELEMENT_NODE) {

        Element newElement =
                newDoc.createElement(thisNode.getNodeName());
        newParent.appendChild(newElement);

        NamedNodeMap attributes = thisNode.getAttributes();
```

Listing 6.9—continued

```
42:         if (attributes.getLength() > 0) {
43:             for (int i=0; i < attributes.getLength(); i++) {
44:             Node thisAttr = attributes.item(i);
45:             newElement.setAttribute(thisAttr.getNodeName(),
46:                                     thisAttr.getNodeValue());
47:             }
48:         }
49:
50:         NodeList thisKids = thisNode.getChildNodes();
51:         for (int i=0; i < thisKids.getLength(); i++) {
52:             processNode(thisKids.item(i), out, newElement,
53:                                          newDoc, spacer+"--");
54:         }
55:
56:     } else if (thisNode.getNodeType() == thisNode.TEXT_NODE) {
57:         Node newNode = newDoc.createTextNode(thisNode.getNodeValue());
58:         newParent.appendChild(newNode);
59:     }
60:
61: }
...
```

We had previously added the elements themselves, so all we need to do to complete this copy is to add any attributes or text nodes.

The attributes are added on lines 45 and 46. For each attribute in the original element, we add an identical attribute to the new element. Similarly, we create an identical text node on line 57 and add it to the parent element on line 58.

Now, if we compile and run the servlet, we see a complete copy:

```
<?xml version="1.0" encoding="UTF-8"?>
<orderSystem>
    <orders>
        <order order_id="To1010mC24980190282174342At">
            <order_status>open</order_status>
            <item product_id="RC2342">
                <quantity>5</quantity>
            </item>
        </order>
        <order order_id="To1010mC7161452772864825At">
            <order_status>open</order_status>
            <item product_id="RC2342">
                <quantity>3</quantity>
            </item>
            <item product_id="QA3452">
                <quantity>1</quantity>
            </item>
        </order>
    </orders>
</orderSystem>
```

Adding the Products to the Document

Now that we have a complete copy of the `orders` elements, we need to add the `products` elements as well. We've really done all the hard work already. We just need to start `processNode()` off on the right foot, as in Listing 6.10.

Listing 6.10—Adding `products.xml`

```
...
72:        DOMParser parser = new DOMParser();
73:        parser.parse("/files/orders.xml");
74:        Document orders = parser.getDocument();
75:
76:        Document newDoc = new DocumentImpl();
77:        Element orderSystem = newDoc.createElement("orderSystem");
78:        newDoc.appendChild(orderSystem);
79:
80:        Node orderRoot = orders.getFirstChild();
81:        processNode(orderRoot, out, orderSystem, newDoc, "--");
82:
83:        parser.parse("/files/products.xml");
84:        Document products = parser.getDocument();
85:        Node productRoot = products.getFirstChild();
86:        processNode(productRoot, out, orderSystem, newDoc, "--");
87:
88:        OutputFormat format = new OutputFormat(newDoc, "UTF-8", true);
89:        XMLSerializer output = new XMLSerializer(out, format);
90:        output.serialize(newDoc);
...
```


We've already created the parser on line 72, so we don't need to create it again. Instead, we can just `parse()` the new file on line 83. Just as we did before, we get the `Document` object, then look for the root element on line 85, and process it on line 86.

A problem exists, however. If we compile the servlet and run it, we won't see any change. The `orders` nodes are added properly, but none of the `products` nodes appears.

The reason has to do with line 85. When we were getting the root element for the `orders.xml` file, we could just get the first child. If we look at the products file, however, it's a different story. `products.xml` starts with the following:

```
<?xml version="1.0"?>
<?xml-stylesheet href="catalog.xsl" type="text/xsl"?>
<products>
<vendor webvendor="full">
    <vendor_name>Conners Chair Company</vendor_name>
    <advertisement>
        <ad_sentence>
        Conners Chair Company presents their annual big three
        day only chair sale. We're making way for our new
        stock!  All current inventory must go!    Regular prices
```

```
        slashed by up to 60%!
        </ad_sentence>
    </advertisement>
...
</products>
```

We have to keep in mind that the `Document` is everything, not just the elements we're used to dealing with. So, coming as it does just after the document declaration, the style sheet information is actually the first child of the document object.

As we mentioned before, this is a processing instruction, another kind of node for which we haven't accounted in `processNode()`. We can handle this a number of ways. One is to change line 85 to

```
Node productRoot = products.getDocumentElement();
```

or even

```
Node productRoot = products.getElementsByTagName("products").item(0);
```

That would feed us the root element immediately, but it wouldn't help us if other processing instructions existed elsewhere in the document. So, instead, let's modify `processNode()` to handle this situation, as shown in Listing 6.11.

Listing 6.11—Accounting for Processing Instructions

```
...
public void processNode(Node thisNode,
                        PrintWriter out,
                        Node newParent,
                        Document newDoc,
                        String spacer) {

    if (thisNode.getNodeType() == thisNode.ELEMENT_NODE) {

        Element newElement =
                newDoc.createElement(thisNode.getNodeName());
        newParent.appendChild(newElement);

        NamedNodeMap attributes = thisNode.getAttributes();
        if (attributes.getLength() > 0) {
            for (int i=0; i < attributes.getLength(); i++) {
            Node thisAttr = attributes.item(i);
                newElement.setAttribute(thisAttr.getNodeName(),
                                        thisAttr.getNodeValue());
              }
        }

        NodeList thisKids = thisNode.getChildNodes();
        for (int i=0; i < thisKids.getLength(); i++) {
            processNode(thisKids.item(i), out, newElement,
                                          newDoc, spacer+"--");
        }
```

Listing 6.11—continued

```
55:
56:      } else if (thisNode.getNodeType() ==
57:                          thisNode.TEXT_NODE) {
58:          Node newNode =
59:               newDoc.createTextNode(thisNode.getNodeValue());
60:          newParent.appendChild(newNode);
61:      } else if (thisNode.getNodeType() ==
62:                          thisNode.PROCESSING_INSTRUCTION_NODE) {
63:          Node nextNode = thisNode.getNextSibling();
64:          if (nextNode == null) {
65:              // The document is finished.
66:          } else {
67:              processNode(nextNode, out, newParent, newDoc, spacer);
68:          }
69:      }
70:  }
...
```

We really are just adding one more condition on lines 61 and 62 to check for processing instruction nodes the same way we checked for element nodes, attribute nodes, and text nodes. If we find one, what we really want isn't the node itself, but the next node in line. Keeping with the parent/child theme, this would be the node's sibling. So, to determine the next node to process, we use the `getNextSibling()` function. (To move up the line, we could use `getPreviousSibling()`.)

Of course, if this is the last node in the document, we get an error if we try to process a nonexistent sibling. In that case, `getNextSibling()` returns `null`, so we check for it on line 64.

If a sibling does exist, we need to process it. We must be careful, however, about how we do that with the recursion. Our method signature is

```
public void processNode(Node thisNode, PrintWriter out, Node newParent,
➥Document newDoc, String spacer)
```

Because we didn't process `thisNode` this time around, we didn't move up or down the tree. Therefore, the only one of these parameters that should change is `thisNode`, which should now be the sibling. We make the call on line 67.

Now, if we compile and run the servlet, it adds both documents to `orderSystem`.

Cleaning Up

Before we move on, however, let's do a little cleanup. First, because we aren't displaying the `Document`, we don't need the `spacer` anymore. Second, we did a good thing by moving to the next node if we stumbled across a processing instruction node. Let's modify `processNode()` to do the same for any node we don't want to process directly.

Listing 6.12 is the complete servlet up to this point.

Listing 6.12—ReviewOrder.java to This Point

```
import java.io.*;
import javax.servlet.*;
import javax.servlet.http.*;
import org.apache.xerces.parsers.DOMParser;
import org.w3c.dom.Document;
import org.apache.xerces.dom.DocumentImpl;
import org.w3c.dom.Element;
import org.w3c.dom.Node;
import org.w3c.dom.NodeList;
import org.w3c.dom.NamedNodeMap;
import org.apache.xml.serialize.XMLSerializer;
import org.apache.xml.serialize.OutputFormat;

public class ReviewOrder extends HttpServlet {

  public String getNodeTypeName(int type) {

      String[] nodeTypeNames = { "No node type 0",
                                 "ELEMENT_NODE",
                                 "ATTRIBUTE_NODE",
                                 "TEXT_NODE",
                                 "CDATA_SECTION_NODE",
                                 "ENTITY_REFERENCE_NODE",
                                 "ENTITY_NODE",
                                 "PROCESSING_INSTRUCTION_NODE",
                                 "COMMENT_NODE",
                                 "DOCUMENT_NODE",
                                 "DOCUMENT_TYPE_NODE",
                                 "DOCUMENT_FRAGMENT_NODE",
                                 "NOTATION_NODE" };
      return nodeTypeNames[type];
  }

  public void processNode(Node thisNode,
                          PrintWriter out,
                          Node newParent,
                          Document newDoc) {

      if (thisNode.getNodeType() == thisNode.ELEMENT_NODE) {

          Element newElement =
                  newDoc.createElement(thisNode.getNodeName());
          newParent.appendChild(newElement);

          NamedNodeMap attributes = thisNode.getAttributes();
          if (attributes.getLength() > 0) {
              for (int i=0; i < attributes.getLength(); i++) {
                  Node thisAttr = attributes.item(i);
                  newElement.setAttribute(thisAttr.getNodeName(),
                                          thisAttr.getNodeValue());
```

Listing 6.12—continued

```
              }
        }

        NodeList thisKids = thisNode.getChildNodes();
        for (int i=0; i < thisKids.getLength(); i++) {
            processNode(thisKids.item(i), out, newElement,
                                          newDoc);
        }

    } else if (thisNode.getNodeType() ==
                       thisNode.TEXT_NODE) {
        Node newNode =
             newDoc.createTextNode(thisNode.getNodeValue());
        newParent.appendChild(newNode);
    } else {
        Node nextNode = thisNode.getNextSibling();
        if (nextNode == null) {
            // The document is finished.
        } else {
            processNode(nextNode, out, newParent, newDoc);
        }
    }
}

public void doGet(HttpServletRequest request,
                  HttpServletResponse response)
           throws IOException, ServletException
  {
  response.setContentType("text/html");
  PrintWriter out = response.getWriter();

  try {

      DOMParser parser = new DOMParser();
      parser.parse("/files/orders.xml");
      Document orders = parser.getDocument();

      Document newDoc = new DocumentImpl();
      Element orderSystem = newDoc.createElement("orderSystem");
      newDoc.appendChild(orderSystem);

      Node orderRoot = orders.getFirstChild();
      processNode(orderRoot, out, orderSystem, newDoc);

      parser.parse("/files/products.xml");
      Document products = parser.getDocument();
      Node productRoot = products.getFirstChild();
      processNode(productRoot, out, orderSystem, newDoc);

      OutputFormat format = new OutputFormat(newDoc, "UTF-8", true);
      XMLSerializer output = new XMLSerializer(out, format);
      output.serialize(newDoc);
```

Listing 6.12—continued

```
98:
99:     } catch (org.xml.sax.SAXException SAXe) {
100:        out.print("There was a problem with the source"
101:            + " document.");
102:    } catch (IOException IOe) {
103:        out.print("There was an IO error. Make sure the file"
104:            + " exists and is readable.");
105:    } catch (Exception e) {
106:        out.print("There was an error: "+e.getMessage());
107:    }
108:  }
109:}
```

The changes here aren't too substantial. On line 60, we remove the `if` statement to make this an `else` clause—if all else fails, the method moves on to the next sibling. Otherwise, we just remove the references to the spacer on lines 33, 52, 65, 88, and 93.

Adding Namespaces

Now that we've got all our data added to the document, it's time to segregate it into namespaces so we can work with it.

When it comes to namespaces, an element or attribute can find itself in three possible situations. The first is an *explicit* namespace, in which the namespace is declared and a prefix is used. In a situation such as this, our `orderSystem` document might look like Listing 6.13.

Listing 6.13—Explicit Namespace Declarations

```
<?xml version="1.0" encoding="UTF-8"?>
<orderSystem>
   <ord:orders xmlns:ord="http://www.nicholaschase.com/orders/ ">
       <ord:order order_id="To1010mC24980190282174342At">
           <ord:order_status>open</ord:order_status>
           <ord:item product_id="RC2342">
               <ord:quantity>5</ord:quantity>
           </ord:item>
       </ord:order>
...
       </ord:order>
   </ord:orders>
   <prod:products xmlns:prod="http://www.nicholaschase.com/products/">
       <prod:vendor webvendor="full">
           <prod:vendor_name>Conners Chair Company</prod:vendor_name>
...
   </prod:products>
</orderSystem>
```

In this case, both the prod and ord namespaces are declared within their relevant elements. From there, the prefix is used in each element.

We could also have declared both namespaces within the orderSystem element, as in Listing 6.14.

Listing 6.14—Explicit Namespace Declarations (Redux)

```
<?xml version="1.0" encoding="UTF-8"?>
<orderSystem xmlns:ord="http://www.nicholaschase.com/orders/"
             xmlns:prod="http://www.nicholaschase.com/products/">
    <ord:orders>
        <ord:order order_id="To1010mC24980190282174342At">
            <ord:order_status>open</ord:order_status>
            <ord:item product_id="RC2342">
                <ord:quantity>5</ord:quantity>
            </ord:item>
        </ord:order>
...
        </ord:order>
    </ord:orders>
    <prod:products>
        <prod:vendor webvendor="full">
            <prod:vendor_name>Conners Chair Company</prod:vendor_name>
...
    </prod:products>
</orderSystem>
```

In either of these cases, orders and its children are part of the http://www.nicholaschase.com/orders/ namespace, and products and its children are part of the http://www.nicholaschase.com/products/ namespace. It's important to note that orderSystem itself is not part of any namespace, because it doesn't have a prefix, and no default namespace is declared for it.

The default namespace comes in handy when we have a lot of elements that are part of one namespace and just a few in a second. For instance, (for now) the products element has a lot more information than the orders element, so we can make that the default namespace, as in Listing 6.15.

Listing 6.15—Default Namespaces

```
<?xml version="1.0" encoding="UTF-8"?>
<orderSystem xmlns:ord="http://www.nicholaschase.com/orders/"
             xmlns="http://www.nicholaschase.com/products/">
    <ord:orders>
        <ord:order order_id="To1010mC24980190282174342At">
            <ord:order_status>open</ord:order_status>
            <ord:item product_id="RC2342">
                <ord:quantity>5</ord:quantity>
            </ord:item>
        </ord:order>
...
```

Listing 6.15—continued

```
17:         </ord:order>
18:     </ord:orders>
19:     <products>
20:         <vendor webvendor="full">
21:             <vendor_name>Conners Chair Company</prod:vendor_name>
...
160:    </products>
161:</orderSystem>
```

In this case, on line 1a we define the default namespace by declaring it with no prefix. From there, every element that doesn't have a prefix will be part of this namespace.

Of course, that includes `orderSystem`, which isn't what we want. So, to be more accurate, we can move the default declaration as shown in Listing 6.16.

Listing 6.16—Default Namespaces (Redux)

```
<?xml version="1.0" encoding="UTF-8"?>
<orderSystem xmlns:ord="http://www.nicholaschase.com/orders/">
    <ord:orders>
        <ord:order order_id="To1010mC24980190282174342At">
            <ord:order_status>open</ord:order_status>
            <ord:item product_id="RC2342">
                <ord:quantity>5</ord:quantity>
            </ord:item>
        </ord:order>
...
        </ord:order>
    </ord:orders>
    <products xmlns="http://www.nicholaschase.com/products/">
        <vendor webvendor="full">
            <vendor_name>Conners Chair Company</vendor_name>
...
    </products>
</orderSystem>
```

In this case, the default namespace exists only within the scope of the products element.

`orderSystem`, on the other hand, is not part of any namespace, including the default namespace. That's fine, because we don't really need it, but it's important to remember the distinction.

It becomes even more important when we realize that another group of information exists that is not part of any namespace right now, and it's something we do need: our attributes.

When it comes to namespaces, attributes are handled a little strangely. First of all, attributes are never part of the default namespace. Any attribute that doesn't have a prefix—whether or not its element is any namespace—is in no namespace at all. This means that if we want our products' attributes to be in the same namespaces as their elements, we must use the prefixes, as in Listing 6.17.

Listing 6.17—Explicit Namespace Declarations (Redux)

```
<?xml version="1.0" encoding="UTF-8"?>
<orderSystem xmlns:ord="http://www.nicholaschase.com/orders.html"
             xmlns:prod="http://www.nicholaschase.com/products.html">
    <ord:orders>
        <ord:order ord:order_id="To1010mC24980190282174342At">
            <ord:order_status>open</ord:order_status>
            <ord:item ord:product_id="RC2342">
                <ord:quantity>5</ord:quantity>
            </ord:item>
        </ord:order>
...
    </ord:orders>
    <prod:products>
        <prod:vendor prod:webvendor="full">
            <prod:vendor_name>Conners Chair Company</prod:vendor_name>
...
    </prod:products>
</orderSystem>
```


Now, we need to add this functionality to `ReviewOrder`. In Listing 6.18, we modify `processNode()` to create elements and attributes with namespaces.

Listing 6.18—`ReviewOrder.java`: Adding Namespaces to Elements and Attributes

```
...
import org.w3c.dom.Element;
import org.w3c.dom.Node;
import org.w3c.dom.NodeList;
import org.w3c.dom.NamedNodeMap;
import org.w3c.dom.Attr;
...
 public void processNode(Node thisNode,
                         PrintWriter out,
                         Node newParent,
                         DocumentImpl newDoc,
                         String namespaceURI,
                         String ns) {

    if (thisNode.getNodeType() == thisNode.ELEMENT_NODE) {

        Element newElement =
                newDoc.createElementNS(namespaceURI,
                                       ns+thisNode.getNodeName());
        newParent.appendChild(newElement);

        NamedNodeMap attributes = thisNode.getAttributes();
        if (attributes.getLength() > 0) {
            for (int i=0; i < attributes.getLength(); i++) {
```

Listing 6.18—continued

```
                Node thisAttr = attributes.item(i);
                Attr thisAttrObj =
                    newDoc.createAttributeNS(namespaceURI,
                              ns+thisAttr.getNodeName());
                thisAttrObj.setValue(thisAttr.getNodeValue());
                newElement.setAttributeNode(thisAttrObj);
            }
        }

        NodeList thisKids = thisNode.getChildNodes();
        for (int i=0; i < thisKids.getLength(); i++) {
            processNode(thisKids.item(i), out, newElement,
                                  newDoc, namespaceURI, ns);
        }

    } else if (thisNode.getNodeType() ==
                     thisNode.TEXT_NODE) {
        Node newNode =
             newDoc.createTextNode(thisNode.getNodeValue());
        newParent.appendChild(newNode);
    } else {
        Node nextNode = thisNode.getNextSibling();
        if (nextNode == null) {
            // The document is finished.
        } else {
            processNode(nextNode, out, newParent, newDoc,
                                   namespaceURI, ns);
        }
    }
}

...
         Document orders = parser.getDocument();

         DocumentImpl newDoc = new DocumentImpl();
         Element orderSystem = newDoc.createElement("orderSystem");
         newDoc.appendChild(orderSystem);

        Node orderRoot = orders.getFirstChild();
        processNode(orderRoot, out, orderSystem, newDoc,
              "http://www.nicholaschase.com/orders/", "ord:");

        parser.parse("/files/products.xml");
        Document products = parser.getDocument();
        Node productRoot = products.getFirstChild();
        processNode(productRoot, out, orderSystem, newDoc,
              "http://www.nicholaschase.com/products/", "prod:");

        OutputFormat format = new OutputFormat(newDoc, "UTF-8", true);
        XMLSerializer output = new XMLSerializer(out, format);
...
```

The first thing we do is to add the namespace and the prefix to the signature of `processNode()`, on lines 34 and 35. `processNode()` just sees them as strings to be added to the elements, even though we know there is something special about them.

We actually add these parameters to the method call on lines 97 and 103. Notice that we haven't concerned ourselves very much about which URIs we use, as long as they're unique. There's nothing special about the URI.

Moving back into `processNode()`, we want to do two things: add namespace information to the elements, and add namespace information to the attributes.

For the elements, we change our `createElement()` call to `createElementNS()`. In doing that, we add both the namespace and the prefix to the call. This, in turn, adds the prefix to our output.

We must consider one more thing, however. The `createElementNS()` method is not implemented in `Document`; it's implemented in `DocumentImpl`. Therefore, we must ensure that `newDoc` is a `DocumentImpl`. We take care of that by changing the parameter declaration on line 33.

Finally, to accommodate our attributes, we made some changes on lines 48 through 52. On lines 48 through 50, we use the `DocumentImpl` object to create a new attribute with a namespace, just as we did with the element. Whereas before, when we created the attribute it was complete—it had a value and was already attached to an element—this is just a blank attribute with a name and no value. So, on line 51, we give it a value, and then on line 52, we add the attribute node to our new element.

Finally, on lines 58, 59, 72, and 73, we carry the namespace information through to the next level of the tree.

If we compile the servlet and try to run it with Internet Explorer, we get an error, as in Figure 6.3.

If we take a look at the source, we find that something is missing:

```
<?xml version="1.0" encoding="UTF-8"?>
<orderSystem>
    <ord:orders>
        <ord:order ord:order_id="To1010mC24980190282174342At">
            <ord:order_status>open</ord:order_status>
            <ord:item ord:product_id="RC2342">
                <ord:quantity>5</ord:quantity>
            </ord:item>
        </ord:order>
        <ord:order ord:order_id="To1010mC7161452772864825At">
            <ord:order_status>open</ord:order_status>
            <ord:item ord:product_id="RC2342">
                <ord:quantity>3</ord:quantity>
            </ord:item>
            <ord:item ord:product_id="QA3452">
```

```
                <ord:quantity>1</ord:quantity>
            </ord:item>
        </ord:order>
    </ord:orders>
    <prod:products>
        <prod:vendor prod:webvendor="full">
              <prod:vendor_name>Conners Chair </prod:vendor_name>
              <prod:advertisement>
                    <prod:ad_sentence>   Conners Chair Company presents
                    their annual big three day only chair sale.
                    We&apos;re making way for our new stock!  All
                    current inventory must go! Regular prices    slashed
                    by up to 60%!   </prod:ad_sentence>
            </prod:advertisement>
...
</orderSystem>
```

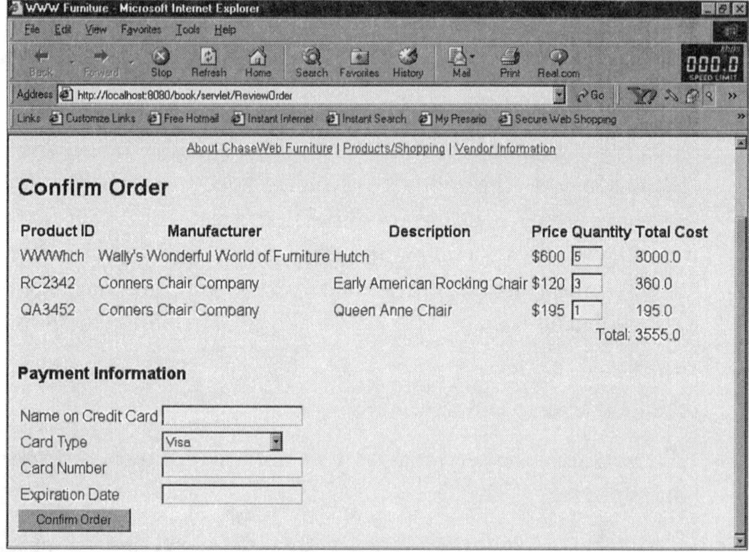

Figure 6.3

The servlet doesn't provide the complete solution yet.

The source might not be available in IE because of the error.

Although the prefixes have been added to each element, the namespaces themselves have not, which asks the question: Why ask for the namespace in, say, `createElementNS()` if it's not going to be used?

Well, even though the prefix is what's immediately obvious in most elements, it's NOT the namespace, but rather an alias for the namespace. The application needs to know what namespace holds the element for other tasks.

EXCURSION

Why Prefixes?

If the namespace URI is the important part, why not use it instead of prefixes? The reason has to do with naming constraints. A URI has characters, such as the colon and slash, which are reserved and can't be used in an element name. Because the prefix becomes part of the name, another solution had to be found, and prefixes fit the bill. Besides, they are certainly much more convenient to use!

So, how do we get the namespace information into the document? Fortunately for us, it's just an attribute—admittedly an important one. Because we don't want to be declaring each namespace repeatedly, we can put the information into the `orderSystem` element, and it will carry through to all our elements. We do this in Listing 6.19.

Listing 6.19—`ReviewOrder.java`: Adding the Namespace Information to `orderSystem`

```
...
        DOMParser parser = new DOMParser();
        parser.parse("/files/orders.xml");
        Document orders = parser.getDocument();

        DocumentImpl newDoc = new DocumentImpl();
        Element orderSystem = newDoc.createElement("orderSystem");
        orderSystem.setAttribute("xmlns:ord",
                          "http://www.nicholaschase.com/orders/");
        orderSystem.setAttribute("xmlns:prod",
                          "http://www.nicholaschase.com/products/");
        newDoc.appendChild(orderSystem);

        Node orderRoot = orders.getFirstChild();
         processNode(orderRoot, out, orderSystem, newDoc,
              "http://www.nicholaschase.com/orders/", "ord:");
...
```

Now we can compile and run the servlet successfully, with the following source code:

```
<?xml version="1.0" encoding="UTF-8"?>
<orderSystem xmlns:ord="http://www.nicholaschase.com/orders/"
          xmlns:prod="http://www.nicholaschase.com/products/">
    <ord:orders>
        <ord:order ord:order_id="To1010mC24980190282174342At">
            <ord:order_status>open</ord:order_status>
            <ord:item ord:product_id="RC2342">
                <ord:quantity>5</ord:quantity>
            </ord:item>
...
```

Retrieving Namespace Information

Now that we've added namespace information to our elements, at some point we might want to get it back out again. Xerces provides for this possibility with the `NamespaceSupport` object. For example, we can analyze `orderSystem` and its two children, `ord:orders` and `prod:products`, with the code in Listing 6.20.

Listing 6.20—`ReviewOrder.java`: Retrieving Namespace Information

```
...
import org.w3c.dom.Element;
import org.w3c.dom.Node;
import org.w3c.dom.NodeList;
import org.w3c.dom.NamedNodeMap;
import org.w3c.dom.Attr;
import org.xml.sax.helpers.NamespaceSupport;
...
                processNode(nextNode, out, newParent, newDoc,
                                        namespaceURI, ns);
            }
        }
    }

    public void showNamespace(NamespaceSupport ns,
                             Node thisNode, PrintWriter out) {
        String nameParts[] = {"namespaceURI", "element name", "raw name"};
        ns.processName(thisNode.getNodeName(), nameParts, false);
        out.print(nameParts[1] + ": " + nameParts[0] + "<br />");
    }

    public void doGet(HttpServletRequest request,
...
//        OutputFormat format = new OutputFormat(newDoc, "UTF-8", true);
//        XMLSerializer output = new XMLSerializer(out, format);
//        output.serialize(newDoc);

          NamespaceSupport ns = new NamespaceSupport();
          ns.pushContext();
          ns.declarePrefix("", "http://www.w3.org/1999/xhtml");
          ns.declarePrefix("prod",
                    "http://www.nicholaschase.com/products/");
          ns.declarePrefix("ord",
                    "http://www.nicholaschase.com/orders/");

          showNamespace(ns, orderSystem, out);
          NodeList orderSystemKids = orderSystem.getChildNodes();
          for (int i=0; i < orderSystemKids.getLength(); i++) {
                showNamespace(ns, orderSystemKids.item(i), out);
          }

      ns.popContext();

```

Listing 6.20—continued

```
136:    } catch (org.xml.sax.SAXException SAXe) {
137:        out.print("There was a problem with the source"
...
```

We output some text other than the serialized document, so to prevent errors, we must comment that out on lines 116 through 118. After creating the `NamespaceSupport` object on line 120, we set the context on line 121. This is very important because namespaces have scope. For instance, if suites were in a namespace different from products, we could redefine the meaning of the `prod:` prefix on the suite element. In that case, when we got to the suite element, we could push a new context. This terminology comes from stacks, where we push an object on the top, and then when we're done, we pop it off again. Similarly, when we are done with the suite element, we could pop the context, as on line 134, to go back to the previous context.

In this case, however, we have only one context. On lines 122 through 126, we declare three namespaces: one default and two explicitly. On lines 128 through 132, we display the namespace information for `orderSystem` and its two children, `orders` and `products`; then, we clear the `NamespaceSupport` object on line 134.

The `showNamespace()` method on lines 78 through 83 is pretty straightforward. On line 80, we create the array into which we will insert the information from the `NamespaceObject`. The array will have three pieces of data in it—all of them strings—and we need to initialize it before we can use it.

Line 81 is actually doing the work. It takes the name of the node (which is the raw name) and looks for a prefix. If it finds one, it compares it to the declared prefixes to get a namespace URI, which we print on line 82.

The results of saving and running this servlet are as follows, with the output of the final `document` being replaced by information on the namespaces of our three main nodes:

```
orderSystem: http://www.w3.org/1999/xhtml
orders: http://www.nicholaschase.com/orders/
products: http://www.nicholaschase.com/products/
```

Notice that because we declare a default namespace on line 122, the servlet knows where to put `orderSystem`, which doesn't have a prefix. Without that declaration, the `namespaceURI` would simply be blank.

If you've previously displayed the XML file, you might need to quit IE and restart it to display this page. Otherwise, IE believes it's still XML—badly written XML.

Because we don't really need this functionality to review the order, we'll return the servlet to its original state.

Creating the Review Page

Now that we've gotten our document together, we can finally put together our order review page. To do this, we need to process our document through two different style sheets. The first is to gather the data, which we'll then massage slightly. The second is to format the results.

The trick is creating a style sheet that relates data from our two namespaces together.

Ultimately, we're looking for a page similar to Figure 6.4.

Figure 6.4

The completed review page is shown here.

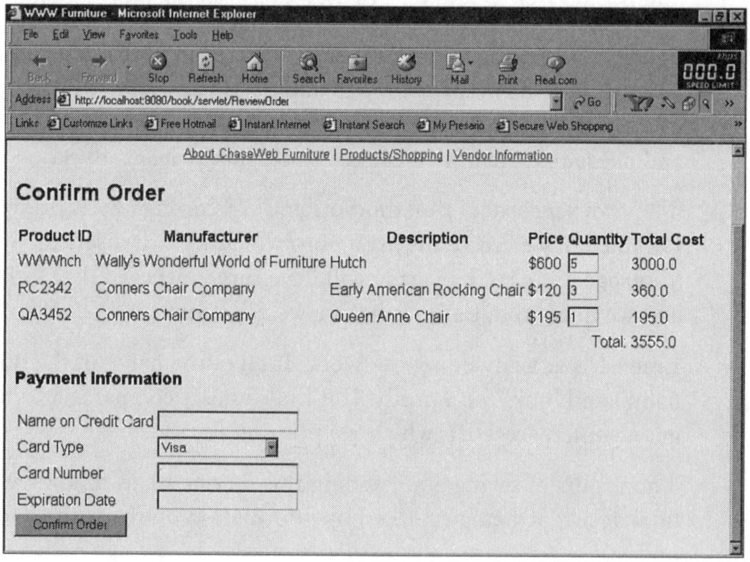

Let's start by setting up a simple style sheet to make sure everything's working properly. First, we set up the servlet to display the results, as shown in Listing 6.21.

Listing 6.21—`ReviewOrder.java`: Outputting to the Style Sheet

```
...
import org.apache.xml.serialize.OutputFormat;
import javax.xml.transform.TransformerFactory;
import javax.xml.transform.Transformer;
import javax.xml.transform.dom.DOMSource;
import javax.xml.transform.stream.StreamSource;
import javax.xml.transform.stream.StreamResult;

public class ReviewOrder extends HttpServlet {
...
```

Listing 6.21—continued

```
107:        processNode(productRoot, out, orderSystem, newDoc,
108:              "http://www.nicholaschase.com/products/", "prod:");
109:
110:        TransformerFactory transFactory =
111:                 TransformerFactory.newInstance();
112:        Transformer transformer = transFactory.newTransformer(
113:                              new StreamSource("/files/ReviewOrder.xsl"));
114:        transformer.transform(new DOMSource(orderSystem),
115:                                                new StreamResult(out));
116:
117:    } catch (org.xml.sax.SAXException SAXe) {
118:        out.print("There was a problem with the source"
...
```

This time we've completely removed the serialization because we won't need it anymore. Instead, on lines 110 through 115 we do the same thing we've been doing all along, in converting our output using a style sheet.

Now, we're ready to put together the style sheet. Let's start with something simple just to make sure everything is working. In Listing 6.22, we just output the `product_ids` we'll be working with.

Listing 6.22—`ReviewOrder.xsl`: Outputting the `product_ids`

```
0: <?xml version="1.0"?>
1: <xsl:stylesheet version="1.0"
2:      xmlns:xsl="http://www.w3.org/1999/XSL/Transform"
3:      xmlns:prod="http://www.nicholaschase.com/products/"
4:      xmlns:ord="http://www.nicholaschase.com/orders/">
5:
6: <xsl:template match="text()">
7:     <xsl:apply-templates />
8: </xsl:template>
9:
10:<xsl:template match="item">
11:    <xsl:value-of select="@product_id" />
12:    <br />
13:</xsl:template>
14:
15:</xsl:stylesheet>
```

The first thing to notice about this style sheet is that we've gone ahead and declared our namespaces in the top-level element, `xsl:stylesheet`. If we didn't, we'd get errors in trying to process our document because the XSL processor wouldn't know what to do with the prefixes.

On lines 6 through 8, we have a simple template to send our text nodes off for processing. (This also prevents them from just being displayed at the bottom of the document if we don't have a template dealing with them.)

Finally, on lines 10 through 13, we do the real work—finding the order items and displaying the `product_id` attribute. Notice that we have included the prefix.

Now, if we were to compile the servlet and call it with the browser, we wouldn't get an error, but we wouldn't see any results, either. The reason is that we left out the prefixes. The element item is a different animal from the element `ord:item`. In Listing 6.23, we complete the first part of the puzzle.

Listing 6.23—`ReviewOrder.xsl`: Outputting the `product_ids`

```
0: <?xml version="1.0"?>
1: <xsl:stylesheet version="1.0"
2:       xmlns:xsl="http://www.w3.org/1999/XSL/Transform"
3:       xmlns:prod="http://www.nicholaschase.com/products/"
4:       xmlns:ord="http://www.nicholaschase.com/orders/">
5:
6: <xsl:template match="text()">
7:      <xsl:apply-templates />
8: </xsl:template>
9:
10:<xsl:template match="ord:item">
11:     <xsl:value-of select="@ord:product_id" />
12:     <br />
13:</xsl:template>
14:
15:</xsl:stylesheet>
```

Now, if we reload the page, we see the three `product_ids` in our sample `orders.xml` file.

The next step is simple. We need the quantity displayed; we add that in Listing 6.24.

Listing 6.24—`ReviewOrder.xsl`: Adding the Quantity

```
...
10:<xsl:template match="ord:item">
11:     <xsl:value-of select="@ord:product_id" />
12:     <br />
13:     <xsl:value-of select="ord:quantity" />
14:     <br />
15:     <hr />
16:</xsl:template>
...
```

There's nothing special about line 13. We simply retrieve the `quantity` element, which is a child of `item`. We also add another line break and a horizontal rule between items, just to make things a little more readable.

Now things get interesting. What we want now is the `vendor_name` for the product that has the `product_id` in question. Our challenge is to feed that `product_id` to the expression somehow. Back in Chapter 4, "Getting Serious: XSL Processors and

Server-Side Processing," we used a parameter passed into the style sheet from the servlet, but that won't do us any good here because it needs to change with each item.

To accomplish this, we must do something similar, as in Listing 6.25.

Listing 6.25—`ReviewOrder.xsl`: Using `call-template` to Change Parameters

```
...
10:<xsl:template match="ord:item">
11:    <xsl:value-of select="@ord:product_id" />
12:    <br />
13:    <xsl:value-of select="ord:quantity" />
14:    <br />
15:    <xsl:call-template name="vendor_name">
16:        <xsl:with-param name="vProduct_id">
17:            <xsl:value-of select="@ord:product_id" />
18:        </xsl:with-param>
19:    </xsl:call-template>
20:    <br />
21:    <hr />
22:</xsl:template>
23:
24:<xsl:template name="vendor_name">
25:    <xsl:param name="vProduct_id"></xsl:param>
26:    <xsl:value-of select="//prod:vendor[self::node()
➥//prod:product_id=$vProduct_id]/prod:vendor_name" />
27:</xsl:template>
28:
29:</xsl:stylesheet>
```

On lines 24 through 27, we create a special template. Notice that it has no match attribute; instead it has a name, so we can call it directly. When it is called, we've defined a parameter, `vProduct_id`, on line 25. This parameter exists only in the scope of this template.

It's used on line 26, when we select the data.

Let's take that select one step at a time. Starting at the right, we look for a `vendor_name`. That `vendor_name` must have a parent that is not only a `vendor`, but a `vendor` that satisfies the expressions in the brackets.

Let's look at that expression: `self::node()`. We've already seen that expression—it's the context node, so wherever you go, there you are. This node must have a descendant (not necessarily a direct child, but a descendant) that is a `product_id` and has a value equal to the `vProduct_id` parameter.

But where does that value come from? We've defined it, but we didn't even give it a real value.

That actually happens on lines 15 through 19. First, we tell the processor that we want to use our new template, `vendor_name`, and then we specify a value for its parameter, `vProduct_id`. That value should be equal to the `product_id` attribute, so that's what we specify on line 17. Note that this is the `product_id` attribute for the item we happen to be dealing with at the moment.

So, if we were to refresh the page, for every item, the processor would look for a `vendor_name` that satisfies our conditions and then print it. The results look similar to Figure 6.5.

Figure 6.5

Now we can do a search between data sets.

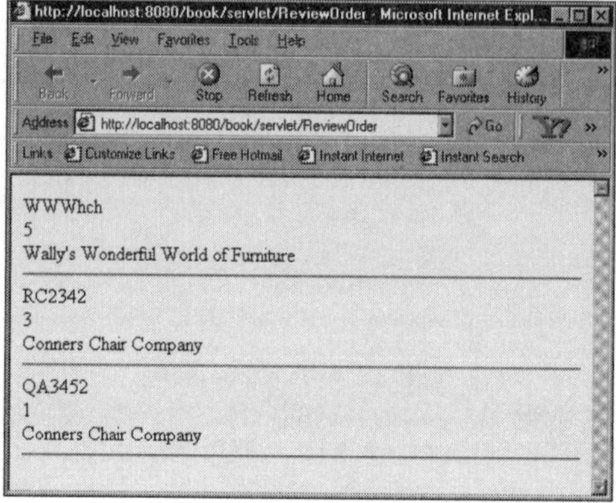

The next step is to gather the `short_desc` of the item. We can use a similar technique, shown in Listing 6.26.

Listing 6.26—`ReviewOrder.xsl`: Adding the `short_desc`

```
...
17:             <xsl:value-of select="@ord:product_id" />
18:         </xsl:with-param>
19:     </xsl:call-template>
20:     <br />
21:     <xsl:call-template name="short_desc">
22:         <xsl:with-param name="vProduct_id">
23:             <xsl:value-of select="@ord:product_id" />
24:         </xsl:with-param>
25:     </xsl:call-template>
26:     <br />
27:     <hr />
28:</xsl:template>
29:
30:<xsl:template name="vendor_name">
31:     <xsl:param name="vProduct_id"></xsl:param>
32:     <xsl:value-of select="//prod:vendor[self::node()
➥//prod:product_id=$vProduct_id]/prod:vendor_name" />
33:</xsl:template>
34:
```

Listing 6.26—continued

```
35:<xsl:template name="short_desc">
36:     <xsl:param name="vProduct_id"></xsl:param>
37:     <xsl:value-of select="//prod:short_desc
➥[preceding-sibling::prod:product_id=$vProduct_id]" />
38:</xsl:template>
39:
40:</xsl:stylesheet>
```

Lines 21 through 25 are the same as for `vendor_name`, and lines 35 through 38 are the same except for the expression on line 37.

Let's take it from the top. We look for a `prod:short_desc` element that's anywhere in the document, but it must satisfy the expression in brackets.

`Preceding-sibling::prod:product_id` signifies any sibling of `prod:short_desc` that comes earlier in the document, as long as it's a `prod:product_id` element. It also must be equal to the `product_id` with which we're working.

We're almost there! Now we need the price. We use the same technique, changing only the expression of what we're looking for in Listing 6.27.

Listing 6.27—Adding the Price

```
...
            </xsl:with-param>
        </xsl:call-template>
        <br />
        <xsl:call-template name="price">
            <xsl:with-param name="vProduct_id">
                <xsl:value-of select="@ord:product_id" />
            </xsl:with-param>
        </xsl:call-template>
        <br />
        <hr />
</xsl:template>

...
        <xsl:value-of select="//prod:short_desc
➥[preceding-sibling::prod:product_id=$vProduct_id]" />
</xsl:template>

<xsl:template name="price">
        <xsl:param name="vProduct_id"></xsl:param>
        <xsl:value-of select="//prod:price
➥[preceding-sibling::prod:product_id=$vProduct_id and
 ➥attribute::prod:pricetype='retail']" />
</xsl:template>

</xsl:stylesheet>
```

Again, the important part here is on line 48, where we determine which node to grab. In this case, we want any `prod:price` in the document that meets our criteria, which are twofold.

First, we need to ensure that we're in the correct product, which we do with the same `preceding-sibling` expression we used for the description. At that point, we need to narrow it down to only `prod:price` elements that have a `prod:pricetype` attribute with a value of `retail`.

When we're done with this, we'll have output similar to Figure 6.6.

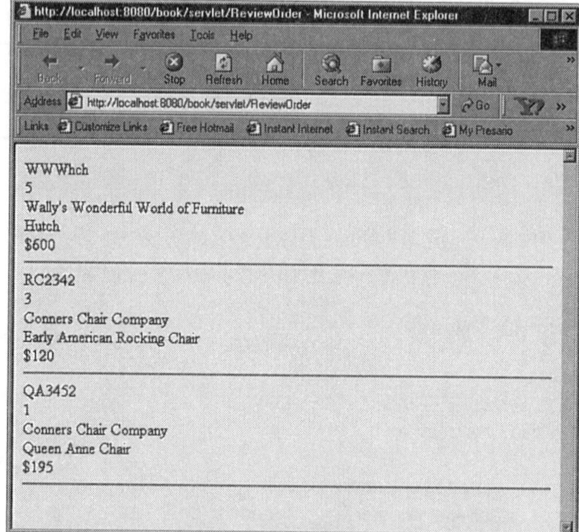

Figure 6.6

This shows how to retrieve order data.

Working with the Results of the Transformation

Now that we've retrieved the information, we still need to massage it. We need to add extended prices based on quantity for each item, as well as a final total price. To do that, we must get the results of the first transformation as a document, instead of just the output text. Therefore, we need to make some changes to both the servlet and the style sheet. Listing 6.28 shows the changes to `ReviewOrder.java`.

Listing 6.28—`ReviewOrder.java`: Outputting the Temporary Document

```
...
        Node productRoot = products.getFirstChild();
        processNode(productRoot, out, orderSystem, newDoc,
              "http://www.nicholaschase.com/products/", "prod:");

        TransformerFactory transFactory =
                 TransformerFactory.newInstance();
        Transformer transformer = transFactory.newTransformer(
                           new StreamSource("/files/ReviewOrder.xsl"));
```

Listing 6.28—continued

```
114:
115:        DOMResult domResult = new DOMResult();
116:
117:        transformer.transform(new DOMSource(orderSystem), domResult);
119:
120:        Document tempDoc = new DocumentImpl();
121:        tempDoc = (Document)domResult.getNode();
122:
123:        OutputFormat format = new OutputFormat(tempDoc, "UTF-8", true);
124:        XMLSerializer output = new XMLSerializer(out, format);
125:        output.serialize(tempDoc);
126:
127:    } catch (org.xml.sax.SAXException SAXe) {
128:        out.print("There was a problem with the source"
...
```

First, we're not outputting the results of the transformation to a stream anymore. Instead, we want a DOM object, so on line 115, we create the `DOMResult` that we output to on line 117.

Next, we're ready to create the temporary `Document` on line 120. Remember, we can't instantiate a `Document` directly because it's an interface. On line 121, we extract the `Document` from the result. Because this actually comes to us as a `Node`, we need to case it as a `Document`.

Lines 123 through 125 should look familiar because they're the same lines we deleted a few steps back. This time, we output `tempDoc`.

Now that we have a `Document` to output, let's look at the changes to `ReviewOrder.xsl` in Listing 6.29.

Listing 6.29—Adapting `ReviewOrder.xsl` to Output a Document

```
<?xml version="1.0"?>
<xsl:stylesheet version="1.0"
      xmlns:xsl="http://www.w3.org/1999/XSL/Transform"
        xmlns:prod="http://www.nicholaschase.com/products/"
        xmlns:ord="http://www.nicholaschase.com/orders/">

<xsl:template match="/">
    <tempDoc>
        <xsl:apply-templates />
    </tempDoc>
</xsl:template>

<xsl:template match="text()">
    <xsl:apply-templates />
</xsl:template>

<xsl:template match="ord:item">
```

Listing 6.29—continued

```
17:     <xsl:copy-of select="@ord:product_id" />
18:     <xsl:copy-of select="ord:quantity" />
19:     <xsl:call-template name="vendor_name">
20:         <xsl:with-param name="vProduct_id">
21:             <xsl:value-of select="@ord:product_id" />
22:         </xsl:with-param>
23:     </xsl:call-template>
24:     <xsl:call-template name="short_desc">
25:         <xsl:with-param name="vProduct_id">
26:             <xsl:value-of select="@ord:product_id" />
27:         </xsl:with-param>
28:     </xsl:call-template>
29:     <xsl:call-template name="price">
30:         <xsl:with-param name="vProduct_id">
31:             <xsl:value-of select="@ord:product_id" />
32:         </xsl:with-param>
33:     </xsl:call-template>
34:</xsl:template>
35:
36:<xsl:template name="vendor_name">
37:     <xsl:param name="vProduct_id"></xsl:param>
38:     <xsl:copy-of select="//prod:vendor[self::node()//
➥prod:product_id=$vProduct_id]/prod:vendor_name" />
39:</xsl:template>
40:
41:<xsl:template name="short_desc">
42:     <xsl:param name="vProduct_id"></xsl:param>
43:     <xsl:copy-of select="//prod:short_desc[preceding-sibling::
➥prod:product_id=$vProduct_id]" />
44:</xsl:template>
45:
46:<xsl:template name="price">
47:     <xsl:param name="vProduct_id"></xsl:param>
48:     <xsl:copy-of select="//prod:price[preceding-sibling::
➥prod:product_id=$vProduct_id and attribute::prod:pricetype='retail']" />
49:</xsl:template>
50:
51:</xsl:stylesheet>
```

You should notice a few things here. First, on lines 6 through 10, we create a root element for our new document. All our upcoming elements will be descendants of this root.

Next, everywhere we actually output content, we've changed `value-of` to `copy-of`. This is because we want an actual copy of the element, not just the string that represents the content. Where we send parameters, however, we've left it as `value-of`. In that case, we DO want just the string, because we're dropping it into an expression.

We've also removed all those break tags because we don't need them anymore. If we compile and run the servlet, the results look similar to Listing 6.30.

Listing 6.30—Our Results, As Serialized in `tempDoc`

```
<?xml version="1.0" encoding="UTF-8"?>
<tempDoc ord:product_id="WWWhch"
    xmlns:ord="http://www.nicholaschase.com/orders/"
➥xmlns:prod="http://www.nicholaschase.com/products/">
    <ord:quantity xmlns:prod="http://www.nicholaschase.com/products/">5
➥</ord:quantity>
    <prod:vendor_name
        xmlns:prod="http://www.nicholaschase.com/products/">
        Wally&apos;s Wonderful World of Furniture  </prod:vendor_name>
    <prod:short_desc xmlns:prod="http://www.nicholaschase.com/products/">Hutch
➥</prod:short_desc>
    <prod:price prod:pricetype="retail"
➥xmlns:prod="http://www.nicholaschase.com/products/">$600</prod:price>
    <ord:quantity ord:product_id="RC2342"
➥xmlns:prod="http://www.nicholaschase.com/products/">3</ord:quantity>
    <prod:vendor_name
        xmlns:prod="http://www.nicholaschase.com/products/">Conners
        Chair Company</prod:vendor_name>
    <prod:short_desc
        xmlns:prod="http://www.nicholaschase.com/products/">Early
        American Rocking Chair</prod:short_desc>
    <prod:price prod:pricetype="retail"
➥xmlns:prod="http://www.nicholaschase.com/products/">$120</prod:price>
    <ord:quantity ord:product_id="QA3452"
➥xmlns:prod="http://www.nicholaschase.com/products/">1</ord:quantity>
    <prod:vendor_name
        xmlns:prod="http://www.nicholaschase.com/products/">Conners
        Chair Company</prod:vendor_name>
    <prod:short_desc
        xmlns:prod="http://www.nicholaschase.com/products/">Queen Anne Chair
➥</prod:short_desc>
    <prod:price prod:pricetype="retail"
➥xmlns:prod="http://www.nicholaschase.com/products/">$195</prod:price>
</tempDoc>
```

Now, this is close, but it still looks a little funny.

Notice the fact that Xalan puts the namespace declarations in every element, underscoring the fact that different applications handle these things differently.

Much more important than that, however, is the fact that the `product_id` isn't being handled properly. It's just being absorbed by whichever element begins before it. That's because it's an attribute before we copy it, so it's an attribute after we copy it. To bring it out on its own, we need to give it its own element, as in Listing 6.31.

Listing 6.31—`ReviewOrder.xsl`: Making `product_id` and Item Elements

```
...
    <xsl:apply-templates />
</xsl:template>

```

Listing 6.31—continued

```
16:<xsl:template match="ord:item">
17:    <xsl:element name="ord:item">
18:        <xsl:element name="ord:product_id">
19:            <xsl:value-of select="@ord:product_id" />
20:        </xsl:element>
21:        <xsl:copy-of select="ord:quantity" />
22:        <xsl:call-template name="vendor_name">
...
35:            </xsl:with-param>
36:        </xsl:call-template>
37:    </xsl:element>
38:</xsl:template>
...
```

The changes here are straightforward. Because we're sticking with the prefixes on all our other elements, we keep it in the name we give to the new element on lines 18 and 20. On line 19, we change it back to `value-of` because now that we are setting the content for an element, we do want the string.

We also group each item into its own element on lines 17 and 37, but because we want actual elements, we've left the rest of our elements as `copy-of`.

The results look like Listing 6.32.

Listing 6.32—The Changes to Our Results

```
<?xml version="1.0" encoding="UTF-8"?>
<tempDoc xmlns:ord="http://www.nicholaschase.com/orders/"
xmlns:prod="http://www.nicholaschase.com/products/">
    <ord:item>
        <ord:product_id>WWWhch</ord:product_id>
        <ord:quantity xmlns:prod="http://www.nicholaschase.com/products/">5
➥</ord:quantity>
        <prod:vendor_name
            xmlns:prod="http://www.nicholaschase.com/products/">
            Wally&apos;s Wonderful World of Furniture  </prod:vendor_name>
        <prod:short_desc xmlns:prod="http://www.nicholaschase.com/products/">
➥Hutch</prod:short_desc>
        <prod:price prod:pricetype="retail"
xmlns:prod="http://www.nicholaschase.com/products/">$600</prod:price>
    </ord:item>
    <ord:item>
        <ord:product_id>RC2342</ord:product_id>
        <ord:quantity xmlns:prod="http://www.nicholaschase.com/products/">3
➥</ord:quantity>
        <prod:vendor_name
            xmlns:prod="http://www.nicholaschase.com/products/">Conners
            Chair Company</prod:vendor_name>
        <prod:short_desc
            xmlns:prod="http://www.nicholaschase.com/products/">Early
            American Rocking Chair</prod:short_desc>
```

Listing 6.32—continued

```
        <prod:price prod:pricetype="retail"
➥xmlns:prod="http://www.nicholaschase.com/products/">$120</prod:price>
    </ord:item>
    <ord:item>
        <ord:product_id>QA3452</ord:product_id>
        <ord:quantity xmlns:prod="http://www.nicholaschase.com/products/">1
➥</ord:quantity>
        <prod:vendor_name
            xmlns:prod="http://www.nicholaschase.com/products/">Conners
            Chair Company</prod:vendor_name>
        <prod:short_desc
            xmlns:prod="http://www.nicholaschase.com/products/">Queen
            Anne Chair</prod:short_desc>
        <prod:price prod:pricetype="retail"
➥xmlns:prod="http://www.nicholaschase.com/products/">$195</prod:price>
    </ord:item>
</tempDoc>
```

Working with Our Temporary Document

Now that we have the document, we need to add the extended price and totals to it. Let's start by pulling out the price and quantity information in Listing 6.33.

Listing 6.33—Retrieving Price and Quantity Information

```
...
import org.apache.xerces.dom.ElementImpl;
...

        ElementImpl tempDocRoot = (ElementImpl)tempDoc.getFirstChild();
        NodeList items = tempDocRoot.getElementsByTagName("ord:item");
        for (int i=0; i < items.getLength(); i++) {
            ElementImpl thisItem = (ElementImpl)items.item(i);

            NodeList quantityNodeList =
➥                   thisItem.getElementsByTagName("ord:quantity");
            Node quantityNode = quantityNodeList.item(0).getFirstChild();
            out.print("<br />Quantity="+quantityNode.getNodeValue());

            NodeList priceNodeList =
➥                   thisItem.getElementsByTagName("prod:price");
            Node priceNode = priceNodeList.item(0).getFirstChild();
            out.print("<br />Price="+priceNode.getNodeValue());
        }

        out.print("<br />");

//          OutputFormat format = new OutputFormat(newDoc, "UTF-8", true);
//          XMLSerializer output = new XMLSerializer(out, format);
//          output.serialize(tempDoc);
```

Listing 6.33—continued

```
142:
143:     } catch (org.xml.sax.SAXException SAXe) {
...
```

We will use a method from `ElementImpl` (`getElementsByTagName()`), so instead of creating a node like we normally do, on line 123 we create the `tempDocRoot` object as an `ElementImpl`. On line 124, we use `getElementsByTagName()` to specifically retrieve the `ord:item` elements. Strictly speaking, we could have used `getChildNodes()` instead, but we've achieved the same result.

On lines 125 through 135, we loop through each item, retrieve the `prod:price` and `ord:quantity` elements, and then print their values to the page.

We've also temporarily commented out the section that prints the entire document because we're not ready for that yet. The output should look something like this:

```
Quantity=5
Price=$600
Quantity=3
Price=$120
Quantity=1
Price=$195
```

The next step is to figure the extended cost for each item and quantity. In Listing 6.34, we convert our strings to numbers and do the multiplication.

Listing 6.34—Figuring Extended Costs

```
121:         processor.process(XMLFile, XSLSheet, XMLResult);
122:
123:         float totalCost = 0;
124:         float itemCost = 0;
125:         ElementImpl tempDocRoot = (ElementImpl)tempDoc.getFirstChild();
126:         NodeList items = tempDocRoot.getElementsByTagName("ord:item");
127:         for (int i=0; i < items.getLength(); i++) {
128:             ElementImpl thisItem = (ElementImpl)items.item(i);
129:
130:             NodeList quantityNodeList =
➥                        thisItem.getElementsByTagName("ord:quantity");
131:             Node quantityNode = quantityNodeList.item(0).getFirstChild();
132:             int quantity = Integer.parseInt(quantityNode.getNodeValue());
133:
134:             NodeList priceNodeList =
➥                        thisItem.getElementsByTagName("prod:price");
135:             Node priceNode = priceNodeList.item(0).getFirstChild();
136:             String priceString = priceNode.getNodeValue().substring(1);
137:             float price = Float.valueOf(priceString).floatValue();
138:
139:             itemCost = quantity * price;
140:             out.print("<br />itemCost = "+itemCost);
141:
```

Listing 6.34—continued

```
142:         }
143:
144:         out.print("<br />");
...
```

On lines 123 and 124, we initialize variables we will need later. On line 132, we use the same technique we used in the last chapter to convert our quantity, which is a string, to an integer value.

The `price` is a little more complicated, for two reasons. First of all, we need to remove the dollar sign that's included in the price. To do that, on line 136 we create a new string using the `substring()` method of the `String` object. (Because `getNodeValue()` returns a `String`, we have direct access to that method.) This version of `substring()` takes the index we want to start at. The first letter has an index of 0, so by specifying that we want to start at character 1, we remove the dollar sign.

After we have a `String` that's suitable for conversion to a number, we have an additional issue to deal with. The price isn't an `int` value; it's a double or a float. The `Float` object, however, doesn't provide an easy way to get a float value the way that `Integer` provides an easy way to get an `int` value. Instead, we must first use the `Float` object to create another `Float` object with our `priceString` as the value. After we have that, we can use `floatValue()` to convert the `Float` to a float. That's what line 137 does.

Now that we have our values, on line 139 we multiply them and check the results by printing them out.

We have three steps left before we'll have all our information. First, we have to add the `itemCost` to the `item` element. Second, we have to calculate the running total. Third, we have to add the running total to our `tempDoc`. We tackle all three of these tasks in Listing 6.35.

Listing 6.35—Adding Totals to the Document

```
123:         float totalCost = 0;
124:         float itemCost = 0;
125:         ElementImpl tempDocRoot = (ElementImpl)tempDoc.getFirstChild();
126:         NodeList items = tempDocRoot.getElementsByTagName("ord:item");
127:         for (int i=0; i < items.getLength(); i++) {
128:             ElementImpl thisItem = (ElementImpl)items.item(i);
129:
130:             NodeList quantityNodeList =
➥                        thisItem.getElementsByTagName("ord:quantity");
131:             Node quantityNode = quantityNodeList.item(0).getFirstChild();
132:             int quantity = Integer.parseInt(quantityNode.getNodeValue());
133:
134:             NodeList priceNodeList =
```

Listing 6.35—continued

```
➥                         thisItem.getElementsByTagName("prod:price");
135:             Node priceNode = priceNodeList.item(0).getFirstChild();
136:             String priceString = priceNode.getNodeValue().substring(1);
137:             float price = Float.valueOf(priceString).floatValue();
138:
139:             itemCost = quantity * price;
140:             Node itemCostNode = tempDoc.createElement("ord:itemCost");
141:             Node itemCostText =
➥                        tempDoc.createTextNode(String.valueOf(itemCost));
142:             itemCostNode.appendChild(itemCostText);
143:             thisItem.appendChild(itemCostNode);
144:             totalCost = totalCost + itemCost;
145:
146:         }
147:
148:         Node totalCostNode = tempDoc.createElement("ord:totalCost");
149:         Node totalCostText =
➥                        tempDoc.createTextNode(String.valueOf(totalCost));
150:         totalCostNode.appendChild(totalCostText);
151:         tempDocRoot.appendChild(totalCostNode);
152:
153:         OutputFormat format = new OutputFormat(newDoc, "UTF-8", true);
154:         XMLSerializer output = new XMLSerializer(out, format);
155:         output.serialize(tempDoc);
...
```

Because of the structure of a `Document`, adding a new node with information isn't as simple as it might seem. First, on line 140, we create the node itself, sticking with our naming conventions. Then, on line 141, we create the actual text node separately. Because we now need a `String`, we convert it back using the `String` object.

After we have them both created, we add the text node to the node itself on line 142. Then, we add the whole thing to the item node we are currently processing. On line 144, we begin processing the running total.

The running total is added to the root element the same way the `itemCost` is added to the item element on lines 148 through 151.

If we compile and run the servlet, the results look like the following:

```
<?xml version="1.0" encoding="UTF-8"?>
<tempDoc xmlns:ord="http://www.nicholaschase.com/orders/"
➥xmlns:prod="http://www.nicholaschase.com/products/">
    <ord:item>
        <ord:product_id>WWWhch</ord:product_id>
        <ord:quantity xmlns:prod="http://www.nicholaschase.com/products/">5
➥</ord:quantity>
        <prod:vendor_name
            xmlns:prod="http://www.nicholaschase.com/products/">
            Wally&apos;s Wonderful World of Furniture  </prod:vendor_name>
        <prod:short_desc xmlns:prod="http://www.nicholaschase.com/products/">
```

```
➥Hutch</prod:short_desc>
        <prod:price prod:pricetype="retail"
xmlns:prod="http://www.nicholaschase.com/products/">$600</prod:price>
        <ord:itemCost>3000.0</ord:itemCost>
    </ord:item>
    <ord:item>
        <ord:product_id>RC2342</ord:product_id>
        <ord:quantity xmlns:prod="http://www.nicholaschase.com/products/">3
➥</ord:quantity>
        <prod:vendor_name
            xmlns:prod="http://www.nicholaschase.com/products/">Conners
            Chair Company</prod:vendor_name>
        <prod:short_desc
            xmlns:prod="http://www.nicholaschase.com/products/">Early
            American Rocking Chair</prod:short_desc>
        <prod:price prod:pricetype="retail"
xmlns:prod="http://www.nicholaschase.com/products/">$120</prod:price>
        <ord:itemCost>360.0</ord:itemCost>
    </ord:item>
    <ord:item>
        <ord:product_id>QA3452</ord:product_id>
        <ord:quantity xmlns:prod="http://www.nicholaschase.com/products/">1
➥</ord:quantity>
        <prod:vendor_name
            xmlns:prod="http://www.nicholaschase.com/products/">Conners
            Chair Company</prod:vendor_name>
        <prod:short_desc
            xmlns:prod="http://www.nicholaschase.com/products/">Queen
            Anne Chair</prod:short_desc>
        <prod:price prod:pricetype="retail"
xmlns:prod="http://www.nicholaschase.com/products/">$195</prod:price>
        <ord:itemCost>195.0</ord:itemCost>
    </ord:item>
    <ord:totalCost>3555.0</ord:totalCost>
</tempDoc>
```

Now all we need is a style sheet that displays all this information properly.

The Final Style Sheet

The actual display page needs to do three things: show the user what she has ordered, allow her to change it, and collect payment information.

Let's start off by modifying our servlet to send the output through our new style sheet in Listing 6.36.

Listing 6.36—`ReviewOrder.java`: Outputting to the Final Style Sheet

```
...
            totalCostNode.appendChild(totalCostText);
            tempDocRoot.appendChild(totalCostNode);

        transformer = transFactory.newTransformer
```

Listing 6.36—continued

```
                (new StreamSource("file:///c:/files/confirmOrder.xsl"));
      transformer.transform(new javax.xml.transform.dom.DOMSource(tempDoc),
                                                 new StreamResult(out));

    } catch (org.xml.sax.SAXException SAXe) {
      out.print("There was a problem with the source"
...
```

All these objects were created and used earlier, so we just have to give them new values and use them again.

Now, let's move on to the style sheet. We want something that is informative, but still gets any of the information we might need, now or later. Listing 6.37 shows the basic style sheet.

Listing 6.37—`ConfirmOrder.xsl`

```
<?xml version="1.0"?>
<xsl:stylesheet version="1.0"
    xmlns:xsl="http://www.w3.org/1999/XSL/Transform"
        xmlns:prod="http://www.nicholaschase.com/products/"
        xmlns:ord="http://www.nicholaschase.com/orders/">

<xsl:include href="topinclude.xsl"/>

<xsl:template match="tempDoc">
    <h2>Confirm Order</h2>
     <table>
         <tr>
             <th>Product ID</th>
             <th>Manufacturer</th>
             <th>Description</th>
             <th>Price</th>
             <th>Quantity</th>
             <th>Total Cost</th>
         </tr>
         <xsl:apply-templates select="item" />
         <tr>
             <td align="right" colspan="5">
                 Total:
             </td>
             <td>
                 <xsl:value-of select="totalCost" />
             </td>
         </tr>
    </table>
</xsl:template>

<xsl:template match="//item">
    <tr>
        <td><xsl:value-of select="product_id"/></td>
```

Listing 6.37—continued

```
34:         <td><xsl:value-of select="prod:vendor_name"/></td>
35:         <td><xsl:value-of select="prod:short_desc"/></td>
36:         <td><xsl:value-of select="prod:price"/></td>
37:         <td><xsl:value-of select="ord:quantity"/></td>
38:         <td><xsl:value-of select="itemCost"/></td>
39:    </tr>
40:</xsl:template>
41:
42:</xsl:stylesheet>
```

Because this is a page the user sees, we insert the interface on line 6. As before, this leave us the root element for any additions to the main page. We will display the products as a table, so we add the top row on lines 11 through 18, and then send the `items` off to other templates.

The `items` are picked up by the template on lines 31 through 40, where each piece of information about the item is displayed. Finally, we return to lines 20 through 27, where the last row of the table displays the total cost of the items ordered.

The results look similar to Figure 6.7.

6

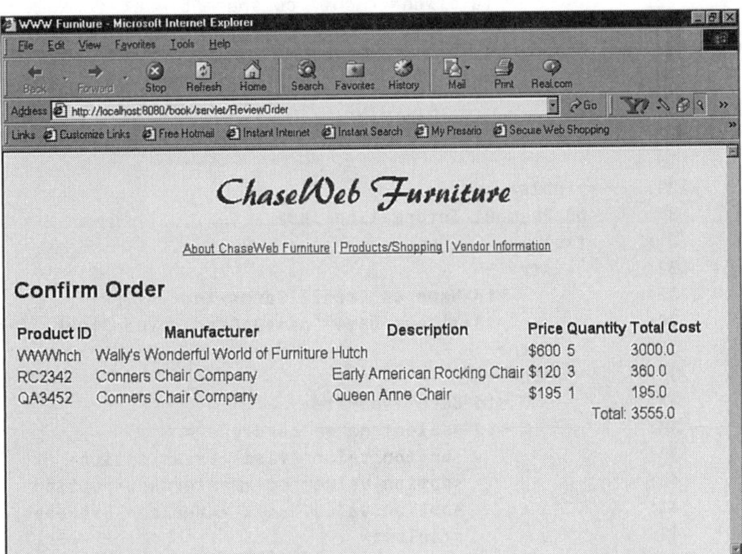

Figure 6.7

Order information is displayed in a table.

Collecting Payment Information

Now, we need to give the user a place to enter his or her credit-card information. Listing 6.38 shows the changes to the style sheet to add a form.

Listing 6.38—`ConfirmOrder.xsl`: Adding a Form

```
<?xml version="1.0"?>
<xsl:stylesheet version="1.0"
        xmlns:xsl="http://www.w3.org/1999/XSL/Transform"
        xmlns:prod="http://www.nicholaschase.com/products/"
        xmlns:ord="http://www.nicholaschase.com/orders/">

<xsl:include href="topinclude.xsl"/>

<xsl:template match="tempDoc">
    <h2>Confirm Order</h2>
    <form action="CompleteOrder" method="get">
    <table>
        <tr>
            <th>Product ID</th>
            <th>Manufacturer</th>
            <th>Description</th>
            <th>Price</th>
            <th>Quantity</th>
            <th>Total Cost</th>
        </tr>
        <xsl:apply-templates select="item" />
        <tr>
            <td align="right" colspan="5">
                Total:
            </td>
            <td>
                <xsl:value-of select="totalCost" />
            </td>
        </tr>
    </table>
    <h3>Payment Information</h3>
    <table>
        <tr>
            <td>Name on Credit Card</td>
            <td><input name="nameOnCard" type="text" /></td>
        </tr>
        <tr>
            <td>Card Type</td>
            <td><select name="cardType">
                <option value="visa">Visa</option>
                <option value="mc">MasterCard</option>
                <option value="amex">American Express</option>
                </select>
            </td>
        </tr>
        <tr>
            <td>Card Number</td>
            <td><input name="cardNumber" type="text" /></td>
        </tr>
        <tr>
            <td>Expiration Date</td>
            <td><input name="expDate" type="text" /></td>
```

Listing 6.38—continued

```
52:        </tr>
53:     </table>
54:
55:    <input type="submit" value="Confirm Order" />
56:    </form>
57:</xsl:template>
58:
59:<xsl:template match="//item">
60:    <tr>
61:        <td><xsl:value-of select="product_id"/></td>
...
```

The form we create on line 10 is no different from the form we used in Chapter 5. We collect payment information on lines 30 through 53, and line 55 is the submit button for the form.

Now that we can see that all this is working, we need to pare the ordered items down to just the items from our session. In Listing 6.39, we get the appropriate `order_id` and limit the items copied to `orderSystem`. This is the final version of `ReviewOrder.java`.

Listing 6.39—`ReviewOrder.java`: Limiting Ourselves to This Order

```
import java.io.*;
import javax.servlet.*;
import javax.servlet.http.*;
import org.apache.xerces.parsers.DOMParser;
import org.apache.xerces.dom.DocumentImpl;
import org.apache.xerces.dom.ElementImpl;
import org.w3c.dom.Document;
import org.w3c.dom.Element;
import org.w3c.dom.Node;
import org.w3c.dom.NodeList;
import org.w3c.dom.NamedNodeMap;
import org.w3c.dom.Attr;
import org.apache.xml.serialize.XMLSerializer;
import org.apache.xml.serialize.OutputFormat;
import javax.xml.transform.TransformerFactory;
import javax.xml.transform.Transformer;
import javax.xml.transform.dom.DOMSource;
import javax.xml.transform.dom.DOMResult;
import javax.xml.transform.stream.StreamSource;
import javax.xml.transform.stream.StreamResult;

public class ReviewOrder extends HttpServlet {

  public String getNodeTypeName(int type) {

      String[] nodeTypeNames = { "No node type 0",
                                 "ELEMENT_NODE",
                                 "ATTRIBUTE_NODE",
```

Listing 6.39—continued

```
                                        "TEXT_NODE",
                                        "CDATA_SECTION_NODE",
                                        "ENTITY_REFERENCE_NODE",
                                        "ENTITY_NODE",
                                        "PROCESSING_INSTRUCTION_NODE",
                                        "COMMENT_NODE",
                                        "DOCUMENT_NODE",
                                        "DOCUMENT_TYPE_NODE",
                                        "DOCUMENT_FRAGMENT_NODE",
                                        "NOTATION_NODE" };
        return nodeTypeNames[type];
    }

    public void processNode(Node thisNode,
                            PrintWriter out,
                            Node newParent,
                            DocumentImpl newDoc,
                            String namespaceURI,
                            String ns)  {

        if (thisNode.getNodeType() == thisNode.ELEMENT_NODE) {

            Element newElement =
                    newDoc.createElementNS(namespaceURI,
                                      ns+thisNode.getNodeName());
            newParent.appendChild(newElement);

            NamedNodeMap attributes = thisNode.getAttributes();
            if (attributes.getLength() > 0) {
                for (int i=0; i < attributes.getLength(); i++) {
                    Node thisAttr = attributes.item(i);
                    Attr thisAttrObj =
                         newDoc.createAttributeNS(namespaceURI,
                                  ns+thisAttr.getNodeName());
                    thisAttrObj.setValue(thisAttr.getNodeValue());
                    newElement.setAttributeNode(thisAttrObj);
                }
            }

            NodeList thisKids = thisNode.getChildNodes();
            for (int i=0; i < thisKids.getLength(); i++) {
                processNode(thisKids.item(i), out, newElement,
                                     newDoc,namespaceURI, ns);
            }

        } else if (thisNode.getNodeType() ==
                          thisNode.TEXT_NODE) {
            Node newNode =
                  newDoc.createTextNode(thisNode.getNodeValue());
            newParent.appendChild(newNode);
        } else {
            Node nextNode = thisNode.getNextSibling();
```

Listing 6.39—continued

```
            if (nextNode == null) {
                // The document is finished.
            } else {
                processNode(nextNode, out, newParent,
                                            newDoc, namespaceURI, ns);
            }
        }
    }

    public void doGet(HttpServletRequest request,
                      HttpServletResponse response)
                throws IOException, ServletException
    {
        response.setContentType("text/html");
        PrintWriter out = response.getWriter();

        try {

            DOMParser parser = new DOMParser();
            parser.parse("/files/orders.xml");
            Document orders = parser.getDocument();

            DocumentImpl newDoc = new DocumentImpl();
            Element orderSystem = newDoc.createElement("orderSystem");
            orderSystem.setAttribute("xmlns:ord",
                             "http://www.nicholaschase.com/orders/");
            orderSystem.setAttribute("xmlns:prod",
                             "http://www.nicholaschase.com/products/");

            newDoc.appendChild(orderSystem);

            HttpSession session = request.getSession(true);
            String session_id = session.getId();

            NodeList allOrders = orders.getElementsByTagName("order");
            for (int i=0; i < allOrders.getLength(); i++) {
                NamedNodeMap attributes = allOrders.item(i).getAttributes();
                Node order_idNode = attributes.item(0);
                String order_id = order_idNode.getNodeValue();
                if (order_id.equals(session_id)) {
                    processNode(allOrders.item(i), out, orderSystem, newDoc,
                       "http://www.nicholaschase.com/orders/", "ord:");
                }
            }

            parser.parse("/files/products.xml");
            Document products = parser.getDocument();
            Node productRoot = products.getFirstChild();
            processNode(productRoot, out, orderSystem, newDoc,
                "http://www.nicholaschase.com/products/", "prod:");

            TransformerFactory transFactory =
```

6

Listing 6.39—continued

```
             TransformerFactory.newInstance();

        Transformer transformer = transFactory.newTransformer
                (new StreamSource("file:///c:/files/reviewOrder.xsl"));

        DOMResult domResult = new DOMResult();

        transformer.transform(new DOMSource(newDoc), domResult);

        Document tempDoc = new DocumentImpl();
        tempDoc = (Document)domResult.getNode();

        float totalCost = 0;
        float itemCost = 0;

        ElementImpl tempDocRoot = (ElementImpl)tempDoc.getFirstChild();
        NodeList items = tempDocRoot.getElementsByTagName("ord:item");
        for (int i=0; i < items.getLength(); i++) {
            ElementImpl thisItem = (ElementImpl)items.item(i);

            NodeList quantityNodeList =
                         thisItem.getElementsByTagName("ord:quantity");
            Node quantityNode=quantityNodeList.item(0).getFirstChild();

            int quantity=Integer.parseInt(quantityNode.getNodeValue());

            NodeList priceNodeList =
                       thisItem.getElementsByTagName("prod:price");
            Node priceNode = priceNodeList.item(0).getFirstChild();

            String priceString = priceNode.getNodeValue().substring(1);
            float price = Float.valueOf(priceString).floatValue();

            itemCost = quantity * price;

            Node itemCostNode = tempDoc.createElement("ord:itemCost");
            Node itemCostText =
                     tempDoc.createTextNode(String.valueOf(itemCost));

            itemCostNode.appendChild(itemCostText);
            thisItem.appendChild(itemCostNode);
            totalCost = totalCost + itemCost;
        }

        Node totalCostNode = tempDoc.createElement("ord:totalCost");
        Node totalCostText =
                  tempDoc.createTextNode(String.valueOf(totalCost));

        totalCostNode.appendChild(totalCostText);
        tempDocRoot.appendChild(totalCostNode);

        transformer = transFactory.newTransformer
```

Listing 6.39—continued

```
184:                (new StreamSource("file:///c:/files/confirmOrder.xsl"));
185:            transformer.transform(new DOMSource(tempDoc),
186:                                  new StreamResult(out));
187:
188:        } catch (org.xml.sax.SAXException SAXe) {
189:            out.print("There was a problem with the source"
190:                + " document.");
191:        } catch (IOException IOe) {
192:            out.print("There was an IO error. Make sure the file"
193:                + " exists and is readable.");
194:        } catch (Exception e) {
195:            out.print("There was an error: "+e.getMessage());
196:        }
197:
198:    }
199:}
200:
```

The only thing that really has changed here is that instead of processing all orders, we've made sure that this is our order before we run it through `processNode()`. On line 104, we use `getElementsByTagName()` to get a `NodeList` of all the order elements. Then, on lines 115 through 123, we loop through the list, comparing the `order_id` attribute of each one with the current `session_id` on line 109. After we find it, we can send it through `processNode()` on lines 110 and 111.

This way, only our actual order is in the `orderSystem` document, and we can proceed as normal.

Accepting Payment Information

At this point, we have a page that shows the user his or her order and allows the input of payment information. All that's left is for us to create a servlet to take in that information, and Listing 6.40 is that servlet.

Listing 6.40—`CompleteOrder.java`: Saving Payment Information

```
import java.io.*;
import javax.servlet.*;
import javax.servlet.http.*;
import org.apache.xerces.parsers.DOMParser;
import org.w3c.dom.Document;
import org.w3c.dom.Node;
import org.w3c.dom.NamedNodeMap;
import org.w3c.dom.NodeList;
import org.apache.xml.serialize.XMLSerializer;
import org.apache.xml.serialize.OutputFormat;

public class CompleteOrder extends HttpServlet {

```

Listing 6.40—continued

```
//********* BEGIN doGet() ************
public void doGet(HttpServletRequest request,
                    HttpServletResponse response)
           throws IOException, ServletException
{
  response.setContentType("text/html");
  PrintWriter out = response.getWriter();

  try {

      HttpSession session = request.getSession(true);
      String session_id = session.getId();

      String nameOnCard = request.getParameter("nameOnCard");
      String cardType = request.getParameter("cardType");
      String cardNumber = request.getParameter("cardNumber");
      String expDate = request.getParameter("expDate");

      DOMParser parser = new DOMParser();
      parser.parse("/files/orders.xml");
      Document orders = parser.getDocument();

      NodeList allOrders = orders.getElementsByTagName("order");
      for (int i=0; i < allOrders.getLength(); i++) {
          Node thisOrder = allOrders.item(i);
          NamedNodeMap attributes = thisOrder.getAttributes();
          Node order_idNode = attributes.item(0);
          String order_id = order_idNode.getNodeValue();
          if (order_id.equals(session_id)) {
              Node payment = orders.createElement("payment");

              Node nameOnCardNode = orders.createElement("nameOnCard");
              Node nameText = orders.createTextNode(nameOnCard);
              nameOnCardNode.appendChild(nameText);
              payment.appendChild(nameOnCardNode);

              Node cardTypeNode = orders.createElement("cardType");
              Node cardTypeText = orders.createTextNode(cardType);
              cardTypeNode.appendChild(cardTypeText);
              payment.appendChild(cardTypeNode);

              Node cardNumberNode = orders.createElement("cardNumber");
              Node cardNumberText = orders.createTextNode(cardNumber);
              cardNumberNode.appendChild(cardNumberText);
              payment.appendChild(cardNumberNode);

              Node expDateNode = orders.createElement("expDate");
              Node expDateText = orders.createTextNode(expDate);
              expDateNode.appendChild(expDateText);
              payment.appendChild(expDateNode);

              thisOrder.appendChild(payment);
```

Listing 6.40—continued

```
62:
63:                 Node status =
➥                   orders.getElementsByTagName("order_status").item(0);
64:                 status.setNodeValue("complete");
65:             }
66:         }
67:
68:         OutputFormat format = new OutputFormat(orders, "UTF-8", true);
69:         XMLSerializer output =
➥        new XMLSerializer(new FileWriter("/files/orders.xml"), format);
70:         output.serialize(orders);
71:
72:         Output.returnResult("Thank you for your order!", out);
73:
74:     } catch (Exception e) {
75:         out.print("There has been an error.");
76:     }
77:
78: }
79: //********* END doGet() ************
80:
81: //********* BEGIN doPost() ************
82: public void doPost(HttpServletRequest request,
83:                          HttpServletResponse response)
84:               throws IOException, ServletException
85: {
86:         doGet(request, response);
87: }
88: //********* END doPost() ************
89:}
```


There's nothing really new in this servlet, so let's just take it from the top.

Lines 0 through 6 are simply the necessary imports for `CompleteOrder`.

All the processing within the servlet takes place in `doGet()` this time, so we start out by setting up our response and `PrintWriter` on lines 15 and 16. Then, we open a `try-catch` block to handle most of the work.

On lines 20 and 21, we get the current `session_id` because that's what we used as the `order_ids`. On lines 23 through 26, we retrieve the data from the forms.

Lines 28 through 30 give us the `orders.xml` file as an in-memory document, and on lines 32 through 38 we use exactly the same method we used in `ReviewOrder` to get to our current order. In this case, however, instead of just updating current information, we add a few fields for the payment information.

We start on line 39 by creating a payment element to hold all our information. Next, on line 41, we create an empty element for the name on the card, and on line 42 we create a text node to insert it on line 43. Finally, we add the new node to the payment.

The same steps are repeated on lines 49 through 59, for card type, card number, and expiration date.

After we've added all our information to the payment node, on line 61 we add the payment news itself. Finally, on lines 63 and 64, we update the `order_status` field for the order in question.

We then save the `orders.xml` file on lines 68 through 70.

All that remains now is to output some sort of message to the user. We aren't manipulating style sheets, but we still want to use the basic template that appears throughout the site.

In the last chapter, we did that via a routine called `returnResult()`. It took text and displayed it within the page. We could reuse that routine, but it's not quite generic enough; it only allows us to specify a `product_id`.

Instead, we'll make a copy of that routine in a new class called `Output`. (Notice that since Java is case sensitive, `output` and `Output` are different.) We'll also make it static, as in Listing 6.41.

Listing 6.41—`Output.java`: Creating a Generic Output Routine

```
import java.io.*;
import javax.servlet.*;
import javax.servlet.http.*;
import org.jdom.Element;
import org.jdom.Document;
import org.jdom.JDOMException;
import org.jdom.Namespace;
import org.jdom.output.XMLOutputter;
import org.jdom.input.SAXBuilder;
import java.util.List;
import org.jdom.output.DOMOutputter;
import javax.xml.transform.TransformerFactory;
import javax.xml.transform.Transformer;
import javax.xml.transform.dom.DOMSource;
import javax.xml.transform.stream.StreamResult;

public class Output extends HttpServlet {

  //*******BEGIN returnResult()*********
  public static void returnResult(
                              String msgTxt,
                              PrintWriter out )
  {
      File resultFile = new File("/files/msgText.xml");
      Document resultDoc = getDocument(resultFile, out);
      Element resultText = resultDoc.getRootElement();
      Element msgHere = resultText.getChild("msgHere");
      msgHere.addContent(msgTxt);
      File includeFile = new File("/files/topinclude.xsl");
```

Listing 6.41—continued

```
    Document includeDoc = getDocument(includeFile, out);
    Element styleSheetRoot = includeDoc.getRootElement();

    List templates = styleSheetRoot.getChildren();
    for (int i=0; i < templates.size(); i++) {
        Element thisTemplate = (Element)templates.get(i);
        String thisMatch = thisTemplate.getAttributeValue("match");
        if (thisMatch.equals("/")) {
            Element htmlElement = thisTemplate.getChild("html");
            Element bodyElement = htmlElement.getChild("body");
            Namespace xslns = Namespace.getNamespace("xsl",
                        "http://www.w3.org/1999/XSL/Transform");
            List allContent =
                 bodyElement.getChildren("apply-templates", xslns);
            allContent.set(0, resultText);
            break;
        }
    }

    try {
        org.w3c.dom.Document DOMDoc;
        DOMOutputter DomOut = new DOMOutputter();
        DOMDoc = DomOut.output(includeDoc);

        TransformerFactory transFactory =
             TransformerFactory.newInstance();
        Transformer transformer =
             transFactory.newTransformer(new DOMSource(DOMDoc));
        transformer.transform(new DOMSource(DOMDoc),
                              new StreamResult(out));
    } catch (Exception e) {
        out.print("There was a problem with the transformation. ");
    }
}
//*******END returnResult()*********

//*******BEGIN getDocument() *********
public static Document getDocument(File sourceFile,
                            PrintWriter errorsOut)
{
  try {

      SAXBuilder builder = new SAXBuilder();
      Document document = builder.build(sourceFile);
      return document;

  } catch (JDOMException e) {
      errorsOut.print("There was a problem building the document: "
             +e.getMessage()+"<br />"+
             "Returning blank document.");
      return new Document(new Element("blank"));
  }
```

6

Listing 6.41—continued

```
  }
  //*******END getDocument() *********

}
```

Notice that this routine uses JDOM, but we can still use it from `CompleteOrder`.

We still have to take care of one last detail. This method needs a more flexible version of the style sheet, as shown in Listing 6.42.

Listing 6.42—`msgText.xml`

```
<resultText>
<!-- DO NOT REMOVE msgHere tag! -->
     <msgHere></msgHere>
</resultText>
```

Next Steps

Whew! That's a lot! In this chapter, we covered the nitty-gritty of using DOM for everyday projects. We also talked about namespaces and how to use them, as well as saw some examples.

In this chapter, we enabled the user to check his order before he provides payment information. Then, we gathered that payment information.

In the next chapter, "Product Search: XQL," we take a look at new ways to search through data, as we create a searchable index of keywords and allow users to search using XML databases and persistent DOM, or PDOM.

In this chapter

- *Downloading the GMD-IPSI XQL Engine*
- *Creating the Index File*
- *Creating the Search Page*
- *The Search Results Page*
- *Performing the Search*
- *Next Steps*

Chapter 7

Product Search: XQL

In Chapter 6, "Adjusting Inventory: Using Namespaces and More About DOM," we finalized the order process, using XPath expressions to help us find product information. To do that, we processed our document using an XSL style sheet, and then worked with the resulting document. It worked, but it certainly wasn't the most convenient way of using XPath-type expressions. In this chapter, we're going to look at another way.

If you've ever done any database programming, you're probably familiar with Standard Query Language, or SQL. It's a (mostly) standard way of retrieving information from databases. Here we have XML Query Language.

At the time of this writing, the XML Query specification was still in very early stages, but one early implementation is the GMD-IPSI XQL Engine. XQL was the original draft proposal for what became XML Query, so this implementation will probably change as the specification does, but the techniques we'll look at are useful in any case. (If the possibility of changes concerns you, feel free to skip this chapter. The search is fairly self-contained, and won't affect the remaining chapters.) The GMD-IPSI XQL Engine also includes an implementation of PDOM, or Persistent DOM, another way to store XML information.

XQL is based, for the most part, on XPath, so by now the syntax should be pretty familiar. The difference is that now, instead of building a style sheet and processing it, we're going to use our queries directly on the document, in a much more streamlined way.

To look at this topic, we're going to add a product search to our site. Users will be able to enter a keyword and have it compared to the name and description of each of our products. The result will be a page of links to products that match their search.

Downloading the GMD-IPSI XQL Engine

The XQL engine we're going to use for this part of the project comes from the GMD German National Research Center for Information Technology.

We'll start by downloading and installing the software. Go to

```
http://xml.darmstadt.gmd.de/xql/index.html
```

and click "Download". After you've filled out the form, you'll receive, via email, the username and password needed to download the Zip file.

These links appear to change periodically. If this URL doesn't work, try going to

`http://xml.darmstadt.gmd.de`

and working your way through the links.

After we have the software, installation is simple: Uncompress the files and modify our CLASSPATH. Uncompressing the files to our root directory will put them in

```
C:\gmd-ipsi-xql-engine-1_0_2\
```

```
As you do your own installation you might find it more convenient to change the
name of this directory, but we won't have to type it very often, so let's leave
it alone and go ahead and add it to the classpath in AUTOEXEC.bat. By now our
classpath should look something like this:SET
CLASSPATH=.;c:\xalan\xerces.jar;c:\xalan\xalan.jar;
SET CLASSPATH=%CLASSPATH%c:\tomcat\lib\webserver.jar;c:\tomcat\lib\jasper.jar;
SET CLASSPATH=%CLASSPATH%c:\tomcat\lib\xml.jar;c:\tomcat\lib\servlet.jar;
➥c:\tomcat\lib\tools.jar;
SET CLASSPATH=%CLASSPATH%C:\jdom\build\jdom.jar;
SET CLASSPATH=%CLASSPATH%c:\gmd-ipsi-xql-engine-1_0_2\xqlpdom_1_0_2.jar;
```

We can run that at the command line for now, but we'll have to restart Windows before it will take effect for the Web server.

If you're not running Windows, of course, you won't need the AUTOEXEC.bat file, but the warning still stands: To get the CLASSPATH to take effect for the Web server, it needs to be changed in the environment where it's running.

To make sure that everything is installed properly, we're going to run a batch script that comes with the installation:

```
cd C:\gmd-ipsi-xql-engine-1_0_2\samples\tutorial-examples
demo.bat
```

This should result in a series of outputs demonstrating the various features of XQL and PDOM.

Some platforms will see "Bad command or filename" at the start and end of the script. This is because of a command in the batch script, and does not indicate a problem with the XQL installation.

If you experience problems, such as classes not being found, make sure that the classpath is correct in that particular Command Prompt window. You can check the value for `CLASSPATH` by typing

```
set
```

Creating the Index File

What we're trying to accomplish is for a user to type in a keyword and get back a list of all products that have that keyword as part of the name or the description. Now, we could search the products themselves, but that would mean parsing the entire `products.xml` file and searching through a lot of information that isn't relevant every time someone does a search.

A more efficient way to do it would be to create a file that is ready to search. For instance, we are actually looking for individual words, so this file would have the names and descriptions already broken up that way. This way, we can just search the individual words, and when we find one, we'll have the `product_id` handy—and from there, we can get right to the product itself. When we're finished, we should have a file that looks something like Listing 7.1.

Listing 7.1—Our Final Index File

```
<?xml version="1.0" encoding="UTF-8"?>
<index>
    <entry>
        <product_id>QA3452</product_id>
        <keyword>Queen</keyword>
        <keyword>Anne</keyword>
        <keyword>Chair</keyword>
    </entry>
    <entry>
        <product_id>RC2342</product_id>
        <keyword>Early</keyword>
        <keyword>American</keyword>
        <keyword>Rocking</keyword>
        <keyword>Chair</keyword>
```

Listing 7.1—continued

```
    </entry>
...
    <entry>
        <product_id>39981234</product_id>
        <keyword>Floataway</keyword>
        <keyword>Waterbeds</keyword>
    </entry>
</index>
```

Each entry shows the `product_id` and each of the words in the product name or description. Getting to this point is going to involve the following steps:

```
Read the products.xml file
Find the short_desc and long_desc nodes
Break text nodes into each individual word
Save all nodes to index.xml
Display results
```

The first thing we need to do is go ahead and create an XML `Document` out of the `products.xml` file, as in Listing 7.2.

Listing 7.2—`CreateIndex.xml`: Reading the `products.xml` File

```
import java.io.*;
import java.util.*;
import javax.servlet.*;
import javax.servlet.http.*;
import org.apache.xerces.parsers.*;
import org.w3c.dom.*;
import org.apache.xerces.dom .*;

public class CreateIndex extends HttpServlet {

  public void doGet(HttpServletRequest request,
                      HttpServletResponse response)
                throws IOException, ServletException
    {
    response.setContentType("text/html");
    PrintWriter out = response.getWriter();

    try {

        DOMParser parser = new DOMParser();
        parser.parse("/files/products.xml");
        Document products = parser.getDocument();

        out.print("Done.");

     } catch (org.xml.sax.SAXException SAXe) {
        out.print("There was a problem with the source"
```

```
27:              + " document:" + SAXe.getMessage());
28:      }
29:   }
30:}
```

There's nothing here that we haven't seen before. Lines 0 through 6 bring in the imports that we'll need for the servlet and to parse the file, lines 14 and 15 set the stage for any output we might do (as on line 23), and lines 17 through 28 simply parse the file and create a `Document` out of it.

The next step isn't so routine. We want to pick out a particular set of nodes: the product names and descriptions. This is complicated not only by the fact that we're looking for two different element names (`short_desc` and `long_desc`) but also by the fact that they can appear at different levels of the document, thanks to our `suites`.

To find these nodes, we're going to use XQL, as in Listing 7.3.

Listing 7.3—`CreateIndex.java`: Finding the `short_desc` and `long_desc` Nodes

```
import java.io.*;
import java.util.*;
import javax.servlet.*;
import javax.servlet.http.*;
import org.apache.xerces.parsers.*;
import org.w3c.dom.*;
import org.apache.xerces.dom .*;
import de.gmd.ipsi.xql.*;

public class CreateIndex extends HttpServlet {

  public void doGet(HttpServletRequest request,
                    HttpServletResponse response)
            throws IOException, ServletException
    {
    response.setContentType("text/html");
    PrintWriter out = response.getWriter();

    try {

        DOMParser parser = new DOMParser();
        parser.parse("/files/products.xml");
        Document products = parser.getDocument();

        XQLResult descNodes =
          XQL.execute("//short_desc | //long_desc", products);
        for (int i=0; i < descNodes.getLength(); i++) {

            Node thisDesc = (Node)descNodes.getItem(i);
            String thisDescStr =
              thisDesc.getFirstChild().getNodeValue();

```

Listing 7.3—continued

```
32:            Element thisProduct =
33:              (Element)thisDesc.getParentNode();
34:            Node thisProduct_id =
35:              thisProduct.getElementsByTagName("product_id").item(0);
36:            String thisProduct_idStr =
37:              thisProduct_id.getFirstChild().getNodeValue();
38:
39:            out.print("product_id = " +
40:              thisProduct_idStr + "<br />");
41:            out.print("description = " + thisDescStr + "<br />");
42:        }
43:
44:        out.print("Done.");
45:
46:     } catch (org.xml.sax.SAXException SAXe) {
47:        out.print("There was a problem with the source"
48:            + " document:" + SAXe.getMessage());
49:    }
50:  }
51:}
```

On line 7, we're importing the new XQL classes. This is one of three packages that are included in the distribution we downloaded, and contains all the classes involved with the actual XQL operations.

On line 24, we're getting right down to business. We are creating an `XQLResult` object by executing a query on the `products` document. This query is exactly what it would have been in XPath. We are simply searching for any `short_desc` or `long_desc`, anywhere in the document. (Remember, the `//` means that it can be any child of the root document, no matter how deeply nested.)

The `XQLResult` that we get back is much like the `NodeList` and other `List`-like classes we have been using, in that it has a certain number of items in it, which can then be retrieved by their numerical index. On lines 26 through 42, we're looping through each of the `Node`s that the query returned.

For each one of those `Node`s, we're going to retrieve it on line 28. Because `XQLResult`, like the `List` class we used in Chapter 5, returns an `Object`, we need to cast the item back to `Node`.

After we have the `Node`, we can get the actual value of it. Remember, though, that the `Node` that was returned is the `ELEMENT_NODE`. To get at the text, we have to retrieve the `TEXT_NODE` that is the first child of the element, as on lines 29 and 30.

That takes care of the descriptions, but they aren't going to do us any good unless we also know the `product_id`. To get that, the first thing we have to do is to get the parent of the description, which will be the `product` itself. We do that on lines 32 and 33.

After we have the `product` element, we need to retrieve the `product_id` element. We can use `getElementsByTagName()` to eliminate the need to loop through every single child of the `product`, but that's going to return a `NodeList`, so we need to tell the servlet we actually want the very first item, number 0, as we see on lines 34 and 35.

After we have the `product_id` node, we can retrieve the text on lines 36 and 37, just as we did for the description itself on lines 29 and 30.

Finally, on lines 39 through 41, we print the information to the page so we can be sure that everything is working properly.

If we compile and run the servlet, we should get output something like Listing 7.4.

Listing 7.4—`Product_ids` and Descriptions

```
0: product_id = QA3452
1: description = Queen Anne Chair
2: product_id = RC2342
3: description = Early American Rocking Chair
4: product_id = BR3452
5: description = Bentwood Rocker
6: product_id = CDRS
7: description = Complete Dining Room Set
8: product_id = CDRS
9: description = This five piece dining set features swivel chairs with
➥cushions in five exciting colors.
10:product_id = WWWdrt
11:description = Dining Room Table
12:product_id = WWWsc
13:description = Swivel Chair
14:product_id = WWWhch
15:description = Hutch
16:product_id = HallBench
17:description = Hall Bench
18:product_id = SofaLoveSeat
19:description = Sofa and Love Seat
20:product_id = 3253435
21:description = Sleepeazy Mattresses
22:product_id = 5622345
23:description = CozyComfort Mattresses
24:product_id = 39981234
25:description = Floataway Waterbeds
```

There are a couple of things to notice about this. First, on lines 6 through 9, there are two listings for the same `product`. One is for the `short_desc`, and one is for the `long_desc`. Second, most of our listings don't have a `long_desc`, because there isn't one in the `products.xml` file. By pulling this information out into another file, we save ourselves the trouble of searching for information that isn't there.

Now we need to break the descriptions into individual words. We're going to do that with some standard Java, the `StringTokenizer`, as in Listing 7.5.

Listing 7.5—`CreateIndex.java`: Using `StringTokenizer` to Break Descriptions into Words

```
...
38:
39:            out.print("product_id = " +
40:              thisProduct_idStr + "<br />");
41:
42:            StringTokenizer keywords =
43:              new StringTokenizer(thisDescStr, " ");
44:
45:            while (keywords.hasMoreTokens()) {
46:                String keywordStr = keywords.nextToken();
47:                out.print(keywordStr + "<br />");
48:            }
49:
50:        }
51:
52:        out.print("Done.");
...
```

`StringTokenizer` enables us to take a string and break it into pieces based on a specific delimiter. For instance, if we had a comma-delimited string, we could simply replace the `" "` on line 43 with `","` to tell the `StringTokenizer` that was the character to look for.

What we are doing on lines 42 and 43 is essentially parsing the string, looking for spaces. The result, `keywords`, is similar to a cursor in a database. Before we get to line 45, the "pointer" is above the first item in the list, as in Figure 7.1.

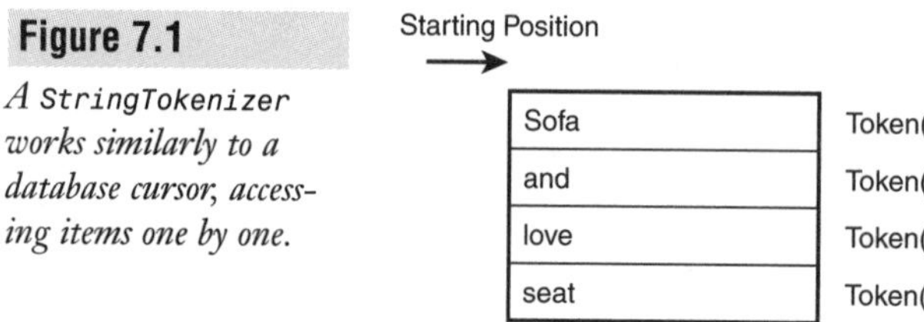

Figure 7.1

A `StringTokenizer` works similarly to a database cursor, accessing items one by one.

When we get to line 45, it can look below, so to speak, to see whether there are more tokens. If there are, we proceed to line 46, where the pointer moves to the `nextToken()`—`Sofa`, in Figure 7.1—and puts that value into `keywordStr`. We then print it on line 47 (along with a `<br />` tag to format the output nicely) and go back to the beginning of the loop, on line 45. From there, the pointer is on the first word in the description (`Sofa`), and looks again, to see whether there are any more tokens—in this case—and this goes on until we get to line 45 and there are no more tokens, and we can proceed to the next node. The results look something like Figure 7.2.

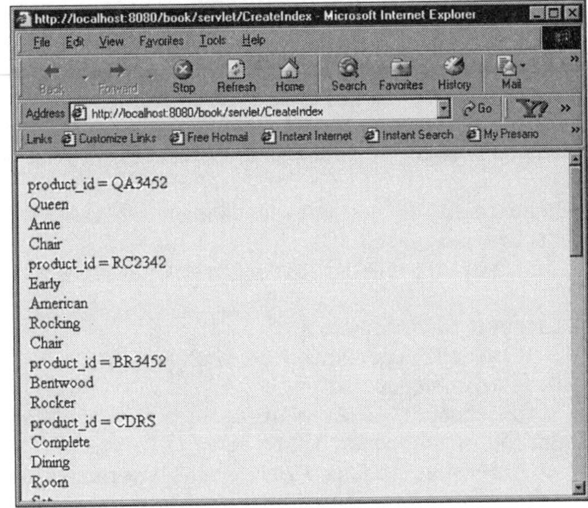

Figure 7.2

The results of using `StringTokenizer` *are shown here.*

Now we need to turn all this into an XML document, as in Listing 7.6.

Listing 7.6—`CreateIndex.java`: Creating the Index Document

```
import java.io.*;
import java.util.*;
import javax.servlet.*;
import javax.servlet.http.*;
import org.apache.xerces.parsers.*;
import org.w3c.dom.*;
import org.apache.xerces.dom .*;
import de.gmd.ipsi.xql.*;
import org.apache.xml.serialize.*;

public class CreateIndex extends HttpServlet {

  public void doGet(HttpServletRequest request,
                    HttpServletResponse response)
              throws IOException, ServletException
    {
    response.setContentType("text/html");
    PrintWriter out = response.getWriter();

    try {

        DOMParser parser = new DOMParser();
        parser.parse("/files/products.xml");
        Document products = parser.getDocument();

        Document index = new DocumentImpl();
        Element indexRoot = index.createElement("index");

        XQLResult descNodes =
```

Listing 7.6—continued

```
           XQL.execute("//short_desc | //long_desc", products);
         for (int i=0; i < descNodes.getLength(); i++) {

             Element entry = index.createElement("entry");

             Node thisDesc = (Node)descNodes.getItem(i);
             String thisDescStr =
               thisDesc.getFirstChild().getNodeValue();

             Element thisProduct =
               (Element)thisDesc.getParentNode();
             Node thisProduct_id =
               thisProduct.getElementsByTagName("product_id").item(0);
             String thisProduct_idStr =
               thisProduct_id.getFirstChild().getNodeValue();

             Element product_id = index.createElement("product_id");
             Node product_idTxt =
               index.createTextNode(thisProduct_idStr);
             product_id.appendChild(product_idTxt);
             entry.appendChild(product_id);

             StringTokenizer keywords =
               new StringTokenizer(thisDescStr, " ");

             while (keywords.hasMoreTokens()) {
                 String keywordStr = keywords.nextToken();
                 Element keyword = index.createElement("keyword");
                 Node keywordTxt = index.createTextNode(keywordStr);
                 keyword.appendChild(keywordTxt);
                 entry.appendChild(keyword);

             }

             indexRoot.appendChild(entry);
         }

         index.appendChild(indexRoot);

         OutputFormat format = new OutputFormat(index, "UTF-8", true);
         XMLSerializer output = new XMLSerializer(out, format);
         output.serialize(index);

      } catch (org.xml.sax.SAXException SAXe) {
         out.print("There was a problem with the source"
             + " document:" + SAXe.getMessage());
      }
   }
}
```

This time around, instead of outputting the actual data, we're going to create the `Document` and output it to the page, so on line 8, we'll import the `serialize` package.

On line 25, we're creating the actual `Document` itself, and on line 26 we're creating the root element.

According to our target structure in Listing 7.1, each description is going to have its own node, so on line 32 we'll create the `entry` element. Lines 34 through 43 are pulling out the `product_id` and description, just as they were before, but now, instead of simply outputting the information to the page, we're going to go ahead and add it to `index`.

On line 45, we create the `product_id` element, which we populate on lines 46 through 48. We then add that to the entry on line 49. We add the `keywords` the same way, on lines 56 through 59, as they're created by the `StringTokenizer`.

When the `entry` is complete, we add it to the `indexRoot` on line 63. Finally, when all the entries have been created, we add the root element to the document on line 66.

Lines 68 through 70 are where we output the document to the page, just as we have done in previous chapters.

The result is shown in Figure 7.3.

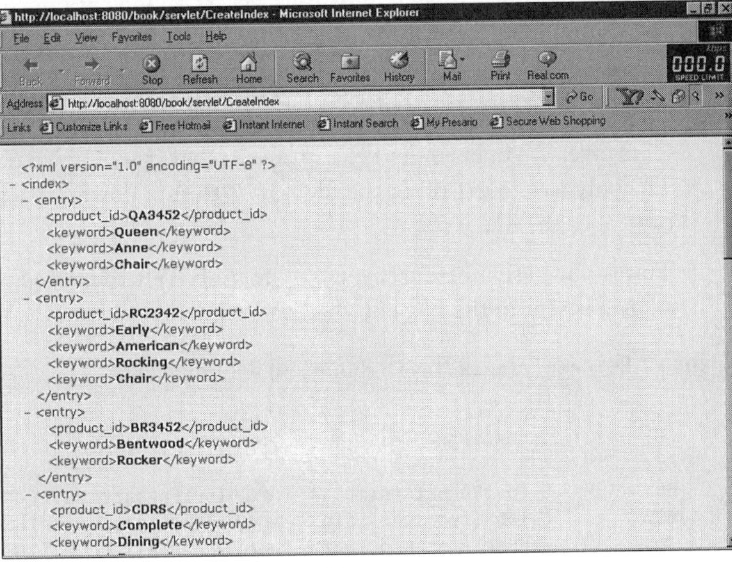

Figure 7.3

Here is a look at our index document.

All that's left to do now is save the document to a file, as in Listing 7.7.

Listing 7.7—`CreateIndex.java`: Saving the Document to a File

```
...
65:
66:         index.appendChild(indexRoot);
67:
68:         OutputFormat format = new OutputFormat(index, "UTF-8", true);
69:         FileWriter indexFile = new FileWriter("/files/index.xml");
70:         XMLSerializer output = new XMLSerializer(indexFile, format);
71:         output.serialize(index);
72:
73:         out.print("Done.");
74:
75:      } catch (org.xml.sax.SAXException SAXe) {
76:         out.print("There was a problem with the source"
77:             + " document:" + SAXe.getMessage());
78:     }
79:   }
80:}
```

This time, instead of sending the output to the page, we're creating a `FileWriter` to send it to on line 69, attached to our `index.xml` file. We've also added a line of output so the browser has something to display.

There is still one problem here, however. If we look at the contents of the `index.xml` file, we find that there aren't any. And if that wasn't strange enough, we also find that we can't delete the file and start over because it's in use by another process. Another process?

Of course. We opened the file with the `FileWriter`, but we never closed it again. The only way to get rid of the file now is to shut down Tomcat, which is what has control of the file.

This is obviously not an acceptable situation. What we need to do is make sure that all data is sent to the file, and that it's closed and released, as in Listing 7.8.

Listing 7.8—`CreateIndex.java`: Releasing the File

```
...
        index.appendChild(indexRoot);

        OutputFormat format = new OutputFormat(index, "UTF-8", true);
        FileWriter indexFile = new FileWriter("/files/index.xml");
        XMLSerializer output = new XMLSerializer(indexFile, format);
        output.serialize(index);

        indexFile.flush();
        indexFile.close();

        out.print("Done.");
```

Listing 7.8—continued

```
77:
78:     } catch (org.xml.sax.SAXException SAXe) {
79:        out.print("There was a problem with the source"
80:            + " document:" + SAXe.getMessage());
81:    }
82:  }
83:}
```

On line 73, we `flush()` the buffer, which sends all data to the file, and on line 74 we `close()` it, which releases it for further use.

Creating the Search Page

Now we have the index file, so we'll move on to creating the search itself. We want it to be available from anywhere on the site, so the simplest thing to do would be to add it to the main style sheet. This way, it appears on any of our pages.

To start with, point your browser to

`http://localhost:8080/book/servlet/TransformServlet?product_id=3253435`

This gives us a good starting point. We want to put the form box in the top line of links, just after "Vendor Information." To do that, we can make the change to `topinclude.xsl`, as in Listing 7.9.

Listing 7.9—Adding the Search Form to `topinclude.xsl`

```
<?xml version="1.0"?>
<xsl:stylesheet version="1.0"
    xmlns:xsl="http://www.w3.org/1999/XSL/Transform">

<xsl:template match="/">
<html>
<head>
    <title>WWW Furniture</title>
</head>
<body style="background-color: F6F6F6;
                 font-family: Arial;font-size:10pt;">

     <center>
     <img src="file:///c:/files/chasewebfurniture.gif"
                              alt="ChaseWeb Furniture Logo"/>
     </center>

     <p align="center">
         <a href="index.html">About ChaseWeb Furniture</a>
         |
         <a href="TransformServlet?product_id=all">Products/Shopping</a>
         |
         <a href="TransformServlet?product_id=all">Vendor Information</a>
```

Listing 7.9—continued

```
           |
           Product Search: <form action="SearchResults" method="get">
                           <input type="text" name="key" />
                           </form>
    </p>

    <xsl:apply-templates/>

</body>
</html>
</xsl:template>
...
```

This seems simple enough. We drop it into the template, and then refresh the browser as in Figure 7.4. When we do that, however, we don't see things quite the way we wanted them. Instead of having everything on one line, the text box has dropped down to the next line all by itself. It doesn't seem to be related to the line length, so what can it be?

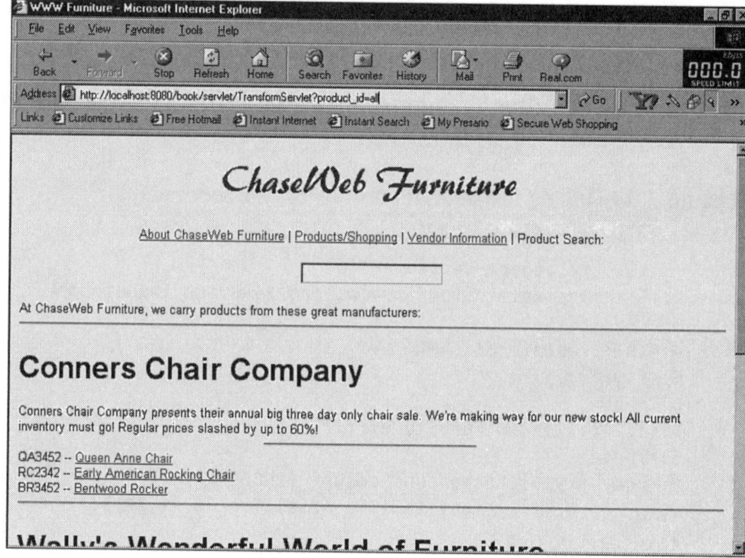

Figure 7.4

The search box doesn't appear next to `Vendor Information`*, where we expected it.*

Remember in Chapter 1 we talked about block elements versus inline elements? Well, `<form></form>` is a block element, so it's going to start on a new line. Fortunately, this is a quick fix, as shown in Listing 7.10.

Listing 7.10—Adjusting the Search Form

```
...
    <center>
    <img src="file:///c:/files/chasewebfurniture.gif"
```

Listing 7.10—continued

```
                                    alt="ChaseWeb Furniture Logo"/>
     </center>

     <p align="center">
      <form action="SearchResults" method="get">
      <a href="index.html">About ChaseWeb Furniture</a>
         |
         <a href="TransformServlet?product_id=all">Products/Shopping</a>
         |
         <a href="TransformServlet?product_id=all">Vendor Information</a>
         |
      Product Search: <input type="text" name="key" />
      </form>
     </p>

     <xsl:apply-templates/>

</body>
</html>
</xsl:template>
...
```

By moving the <form> tag to the head of the line, it all becomes one big block, which is what we wanted. Because there are no other forms on this line, it doesn't affect anything but the format.

Because the entire form consists of a single text box, we don't need a submit button, because browsers will automatically submit when the user presses the Enter key. You might find, however, that you want to put one in anyway to enhance usability.

The Search Results Page

Now that we have our form, we need to provide an action for it. First, we'll create the SearchResults servlet, which echoes back our entry, as in Listing 7.11.

Listing 7.11—SearchResults.java: Creating the Servlet

```
import java.io.*;
import javax.servlet.*;
import javax.servlet.http.*;

public class SearchResults extends HttpServlet {

  public void doGet(HttpServletRequest request,
                        HttpServletResponse response)
                throws IOException, ServletException
  {
   response.setContentType("text/html");
   PrintWriter out = response.getWriter();

```

Listing 7.11—continued

```
13:  String key = request.getParameter("key");
14:  out.print("Results for keyword: " + key + "<br /><br />");
15:
16:  }
17:
18:
19:  public void doPost(HttpServletRequest request,
20:                     HttpServletResponse response)
21:              throws IOException, ServletException
22:  {
23:      doGet(request, response);
24:  }
25:}
```

This is our standard servlet, with a couple of additions. On line 13, we're retrieving the keyword that the user has entered into the form so we can make sure we don't have a typo somewhere in the process. On line 14, we're simply outputting it.

Also, on lines 19 through 24 we've added `doPost()`, in case we decide to change the method on the form at some point.

Although this does work, it certainly isn't pretty, outputting just a line of text. What we really need is a page that fits in with our overall look. One way to do that would be to use our `topinclude.xsl` style sheet, as in Listing 7.12.

Listing 7.12—`SearchResults.java`: Using `topinclude.xsl`

```
import java.io.*;
import javax.servlet.*;
import javax.servlet.http.*;
import javax.xml.transform.*;
import javax.xml.transform.dom.*;
import javax.xml.transform.stream.*;
import org.w3c.dom.*;
import org.apache.xerces.dom.*;
import org.apache.xml.serialize.*;

public class SearchResults extends HttpServlet {

  public void doGet(HttpServletRequest request,
                    HttpServletResponse response)
             throws IOException, ServletException
  {
    response.setContentType("text/html");
    PrintWriter out = response.getWriter();

    try {

          Document page = new DocumentImpl();

          TransformerFactory transFactory =
```

Listing 7.12—continued

```
24:              TransformerFactory.newInstance();
25:          Transformer transformer =
26:              transFactory.newTransformer(
27:                    new StreamSource("/files/topinclude.xsl"));
28:
29:          DOMResult result = new DOMResult();
30:
31:          transformer.transform(new DOMSource(page),
32:                                result);
33:
34:          page = (Document)result.getNode();
35:
36:          Node body = page.getElementsByTagName("body").item(0);
37:
38:          String key = request.getParameter("key");
39:
40:          Node bodyText =
41:              page.createTextNode("Results for keyword: "+key);
42:          body.appendChild(bodyText);
43:
44:          OutputFormat format = new OutputFormat(page, "UTF-8", true);
45:          XMLSerializer output = new XMLSerializer(out, format);
46:          output.serialize(page);
47:
48:      } catch (Exception e) {
49:          out.print("There was a problem with the source"
50:              + " document:" + e.getMessage());
51:      }
52:  }
...
```

Now, we've kind of pulled a fast one here. What we wanted was to stay consistent with the `topinclude.xsl` style sheet, but we don't necessarily want to write a new style sheet to go with it. So instead, we've created the base document, and then added content to it. Let's take a look at how we did it.

Lines 3 through 8, of course, are the imports that we need to pull this off.

The first thing that we're doing is on line 21, when we create an empty `Document` that represents our page. At this point, there's nothing whatsoever in it. Then, on lines 23 through 34, we're using the now-familiar style sheet processing code to run `page` through `topinclude.xsl`.

Now, under normal circumstances, `topinclude.xsl` isn't going to add any content to the output, even if we had any, which we don't. All that is handled by the style sheets that include `topinclude.xsl`. All the style sheet adds is the basic frame of the page. But by extracting `page` from our `DOMResult`, we wind up with a `Document` that includes all our navigation, and so on. If `topinclude.xsl` ever changes, this page will be automatically updated.

Now, that's all well and good, but now we do want to add content, so how do we do it? Well, the first thing we do is remember that this page is just another XML document. Granted, it's an XML document that means something special to the browser, but it's an XML document just the same. So, to add content, we are going to locate the `body` element on line 236.

From there, on lines 40 and 41, we are creating a text node that we then add to the `body` on line 42.

Now we have our complete document, and all that remains is for us to output the XHTML to the browser. That's what we're doing on lines 44 through 46, as we've done countless times before. It's just that this time, the browser knows what to do with it, so we wind up with a real page, such as Figure 7.5.

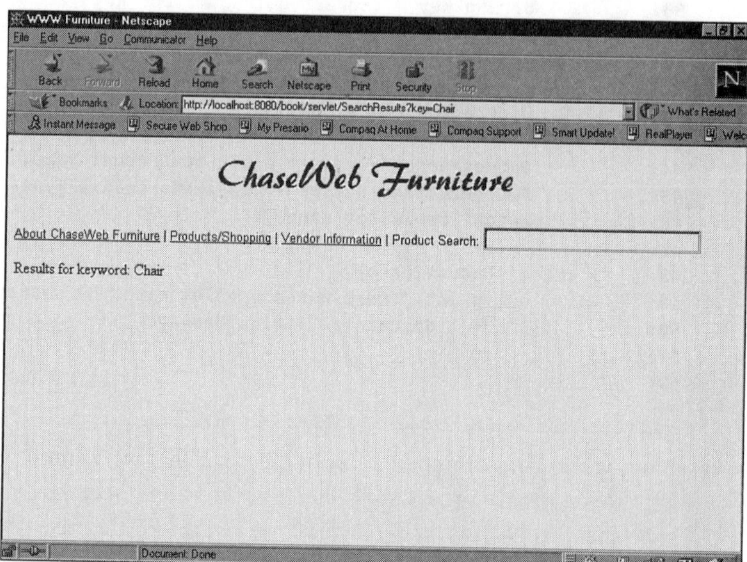

Figure 7.5

This page appears as output to the browser.

Performing the Search

Now that we have a nice-looking results page, it would be handy to have some results to actually put on it. In Listing 7.13, we're performing the basic search against `index.xml` to locate our `product_ids`.

Listing 7.13—Performing the Search

```
import java.io.*;
import javax.servlet.*;
import javax.servlet.http.*;
import org.apache.xalan.xslt.*;
import org.w3c.dom.*;
import org.apache.xerces.dom.*;
```

Listing 7.13—continued

```
6: import org.apache.xml.serialize.*;
7: import org.apache.xerces.parsers.*;
8: import de.gmd.ipsi.xql.*;
...

34:       Node bodyText =
35:            page.createTextNode("Results for keyword: "+key);
42:       body.appendChild(bodyText);
43:       body.appendChild(page.createElement("p"));
44:
45:       DOMParser parser = new DOMParser();
46:       parser.parse("/files/index.xml");
47:       Document index = parser.getDocument();
48:
49:       XQLResult results =
50:             XQL.execute("//entry[keyword='"+key+"']/product_id",
51:                                                        index);
52:       if (results.getLength() > 0) {
53:
54:           body.appendChild(page.createTextNode("Products:  "));
55:           body.appendChild(page.createElement("br"));
56:
57:           for (int i=0; I < results.getLength(); i++) {
58:               Node product_id = (Node)results.getItem(i);
59:               String product_idStr =
60:                   product_id.getFirstChild().getNodeValue();
61:               body.appendChild(page.createTextNode(product_idStr));
62:               body.appendChild(page.createElement("br"));
63:           }
64:
65:       } else {
66:
67:           body.appendChild(
68:                       page.createTextNode("No products found."));
69:
70:       }
71:
72:       OutputFormat format = new OutputFormat(page, "UTF-8", true);
73:       XMLSerializer output = new XMLSerializer(out, format);
74:       output.serialize(page);
75:
76:     } catch (org.xml.sax.SAXException SAXe) {
77:         out.print("There was a problem with the source"
78:             + " document:" + SAXe.getMessage());
79:     }
80:   }
...
```

On lines 7 and 8, we've added the package we need to read the `index.xml` file, as well as the package we need to do the search itself.

On line 43, we're adding a `p` tag to the page to space the "Results" heading from the actual results a bit. Notice that we don't have to explicitly create the node. Instead, we can just create it at the point that we need it. We'll use this extensively in the servlet, because everything we're adding to the body element is just text or XHTML. We're not going to do any further manipulation after it becomes part of the page.

On lines 45 through 47, we retrieve the `index` document, and on line 49 through 51 we perform the actual search.

Let's take a closer look at that expression. In all the expressions we have built up to now, the bracketed section (`[keyword = '"+key+"']`) has been the last item. Now it's here in the middle. The difference lies in what it is that we are trying to find.

It should be clear by now that if we asked for

```
//entry
```

we're looking for an `entry` anywhere in the document. If we had asked for

```
//entry/product_id
```

we would be looking for any `product_id` that is a direct descendant (immediate child) of an `entry` element. In previous attempts, we might have had an expression something like

```
//entry/product_id[@myAtt='myValue']
```

or

```
//entry[product_id='QA3452']
```

where the former will give us only `product_id` children of `entrys`, where the `product_id` has a `myAtt` attribute of `myValue`, and the latter will give us only the `entrys` with a `product_id` child of `QA3452`.

The common thread is that the section in brackets is a filter. It takes everything that has come before and filters it down based on the criteria we give it.

So, in the case of

```
//entry[keyword='"+key+"']/product_id
```

the section in brackets is going to filter down the `entrys` that are originally found. For instance, if we entered a keyword of `Chair`, the XQL expression will be

```
//entry[keyword='Chair']/product_id
```

Let's look at this conceptually. First, all the `entrys` will be retrieved, wherever they might be in the document. Then they will be filtered so that only those with a `keyword` child with a value of `Chair` are retained. From there, any `product_id` children of those `entrys` are returned.

This way, we can actually do a query based on the sibling of what we want to return.

On line 52, we're testing to see whether we actually have any results. If so, we'll first add some text for a heading, and a break tag for the end of the line.

Next, we'll loop through all the items that were found on lines 57 through 63, and output them to the page. Finally, if there weren't any results, on lines 67 and 68 we'll output a message for the user.

Now, if we compile and run this servlet with Internet Explorer, we'll get results like Figure 7.6. If we run it with an older version of Netscape Navigator, however, the line breaks, which are constructed as `<br/>`, won't be recognized.

Figure 7.6

The basic search results are shown here.

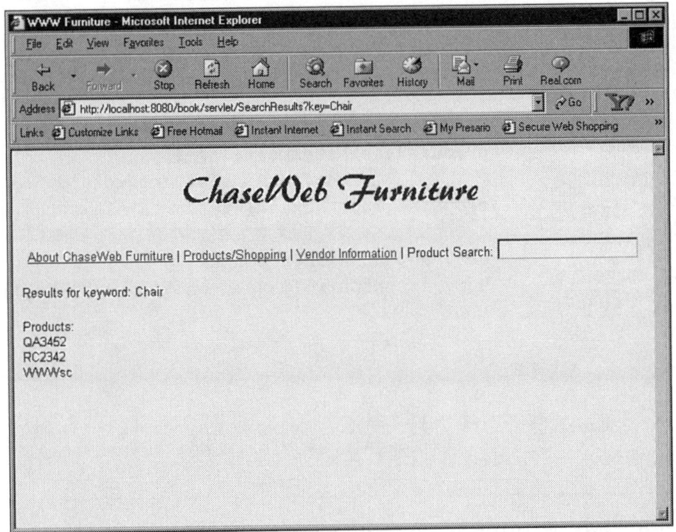

The list of `product_ids` shows us that we're on the right track, but we still need to present this in a way that's going to be useful for the user, as in Listing 7.14.

Listing 7.14—Turning the `product_ids` into Links

```
...
44:
45:     DOMParser parser = new DOMParser();
46:     parser.parse("/files/index.xml");
47:     Document index = parser.getDocument();
48:
49:     XQLResult results =
50:           XQL.execute("//entry[keyword='"+key+"']/product_id",
51:                                                       index);
52:     if (results.getLength() > 0) {
53:
54:         body.appendChild(page.createTextNode("Products:  "));
55:         body.appendChild(page.createElement("br"));
56:
```

Listing 7.14—continued

```
          parser.parse("/files/products.xml");
          Document products = parser.getDocument();

          for (int i=0; i < results.getLength(); i++) {
              Node product_id = (Node)results.getItem(i);
              String product_idStr =
                  product_id.getFirstChild().getNodeValue();

              XQLResult product =
XQL.execute("//product[product_id='"+product_idStr+"']/short_desc",
                                         products);
              Node nameNode = (Node)product.getItem(0);
              String name = nameNode.getFirstChild().getNodeValue();

              Element prodLink = page.createElement("a");
              prodLink.setAttribute("href",
                       "TransformServlet?product_id="+product_idStr);
              prodLink.appendChild(page.createTextNode(name));

              body.appendChild(prodLink);
              body.appendChild(page.createElement("br"));
          }

      } else {

          body.appendChild(
                   page.createTextNode("No products found."));
...
```

Ultimately, we want to wind up with a page like Figure 7.7.

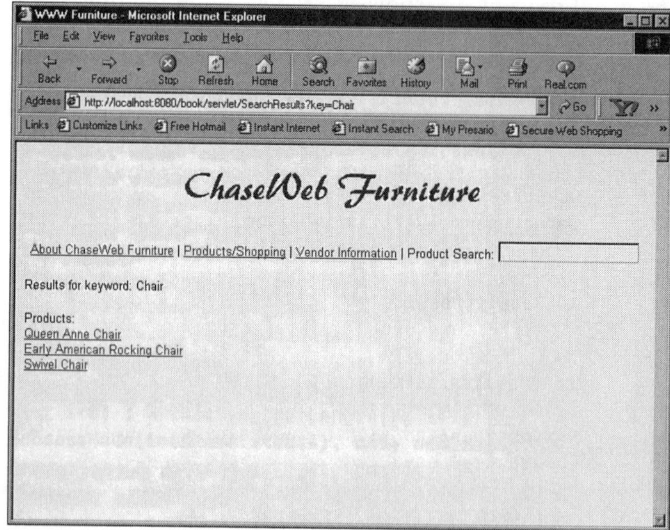

Figure 7.7

Ultimately, we want our search results page to look something like this.

To do that, we're going to need more information than just the `product_id`, so on lines 57 and 58, we'll get the information in `products.xml`. (We already created the parser on line 45, so we don't have to do it again.)

On lines 65 through 67, we'll run another query. This time, we'll first find all the `product` nodes that have a `product_id` that matches the one we're looking at, and then we'll pull out the name, contained in the `short_desc` node, on lines 68 and 70.

Next, we'll need to create the link. On line 65, we're creating an `a` element; then we're adding the destination as an `href` attribute on lines 66 and 67, and finally the content of the element itself on line 68.

We add the link to the body and a break tag to separate them all, and the product search is complete!

EXCURSION

Why Not Create the Elements Manually?

It might be tempting to get around the browser compatibility problem by simply building the tags ourselves as in

```
Body.appendChild(page.createTextNode("<br />");
```

The only problem with that is that the servlet doesn't know that we're doing that because we want the text to be interpreted as a tag, so instead it gets output to the browser as

```
&lt;br /&gt;
```

which to the browser means to actually display the tag instead of evaluating it. So, what we see on the screen is

```
Queen Anne Chair<br />Early American Rocking Chair<br />Swivel Chair<br />
```

This is because of the nature of XML. Any of the normally "problem" characters, such as <, >, and &, are escaped, or changed into their browser-safe equivalents.

Enhancing the Search

Now we have a search that will look for an exact match, but what about giving our users the chance to enter only part of a word? Because XQL is extensible, we can do that. The GMD-IPSI XQL engine has an additional function, `$contains$`, which will let us look for a partial match, as in Listing 7.15.

Listing 7.15—Accommodating a Partial Search

```
...
45:      DOMParser parser = new DOMParser();
46:      parser.parse("/files/index.xml");
47:      Document index = parser.getDocument();
48:
```

Listing 7.15—continued

```
49:        XQLResult results =
50:              XQL.execute("//entry[keyword $contains$ '"+key+"']/product_id",
51:                                                                   index);
52:        if (results.getLength() > 0) {
53:
54:            body.appendChild(page.createTextNode("Products:  "));
...
```

All we did was change the = to `$contains$` on line 44. This tells the XQL engine to look for a partial match. Now we can do a partial match. For instance, `Cha` will now provide results, where it didn't before.

Version 1.0.2 of the XQL engine contains a bug that causes an error if we use `$contains$` to search for a partial match that would have worked if not for case differences. For instance, `Cha` returns results; `cha` returns an error. (A totally wrong keyword produces the "no results" message, as expected.)

For this reason, this feature probably shouldn't be used on a production site until it's fixed, or unless you are going to trap for the error.

Next Steps

In this chapter, we looked at another way of getting information out of XML files, XQL. XQL enables us to query our XML files much more easily, and we used it to create a product search that uses a separate index file. We also looked briefly at manipulating XHTML documents from within our servlets.

In Chapter 8, "Updating Inventory: SQL Databases and SAX," we're going to look at the problem from an entirely different perspective. We'll look at legacy SQL databases, and how we can manipulate them with Java and XML. We'll also take a closer look at SAX as we update inventory based on the sales that come in over the Web.

In this chapter

Chapter 8

Updating Inventory: SQL Databases and SAX

Until now, we've been concentrating on the user experience, and the browser end of the equation. Now it's time for us to step back and take a look under the hood.

I think we can say with a fair degree of certainty that there isn't a single significantly large site in the Web today that doesn't use a back-end database in some way, even if that database isn't directly connected to the Web site. It may have databased content in it, or it may have accounting information, but in some way, it's related to the functioning of the site.

In our case, we're going to assume that part of the ChaseWeb Furniture Company's infrastructure is an inventory database that's updated by vendors when stock is received. Unlike the XQL database we worked with in the last chapter, however, this is an SQL legacy database. We're going to look at how we get information into and out of these databases using Java, and how that relates to our XML.

To do that, we're going to extract information from the `products.xml` file to create the database in the first place; then we're going to use the Simple API for XML (SAX) to retrieve information from the `orders.xml` file to update that database. Finally, we're going to use the database to update the `products.xml` file, completing the circle.

Connecting to the Database: JDBC, ODBC, and SQL

Once upon a time, every database was a land unto itself. There was very little standardization, and what worked in one database was virtually guaranteed not to work in another. And forget about having them talk to each other, unless you were willing to spend a great deal of time and money.

Fortunately, that's no longer the case for the major databases. In the late 1980s and early 1990s, the database industry agreed on a Standard Query Language, or SQL, which is used to put data into the database, and to get it out again.

Also in the 1990s, Microsoft created the Open Database Connectivity standard, or ODBC. ODBC is a standard API that vendors can write to that allows any program to talk to any ODBC-compliant database. All that was needed was the ODBC Driver, as shown in Figure 8.1. As it became an accepted standard, most database vendors saw to it that there were ODBC drivers for their products.

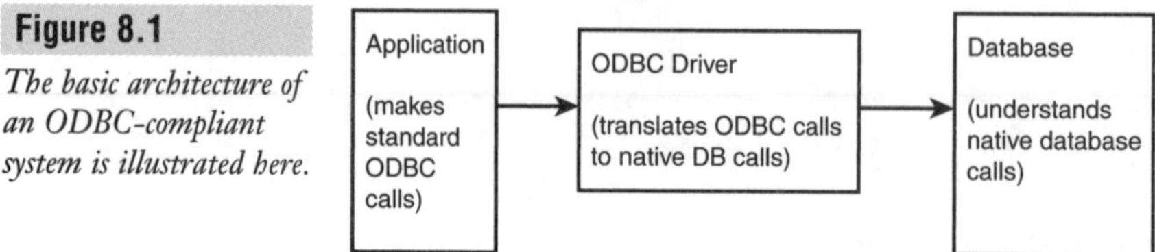

Figure 8.1

The basic architecture of an ODBC-compliant system is illustrated here.

Of course, if we're writing an application in Java, we also want to access the database. To achieve this, Sun created JDBC, which serves much of the same function as ODBC. Using it, Java programmers could simply write their code without worrying about the details of connecting to the database.

But what if you don't have a JDBC driver for your database? No problem—as long as the database is ODBC compliant. Sun included, as part of the JDBC Java classes, a JDBC-ODBC bridge, which translates between the two, as in Figure 8.2.

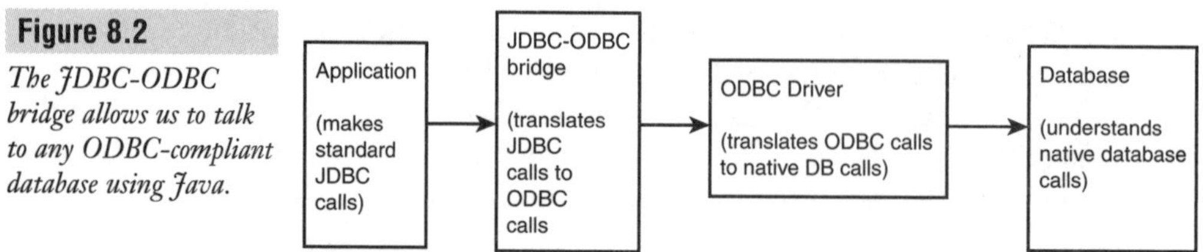

Figure 8.2

The JDBC-ODBC bridge allows us to talk to any ODBC-compliant database using Java.

Creating the Inventory Database

The first thing we need to do is to create the inventory database. To do that, we're going to create a connection to our database, and then execute an SQL statement to create the table.

Creating the ODBC Connection

Because we're going to be using the JDBC-ODBC bridge, we need to create an ODBC connection. To make things simple, it doesn't matter what database you use, as long as you can create an ODBC connection to it.

Setting up an ODBC connection on a Microsoft Windows system involves the following steps:

1. Create the database, if necessary. We can use a text database, so we can create it on the fly, so to speak. A Microsoft Access database can also be created this way, even if you don't have the actual software on your machine.
2. Choose Start/Settings/Control Panel. This will open a window of control panels, one of which will be ODBC Data Sources, ODBC Administrator, or something similar. Double-click this icon to open the control panel.
3. Click the System DSN tab, as in Figure 8.3.

Figure 8.3

The ODBC Data Source Administrator appears as shown.

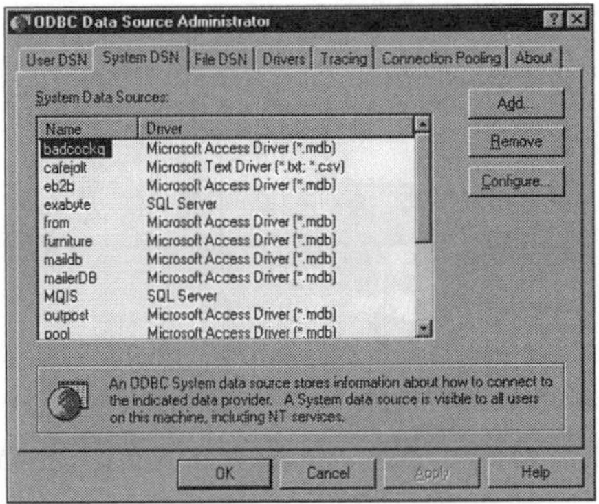

4. Choose a database format, as in Figure 8.4. The formats that you have available will be determined by what drivers are installed in your machine. Drivers are typically installed with programs that use databases, such as Microsoft Visual InterDev, or with the databases themselves. In most cases, the simplest to use will be the Microsoft Access or Text drivers.

Figure 8.4

Choose a database format for your Data Source Name.

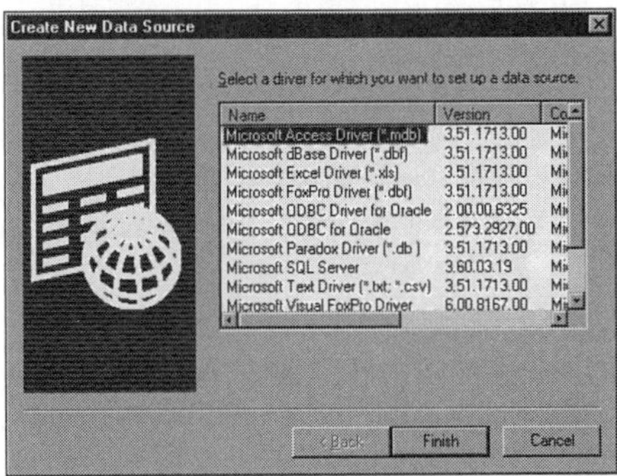

EXCURSION

Which Driver Should I Use?

In general, it makes no difference which ODBC driver you use. In fact, that was the whole point of ODBC—to enable programmers to write their code without worrying about which database it would be run against.

Which driver you use is going to be determined by three factors:

- What software is available to your machine. Although you can actually create a Microsoft Access database even if you don't have Access installed in your machine, you couldn't create an Oracle database without having Oracle installed, but if there is an Oracle instance running on an accessible machine, you could create an ODBC Connection to utilize it.
- What drivers are available on your machine. Some drivers, such as Microsoft Access, are installed with Windows. Others, such as the Oracle drivers or even the Text driver, are installed with other software.
- What development environment you prefer. If you feel comfortable using Access to start out, you shouldn't have to use SQL Server just because it's there.

5. If no existing databases are available, choose Microsoft Access and click `Create` to create a new database—even if Access isn't installed on your machine.
6. Click `Add` and follow the instructions. Instructions will vary based on the type of driver.
7. When the DSN is created, click `OK` to close the window.

How We Connect to a Database

When we want to connect to a database with Java, we need three things:

- The database
- The JDBC driver for the database (or, in our case, the JDBC-ODBC Bridge)
- A DriverManager object, which actually uses the driver to access to the database

The database should already have been created, either before or during DSN creation, so now we'll look at loading the JDBC driver, as in Listing 8.1.

Many, many people have made entire careers out of creating and manipulating databases, so we're certainly not going to be able to tell you all you'll ever need to know in this book. There are plenty of good books out there, depending on which database you're using.

For now, however, we just need an empty database, which we can create with the DSN.

Listing 8.1—Loading the JDBC Driver

```
0:import java.sql.*;
1:
2:public class CreateTable {
3:
4:    public static void main(String[] args) {
5:
6:        try {
7:            Class.forName("sun.jdbc.odbc.JdbcOdbcDriver");
8:        } catch (ClassNotFoundException e) {
9:            System.out.println("There was a problem loading " +
10:                 "the database driver.");
11:         }
12:
13:    }
14:
15:}
```

Notice that we aren't dealing with a servlet here. All the processing we do in this chapter will use a Java application, so of course, we need a public, static, `main()` method.

The major new item here is line 7. Let's backtrack before we look at it.

In the course of building our project, we've seen two different ways to create an object. The first was to use the new keyword and a constructor, as in

```
DocumentImpl products = new DocumentImpl();
```

The second was to use a creation method from another object, as in

```
Element newProduct = products.createElement("newproduct");
```


Some classes are created automatically when the application starts, and we don't need to create an instance of them to use their static methods. For example, we don't need to create a `System` object to use `System.out.print()`.

In this case, we want to tell the Java Virtual Machine to load the JDBC driver class we want to use—but we want to do it from within our application. That's what we're doing on line 7.

This is a third way to create an object, known as dynamically loading a class. When we use the static `forName()` method of the `Class` class, the `Class` object tries to find the named class. If it finds it, it loads it, and then links it in with the rest of the application, so it's available for use. If there's a problem, it throws a `ClassNotFoundException`.

Now that we've loaded the driver, we need to create the connection to the database, as in Listing 8.2.

Listing 8.2—Creating the Connection to the Database

```
0:import java.sql.*;
1:
2:public class CreateTable {
3:
4:    public static void main(String[] args) {
5:
6:        try {
7:            Class.forName("sun.jdbc.odbc.JdbcOdbcDriver");
8:        } catch (ClassNotFoundException e) {
9:            System.out.println("There was a problem loading " +
10:                "the database driver.");
11:            return;
12:        }
13:
14:        try {
15:            String URL = "jdbc:odbc:furniture";
16:            String username = "";
17:            String password = "";
18:
19:            Connection furnDB = null;
20:            furnDB = DriverManager.getConnection (URL,
21:                                                   username,
22:                                                   password);
23:        } catch (SQLException e) {
24:            System.out.println("There was a problem connecting to " +
25:               "the database.");
26:        }
27:
28:    }
29:
30:}
```

In previous chapters, when we had several tasks that needed a `try/catch` block, we put them all together into one. In this case, we're actually splitting them out into different blocks.

The only trouble with this is that the whole purpose of a `try/catch` block is that if an error occurs, we can handle it and move on with the rest of the application. In this case, however, if there is an error loading the driver, we don't want to go on with the rest of the application. Instead, we want to exit the `main()` method, which will kick us out of the application altogether. That's what we're doing on line 11 with the `return` statement. After the error message is printed, the application will simply end.

Lines 14 through 26 are where we're creating a connection to the database.

On line 15, we're defining the location of the database itself. All locations in Java are defined in terms of URIs, or, in this case, URLs, so that's what we're defining on line 15. Of course, at first glance, it doesn't look much like most URLs we're used to seeing, but it's really not all that different.

The most common URLs we see look something like

```
http://www.mcp.com
```

The `http:` is not just a random sequence of characters. It actually means something. In this case, it means to use the `http` protocol to access the location `//www.mcp.com`. Other URLs might look like

```
ftp://www.mcp.com
```

or

```
mailto:javafs@nicholaschase.com
```

All that those first characters are doing is telling the browser (in most cases) which protocol to use. In our case, we have

```
jdbc:odbc:furniture
```

The first string is telling our application to use the `jdbc` protocol to reach the location `odbc:furniture`. The fact that this location also starts with a protocol is no accident. We're using the JDBC-ODBC bridge, so what we're accessing with JDBC is actually an ODBC data source. In this case, it's the DSN `furniture`.

If you're using Access or text, chances are you won't be securing your database with a username and password; however, it's not unusual to take that step to protect our data, so we'll go ahead and leave that in, even though we won't be assigning them data.

On line 19, we're creating a database `Connection` object called `furnDB`, but we're not assigning anything to it yet. Instead, we're creating the actual object on lines 20 through 22, using the static `DriverManager` method `getConnection()`.

8

If there is any problem creating the connection, a `SQLException` will be thrown, and we'll get our error message. Because this is the last item in the application anyway, we haven't worried about a return statement.

Now it's time for us to actually create our table.

EXCURSION

The Enterprise Database

What we are doing with this chapter is creating and manipulating an SQL database to maintain inventory quantities. Although we're just going to create a single inventory table, this information would normally be contained in a company's enterprise systems, possibly along with information on other company functions, such as product data, store information, employee data, and so on.

Because we're not going to be working with any of that data, we're not going to create tables for it, but you should keep in mind that the techniques we see here could just as easily be applied to a much larger system.

The `inventory` table needs to accommodate not just how many pieces of a particular item we have, but also whether it's in a showroom or a warehouse, and what color it is, just as we have it stored in the `products.xml` file. To create this table, we're going to use a create script. This is an SQL command that tells the database to create the table, and also tells it how.

A create script can be executed just as any other command can, so we can do it from our application instead of actually opening up, say, Microsoft Access. (In fact, we don't even need to have Access on our machine, as long as we have the driver for it.)

In this case, the create script will look something like this:

```
create table inventory (product_id  text,
                        location    text,
                        color       text,
                        inv         number)
```

The exact datatypes will vary with your database, but the syntax is basically the same. In Listing 8.3, we create the `inventory` table.

Listing 8.3—Creating the `inventory` Table

```
import java.sql.*;

public class CreateTable {

    public static void main(String[] args) {

        try {
            Class.forName("sun.jdbc.odbc.JdbcOdbcDriver");
        } catch (ClassNotFoundException e) {
            System.out.println("There was a problem loading " +
                "the database driver.");
             return;
         }

         Connection furnDB = null;
         try {
             String URL = "jdbc:odbc:furniture";
             String username = "";
             String password = "";

             furnDB = DriverManager.getConnection (URL,
                                                   username,
                                                   password);
         } catch (SQLException e) {
             System.out.println("There was a problem connecting to " +
                "the database.");
             return;
         }

         try {
```

Listing 8.3—continued

```
30:
31:             Statement sql = furnDB.createStatement();
32:
33:             String sqlTxt = "create table inventory ("+
34:                             "product_id text,"+
35:                             "location text,"+
36:                             "color text,"+
37:                             "inv number)";
38:
39:             sql.execute(sqlTxt);
40:
41:         } catch (SQLException e) {
42:             System.out.print("Error executing SQL: "
43:                 + e.getMessage());
44:             return;
45:         }
46:
47:         try {
48:             furnDB.close();
49:         } catch (SQLException e) {
50:             System.out.print("Couldn't close database.");
51:         }
52:     }
53:
54:}
```

The first thing we've done, on line 14, is to move the declaration of the `furnDB` object out of its `try/catch` block so that it's available to the rest of the application. We've also added a `return` statement to line 26, because we can't create the table if we can't connect to the database.

In line 31, we're creating a new kind of object, an SQL `Statement`. The `Statement` object is where we'll actually do the work of interacting with the database, as we do on line 39, where we actually `execute` the create script, which we put together on lines 33 through 37.

Finally, on lines 47 though 51, we close the database when we're finished with it.

Compile and run this application, and then check your database. You should see a new inventory table.

What we've done here is pretty simple and straightforward, but many other types of statements, such as `selects`, `updates`, and `deletes`, can be done in a similar way, as we'll soon see.

Creating the Initial Inventory

Now that we have the table created, we need to populate it. Normally, this would have been done long before we ever got to the point of even having `*.xml` files to work with, but we're going to give this table a base of the information in the `products.xml` file. Later, we'll look at adjusting it based on vendor information and orders, and then updating the `products.xml` file accordingly.

Let's start with the basics. In Listing 8.4, we'll create the application to access the database.

Listing 8.4—`CreateInventory.java`: Connect to the Database

```
import java.sql.*;

public class CreateInventory {

    public static void main(String[] args) {

        try {
            Class.forName("sun.jdbc.odbc.JdbcOdbcDriver");
        } catch (ClassNotFoundException e) {
            System.out.println("There was a problem loading " +
                "the database driver.");
             return;
         }

         Connection furnDB = null;
         try {
             String URL = "jdbc:odbc:furniture";
             String username = "";
             String password = "";

             furnDB = DriverManager.getConnection (URL,
                                                   username,
                                                   password);
         } catch (SQLException e) {
             System.out.println("There was a problem connecting to " +
                "the database.");
             return;
         }

         try {
             furnDB.close();
         } catch (SQLException e) {
             System.out.print("Couldn't close database.");
         }
    }

}
```

This is just our `CreateTable.java` file, with the SQL statement removed.

What we want to do is use DOM to read the `products.xml` file and give us the initial inventory. In Listing 8.5, we begin that process.

Listing 8.5—`CreateInventory.java`: Getting the `products.xml` Information

```
import java.sql.*;
import org.apache.xerces.parsers.*;
import org.apache.xerces.dom.*;
import org.w3c.dom.*;

public class CreateInventory {

    public static void main(String[] args) {

        try {
            Class.forName("sun.jdbc.odbc.JdbcOdbcDriver");
        } catch (ClassNotFoundException e) {
            System.out.println("There was a problem loading " +
               "the database driver.");
            return;
        }

        Connection furnDB = null;
        try {
            String URL = "jdbc:odbc:furniture";
            String username = "";
            String password = "";

            furnDB = DriverManager.getConnection (URL,
                                                  username,
                                                  password);
        } catch (SQLException e) {
            System.out.println("There was a problem connecting to " +
               "the database.");
            return;
        }

        try {
            DOMParser parser = new DOMParser();
            parser.parse("/files/products.xml");
            Document productDoc = parser.getDocument();

            Element productRoot = productDoc.getDocumentElement();
            NodeList products =
                   productRoot.getElementsByTagName("product");
            for (int i=0; i < products.getLength(); i++) {
                Element thisProduct = (Element)products.item(i);
                Element thisProduct_id = (Element)thisProduct
                       .getElementsByTagName("product_id").item(0);
                String product_id =
                       thisProduct_id.getFirstChild().getNodeValue();
                System.out.print("\nInventory for product "+
                       product_id+"\n");

                NodeList inventoryElements =
                       thisProduct.getElementsByTagName("inventory");
```

Listing 8.5—continued

```
51:                 for (int j=0; j < inventoryElements.getLength(); j++) {
52:                     Element thisInventory =
53:                           (Element)inventoryElements.item(j);
54:                     String thisColor =
55:                           thisInventory.getAttribute("color");
56:                     System.out.print("color="+thisColor+" | ");
57:
58:                     String thisLocation =
59:                           thisInventory.getAttribute("location");
60:                     System.out.print("location="+thisLocation+" | ");
61:
62:                     String thisInv =
63:                           thisInventory.getFirstChild().getNodeValue();
64:                     System.out.print("inventory="+thisInv+"\n");
65:                 }
66:             }
67:
68:         } catch (java.io.IOException e) {
69:             System.out.print("There was a problem reading products.xml.");
70:         } catch (org.xml.sax.SAXException e) {
71:             System.out.print("There was a problem parsing products.xml.");
72:         }
73:
74:         try {
75:             furnDB.close();
76:         } catch (SQLException e) {
77:             System.out.print("Couldn't close database.");
78:         }
79:     }
80:
81:}
```

On lines 1 through 3, we're importing the classes we're going to need to parse and manipulate the data from the file. The work is actually done on lines 32 through 72.

On lines 33 through 35, we parse the file, as usual, extracting the root element on line 37. On line 28, we're actually getting all the product nodes in the file, no matter what level they're on, using `getElementsByTagName()`.

After we have the list of products, we loop through them on lines 40 through 72. Line 41 gets this current product element. From there, we tell the application to look for a `product_id` element within the `product` on lines 42 and 43. Because there should be only one, we're pretty safe just requesting the first one on the list.

Of course, that is going to return us an element, so on lines 44 and 45, we get the text node that is its first child, and take the value as the `product_id`. We'll then output that information.

After we have the product information, we need the inventory elements. There can be any number of them for a particular product, because we broke it out by color and location. On lines 49 and 50, we're getting the whole list of inventory elements for this product, and on lines 51 through 65, we're getting the color and location attributes and the actual value, and then outputting everything to the screen.

If we compile and run this application, we should get results something like this:

```
Inventory for product QA3452
color=royal blue | location=warehouse | inventory=11.0
color=royal blue | location=showroom | inventory=4.0
color=flower print | location=warehouse | inventory=16.0
color=flower print | location=showroom | inventory=3.0
color=seafoam green | location=warehouse | inventory=20.0
color=teal | location=warehouse | inventory=14.0
color=burgundy | location=warehouse | inventory=34.0

Inventory for product RC2342
color= | location=warehouse | inventory=40.0
color= | location=showroom | inventory=2.0

Inventory for product BR3452
color= | location=showroom | inventory=3.0

Inventory for product WWWdrt
color= | location=warehouse | inventory=132.0

Inventory for product WWWsc
color= | location=warehouse | inventory=300.0

Inventory for product WWWhch
color= | location=warehouse | inventory=232.0

Inventory for product HallBench
color= | location=warehouse | inventory=143.0
color= | location=showroom | inventory=5.0

Inventory for product SofaLoveSeat
color=magnolia print | location=showroom | inventory=3.0
color=magnolia print | location=warehouse | inventory=36.0
color=nautical print | location=warehouse | inventory=1.0
color=nautical print | location=showroom | inventory=432.0

Inventory for product 3253435
color= | location=showroom | inventory=23.0
color= | location=warehouse | inventory=15.0

Inventory for product 5622345

Inventory for product 39981234
```

Note that the last two products don't seem to have any inventory information, but their product_ids are showing up. We'll need to make sure that when we actually insert records into the database, they aren't incomplete. Also notice that there are some situations in which there is no color information. We'll need to keep that in mind later, when we try to update the table.

Inserting Data

Now that we've extracted the data from the products.xml file, we need to insert it into the database. SQL has a standard syntax for insert statements. For instance, to insert the data for the teal version of QA3452, we could use

```
insert into inventory values ('QA3452', 'warehouse', 'teal', 14)
```

Because all the fields have data, we don't need to specify the names of the columns. This could be a problem later, however, if we ever changed the definition of the table, say, to add a backordered flag. It's much better practice to use a statement like

```
insert into inventory (product_id, location, color, inv) values
➥('QA3452', 'warehouse', 'teal', 14)
```

This way, if anything outside these columns changes, the statement will still be accurate. For instance, we could add product WWWdrt with

```
insert into inventory (product_id, location, inv) values
➥ ('WWWdrt', 'warehouse', 132)
```

In Listing 8.6, we'll create the insert statements and execute them against the database.

Listing 8.6—CreateInventory.java: Inserting Records into the Database

```
import java.sql.*;
import org.apache.xerces.parsers.*;
import org.apache.xerces.dom.*;
import org.w3c.dom.*;

public class CreateInventory {

    public static void insertInventory(String product_id,
                                       String color,
                                       String location,
                                       String inv)
    {
        String sqlTxt = "insert into inventory " +
                        "(product_id, color, location, inv) values " +
                        "('"+product_id+"', '"+color+"', " +
                        " '"+location+"', "+inv+")";
        System.out.println(sqlTxt);

        Statement sql = furnDB.createStatement();
        sql.execute(sqlTxt);

```

Listing 8.6—continued

```
}

public static void main(String[] args) {

…

    Connection furnDB = null;
    try {
        String URL = "jdbc:odbc:furniture";
        String username = "";
        String password = "";

        furnDB = DriverManager.getConnection (URL,
                                              username,
                                              password);
    } catch (SQLException e) {
        System.out.println("There was a problem connecting to " +
           "the database.");
        return;
    }

    try {
…
            String product_id =
                   thisProduct_id.getFirstChild().getNodeValue();

            NodeList inventoryElements =
                   thisProduct.getElementsByTagName("inventory");
            for (int j=0; j < inventoryElements.getLength(); j++) {
                Element thisInventory =
                      (Element)inventoryElements.item(j);
                String thisColor =
                      thisInventory.getAttribute("color");

                String thisLocation =
                      thisInventory.getAttribute("location");

                String thisInv =
                       thisInventory.getFirstChild().getNodeValue();

                insertInventory(product_id, thisColor,
                                          thisLocation, thisInv);
            }
        }

     } catch (java.io.IOException e) {
     System.out.print("There was a problem reading products.xml.");
     } catch (org.xml.sax.SAXException e) {
     System.out.print("There was a problem parsing products.xml.");
     }

     try {
         furnDB.close();
```

Listing 8.6—continued

```
90:         } catch (SQLException e) {
91:             System.out.print("Couldn't close database.");
92:         }
93:     }
94:
95:}
```

What we're doing here is taking our logic for inserting a `product` and moving it into a separate function. This will give us modularity, so if we were to change the table, or add extra logic, we can do it all in one place.

First, however, let's take a look at what we have. We've removed the output statements, but we've added a call to the `insertInventory()` method on lines 77 and 78. That method, on lines 7 through 21, takes the relevant information, creates the SQL statement on lines 12 through 15, and executes it on line 19.

There are, however, two problems with the application as it's written.

First of all, `furnDB` doesn't exist in the scope of `insertInventory()`. Instead, we need to make it a static member of the class, so it's available everywhere.

The second change has to do with error checking. The `sql.execute` method has the potential to throw an `SQLException`. Previously, what we've done is to encase our login in a `try/catch` block, but we have a second option, which would be to throw the exception from the function, and then catch it back in the main block.

Listing 8.7 shows both of these changes.

Listing 8.7—`CreateInventory.java`: Catching the Exception

```
import java.sql.*;
import org.apache.xerces.parsers.*;
import org.apache.xerces.dom.*;
import org.w3c.dom.*;

public class CreateInventory {

    static Connection furnDB = null;
    static Statement sql = null;
    static String sqlTxt = "";

    public static void insertInventory(String product_id,
                                 String color,
                                 String location,
                                 String inv) throws SQLException
    {

        if (color.equals("")) {
            color = "none";
        }
```

Listing 8.7—continued

```
        sqlTxt = "insert into inventory " +
                 "(product_id, color, location, inv) values " +
                 "('"+product_id+"',  '"+color+"', " +
                 "  '"+location+"', "+inv+")";
        System.out.println(sqlTxt);

        sql.execute(sqlTxt);

    }

    public static void main(String[] args) {

…
        try {
            String URL = "jdbc:odbc:furniture";
            String username = "";
            String password = "";

            furnDB = DriverManager.getConnection (URL,
                                                  username,
                                                  password);
            sql = furnDB.createStatement();

        } catch (SQLException e) {
            System.out.println("There was a problem connecting to " +
               "the database.");
            return;
        }

        try {
…
                    String thisInv =
                           thisInventory.getFirstChild().getNodeValue();

                    insertInventory(product_id, thisColor,
                                              thisLocation, thisInv);

                }
            }

        } catch (java.io.IOException e) {
            System.out.print("There was a problem reading products.xml.");
        } catch (SQLException e) {
            System.out.print("There was a problem with the SQL string: "+
                                                                sqlTxt);
        } catch (org.xml.sax.SAXException e) {
            System.out.print("There was a problem parsing products.xml.");
        }

        try {
            furnDB.close();
        } catch (SQLException e) {
```

Listing 8.7—continued

```
103:            System.out.print("Couldn't close database.");
104:        }
105:    }
106:
107:}
```

The first thing that we've done here is to take `furnDB` and move it out to be a static object, so we can call it from within any of our methods. We've done the same with `sql`, so that we can create it just once, on line 49, and just use it over and over. From a programming standpoint, it doesn't matter which way we do it, but it does from an efficiency standpoint. Every time we create a new object, there's overhead involved—processing power, memory, and so on. If we can just create it once, that's much more efficient. We've also moved `sqlTxt` out so that we can print it with our exception in lines 93 through 95.

Let's take a moment to look at that exception. We're throwing it from the `insertInventory()`method, so if it occurs there, we will return to the `main()` method—specifically to the `try/catch` block where `insertInventory()` was called. It's then up to that block to deal with it, so we're catching it on lines 93 through 95. This is the general progression of exceptions. They propagate outward until they're handled, or until the application is terminated by an error.

Finally, on lines 17 through 19, we've added a bit of business logic that ensures there's always something in the `color` column.

Now we can compile and run this application. To run the application, remember we type

```
java CreateInventory
```

We should get output of

```
insert into inventory (product_id, color, location, inv) values
➥('QA3452',  'royal blue',  'warehouse', 11.0)
insert into inventory (product_id, color, location, inv) values
➥('QA3452',  'royal blue',  'showroom', 4.0)
insert into inventory (product_id, color, location, inv) values
➥('QA3452',  'flower print',  'warehouse', 16.0)
insert into inventory (product_id, color, location, inv) values
➥('QA3452',  'flower print',  'showroom', 3.0)
insert into inventory (product_id, color, location, inv) values
➥('QA3452',  'seafoam green',  'warehouse', 20.0)
insert into inventory (product_id, color, location, inv) values
➥('QA3452',  'teal',  'warehouse', 14.0)
insert into inventory (product_id, color, location, inv) values
➥('QA3452',  'burgundy',  'warehouse', 34.0)
insert into inventory (product_id, color, location, inv) values
```

```
➥('RC2342',   'none',   'warehouse', 40.0)
insert into inventory (product_id, color, location, inv) values
➥('RC2342',   'none',   'showroom', 2.0)
insert into inventory (product_id, color, location, inv) values
➥('BR3452',   'none',   'showroom', 3.0)
insert into inventory (product_id, color, location, inv) values
➥('WWWdrt',   'none',   'warehouse', 132.0)
insert into inventory (product_id, color, location, inv) values
➥('WWWsc',   'none',   'warehouse', 300.0)
insert into inventory (product_id, color, location, inv) values
➥('WWWhch',   'none',   'warehouse', 232.0)
insert into inventory (product_id, color, location, inv) values
➥('HallBench',   'none',   'warehouse', 143.0)
insert into inventory (product_id, color, location, inv) values
➥('HallBench',   'none',   'showroom', 5.0)
insert into inventory (product_id, color, location, inv) values
➥('SofaLoveSeat',   'magnolia print',   'showroom', 3.0)
insert into inventory (product_id, color, location, inv) values
➥('SofaLoveSeat',   'magnolia print',   'warehouse', 36.0)
insert into inventory (product_id, color, location, inv) values
➥('SofaLoveSeat',   'nautical print',   'warehouse', 1.0)
insert into inventory (product_id, color, location, inv) values
➥('SofaLoveSeat',   'nautical print',   'showroom', 432.0)
insert into inventory (product_id, color, location, inv) values
➥('3253435',   'none',   'showroom', 23.0)
insert into inventory (product_id, color, location, inv) values
➥('3253435',   'none',   'warehouse', 15.0)
```

Looking at the database should also show the data in the inventory table.

Introduction to SAX: Adjusting Inventory

This is the state we can assume that we'd be in on an ongoing basis: The inventory table shows what we have on hand, and the `products.xml` file matches it.

What happens from here is going to depend on our business rules. In many cases, we will interact with our vendors to update inventory for, say incoming shipments. This may be a manual process, where an employee needs to enter the new information, or it could be an automated process, perhaps even using XML. The end result is that additional inventory is added to the totals.

The second thing that happens is that users place orders on the site. In practice, we would probably want to find a way to keep the `products.xml` file updated and check orders against it before we accept them, but we're going to look at a compromise solution.

We're going to assume that the inventory database is updated with incoming stock, so in order to keep it accurate, we will have to subtract the items that are ordered through the site. We can then feed the updated totals back to `products.xml`.

This is going to involve reading the `orders.xml` file, figuring out which items have been ordered (and how many), and updating the inventory table with that information. As part of that process, we'll make a copy of the `orders.xml` file, but at no time will we need to change the contents of it, so it's a perfect candidate for the Simple API for XML, or SAX.

Nowhere in this process are we actually archiving the completed orders, which is obviously something that would need to be done on a real site. This could be done using the same techniques we cover in this chapter, depending on the business requirements.

We will have to do some writing of data, however, because we need to accommodate orders that might be in progress when we attempt this update. Let's take a look at our algorithm.

```
Rename orders.xml to orderUpdate.xml
Read orderUpdate.xml file
Create a Document of the open orders
Save it to orders.xml
Read orderupdate.xml file
Determine how many of each product/color combination have been ordered
Update inventory table
Update products.xml
```

We'll start by renaming the file, using standard Java, as in Listing 8.8. (If you haven't surfed through your site and placed a few orders, do it now. Make sure that some have been completed, even if you have to hand-edit the `orders.xml` file to set the status.)

Always make a copy of the original file if there's a chance that it could be damaged or destroyed, as in this case with `orders.xml`.

Listing 8.8—`UpdateInventory.java`: Renaming the `orders.xml` File

```
import java.io.*;

public class UpdateInventory extends Object {

    public static void main (String[] args) {

        String origOrders = "/files/orders.xml";
        String newOrders = "/files/ordersUpdate.xml";

        File ordersFile = new File(origOrders);
```

Listing 8.8—continued

```
10:         File newOrdersFile = new File(newOrders);
11:         ordersFile.renameTo(newOrdersFile);
12:
13:     }
14:
15:}
```

This should be pretty straightforward by now. Again, we're creating an application. On lines 6 and 7, we set our filenames and locations. The `renameTo()` method on line 11 takes only a `File` as an argument, so after we create the original `orders` file, we'll create a new one for the new location.

Now, we want to remove the orders that are completed, and then save the rest back to `orders.xml`, as we do in Listing 8.9.

Listing 8.9—`UpdateInventory.java`: Extracting the Open Orders

```
import java.io.*;
import org.apache.xerces.parsers.*;
import org.apache.xerces.dom.*;
import org.w3c.dom.*;
import org.apache.xml.serialize.*;

public class UpdateInventory extends Object {

    public static void main (String[] args) {

        String origOrders = "/files/orders.xml";
        String newOrders = "/files/ordersUpdate.xml";

        File oldUpdateFile = new File(newOrders);
        oldUpdateFile.delete();

        File newOrdersFile = new File(newOrders);
        File ordersFile = new File(origOrders);
        ordersFile.renameTo(newOrdersFile);

        DOMParser parser = new DOMParser();
        try {
            parser.parse("/files/ordersUpdate.xml");
        } catch (Exception e) {
            System.out.println("Could not parse ordersUpdate.xml.");
            return;
        }

        Document orderDoc = parser.getDocument();
        Element orderRoot = orderDoc.getDocumentElement();
        NodeList orders = orderRoot.getElementsByTagName("order");
        for (int i=0; i < orders.getLength(); i++) {

            Element thisOrder = (Element)orders.item(i);
```

Listing 8.9—continued

```
34:            Node thisStatus = thisOrder
35:                  .getElementsByTagName("order_status").item(0);
36:            String thisStatusStr =
37:                       thisStatus.getFirstChild().getNodeValue();
38:            if (!thisStatusStr.equals("open")) {
39:                 orderRoot.removeChild(thisOrder);
40:            }
41:        }
42:
43:        try {
44:            OutputFormat format =
45:                                 new OutputFormat(orderDoc, "UTF-8", true);
46:            XMLSerializer output =
47:                  new XMLSerializer(new FileWriter("/files/orders.xml"),
48:                                        format);
49:            output.serialize(orderDoc);
50:        } catch (IOException e) {
51:            System.out.print("Couldn't replace orders.xml.");
52:        }
53:
54:    }
55:
56:}
```

We've added a lot of code here, but very little of it is actually new. Now that we have compiled and run this application once, it would be good to delete the old `ordersUpdate.xml` file before we start, which we're doing on lines 13 and 14.

After the copying is done, we can go ahead and parse the file. On lines 20 through 28, we're doing the same thing we've always done—creating the parser, parsing the file, and retrieving the document object—but we've rearranged it somewhat so that only the parse is actually in the `try/catch` block. We've also set the application to quit if there's a problem parsing the file by adding the `return` statement on line 25.

On line 29, we get the `root` element, and then all the `orders` themselves on line 30. On lines 31 through 41, we're looping through the `orders` looking for those that are not still open.

The way that we do that is to retrieve the `order` element itself on line 33, and then look at the status of this `order` on lines 34 through 37. On line 38, we're checking to see whether the order is still open.

Line 39 is where we're actually removing the element from the tree if the order is not still open. As we've seen before, however, this change isn't going to make any difference unless we serialize the document back out to the file. That's what we're doing on lines 43 through 52.

If we compile and run this application, we should wind up with two files. For example, if we start with an `orders.xml` file that looks like this:

```
<?xml version="1.0" encoding="UTF-8"?>
<orders>
    <order order_id="To1010mC24980190282174342At">
        <order_status>open</order_status>
        <item product_id="RC2342">
            <quantity>5</quantity>
        </item>
    </order>
    <order order_id="To1010mC7161452772864825At">
        <order_status>complete</order_status>
        <item product_id="RC2342">
            <quantity>3</quantity>
        </item>
        <item product_id="QA3452" color="royal blue">
            <quantity>1</quantity>
        </item>
        <item product_id="QA3452" color="flower print">
            <quantity>1</quantity>
        </item>
    </order>
    <order order_id="To1010mC7161452975564999At">
        <order_status>complete</order_status>
        <item product_id="QA3452" color="flower print">
            <quantity>1</quantity>
        </item>
        <item product_id="SofaLoveSeat" color="magnolia print">
            <quantity>2</quantity>
        </item>
    </order>
</orders>
```

we should wind up with an orders.xml file that looks like this:

```
<?xml version="1.0" encoding="UTF-8"?>
<orders>
    <order order_id="To1010mC24980190282174342At">
        <order_status>open</order_status>
        <item product_id="RC2342">
            <quantity>5</quantity>
        </item>
    </order>
</orders>
```

The ordersUpdate.xml file should look just like the original orders.xml file did.

Using SAX to Parse the File

Now that we're ready to start using SAX, let's take a look at how it actually works.

SAX is much the same way. There are certain events, such as the start of an element, that require certain actions. Our job is to define those actions in such a way that as we read through the ordersUpdate.xml file, we can tally up the items that have been ordered so that later on, we can update the database.

The first thing that we have to realize is that the SAX parser, while crucial to this process, doesn't actually do any of the work we need. All it does is fire off events to an event handler, as in Figure 8.5.

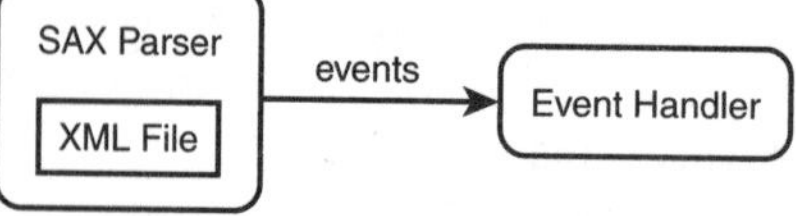

Figure 8.5

A SAX parser has one job: to fire off events to an event handler.

It is our job to create that event handler.

In Listing 8.10, we create the basic application.

Listing 8.10—`parseOrders.java`: The Basic Framework

```
0:import org.xml.sax.helpers.*;
1:import org.xml.sax.*;
2:
3:public class ParseOrders extends DefaultHandler {
4:
5:     public ParseOrders() {
6:         //Not really doing anything...
7:         System.out.println("This is the constructor.");
8:     }
9:
10:     public void callMethod() {
11:         System.out.println("This just demonstrates the method.");
12:     }
13:
14:     public static void main(String[] args) {
15:
16:         ParseOrders update = new ParseOrders();
17:         update.callMethod();
18:
19:     }
20:
21:}
```

Now, every application we've written so far has either extended `HttpServlet`, or it has extended `Object`. Now on line 3, we see that `ParseOrders` is a special kind of object, a `DefaultHandler`. The reason that this makes a difference is that it's actually a `ParseOrders` object that will become the event handler for our SAX parser.

Throughout this book, we have written programs that execute sequentially. Most of them call different functions, but for the most part, our applications have run from beginning to end. Although we have been using the object-oriented nature of Java when we call other code, such as the XML packages or the java packages themselves, we haven't actually taken advantage of it in our own code.

That's about to change.

When this program is run, it is the `main()` function on lines 14 through 19 that is executed. At this point, the only variables and methods that are available to us are those that are declared within the `main()` method and those that are declared as `static`.

When we say that a variable or method is static, we mean that it is available without creating a new instance of the class. You may notice that none of our methods in Listing 8.10 is static. Instead, on line 16, we are creating a `ParseOrders` object called `update`.

When that happens, `java` looks for a constructor that matches the number of arguments provided. In our case, that constructor is on lines 5 through 8. We have just put in a simple output statement, but this is where we would put any variables that need to be set based on how the object is created, or any actions that need to be performed just once at the start of the object's lifetime.

At this point, any of our methods would be available by calling them from the `update` object. For instance, on line 17, we make a call to `callMethod()`, which has been included just for that purpose.

If we compile and run this application, we'll see the following output:

```
This is the constructor.
This just demonstrates the method.
```

We could just as easily create several `ParseOrders` objects, each of which would have their own sets of variables and methods. Let's just look at this briefly in Listing 8.11.

8

Listing 8.11—`ParseOrders.java`: Creating Multiple Objects

```
0:import org.xml.sax.helpers.*;
1:import org.xml.sax.*;
2:
3:public class ParseOrders extends DefaultHandler {
4:
5:    public ParseOrders() {
6:        //Not really doing anything...
7:        System.out.println("This is the constructor.");
8:    }
9:
10:    public ParseOrders(String nameInput) {
11:        System.out.println("I like the name " + nameInput +".");
12:    }
13:
14:    public void callMethod() {
15:        System.out.println("This just demonstrates the method.");
16:    }
17:
18:    public static void main(String[] args) {
19:
```

Listing 8.11—continued

```
20:         ParseOrders update = new ParseOrders();
21:         update.callMethod();
22:
23:         ParseOrders otherObject = new ParseOrders("Toby");
24:
25:         ParseOrders noArg = new ParseOrders();
26:
27:         ParseOrders yesArg = new ParseOrders("Jack");
28:         yesArg.callMethod();
29:
30:     }
31:
32:}
```

Just to make things interesting, we've added a second constructor, which takes a `String` argument, on lines 10 through 12. We've been working with constructors such as

```
new ParseOrders()
```

all along, but Java is smart enough to know that if we supply an argument, as we do on line 23, we need to use the constructor that's ready to handle it. Similarly, it uses the no-argument constructor on line 25, and the new one again on line 27. On line 28, we use our new object to call `callMethod()` once again. The complete output looks like this:

```
This is the constructor.
This just demonstrates the method.
I like the name Toby.
This is the constructor.
I like the name Jack.
This just demonstrates the method.
```

Notice how only the appropriate constructor is executed, and that `callMethod()` is executed only when it is specifically called.

Now that we have our object, we're ready to assign it to a parser, as in Listing 8.12.

Listing 8.12—`ParseOrders.java`: Using the Object

```
import org.xml.sax.helpers.*;
import org.xml.sax.*;

public class ParseOrders extends DefaultHandler {

    public ParseOrders() {
        System.out.println("This is the constructor.");
    }

    public void startElement(java.lang.String uri,
                             java.lang.String localName,
```

Listing 8.12—continued

```
11:                            java.lang.String qName,
12:                            Attributes attributes)
13:                    throws SAXException
14:     {
15:
16:         System.out.println("Starting element: " + localName);
17:
18:     }
19:
20:     public void endElement(java.lang.String uri,
21:                            java.lang.String localName,
22:                            java.lang.String qName)
23:                    throws SAXException  {
24:
25:         System.out.println("Ending element: " + localName);
26:
27:     }
28:
29:     public void characters(char[] ch,
30:                           int start,
31:                           int length)
32:                    throws SAXException  {
33:
34:         System.out.println("Characters for some element");
35:
36:     }
37:
38:     public static void main(String[] args) {
39:
40:         ParseOrders update = new ParseOrders();
41:
42:         try {
43:             XMLReader parser = XMLReaderFactory
44:                .createXMLReader("org.apache.xerces.parsers.SAXParser");
45:
46:             parser.setContentHandler(update);
47:             parser.parse("/files/ordersUpdate.xml");
48:
49:         } catch (Exception e) {
50:             System.out.println("There was a problem parsing the file.");
52:         }
53:     }
54:
55:}
```

On lines 43 and 44, we're creating the SAX parser, or `XMLReader`, using the `XMLReaderFactory`. As we said earlier, all the parser does is fire off events, so on line 46, we set the `contentHandler` for this parser to be our `update` object. That means that when it does fire off events, `update` will be the object that receives them.

8

In Listing 8.13, we add the actual events.

Listing 8.13—ParseOrders.java: The Actual Events

```
import org.xml.sax.helpers.*;
import org.xml.sax.*;

public class ParseOrders extends DefaultHandler {

    public ParseOrders() {
        System.out.println("This is the constructor.");
    }

    public void startElement(String uri,
                             String localName,
                             String qName,
                             Attributes attributes)
                  throws SAXException
     {

         System.out.println("Starting element: " + localName);

     }

     public void endElement(String uri,
                            String localName,
                            String qName)
                  throws SAXException  {

         System.out.println("Ending element: " + localName);

     }

    public void characters(char[] ch,
                           int start,
                           int length)
                throws SAXException  {

        System.out.println("Characters for some element");

    }

    public static void main(String[] args) {

        ParseOrders update = new ParseOrders();

        try {
            XMLReader parser = XMLReaderFactory
               .createXMLReader("org.apache.xerces.parsers.SAXParser");

            parser.setContentHandler(update);
            parser.parse("/files/ordersUpdate.xml");

        } catch (Exception e) {
            System.out.println("There was a problem parsing the file.");
```

Listing 8.13—continued

```
        }

    }

}
```

The first thing to realize is that these are standard events, right out of the API. We didn't make them up, nor did we just decide what arguments are provided. This is what the spec says. When the parser encounters the start of an element, it calls the `startElement()` method. When it sees the end, it calls the `endElement()` method. When it sees any characters at all that are not part of a tag, it calls the `characters()` method. These are the events we will deal with.

First, let's look at what happens if we compile and run the application as is. We should see results like

```
This is the constructor.
Starting element: orders
Characters for some element
Starting element: order
Characters for some element
Starting element: order_status
Characters for some element
Ending element: order_status
Characters for some element
Starting element: item
Characters for some element
Starting element: quantity
Characters for some element
Ending element: quantity
Characters for some element
Ending element: item
Characters for some element
Ending element: order
Characters for some element
Starting element: order
Characters for some element
Starting element: order_status
Characters for some element
Ending element: order_status
Characters for some element
Starting element: item
Characters for some element
Starting element: quantity
Characters for some element
Ending element: quantity
Characters for some element
Ending element: item
Characters for some element
Ending element: order
Characters for some element
Ending element: orders
```

There are a few things we need to keep in mind. First, while the start and end elements tell us what the actual name of the element is, there is no way to automatically know that the start and the end come from the same element. We're going to have to keep track of that ourselves. Similarly, we will also have to keep track of what element these characters belong to—if they belong to an element at all, as opposed to being text between elements.

Strictly speaking, the "text between elements" is part of an element. The root element is made up of many nodes, including what seems like wasted space between elements.

Let's take a look at how this all fits together by having `update` output the `ordersUpdate.xml` file as it sees it, as in Listing 8.14.

Listing 8.14—`ParseOrders.java`: Outputting the `ordersUpdate.xml` File

```
import org.xml.sax.helpers.*;
import org.xml.sax.*;

public class ParseOrders extends DefaultHandler {

    public ParseOrders() {
        System.out.println("This is the constructor.");
    }

    public void startElement(String uri,
                             String localName,
                             String qName,
                             Attributes attributes)
                throws SAXException
    {

        System.out.print("<"+localName+" ");
        for (int i=0; i < attributes.getLength(); i++) {
            System.out.print(attributes.getLocalName(i)+
                " = " + "\"" + attributes.getValue(i)+ "\"" + " ");
        }
        System.out.print(">");

    }

    public void endElement(String uri,
                           String localName,
                           String qName)
                throws SAXException  {

        System.out.print("</"+localName+">");
```

Listing 8.14—continued

```
    }

    public void characters(char[] ch,
                           int start,
                           int length)
                  throws SAXException  {

        String allchar = new String(ch, start, length);
        System.out.print(allchar);
    }

    public static void main(String[] args) {

        ParseOrders update = new ParseOrders();

...
    }

}
```

We haven't actually changed what the events are, just what happens when they are called.

The `startElement()` method will output the start of the tag as well as the name, and then loop through the attributes that have been fed to it. For each one, it will print the name of the attribute, as well as the value. The `"\""` strings are how we tell Java to output a double quote. If we left it there all by itself, Java would think it was the end of our string. The \ is known as an escape character.

Escape character—An escape character is used to change the meaning of a letter or symbol, similar to the way pressing the Escape key on the keyboard can change the meaning of whatever you type next. For instance, with an escape character of \, we can put `\"` in the middle of a string, or tell the system to create a new line of text with `\n`.

The `endElement()` method is simple, outputting the closing tag.

EXCURSION

What Is This `localName` Business?

The SAX API is built to handle not just simple XML files, but also those that contain data from several namespaces. In that case, the qualified name, or `qName`, would consist of both the `uri` and the `localName` information. Because all we care about right now is the `localName`, that's what we're using, but the `uri` information is available to us.

Finally, there is the `characters()` method. This one is a bit more complex because instead of feeding us just a `String`, the parser sends the characters it finds as an array of `char`. In order for us to display them, we need to use them to create a `String` on line 39, and then we display that string on line 40.

All of this produces a more-or-less faithful rendition of our `ordersUpdate.xml` file.

Now that we've looked at all of the pieces, let's start to put them together. In Listing 8.15, we'll pull specific information out of the file.

Listing 8.15—`ParseOrders.java`: Extracting Quantity Information

```
0: import org.xml.sax.helpers.*;
1: import org.xml.sax.*;
2:
3: public class ParseOrders extends DefaultHandler {
4:
5:     public ParseOrders() {
6:
7:     }
8:
9:     String currentElement = "";
10:    String currentProduct_id = "";
11:    String currentColor = "";
12:
13:    public void startElement(String uri,
14:                             String localName,
15:                             String qName,
16:                             Attributes attributes)
17:                throws SAXException
18:    {
19:        currentElement = localName;
20:        if (currentElement.equals("item")) {
21:            currentProduct_id = attributes.getValue(0);
22:            currentColor = attributes.getValue(1);
23:        }
24:    }
25:
26:    public void endElement(String uri,
27:                           String localName,
28:                           String qName)
29:                throws SAXException  {
30:
31:        currentElement = "";
32:
33:    }
34:
35:    public void characters(char[] ch,
36:                           int start,
37:                           int length)
38:               throws SAXException  {
39:
```

Listing 8.15—continued

```
40:         if (currentElement.equals("quantity")) {
41:             String allchar = new String(ch, start, length);
42:             System.out.print(currentProduct_id + "/");
43:             System.out.print(currentColor + ": ");
44:             System.out.println(allchar);
45:         }
46:
47:     }
48:
49:     public static void main(String[] args) {
...
64:     }
65:
66:}
```

Because we will have to keep track of state ourselves, on lines 9 through 11 we're creating variables to hold the current information. When an element starts, the first thing that we do is record what element it is on line 19. If the element is an item, we are also recording the `product_id` and `color` for that element.

This way, when we get down to actual characters, on lines 40 through 45, we'll know what the current element is, because there's no indication from what's passed to the method. The `characters()` method itself needs to look only at the value of the `quantity` element, so we're testing for that on line 40. If it is the `quantity` element, we're outputting the information that we have.

Now, at first glance, it may seem that the `endElement()` method is going to run even if this is not the end of the `currentElement`, and it is, but that's all right. Let's look for a moment at the structure of our file, in Listing 8.16.

Listing 8.16—`ordersUpdate.xml`

```
0: <?xml version="1.0" encoding="UTF-8"?>
1: <orders>
2:     <order order_id="To1010mC24980190282174342At">
3:         <order_status>open</order_status>
4:         <item product_id="RC2342">
5:             <quantity>5</quantity>
6:         </item>
7:     </order>
8:     <order order_id="To1010mC7161452772864825At">
9:         <order_status>complete</order_status>
10:        <item product_id="RC2342">
...
30:</orders>
```

We start out with a `startElement()` event on line 1, so `currentElement` is `orders`. It then changes to `order` on line 2, and again to `order_status` on line 3. Notice that up to this point, we have not hit an `endElement()` event. Next, we have `characters()`, while `currentElement` is still `order_status`, and then finally the `endElement()` event and `currentElement` is set to `""`. Next, we have `startElement()` again, which resets `currentElement` to `item`, and then again on line 5, it's set to "`quantity`", just in time for the characters of that element.

Simply put, characters are always going to belong to the most recent `startElement()` event, and `endElement()` will always come afterward.

If we compile and run the application, we'll see results something like this:

```
RC2342/null: 5
RC2342/null: 3
QA3452/royal blue: 1
QA3452/flower print: 1
QA3452/flower print: 1
SofaLoveSeat/magnolia print: 2
```

(The duplicates aren't an error—that's what's really in the file, remember.)

It seems as though everything is functioning properly, but what about those `nulls`? They're appearing whenever there's no `color` information, but in the database, we set color to `none` in that case. A quick change to the `startElement()` method will take care of that, as in Listing 8.17.

Listing 8.17—`ParseOrders.java`: Cleaning Up Color Information

```
...
    public void startElement(String uri,
                             String localName,
                             String qName,
                             Attributes attributes)
                throws SAXException
    {
        currentElement = localName;
        if (currentElement.equals("item")) {
            currentProduct_id = attributes.getValue(0);
            if (attributes.getLength() > 1) {
                currentColor = attributes.getValue(1);
            } else {
                currentColor = "none";
            }
        }
    }
...
```

Because we know what order the attributes will be found in for the `item` element, we can simply see whether there are any attributes besides the `product_id`, and if there aren't, we can set the `currentColor` accordingly.

Now that we're retrieving the information properly, we could go ahead and update the `inventory` table for each `item`, but that means that we'll be making multiple updates for the same item. It would be much more efficient if we totaled the information and made one big update at the end.

To do that, we need to look at things in a new way. Most programmers are familiar with `arrays`, which store information based on a numerical index. For instance, if we were to represent the string `"hello"` as an array of `char` (as it would be given to us by the `characters()` method), it would look something like this:

```
ch[0] = 'h';
ch[1] = 'e';
ch[2] = 'l';
ch[3] = 'l';
ch[4] = 'o';
```

Now, this is great if you're representing something that's easily linked to a number, such as by position. But what if you want to find it again by a non-numeric value, such as the `product_id`? That's what a `Hashtable` is for.

A `Hashtable` is like an array, but instead of using numeric indexes, we use text values. This allows us to retreive the information much more conveniently.

In Listing 8.18, we'll set up the `Hashtable` using the `product_id`; then when we're done, we'll take into account the `color` information.

Listing 8.18—`ParseOrders.java`: Keeping a Running Total

```
import org.xml.sax.helpers.*;
import org.xml.sax.*;
import java.util.*;

public class ParseOrders extends DefaultHandler {

    public ParseOrders() {

    }

    String currentElement = "";
    String currentProduct_id = "";
    String currentColor = "";
    Hashtable products = new Hashtable();

...

    public void characters(char[] ch,
                           int start,
                           int length)
                throws SAXException  {

        if (currentElement.equals("quantity")) {

            String allchar = new String(ch, start, length);

```

Listing 8.18—continued

```
50:             if (products.containsKey(currentProduct_id)) {
51:
52:                 String currentValue =
53:                        (String)products.get(currentProduct_id);
54:                 int current = new Integer(currentValue).intValue();
55:                 int newint = new Integer(allchar).intValue();
56:                 int subtotal = current + newint;
57:                 products.put(currentProduct_id,
58:                              currentProduct_id.valueOf(subtotal) );
59:
60:             } else {
61:                 products.put(currentProduct_id, allchar);
62:             }
63:         }
64:
65:     }
66:
67:     public static void main(String[] args) {
...
82:     }
83:
84:}
```

The Hashtable class is part of the java.util package, so we'll go ahead and import that on line 2, and create the actual object on line 13.

From there, we move down to characters, which is the only place it matters. Because we're storing our data by product_id, on line 50 we can see whether we've already added an entry for this product by checking to see whether that particular key value is already present.

The first time we hit this point, that will be false, and we'll move down to line 61, where we'll go ahead and put that value into products. The first value is the key, and the second is the value itself. This can be any object, but it can't be a primitive data type, such as int.

If the particular product_id we're working with is already in the products Hashtable, what we want to do is update that value. To do that, we first have to retrieve the actual value, on lines 52 and 53. Without any casting, this would simply be an Object, so we'll have to jump through a couple of hoops before we can do anything useful. First, we'll retrieve it as a String, and then on line 54, we'll use that String to get an int by using the Integer class. In this case, new Integer(currentValue) creates an Integer object which just happens to have no name, and then it is that object that executes its intValue() method to return us an int.

We do the same thing with allchar on line 55. Now we have two ints that we can add together on 56 to give us a subtotal, which we then have to convert back into a string on line 58. (It doesn't matter that we're using an existing `String` object to do this. Because we're feeding it the value we want to convert, absolutely any `String` object will do.) Lines 57 and 58 are just like line 61, except that we're updating a present value instead of adding a new one.

This is all well and good, but it doesn't take into account the `color` information. The simplest way to do that would be to add the `color` to the key, as in Listing 8.19.

Listing 8.19—`ParseObjects.java`: Adding the Color to the `Hashtable`

```
...
13:     Hashtable products = new Hashtable();
14:     String currentKey = "";
15:
16:     public void startElement(String uri,
17:                              String localName,
18:                              String qName,
19:                              Attributes attributes)
20:                   throws SAXException
21:     {
22:         currentElement = localName;
23:         if (currentElement.equals("item")) {
24:             currentProduct_id = attributes.getValue(0);
25:             if (attributes.getLength() > 1) {
26:                 currentColor = attributes.getValue(1);
27:             } else {
28:                 currentColor = "none";
29:             }
30:             currentKey = currentProduct_id + "|" + currentColor;
31:         }
32:     }
33:
...
43:     public void characters(char[] ch,
44:                            int start,
45:                            int length)
46:                 throws SAXException  {
47:
48:         if (currentElement.equals("quantity")) {
49:
50:             String allchar = new String(ch, start, length);
51:
52:             if (products.containsKey(currentKey)) {
53:
54:                 String currentValue =
55:                         (String)products.get(currentKey);
56:                 int current = new Integer(currentValue).intValue();
57:                 int newint = new Integer(allchar).intValue();
58:                 int subtotal = current + newint;
59:                 products.put(currentKey,
60:                              currentKey.valueOf(subtotal) );
61:
62:             } else {
```

Listing 8.19—continued

```
63:                 products.put(currentKey, allchar);
64:             }
65:         }
66:
67:     }
68:
69:     public void showTotals () {
70:
71:         Enumeration allProducts = products.keys();
72:         while (allProducts.hasMoreElements()) {
73:             String thisKey = (String)allProducts.nextElement();
74:             String thisValue = (String)products.get(thisKey);
75:             System.out.print(thisKey+": "+thisValue+"\n");
76:         }
77:
78:     }
79:
80:     public static void main(String[] args) {
81:
82:         ParseOrders update = new ParseOrders();
83:
84:         try {
...
91:         } catch (Exception e) {
92:             System.out.println("There was a problem parsing the file.");
93:             return;
94:         }
95:
96:         update.showTotals();
97:
98:     }
```

Changing the key for the `products` `Hashtable` was easy. We simply created the new variable on line 14, populated it on line 30, and changed `characters()` to look at `currentKey` instead of `currentProduct_id` on lines 52, 55, 59, 60, and 63. This way, it is the combination of the `product_id` and the `color` that determines the key.

We've also added `showTotals()`, which allows us to make sure that things are working properly.

On line 71, we're creating an `Enumeration` based on the keys that are in `products`. (We've dealt with `Enumerations` before, in a simpler form, when we were using `StringTokenizer`.) For every element in the `Enumeration`, we'll look at the key on line 73, and then use it to retrieve the value from our `products` `Hashtable` on line 74. Finally, we'll output the values on line 75.

Of course, this wouldn't do us any good if we didn't actually call it, which we're doing on line 96 (after adding `return` statement in case there's an error parsing the file). This should give us output something like

```
QA3452|flower print: 2
QA3452|royal blue: 1
RC2342|none: 8
SofaLoveSeat|magnolia print: 2
```

Updating the Database

Now that we've got the totals, we're ready to go ahead and save them back to the database. To do that, we'll use the principles we learned earlier in this chapter. First, in Listing 8.20, we'll lay the foundation by connecting to the database and retrieving our information from the `Hashtable`.

Listing 8.20—`ParseOrders.java`: Connecting to the Database

```
import org.xml.sax.helpers.*;
import org.xml.sax.*;
import java.util.*;
import java.sql.*;

public class ParseOrders extends DefaultHandler {

...
    public void showTotals () {

        Enumeration allProducts = products.keys();
        while (allProducts.hasMoreElements()) {
            String thisKey = (String)allProducts.nextElement();
            String thisValue = (String)products.get(thisKey);
            System.out.print(thisKey+": "+thisValue+"\n");
        }

    }

    Connection furnDB = null;
    Statement sql = null;

    public void saveTotals() {
        String URL = "jdbc:odbc:furniture";
        String username = "";
        String password = "";

        try {
            Class.forName("sun.jdbc.odbc.JdbcOdbcDriver");
        } catch (ClassNotFoundException e) {
            System.out.println("Problem loading the database driver.");
            return;
        }

        try {
            furnDB = DriverManager.getConnection (URL,
                                                  username,
```

8

Listing 8.20—continued

```
                                                      password);
            sql = furnDB.createStatement();

            Enumeration allProducts = products.keys();
            while (allProducts.hasMoreElements()) {
                String thisKey = (String)allProducts.nextElement();

                StringTokenizer tokenizer =
                         new StringTokenizer(thisKey, "|");
                String thisProduct = tokenizer.nextToken();
                String thisColor = tokenizer.nextToken();

                String thisValue = (String)products.get(thisKey);

                System.out.println(thisProduct+", "+thisColor+": "
                                                      +thisValue);

            }

            furnDB.close();
        } catch (Exception e) {
            System.out.println("Problem updating the database.");
            return;
        }

    }

    public static void main(String[] args) {

        ParseOrders update = new ParseOrders();

        try {
            XMLReader parser = XMLReaderFactory
               .createXMLReader("org.apache.xerces.parsers.SAXParser");

            parser.setContentHandler(update);
            parser.parse("/files/ordersUpdate.xml");

        } catch (Exception e) {
            System.out.println("There was a problem parsing the file.");
            return;
        }

        update.saveTotals();

    }

}
```

Most of the `saveTotals()` method should be familiar from earlier in the chapter.

On lines 81 and 82, we create the database connection and the statement outside the method so we can use it in any additional functions, as we did before. On lines 85 through 87, we set up the database connection information, and on lines 89 through 94 we load the driver. On lines 97 through 100, we create the database `Connection` and the `Statement`.

Lines 102 through 116 are similar to `showTotals()`, in that we're looping through the elements of the `Hashtable`, except that on lines 106 through 109, we're breaking down the key value based on the fact that we used a `|` as the delimiter. We know there are only two values, so we don't need to create a loop. Finally, on line 111 we're retrieving the actual inventory value, and everything is displayed on lines 113 and 114. On line 118, we close the database `Connection`.

Now we're ready to actually update the database. To do that, we need to use a third type of SQL statement, the `update` statement.

An `update` statement has several parts. Typically, it consists of the name of the table we want to update, which columns and what their new values should be, and a `where` clause. The `where` clause is designed to determine which rows should actually be updated. For instance, to update our SofaLoveSeat, we would—if someone had bought two Sofa Love Seats—have an update statement like

```
update inventory set inv = (inv - 2) where product_id = 'SofaLoveSeat'
➥and color = 'magnolia print'
```

This tells the database that we want to update the `inventory` table, that we want to change the value of the `inv` column, and that we want the new value to be the current value minus 2. It also filters out any rows that don't meet the criteria of the `where` clause, so we should get just our one row.

In Listing 8.21, we'll add this functionality to the application.

Listing 8.21—`ParseOrders.java`: Updating the Database

```
...
80:
81:     Connection furnDB = null;
82:     Statement sql = null;
83:
84:     public void update(String thisProduct_id,
85:                        String thisColor,
86:                        String thisValue) throws SQLException {
87:
88:        String sqlTxt = "update inventory set inv = (inv - " +
89:              thisValue +") where product_id = '"+thisProduct_id+"' "+
90:              " and color = '"+ thisColor+"'";
91:        System.out.println(sqlTxt);
92:
93:        int numFound = sql.executeUpdate(sqlTxt);
```

Listing 8.21—continued

```
94:
95:         if ( numFound == 0 ) {
96:             System.out.print(thisProduct_id + "|" + thisColor +
97:                  " not found.");
98:         }
99:
100:     }
101:
102:     public void saveTotals() {
...
121:             while (allProducts.hasMoreElements()) {
122:                 String thisKey = (String)allProducts.nextElement();
123:
124:                 StringTokenizer tokenizer =
125:                           new StringTokenizer(thisKey, "|");
126:                 String thisProduct = tokenizer.nextToken();
127:                 String thisColor = tokenizer.nextToken();
128:
129:                 String thisValue = (String)products.get(thisKey);
130:
131:                 update(thisProduct, thisColor, thisValue);
132:
133:             }
134:
135:             furnDB.close();
...
```

We make the call on line 131, but lines 84 through 100 are where we're actually doing the work. We're creating a method where we take in the `product_id`, `color`, and `value`, and then build the SQL to update the database with it. That's what we're doing on line 88 through 90, as we discussed previously. In line 91, we're outputting it so we can make sure everything is running properly.

On line 93, we're doing something a little different. Earlier, when we were inserting records into the database, we used the `execute()` method. Now we're using the `executeUpdate()` method. This gives us the advantage that it returns an `int` value telling us how many rows were affected—how many rows matched our `where` clause.

This is important because there's always a possibility that we're trying to update a record that doesn't exist. If that happens, there won't be an error—we just won't have made any changes to the database. So, on lines 95 through 98, we're checking to see whether any rows were affected, and if not, we're outputting a message.

Of course, that's not necessarily what we really want to do. After all, we need to make sure that these `orders` affect inventory, so if they don't already exist, we're going to add them to the database, as in Listing 8.22. We'll also fix a particular logic problem: If there is an entry for `showroom` and `warehouse`, both entries are being updated with the same information.

Listing 8.22—`ParseOrders.java`: Adding Missing Records to the Database

```
...
81:     Connection furnDB = null;
82:     Statement sql = null;
83:
84:     public void update(String thisProduct_id,
85:                        String thisColor,
86:                        String thisValue) throws SQLException {
87:
88:         String sqlTxt = "update inventory set inv = (inv - " +
89:               thisValue +") where product_id = '"+thisProduct_id+"' "+
90:               " and color = '"+ thisColor+"' " +
91:               " and location = 'warehouse'";
92:         System.out.println(sqlTxt);
93:
94:         int numFound = sql.executeUpdate(sqlTxt);
95:
96:         if ( numFound == 0 ) {
97:             sqlTxt =  "update inventory set inv = (inv - " +
98:               thisValue +") where product_id = '"+thisProduct_id+"' "+
99:               " and color = '"+ thisColor+"' " +
100:               " and location = 'showroom'";
101:              System.out.println(sqlTxt);
102:              numFound = sql.executeUpdate(sqlTxt);
103:          }
104:
105:          if ( numFound == 0 ) {
106:              sqlTxt = "insert into inventory " +
107:                 "(product_id, color, location, inv) values "+
108:                 "('"+thisProduct_id+"', '"+thisColor+"', " +
109:                 "'showroom', -"+thisValue+")";
110:              System.out.println(sqlTxt);
111:              sql.execute(sqlTxt);
112:          }
113:
114:      }
...
```

The first thing that we did was to add one more piece of information to the `where` clause on lines 89 through 91. First, we'll attempt to update the `warehouse` information. If there isn't an entry for the `warehouse`, we'll try to update the `showroom` information on lines 97 through 102.

If the update doesn't find any records there, either, we'll `insert` a record for this product on lines 106 through 111. There are two things to notice about this `insert` statement.

First, we are arbitrarily entering this information against the showroom. There is no particular reason for this. We could just as easily have put it against the warehouse.

Second, we are inserting not the inventory value, but the negative inventory value. This is because we are essentially subtracting from zero. There were no items in stock—now we've sold some, so we have a negative number of them on hand.

If we compile and run this application, we can watch the values in our table decrease. To test the final `insert` statement, manually add a "new" item to the `ordersUpdate.xml` file, and make sure that the record is added to the table.

Retrieving Information from the Database: Backorders

Now that we have the information in the database, let's look at how to get it out again. To do this, we're going to look at our backorders—products for which we have a negative number on hand.

In Listing 8.23, we'll select a set of records and output them to the screen.

Listing 8.23—`ParseOrders.java`: Selecting Records

```
...
                String thisValue = (String)products.get(thisKey);

                update(thisProduct, thisColor, thisValue);

            }

        } catch (Exception e) {
            System.out.println("Problem updating the database.");
            return;
        }

    }

    public void showBackorders() {

        String sqlTxt = "select product_id, color, inv from "+
                  "inventory where inv < 0";
        try {
            ResultSet backorders = sql.executeQuery(sqlTxt);

            while (backorders.next()){
                System.out.println(backorders.getString(1)+", " +
                                   backorders.getString(2)+", " +
                                   backorders.getString(3));
            }

            furnDB.close();

        } catch (SQLException e) {
```

Listing 8.23—continued

```
168:             System.out.println("Could not select from database.");
169:             return;
170:         }
171:
172:     }
173:
174:     public static void main(String[] args) {
175:
...
189:
190:         update.saveTotals();
191:         update.showBackorders();
192:
193:     }
194:
195: }
```

Rather than setting up the database all over again, we've moved the `furnDB.close()` statement out of `saveTotals()` and into our new `showBackorders()` method, on line 165.

`showBackorders()` first creates an SQL select statement. As we can see here, a select statement generally shows the columns that we want (or `*` for all columns), the table we're selecting from, and a `where` clause to determine what rows we want.

On line 157, we're using `executeQuery()` to run the SQL statement, because this returns a very special structure called a `ResultSet`. A `ResultSet` is similar to an `Enumeration`, in that we can loop through it, but we have much better control over the data that is in it. Each column is accessible in order, starting with 1 (and not 0). For instance, in our case, if we compile and run this application, we'll get results something like

```
RC2342, none, -16.0
QA3452, royal blue, -3.0
```

This means that the `ResultSet` had a structure something like Table 8.1.

Table 8.1—Updating Columns

Column #1, product_id	*Column #2, color*	*Column #3, inv*
RC2342	none	–16.0
QA3452	royal blue	–3.0

So, as we run through each row on lines 159 through 163, we can pull out each of these values. Because databases can hold such varied types of data, we can decide how we want to see it. In our case, we want it as a `String` so we can output it to the screen, so we use `getString()`.

Now, we do have one more slight problem here. Because we're updating only one inventory record per product/color combination, it's possible to have a negative inventory in that one record, but overall, we still have product. For instance, we see the warehouse has –16 of item RC2342, but if the showroom has 18 of them, the item doesn't have to be backordered. To overcome this problem, we can find the sum for each product/color combination, as we do in Listing 8.24.

Listing 8.24—`ParseOrders.java`: Finding the Sum

```
...
152:     public void showBackorders() {
153:
154:         String sqlTxt = "select product_id, color, sum(inv) from "+
155:                 "inventory group by product_id, color " +
156:                 "having sum(inv) < 0";
157:         try {
158:             ResultSet backorders = sql.executeQuery(sqlTxt);
159:
160:             while (backorders.next()){
161:                 System.out.println(backorders.getString(1)+", " +
162:                                  backorders.getString(2)+", " +
163:                                  backorders.getString(3));
164:             }
...
```

In this case, we are using what is known as a group function. On line 154, we tell the database to add up the values of inv for each group. On line 155, we tell it how to break up those groups, and on line 156 we tell it which of those groups to display. This way, if there are enough items present in either the showroom or the warehouse, an item won't show up on the backorder list.

Completing the Circle

Now we have the database updated, so we need to go back and update the `products.xml` file with the new values. What we're going to do is move through the `products.xml` file, get the `product_id`, `color`, and `location`, and then check the database for the correct inventory value.

In Listing 8.25, we'll start by creating the application and pulling out the appropriate information from `products.xml`.

Listing 8.25—`UpdateProduct.java`: Retrieving Product Information from the XML File

```
import java.util.*;
import java.io.*;
import org.apache.xerces.parsers.*;
import org.apache.xerces.dom.*;
import org.w3c.dom.*;
import org.apache.xml.serialize.*;
```

Listing 8.25—continued

```

public class UpdateProduct extends Object {

    public static void main(String[] args) {

        try {
            DOMParser parser = new DOMParser();
            parser.parse("/files/products.xml");
            Document productDoc = parser.getDocument();

            Element productRoot = productDoc.getDocumentElement();
            NodeList products =
                  productRoot.getElementsByTagName("product");
            for (int i=0; i < products.getLength(); i++) {
                Element thisProduct = (Element)products.item(i);

                Node thisProduct_id = thisProduct
                         .getElementsByTagName("product_id")
                         .item(0);
                String product_id =
                      thisProduct_id.getFirstChild().getNodeValue();

                NodeList inventoryElements =
                      thisProduct.getElementsByTagName("inventory");
                for (int j=0; j < inventoryElements.getLength(); j++) {
                    Element thisInventory =
                           (Element)inventoryElements.item(j);
                    String thisColor =
                           thisInventory.getAttribute("color");
                    String thisLocation =
                           thisInventory.getAttribute("location");

                    System.out.println("product_id = "+product_id);
                    System.out.println("color="+thisColor);
                    System.out.println("location="+thisLocation);
                }
            }

            OutputFormat format =
                 new OutputFormat(productDoc, "UTF-8", true);
            XMLSerializer output =
                 new XMLSerializer(new FileWriter("/files/products.xml"),
                 format);
            output.serialize(productDoc);

        } catch (Exception e) {
            System.out.print("Problem updating document.");
        }

    }

}
```

There is nothing here that we haven't seen before. We import the necessary packages on lines 0 through 5, then parse the document on lines 12 through 14, and grab the document and root element on lines 14 and 16. On lines 17 through 42, we're running through each product in the `products.xml` file, and for each one of them, we're looking at each of the `inventory` elements on lines 28 through 41, printing out the relevant information on lines 38 through 40. The output should look something like this:

```
...
product_id = RC2342
color=
location=warehouse
product_id = RC2342
color=
location=showroom
product_id = BR3452
color=
location=showroom
product_id = WWWdrt
color=
location=warehouse
product_id = WWWsc
color=
location=warehouse
product_id = WWWhch
color=
location=warehouse
product_id = HallBench
color=
location=warehouse
product_id = HallBench
color=
location=showroom
product_id = SofaLoveSeat
color=magnolia print
location=showroom
product_id = SofaLoveSeat
color=magnolia print
location=warehouse
product_id = SofaLoveSeat
color=nautical print
location=warehouse
product_id = SofaLoveSeat
color=nautical print
location=showroom
product_id = 3253435
color=
location=showroom
product_id = 3253435
color=
location=warehouse
```

In Listing 8.26, we'll take the product information and retrieve any information we may have in the database about it, and then update the XML document.

Listing 8.26—`UpdateProduct.java`: Updating the `products.xml` File

```
...
import org.apache.xml.serialize.*;
import java.sql.*;

public class UpdateProduct extends Object {

    public static void main(String[] args) {
        String URL = "jdbc:odbc:furniture";
        String username = "";
        String password = "";

        try {
            Class.forName("sun.jdbc.odbc.JdbcOdbcDriver");
        } catch (Exception e) {
            System.out.println("Problem loading database driver.");
            return;
        }

        Connection furnDB = null;
        Statement sql = null;
        try {
            furnDB = DriverManager.getConnection ( URL,
                                                   username,
                                                   password);
            sql = furnDB.createStatement();
        } catch (SQLException SQLe) {
            System.out.println("Could not open database.");
            return;
        }

        try {
            DOMParser parser = new DOMParser();
            parser.parse("/files/products.xml");
            Document productDoc = parser.getDocument();

            Element productRoot = productDoc.getDocumentElement();
            NodeList products =
                  productRoot.getElementsByTagName("product");
            for (int i=0; i < products.getLength(); i++) {
                Element thisProduct = (Element)products.item(i);

                Node thisProduct_id = thisProduct
                         .getElementsByTagName("product_id")
                         .item(0);
                String product_id =
                      thisProduct_id.getFirstChild().getNodeValue();

                NodeList inventoryElements =
```

Listing 8.26—continued

```
                  thisProduct.getElementsByTagName("inventory");
            for (int j=0; j < inventoryElements.getLength(); j++) {
                Element thisInventory =
                       (Element)inventoryElements.item(j);
                String thisColor =
                       thisInventory.getAttribute("color");
                if (thisColor.equals("")) {
                    thisColor = "none";
                }
                String thisLocation =
                       thisInventory.getAttribute("location");

                String sqlTxt = "select inv from inventory " +
                    "where product_id = '"+product_id+"' and "+
                    "color = '"+thisColor+"' and "+
                    "location = '"+thisLocation+"'";

                ResultSet results = null;
                try {

                    results = sql.executeQuery(sqlTxt);

                } catch (SQLException e) {
                    System.out.println("Problem selecting data.");
                }
                if (results.next()) {
                    System.out.println("Found "+product_id +
                          ", "+thisColor+", "+thisLocation);
                    String thisValue = results.getString(1);
                    Node newInv =
                          productDoc.createTextNode(thisValue);
                    thisInventory.replaceChild(newInv,
                                thisInventory.getFirstChild());
                } else {
                    System.out.println("Didn't find :"+product_id +
                          ", "+thisColor+", "+thisLocation);
                    Node newInv = productDoc.createTextNode("0");
                    thisInventory.replaceChild(newInv,
                                thisInventory.getFirstChild());
                }
            }
        }

        try {
            furnDB.close();
        } catch (SQLException e) {
            System.out.println("Could not close database.");
        }

         OutputFormat format =
              new OutputFormat(productDoc, "UTF-8", true);
```

Listing 8.26—continued

```
103:            XMLSerializer output =
104:                new XMLSerializer(new FileWriter("/files/products.xml"),
105:                format);
106:            output.serialize(productDoc);
107:
108:        } catch (Exception e) {
109:            System.out.print("Problem updating document.");
110:        }
111:
112:    }
113:
114:}
```

Most of this should be familiar. On line 6, we're importing the `java.sql` package, and then on lines 11 through 32 we set up the database `Connection`.

In lines 58 through 60, we're correcting for the fact that if there is no `color` information, it will be listed in the database as `"none"`.

On lines 64 through 67, we're creating the SQL statement based on the information we've gleaned from this particular `inventory` element. On lines 69 through 76, we're creating the `ResultSet`.

If the `ResultSet` has records, then `next()` is going to return a value of `true`, because there is a next record to go to. When we call it, the `ResultSet` automatically advances to that next record. So, we know we have information, and we're outputting a message to that effect on lines 78 and 79. On line 80, we're actually retrieving the value, which we're using to create a new text node on lines 81 and 82. Finally, on lines 83 and 84, we replace the old text node with the new one we just created, effectively updating the tree.

If `next()` returns `false`, we are outputting a message on lines 86 and 87, and then creating a text node of `0` and replacing the old inventory, because we obviously have no stock for that item. (We can test that function by deleting a row out of the `inventory` table.)

Finally, on lines 95 through 99, we close the database. The output looks something like this:

```
Didn't find :QA3452, royal blue, warehouse
Found QA3452, royal blue, showroom
Found QA3452, flower print, warehouse
Found QA3452, flower print, showroom
Found QA3452, seafoam green, warehouse
Found QA3452, teal, warehouse
Found QA3452, burgundy, warehouse
Found RC2342, none, warehouse
Found RC2342, none, showroom
Found BR3452, none, showroom
```

```
Found WWWdrt, none, warehouse
Found WWWsc, none, warehouse
Found WWWhch, none, warehouse
Found HallBench, none, warehouse
Found HallBench, none, showroom
Found SofaLoveSeat, magnolia print, showroom
Found SofaLoveSeat, magnolia print, warehouse
Found SofaLoveSeat, nautical print, warehouse
Found SofaLoveSeat, nautical print, showroom
Found 3253435, none, showroom
Found 3253435, none, warehouse
```

It's also a good idea to check the `products.xml` file to make sure that everything is functioning properly. For instance, in writing this section, I had a typo that caused me to insert the `product_id` instead of the `inventory` value.

Next Steps

In this chapter, we've looked at using JDBC to access our legacy SQL database in order to interface with enterprise data. We also looked at SAX as an alternative to DOM when we don't need to modify the XML data, as well as the object-oriented techniques necessary to use it.

This chapter is a fairly simplified look at these tasks. You'll want to make your applications much more robust and apply your own business rules to them, but all of the concepts are here for you.

At this point, we have fairly complete functionality. We have a site where users can search for products, view their information, and order them. This information is then used to update inventory levels. Some things that we don't have are any graphical design whatsoever, as well as pages that are normally "static," such as "help" information. In the real world, we would also want to bulletproof these programs to a much greater degree, as well as increase the security of our users' credit-card information. And while we're at it, we'll probably want to process those credit-card transactions so we can get paid!

Now that we've pretty well accomplished what it was we set out to do, in Chapter 9, "Other Applications for XML (SOAP)," we'll look at where XML is going and what else you can do with it.

Chapter 9

In this chapter

Other Applications for XML (SOAP)

At this point, we have built a complete e-commerce–capable Web site using XML. Everything we've done, however, could have been done using existing technologies and languages. In this chapter, we're going to look at other uses for XML, which utilize the power of such a flexible environment.

For instance, we're going to start by looking at displaying content using a different style sheet depending on how the user is accessing the site, which enables us to create a special version of our pages for mobile phones and other devices.

We'll then move on to creating Adobe PDF documents, which can be used not only for displaying a page precisely as we intended, no matter what browser is being used, but can also be used for creating a paper version of our catalog. To do this, we'll examine XSL Formatting Objects.

From there, we'll look at some of XML's hidden power: data exchange. We'll create a small application using the *Simple Object Access Protocol (SOAP)* to allow us to exchange information on inventory with our vendors.

Finally, we'll look at the future direction of XML.

Browser Detection

If you've been doing Web development for any significant period of time, you are already aware that there is a significant difference between browsers and the way that they implement the more complex features of HTML and scripting languages such as ECMAScript (formerly known as JavaScript). Many a long night has been spent by Web programmers trying to make sure that their sites will function properly on all browsers.

There are two schools of thought when it comes to this. The first is to create a page that is written in such a way that it won't cause problems in any browser. That's what we've been doing with our simple layouts. This also known as playing to the lowest common denominator.

Finding the lowest common denominator was hard enough to do when we just had similar browsers, such as Netscape and Microsoft Internet Explorer to worry about, but now that we are adding other devices, such as mobile phones, to the mix, it's just about impossible.

EXCURSION

The Modularization of the Web

The disparity of capabilities among Web browsers and devices is something that has long been recognized, and now something is being done about it.

When HTML was reformulatd as XHTML, it was with an eye toward modularizing the language. This way, the makers of a device can choose a specific set of capabilities to support, and developers will know precisely what can and cannot be done. For instance, as the time of this writing, XHTML 1.1 Basic has become a W3C Recommendation, and work is continuing on other modules.

In addition to this, the W3C is also working on Composite Capabilities/Preference Profiles, which will allow a developer to know exactly what platform, application, and capabilities an application is running within.

That leaves us with our second option, which is to create different versions of our pages, and then dole them out to the appropriate browsers. This allows us to do whatever the target browser can handle, as opposed to being limited to the most primitive browser in our target audience. It also allows us to create pages that might be completely different, such as those for mobile phones and other devices.

The first thing that is absolutely necessary to deliver different pages to different browsers is to be able to tell which browser it is that we're dealing with. We can do that by looking at the actual structure of an HTTP request.

Request Headers

Until now, we've been dealing with HTTP requests as objects, but we haven't really taken a look at how they're structured. Actually, they're a series of text messages in a particular format. For instance, we might have a request that looks something like this:

```
GET /book/servlet/TransformServlet HTTP/1.1
Host: 216.2.13.156
User-Agent: Mozilla/5.0 (Windows; U; Win98; en-US; m18) Gecko/20001108
➥Netscape6/6.0
Accept: */*
Accept-Encoding: gzip,deflate,compress,identity
Host: localhost:8080
Accept-Language: en
Keep-Alive: 300
Connection: keep-alive
```

In this case, the first line is the actual request, and the other lines are information about it, such as the host machine we're coming from and the default language we are looking for.

All these lines are headers, and because they're so predictable, we can look at them to retrieve specific information. A sample servlet that looks at the headers of a request is actually included with the Tomcat installation. To take a look at it, start the Tomcat server, and then point your browser to

```
http://localhost:8080/book/servlet/RequestHeaderExample
```

You should get a response similar to Figure 9.1.

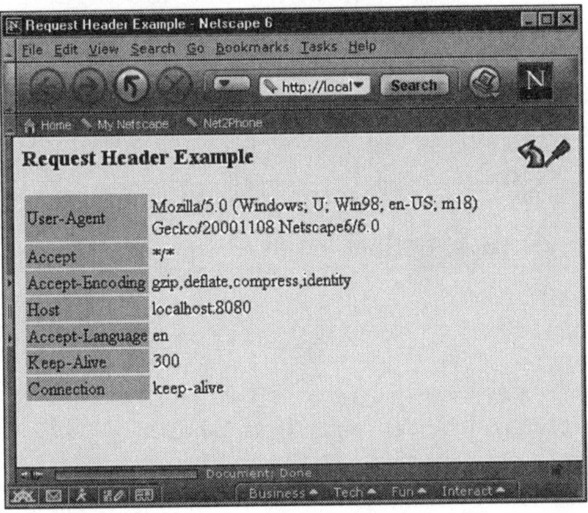

Figure 9.1

Shown are headers for a sample request, from Netscape 6.

Headers can be used to track where a user is geographically (to some extent), the page that contained the link clicked by the user to get there, or, in the case of the user-agent header, the browser that they're using.

For instance, I've run the example in Netscape 6. If I were to run it in Internet Explorer 5.5, I would get different results, such as shown in Figure 9.2.

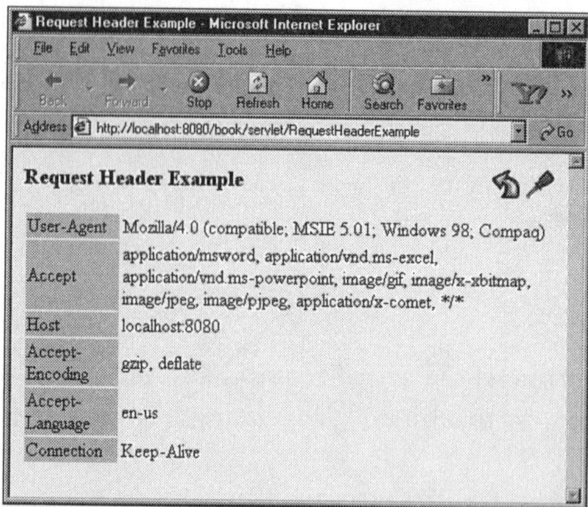

Figure 9.2

Shown here are headers for a sample request, from Internet Explorer.

This difference is what's going to allow us to display our data in a way that's customized for the user's browser.

What we're going to do is use the `User-Agent` header to determine which type of browser the user has, and then decide what group of browsers it belongs to. For instance, Netscape 6.0 and Netscape 4.7 have very different `User-Agent` headers, but they're both Netscape browsers. Also, other information that is operating in a system-specific manner can be included in this value.

What we're going to do is compare the `User-Agent` to a list of groups, each of which contains text identifying the group. Let's start with a basic servlet that retrieves the `User-Agent` header, as in Listing 9.1.

Listing 9.1—`DetectBrowser.java`: Getting the `User-Agent`

```
import java.io.*;
import javax.servlet.*;
import javax.servlet.http.*;

public class DetectBrowser extends HttpServlet {

    public void doGet(HttpServletRequest request,
                      HttpServletResponse response)
        throws IOException, ServletException
    {
        response.setContentType("text/html");
        PrintWriter out = response.getWriter();

        out.print("<html>");
        out.print("<body>");

        String target = request.getHeader("User-Agent");
        out.print("<p>"+target+"</p>");

```

Listing 9.1—continued

```
19:         out.print("</body>");
20:         out.print("</html>");
21:     }
22:}
```

Lines 10 and 11 set the mime-type for the response and create the PrintWriter that we'll use to send the response to the browser, and on lines 13 and 14 we output the beginnings of our HTML.

The key is on line 16, where we are retrieving the `User-Agent` header from the request, and then outputting it on line 17. If we save the file in Tomcat's classes directory, and then compile it, we can see the different results from different browsers, as in Figure 9.3, where I called the servlet in all the different browsers I had access to at this time.

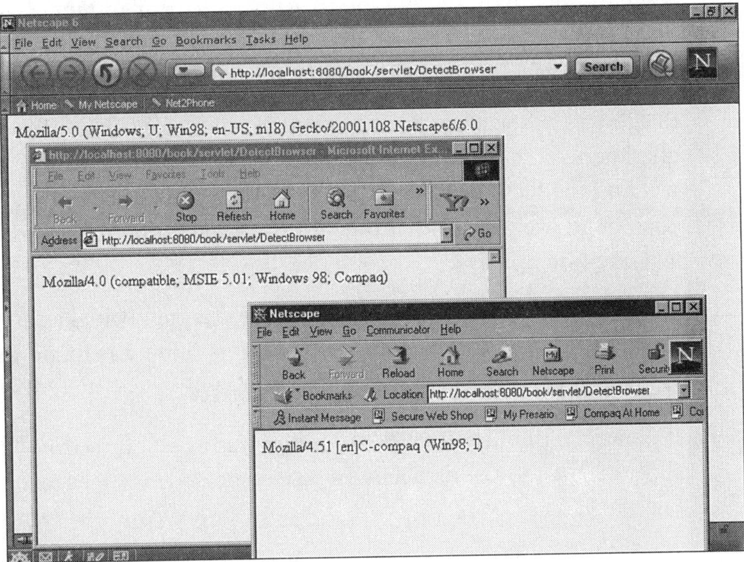

Figure 9.3

Different browsers have different `User-Agents`*.*

Resource Bundles

Now that we have the `User-Agent`, we need a list of groups and identifying strings. Just such a file actually comes with Xalan, so, instead of re-creating it, we'll just make a copy of it and put it into the classes directory. Assuming that Xalan is installed at

```
c:\xalan
```

the file that we want is

```
c:\xalan\samples\media.properties
```

Go ahead and copy this file into the classes directory with `DetectBrowser.class`. The important portion of this file looks like Listing 9.2.

Listing 9.2—media.properties

```
MSIE=explorer
MSPIE=pocketexplorer
HandHTTP=handweb
Mozilla=netscape
Lynx=lynx
Opera=opera
Java=java
AvantGo=avantgo
Nokia=nokia
UP.Browser=up
DoCoMo=imode
```

The left side of each line shows the string to look for, whereas the right side is the name of the group we're going to assign it to. For instance, any browser that sends a `User-Agent` containing the string `MSIE` is going to be part of the `explorer` group.

This `.properties` file is a kind of `ResourceBundle`. `ResourceBundles` are built into Java to allow us to specify properties outside our classes. This class was meant to help programmers deal with internationalization. For instance, in the classes directory, you will find the files `LocalStrings.properties` and `LocalStrings_es.properties`. If we open them, we will see that they list the same properties, but that one is in English, and one is in Spanish.

When the `RequestHeaderExample` servlet was run, it looked to this file for the title of the page. In `LocalStrings.properties`, this value was found in the line

```
requestheader.title=Request Header Example
```

If, however, the Locale of the program was `es_ES`, Java would have automatically appended `_es` to the name, and opened `LocalStrings_es.properties`, where the line was

```
requestheader.title=Ejemplo de Cabecera de Request
```

This way, the servlet automatically gets the right information.

> `ResourceBundles` are usually classes that list property values, but if the system doesn't find a class, it will look for a `.properties` file as a last resort.

In Listing 9.3, we're going to open the media `ResourceBundle` and look at the values it contains.

Listing 9.3—`DetectBrowser.java`: Opening the `ResourceBundle`

```
0: import java.io.*;
1: import javax.servlet.*;
2: import javax.servlet.http.*;
3: import java.util.*;
4:
5: public class DetectBrowser extends HttpServlet {
6:
7:
8:     public void doGet(HttpServletRequest request,
9:                       HttpServletResponse response)
10:        throws IOException, ServletException
11:    {
12:        response.setContentType("text/html");
13:        PrintWriter out = response.getWriter();
14:
15:        out.print("<html>");
16:        out.print("<body>");
17:
18:        String target = request.getHeader("User-Agent");
19:        out.print("<p>"+target+"</p>");
20:
21:        ResourceBundle media = ResourceBundle.getBundle("media");
22:        Enumeration browsers = media.getKeys();
23:        while (browsers.hasMoreElements()) {
24:            String thisBrowser = (String)browsers.nextElement();
25:            out.print(thisBrowser);
26:            out.print("=");
27:            out.print(media.getString(thisBrowser));
28:            out.print("<br />");
29:        }
30:
31:        out.print("</body>");
32:        out.print("</html>");
33:    }
34:}
```


On line 3, we're importing the `java.util.*` package, which contains the `ResourceBundle` class.

On line 21, we actually retrieve the information in the `media.properties` file by calling for the `media` `ResourceBundle`. Java will automatically search for the `media.properties` file in the same directory as the class. We're retrieving the keys on line 22. This is the list of items on the left side of the =, which we'll be searching for in the `User-Agent` string.

On lines 23 through 29, we're looking through the browsers' `Enumeration`, retrieving the current key on line 24. This key is used to retrieve the actual value on line 27, using `getString()`. A `ResourceBundle` can also be used to retrieve objects, using getObject. (This is, of course, only when the `ResourceBundle` is a class, and not a text file.)

So, now we've retrieved the values, and printed them to the page. The resulting output should look like Figure 9.4.

Figure 9.4

Entries listed in `media.properties` *are shown here.*

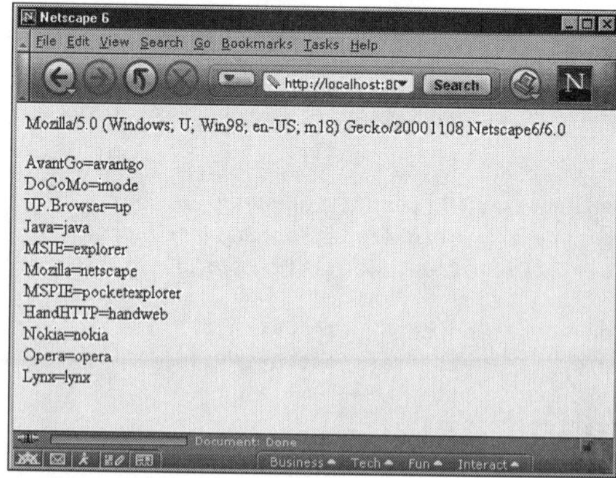

Notice that the order they appear in here is different from the order in which they appear in the file. For our purposes, this is fine (as long as `explorer` appears before `netscape`, for reasons we'll discuss in a moment) but if you need to have the exact order, you will need to find another way to access the information, such as reading in the file directly and parsing it yourself. (Or, an XML document would be handy.)

Now, if you've forgotten to move the `media.properties` file before running the servlet, or if you've tried to change the order of entries, you will have noticed something: Nothing you do seems to have any effect. This is because the `ResourceBundle` is treated as a class external to the servlet, and Tomcat doesn't dynamically reload it. To get the changes to take effect, you can either restart Tomcat or (more conveniently) recompile the servlet.

Now that we have the list, in Listing 9.4, we'll compare it to our `User-Agent` to get the appropriate group.

Listing 9.4—`BrowserDetect.java`: Comparing the List to the `User-Agent`

```
...
        String target = request.getHeader("User-Agent");
        out.print("<p>"+target+"</p>");

        ResourceBundle media = ResourceBundle.getBundle("media");
        Enumeration browsers = media.getKeys();

        boolean found = false;
        while (browsers.hasMoreElements() && !found) {
            String thisBrowser = (String)browsers.nextElement();
            if (target.indexOf(thisBrowser) > -1) {
```

Listing 9.4—continued

```
28:                 found = true;
29:                 out.print("It IS "+media.getString(thisBrowser));
30:             } else {
31:                 out.print("It isn't "
32:                           +media.getString(thisBrowser)+"<br />");
33:             }
34:         }
35:
36:         out.print("</body>");
37:         out.print("</html>");
38:     }
39:}
```

In Listing 9.4, we want to loop through each type of browser, stopping when we get a match. So, on line 24, we'll create a flag, `found`, which is set to `false` as long as we haven't found the right browser yet. We've then added this flag to the condition on line 25.

The `&&` symbol is a logical `and`. That means that in order for the condition to be true, the expressions on both sides have to be true. As long as there are more elements to look at, the left side will be true, and as long as `found` is false, its opposite—`!found`—will be true. So, as long as we have items to look at and we haven't found it yet, we'll keep going.

Line 27 is where we're doing the actual comparison. Every String has the `indexOf()` method, which searches for the character or characters within itself and returns the starting position. If the substring isn't present in the string, `indexOf()` returns –1. For instance, in the case:

```
String myString = "test";
int position = myString.indexOf("e");
```

the value of position would be 1. (Because this is a zero-based operation, the first "t" would be at position 0.)

So, if the value of MSIE was not present in the `User-Agent`, which is now stored in `target`, `target.indexOf("MSIE")` would return `-1`.

If the value is found in our `User-Agent`, we'll set our `found` flag to `true` and print out the message saying so. When we get back to line 25, `found` will be true, so `!found` will be `false`, and the whole condition—`browsers.hasMoreElements() && !found`—will be `false`, ending the loop.

If it's not found, we'll simply output a message and keep looking.

The output, of course, is going to depend on what browser we use to call up the servlet, as illustrated in Figure 9.5.

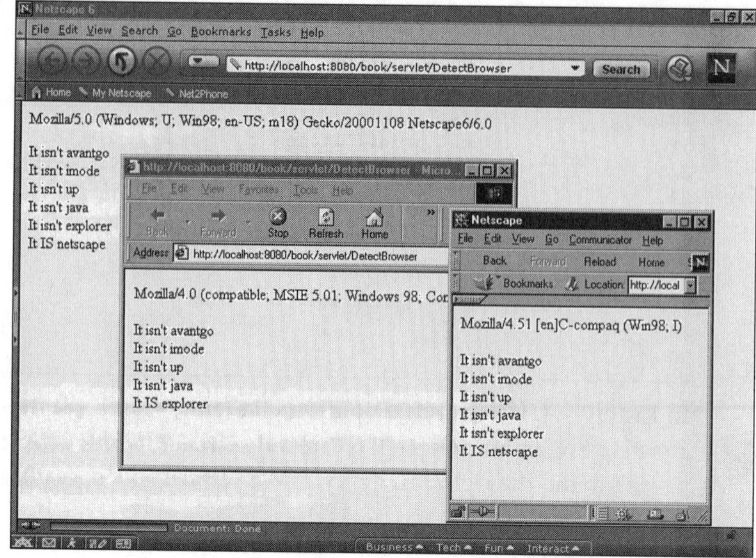

Figure 9.5

Different browsers produce different results.

Notice that both Netscape 4.7 and Netscape 6.0 are recognized as `netscape`, but that Internet Explorer is recognized as `explorer`. Remember earlier when we said that the order wasn't important as long as `explorer` came first? That was because all three of these browsers were based on Mozilla, so all three of them have it in the `User-Agent`. Because we stop looking when we find the right group, however, Internet Explorer isn't mistaken for the Netscape.

Media

Now that we know what group our browser is in, what good does it do us?

Fortunately, the authors of the XSLT specification had this very idea in mind, and created a way for us to easily designate different style sheets for different browsers.

Back in Chapter 2, "Product Pages: Transforming XML in the Browser Using XSL," we created our first XML file, `products.xml`, and associated it with a style sheet, `catalog.xsl`. That association looked like Listing 9.5.

Listing 9.5—`products.xml`: Associating a Style Sheet

```
<?xml version="1.0" encoding="UTF-8"?>
<?xml-stylesheet href="catalog.xsl" type="text/xsl"?>

<products>
    <vendor webvendor="full">
        <vendor_name>Conners Chair</vendor_name>
...
```

We later used the style sheet `allproducts.xsl`, which is what we want to use now. In Listing 9.6, we'll change that association.

Listing 9.6—`products.xml`: Associating a New Style Sheet

```
<?xml version="1.0" encoding="UTF-8"?>
<?xml-stylesheet href="allproducts.xsl" type="text/xsl"?>

<products>
    <vendor webvendor="full">
        <vendor_name>Conners Chair</vendor_name>
...
```

In all our servlets so far, we have been specifically indicating the style sheet we want to use, but we could just as easily read this association from the file. In Listing 9.7, we're creating a basic servlet that will get the associated style sheet and transform the file using it.

Listing 9.7—`ShowCatalog.java`: Getting the Associated Style Sheet

```
import java.io.*;
import javax.servlet.*;
import javax.servlet.http.*;
import org.apache.trax.*;
import org.xml.sax.InputSource;

public class ShowCatalog extends HttpServlet {

    public void doGet(HttpServletRequest request,
                      HttpServletResponse response)
        throws IOException, ServletException
    {

    response.setContentType("text/html");
    PrintWriter out = response.getWriter();

    try {

        Processor processor = Processor.newInstance("xslt");

        InputSource[] XSLSheet =
             processor.getAssociatedStylesheets(
               new InputSource("file:///c:/files/products.xml"),
                                               null, null, null);

        Templates templates = processor.processMultiple(XSLSheet);

        Transformer transformer = templates.newTransformer();
        transformer.transform(
              new InputSource("file:///c:/files/products.xml"),
                                                 new Result(out));

    } catch (Exception e) {
```

Listing 9.7—continued

```
33:         out.print("There was a problem transforming the file.");
34:     }
35:
36:     }
37:}
```

Most of this is the standard work we've been doing all along. Lines 0 through 4 are the necessary imports. On lines 13 and 14, we set the MIME-type for the response, and then create the `PrintWriter` for our output.

On line 18, we're creating the XSLT processor, and on lines 25 through 30, we're doing the actual processing and outputting the results to the page.

The interesting thing is on lines 20 through 23, where we're assigning the style sheet. Rather than designating a particular file, as we've been doing until now, we're asking the servlet to see what file is listed in the XML document itself. The first input for `getAssociatedStylesheets()` is, of course, an `InputSource` based on the XML document itself. It's the second input, `media`, that is going to allow us to choose a different style sheet depending on our browser. For now, `media`, `title`, and `charset` are all set to `null`, because we have only one style sheet.

This function is designed to return an array of matching style sheets, so to accommodate that, on line 25 we're using `processMultiple` instead of the more familiar process. In our case, we have only one style sheet anyway, but this is Java; we play the objects we're dealt.

The next thing that we're going to do is create a second style sheet, say, for Netscape users. Make a copy of `allproducts.xsl` and call it `allproducts_ns.xsl`; then make the additions shown in Listing 9.8.

Listing 9.8—`allproducts_ns.xsl`: Customizing the Style Sheet

```
...
<xsl:template match="products">

    <h2 align="center">Welcome Netscape Users!</h2>
    <h3 align="center">Please check out our special deals!</h3>

    At ChaseWeb Furniture, we carry products from these great manufacturers:
    <xsl:apply-templates/>
</xsl:template>
...
```

Normally, the changes would have much more to do with layout and script capabilities, but because we're keeping things simple, we'll just display a message.

Now we need to add this new style sheet to the `products.xml` file. We'll do this in Listing 9.9.

Listing 9.9—products.xml: Associating the New Style Sheet

```
0:<?xml version="1.0" encoding="UTF-8"?>
1:<?xml-stylesheet href="allproducts_ns.xsl" media="netscape"
2:         alternate="yes" type="text/xsl" ?>
3:<?xml-stylesheet href="allproducts.xsl" type="text/xsl"?>
4:
5:<products>
6:    <vendor webvendor="full">
7:       <vendor_name>Conners Chair</vendor_name>
...
```

On lines 2 and 3, we have added a new style sheet association with two important attributes. The first, `media`, will allow us to designate a choice using the media parameter of `getAssociatedStyleSheets()`. The second, `alternate`, allows us to specify our default style sheet.

> `getAssociatedStyleSheets()` ignores the `alternate` attribute and simply uses the last entry if no `media` is chosen, where Internet Explorer ignores the alternate attribute and chooses the first entry.
>
> This means it's important to know where the XML document will be used (in the client or on the server) if you are relying on this information, so you can order it appropriately.

Now we can add in our browser detection routine to allow the servlet to choose the proper style sheet to display. In Listing 9.10, we'll incorporate those changes.

Listing 9.10—ShowCatalog.java: Adding Browser Detection

```
import java.io.*;
import javax.servlet.*;
import javax.servlet.http.*;
import org.apache.trax.*;
import org.xml.sax.InputSource;
import java.util.*;

public class ShowCatalog extends HttpServlet {

    public void doGet(HttpServletRequest request,
                      HttpServletResponse response)
        throws IOException, ServletException
    {

    response.setContentType("text/html");
    PrintWriter out = response.getWriter();

    String target = request.getHeader("User-Agent");

```

Listing 9.10—continued

```
19:     ResourceBundle media = ResourceBundle.getBundle("media");
20:     Enumeration browsers = media.getKeys();
21:
22:     boolean found = false;
23:
24:     String mediaStr = "";
25:     while (browsers.hasMoreElements() && !found) {
26:         String thisBrowser = (String)browsers.nextElement();
27:         if (target.indexOf(thisBrowser) > -1) {
28:             found = true;
29:             mediaStr = media.getString(thisBrowser);
30:         }
31:     }
32:
33:     try {
34:
35:         Processor processor = Processor.newInstance("xslt");
36:
37:         InputSource[] XSLSheet =
38:              processor.getAssociatedStylesheets(
39:                new InputSource("file:///c:/files/products.xml"),
40:                                                mediaStr, null, null);
41:
42:         Templates templates = processor.processMultiple(XSLSheet);
43:
44:         Transformer transformer = templates.newTransformer();
45:         transformer.transform(
46:               new InputSource("file:///c:/files/products.xml"),
47:                                                    new Result(out));
48:
49:     } catch (Exception e) {
50:         out.print("There was a problem transforming the file.");
51:     }
52:
53:     }
54:}
```

We've really just combined what we did earlier in this chapter, adding the import for the `ResourceBundle` on line 5, and the actual choice of `media` on lines 17 through 31. With the `if-then` statement on lines 16 through 30, we've cut the code down so that it just assigns the value of the `media` to a variable so we can use it on lines 39 and 40.

By adding a value for `media`, we're telling `getAssociatedStylesheets` to choose a style sheet that has only this particular `media` listed. Now, if we pull up the page in Netscape, we'll see our new results. Unfortunately, if we pull it up in Internet Explorer, we'll see an error. Let's take a look at the reason.

On line 42, we're going to process whatever style sheets were found by `getAssociatedStylesheets()` on lines 37 through 40. That's fine—as long as at least one style sheet was found, as it is when the `media` is Netscape. When we call the page in Internet Explorer, however, there are no matches; `getAssociatedStylesheets()` doesn't pick the default page. Instead, `XSLSheets` remains empty, causing an error on line 42.

Now, we could solve the problem by adding another listing with `explorer` as the `media`, but that doesn't really solve the problem, because we always want to have a default style sheet, in case `media.properties` doesn't pick up a particular browser.

So, instead, in Listing 9.11, we'll take care of the problem of choosing the default style sheet.

Listing 9.11—`ShowCatalog.java`: Choosing the Default Style Sheet

```
0: import java.io.*;
1: import javax.servlet.*;
2: import javax.servlet.http.*;
3: import org.apache.trax.*;
4: import org.xml.sax.InputSource;
5: import java.util.*;
6:
7: public class ShowCatalog extends HttpServlet {
8:
9:     public void doGet(HttpServletRequest request,
10:                          HttpServletResponse response)
11:        throws IOException, ServletException
12:    {
13:
14:    response.setContentType("text/html");
15:    PrintWriter out = response.getWriter();
16:
17:    String target = request.getHeader("User-Agent");
18:
19:    ResourceBundle media = ResourceBundle.getBundle("media");
20:    Enumeration browsers = media.getKeys();
21:
22:    boolean found = false;
23:
24:    String mediaStr = "";
25:    while (browsers.hasMoreElements() && !found) {
26:        String thisBrowser = (String)browsers.nextElement();
27:        if (target.indexOf(thisBrowser) > -1) {
28:            found = true;
29:            mediaStr = media.getString(thisBrowser);
30:        }
31:    }
32:
33:    try {
34:
35:        Processor processor = Processor.newInstance("xslt");
36:
37:        InputSource[] XSLSheet =
```

Listing 9.11—continued

```
38:             processor.getAssociatedStylesheets(
39:               new InputSource("file:///c:/files/products.xml"),
40:                                              mediaStr, null, null);
41:
42:         Templates templates;
43:         try {
44:             templates = processor.processMultiple(XSLSheet);
45:         } catch (Exception e) {
46:            XSLSheet = processor.getAssociatedStylesheets(
47:                new InputSource("file:///c:/files/products.xml"),
48:                                                  null, null, null);
49:            templates = processor.processMultiple(XSLSheet);
50:         }
51:
52:         Transformer transformer = templates.newTransformer();
53:         transformer.transform(
54:               new InputSource("file:///c:/files/products.xml"),
55:                                                  new Result(out));
56:
57:     } catch (Exception e) {
58:         out.print("There was a problem transforming the file.");
59:     }
60:
61:     }
62:}
```

In this case, the easiest way to know whether there is going to be a problem is to simply do it and catch the exception. That's what we're doing on lines 43 through 50.

First, on line 42, we're declaring templates outside the `try-catch` block so we can use it later, when we're ready to transform the XML document itself. Then, on lines 43 and 45, we've enclosed the statement in question in a `try` block.

If there was a style sheet found, this will proceed with no problem. On the other hand, if no style sheet with the current `media` was found, we will explicitly look for the default style sheet on lines 46 through 48, and then try to process it (again) on line 49.

If we compile the servlet and open it in Internet Explorer (or any browser that doesn't have its own style sheet), we'll now get the default style sheet.

Two browsers—one URL, two different pages—are shown in Figure 9.6. That's the name of the game.

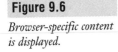

Figure 9.6

Browser-specific content is displayed.

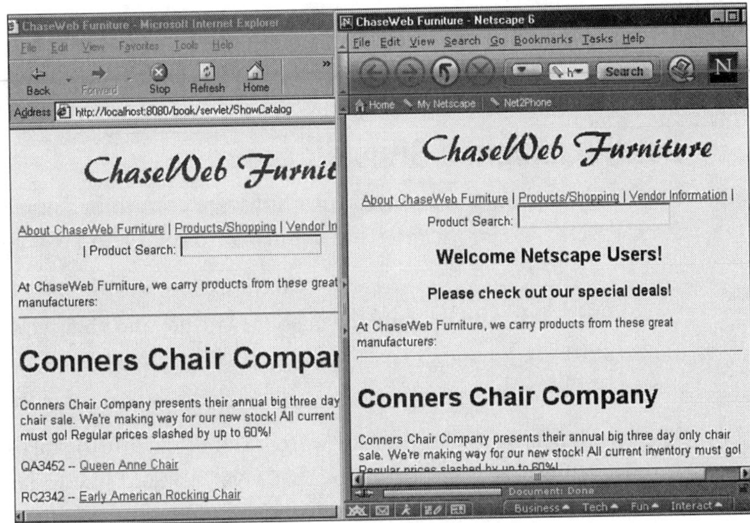

Of course, this is an extremely simplistic example. In most cases, the differences between style sheets involve the way that the content or the XHTML is structured. Take, for example, mobile phones.

Mobile Phones

One major reason to use XML for a Web site or Web-enabled application is the capability to adapt content for viewing over mobile phones and other devices.

In some ways, providing content for mobile phones is just like providing it for a traditional browser; both use marked-up content. That's about where the similarity ends right now, however.

Web-enabled mobile phones do have a browser, but they have some extremely tight restrictions. Pages must be very small to fit both the screen and the tiny amount of available bandwidth (current phones can move as slowly as 9Kbps), and there are no large, color, graphics.

Even the language is different. At the time of this writing, HDML, or Handheld Device Markup Language, was being replaced by WML, or Wireless Markup Language, just as HTML was being supplanted by XML. Both bear similarities to their traditional counterparts, but the vocabularies are extremely different.

To take a look at what's involved in serving content to mobile phones, we're going to download a simulator for the UP.browser from Phone.com. This browser is supported in many of today's mobile phones in Europe, with major coverage in the

United States expected in 2001. The simulator enables us to develop some WML pages, or decks, based on the catalog page we've been using in this chapter, and test them out.

Downloading the Simulator

Phone.com recently combined with Software.com to become openwave.com, but the UP.SDK, which includes the simulator, should still be available at `http://developer.phone.com`.

You will need to sign up, but the account is free, and then you will be given the opportunity to download the UP.SDK. For the purposes of this book, we will use version 4.0.

After you've downloaded the software, double-click it to start the installer. When the installer is finished, check the box that says "I would like to launch the UP.SDK Simulator" and click the Finish button.

The simulator itself looks and works much like a normal Web-enabled phone (without the calls, of course!), with the black buttons just below the screen serving as the OK or Back buttons, as in Figure 9.7.

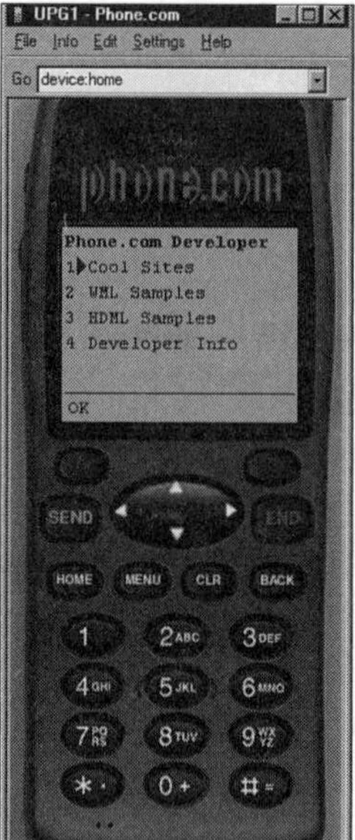

Figure 9.7

This is the UP.SDK simulator.

To maneuver on the pages, use the up and down arrows. To select a highlighted choice, click OK.

Take a few moments to familiarize yourself with how the phone works. Notice that the screen is pretty small, so we don't have too much real estate to work with. Also, notice that although there are applications and even some scripting, the layouts and actions are pretty simple. Eventually, wireless devices may catch up with their desktop counterparts, but for now we have a tiny screen and one-bit (black-and-white) graphics to work with.

If you can browse through the applications on the phone without any errors, the installation is complete.

Still, we can provide information for our users.

The WML Page

So far, we've been working with XHTML, which is just one application of XML. In this case, we're going to work with Wireless Markup Language, or WML, another application. WML is similar to XHTML in that it's a tagging language and even some of the formatting tags are the same, but the structure of a WML file is a little different from a traditional HTML page.

For one thing, a WML page isn't really a page at all—it's a deck, so called because it consists of one or more cards. This is because a single page can hold such a small amount of information, it is more convenient to retrieve several at once, cutting down on the number of times the phone has to retrieve information from the server.

We're going to start out with a very simple deck just to make sure we've got everything in the right place, but first we need to make a change to the configuration of the Web server itself. The UP.Simulator doesn't know how to handle traditional XHTML files, which have a MIME-type of `text/html`. Instead, it's looking for a MIME-type of `text/vnd.wap.wml`, so we're going to have to give Tomcat some instructions on how and when to send it.

Normally, as we mentioned in Chapter 3, a Web server knows what MIME-type to output based on the file extension. That's why we had to send it specifically for servlets—there is no file extension. Now there is, but Tomcat doesn't know anything about it. What we need to do is add an instruction to Tomcat's configuration.

For the installation we did in Chapter 3, "Defining the Data Structure: Document Type Definitions, XML Schema, and Parsers," we need to open the file

```
C:\tomcat\conf\web.xml
```

and make the additions shown in Listing 9.12.

Listing 9.12—web.xml: Adding the New MIME-Type

```
        </extension>
        <mime-type>
            video/mpeg2
        </mime-type>
    </mime-mapping>
    <mime-mapping>
        <extension>
            wml
        </extension>
        <mime-type>
            text/vnd.wap.wml
        </mime-type>
    </mime-mapping>
    <welcome-file-list>
```

Notice that this is a complete set, if you will, of elements. We start with the mime-mapping and make sure that we hit the proper children below it.

After this change is made to `web.xml`, save the file and restart Tomcat. Now we're ready to create the actual `wml` file.

In Listing 9.13, we'll create a simple file called `catalog.wml`. To view this file, we need to place it NOT in our traditional classes directory, but in the `book` directory itself, because it's not a servlet. This will become obvious in the URL that we use to access it.

Listing 9.13—catalog.wml: Creating the File

```
<?xml version="1.0"?>
<!DOCTYPE wml PUBLIC "-//WAPFORUM//DTD WML 1.1//EN"
     "http://www.wapforum.org/DTD/wml_1.1.xml">
<wml>
    <card>
        <p>
            ChaseWeb Furniture vendors:
        </p>
        <p>
            <select>
                <option>
                    Conners Chair Company
                </option>
                <option>
                    Wally's Wonderful World of Furniture
                </option>
                <option>
                    Crazy Marge's Furniture Emporium
                </option>
             </select>
         </p>
    </card>
</wml>
```

Starting at the top, we see that this is an XML document, because we have that declaration at the top, on line 0. Next we see the official WML DTD referenced, so this document can be validated.

Next, we see the document itself, on lines 3 through 22. This deck has only one card, on lines 4 through 21, but we'll be adding more in a moment.

The actual XML on lines 5 through 20 might look familiar; all of it is standard XHTML, but it's being used slightly differently than we might see it in a traditional Web page. For instance, notice that the `<p>` tags enclose the entire page, when normally, we would expect them to enclose just the descriptive text at the top. The DTD, however, forbids a `<select>` element as a direct child of `<card>`. It must be a child of either `<p>` or `<do>`, which is beyond the scope of this chapter.

Also, notice that there is a select list and options, but no `<form>`! If we look at the output in Figure 9.8, however, we will see that these options are treated differently from our straight text. The fact that they are options cues the browser to highlight them as choices, which we can choose by moving the cursor up or down.

Figure 9.8

The browser knows that `<options>` *are user choices.*

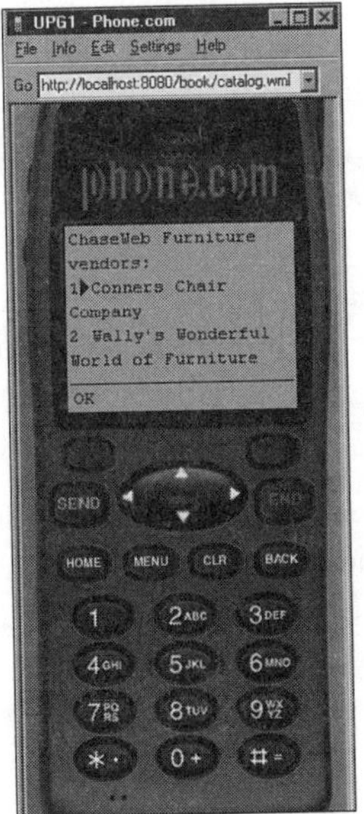

Also notice that because of the small window, we weren't able to fit all our choices on the first page. Although we can scroll down with the down arrow, we might want to go ahead and make sure that each of our choices takes only one line. We can do that quickly in Listing 9.14.

Listing 9.14—`catalog.wml`: Changing the Format

```
0: <?xml version="1.0"?>
1: <!DOCTYPE wml PUBLIC "-//WAPFORUM//DTD WML 1.1//EN"
2:        "http://www.wapforum.org/DTD/wml_1.1.xml">
3:<wml>
4:     <card title="ChaseWeb Vendors">
5:         <p>
6:             ChaseWeb Furniture vendors:
7:         </p>
8:         <p mode="nowrap">
9:             <select>
10:                 <option>
11:                     Conners Chair Company
12:                 </option>
13:                 <option>
14:                     Wally's Wonderful World of Furniture
15:                 </option>
16:                 <option>
17:                     Crazy Marge's Furniture Emporium
18:                 </option>
19:             </select>
20:         </p>
21:     </card>
22:</wml>
```

On line 4, we've added a `title` to the card. Even though we won't see it in this browser, we never know when this page might be accessed by a device that will display it. Secondly, on line 8, we've told the browser not to wrap our select options. Of course, this means that not all the names will be seen immediately, because they don't fit on a single line. When the user highlights that line, however, it will flash, showing all the line in turn. We can see the second half of that flashing line in Figure 9.9.

That's all well and good, but now we need to be able to get a list of products, after we choose a vendor. To prevent multiple trips to the server, we're going to put them into additional cards in this deck, as in Listing 9.15.

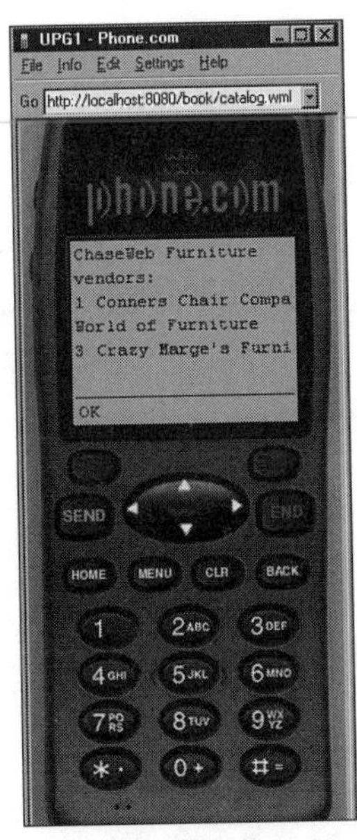

Figure 9.9

If an option is too long to fit on one line, the browser will flash each part in turn, allowing the user to see it all.

Listing 9.15—`catalog.wml`: Adding Product Listings

```
<?xml version="1.0"?>
<!DOCTYPE wml PUBLIC "-//WAPFORUM//DTD WML 1.1//EN"
     "http://www.wapforum.org/DTD/wml_1.1.xml">
<wml>
   <card title="ChaseWeb Vendors">
       <p>
           ChaseWeb Furniture vendors:
       </p>
       <p mode="nowrap">
           <select>
               <option onpick="#conners">
                   Conners Chair Company
               </option>
               <option onpick="#wally">
                   Wally's Wonderful World of Furniture
               </option>
               <option onpick="#marge">
                   Crazy Marge's Furniture Emporium
               </option>
           </select>
       </p>
   </card>
   <card id="conners" title="Conners Chair Company">
       <p>
           Conners Chair Company
       </p>
       <p mode="nowrap">
```

Listing 9.15—continued

```
            <select>
                <option>
                    Queen Anne Chair
                </option>
                <option>
                    Early American Rocking Chair
                </option>
                <option>
                    Bentwood Rocker
                </option>
            </select>
        </p>
    </card>
    <card id="wally" title="Wally's Wonderful World of Furniture">
        <p>
            Wally's Wonderful World of Furniture
        </p>
        <p mode="nowrap">
            <select>
                <option>
                    Complete Dining Room Set
                </option>
                <option>
                    Dining Room Table
                </option>
                <option>
                    Swivel Chair
                </option>
                <option>
                    Hutch
                </option>
                <option>
                    Hall Bench
                </option>
                <option>
                    Sofa and Love Seat
                </option>
            </select>
        </p>
    </card>
    <card id="marge" title="Crazy Marge's Bed Emporium">
        <p>
            Crazy Marge's Bed Emporium
        </p>
        <p mode="nowrap">
            <select>
                <option>
                    Sleepeazy Mattresses
                </option>
                <option>
```

Listing 9.15—continued

```
77:                     CozyComfort Mattresses
78:                 </option>
79:                 <option>
80:                     Floataway Waterbeds
81:                 </option>
82:             </select>
83:         </p>
84:     </card>
85:</wml>
```

On lines 10, 13, and 16, we've added the `onpick` attribute to our options. In actuality, these are not so much attributes as events. When the user chooses one of these options, the browser displays the card with the given `id`. So, if the user picks Wally's Wonderful World of Furniture, the `onpick` event fires, and the browser looks for the `wally` card. The `#` before the name indicates that we're looking for a card in the same deck, as opposed to another deck altogether. This is similar to the way a `#` is used in XHTML to indicate a spot within a page.

The `wally` card, like the other cards, shows the vendor's name and their products. We can then link each of those options to the individual product page, as in Listing 9.16.

Listing 9.16—`catalog.wml`: Adding Links to the Product Pages

```
0: <?xml version="1.0"?>
1: <!DOCTYPE wml PUBLIC "-//WAPFORUM//DTD WML 1.1//EN"
2:      "http://www.wapforum.org/DTD/wml_1.1.xml">
3:<wml>
4:    <card title="ChaseWeb Vendors">
5:        <p>
6:            ChaseWeb Furniture vendors:
7:        </p>
8:        <p mode="nowrap">
9:            <select>
10:                <option onpick="#conners">
11:                    Conners Chair Company
12:                </option>
13:                <option onpick="#wally">
14:                    Wally's Wonderful World of Furniture
15:                </option>
16:                <option onpick="#marge">
17:                    Crazy Marge's Furniture Emporium
18:                </option>
19:            </select>
20:        </p>
21:    </card>
22:    <card id="conners" title="Conners Chair Company">
23:        <p>
24:            Conners Chair Company
25:        </p>
```

9

Listing 9.16—continued

```
        <p mode="nowrap">
            <select>
                <option
        onpick="/book/servlet/TransformServlet?product_id=QA3452">
                    Queen Anne Chair
                </option>
                <option
        onpick="/book/servlet/TransformServlet?product_id=RC2342">
                    Early American Rocking Chair
                </option>
                <option
        onpick="/book/servlet/TransformServlet?product_id=BR3452">
                    Bentwood Rocker
                </option>
            </select>
        </p>
    </card>
    <card id="wally" title="Wally's Wonderful World of Furniture">
        <p>
            Wally's Wonderful World of Furniture
        </p>
        <p mode="nowrap">
            <select>
                <option
        onpick="/book/servlet/TransformServlet?product_id=CDRS">
                    Complete Dining Room Set
                </option>
                <option
        onpick="/book/servlet/TransformServlet?product_id=WWWdrt">
                    Dining Room Table
                </option>
                <option
        onpick="/book/servlet/TransformServlet?product_id=WWWsc">
                    Swivel Chair
                </option>
                <option
        onpick="/book/servlet/TransformServlet?product_id=WWWhch">
                    Hutch
                </option>
                <option
        onpick="/book/servlet/TransformServlet?product_id=HallBench">
                    Hall Bench
                </option>
                <option
        onpick="/book/servlet/TransformServlet?product_id=SofaLoveSeat">
                    Sofa and Love Seat
                </option>
            </select>
        </p>
    </card>
    <card id="marge" title="Crazy Marge's Bed Emporium">
        <p>
```

Listing 9.16—continued

```
78:             Crazy Marge's Bed Emporium
79:         </p>
80:         <p mode="nowrap">
81:             <select>
82:                 <option
83:         onpick="/book/servlet/TransformServlet?product_id=3253435">
84:                     Sleepeazy Mattresses
85:                 </option>
86:                 <option
87:         onpick="/book/servlet/TransformServlet?product_id=5622345">
88:                     CozyComfort Mattresses
89:                 </option>
90:                 <option
91:         onpick="/book/servlet/TransformServlet?product_id=39981234">
92:                     Floataway Waterbeds
93:                 </option>
94:             </select>
95:         </p>
96:     </card>
97:</wml>
```

The additions on lines 29, 33, 37, 50, 54, 58, 62, 66, 70, 83, 87, and 91 will send the browser to another page, because they don't start with `#`.

Of course, if we were to try to access any of those links right now, we'd get an error, because the browser won't know how to interpret the response.

Adapting a Servlet for Wireless Devices

In the Browser Detection and Media sections of this chapter, we looked at using different style sheets for different types of browsers. Now we're going to take that a step farther, creating a new style sheet for our Web phone.

9

Before we can even think about seeing it, however, we need to make a couple of changes. First of all, as we mentioned earlier, the phone isn't going to understand any requests that come back with a MIME-type other than `text/vnd.wap.wml`. So, the first thing we need to do is to tell the servlet to output the appropriate MIME-type. In Listing 9.17, we'll use the `media` value, which we're already checking for, to decide on the appropriate MIME-type.

Listing 9.17—`ShowCatalog.java`: Adjusting the MIME-Type

```
public class ShowCatalog extends HttpServlet {

    public void doGet(HttpServletRequest request,
                      HttpServletResponse response)
        throws IOException, ServletException
    {
```

Listing 9.17—continued

```
13:
14:     String target = request.getHeader("User-Agent");
15:
16:     ResourceBundle media = ResourceBundle.getBundle("media");
17:     Enumeration browsers = media.getKeys();
18:
19:     boolean found = false;
20:
21:     String mediaStr = "";
22:     while (browsers.hasMoreElements() && !found) {
23:         String thisBrowser = (String)browsers.nextElement();
24:         if (target.indexOf(thisBrowser) > -1) {
25:             found = true;
26:             mediaStr = media.getString(thisBrowser);
27:         }
28:     }
29:
30:     String mimetype = "";
31:     if (mediaStr.equals("up")) {
32:         mimetype = "text/vnd.wap.wml";
33:     } else {
34:         mimetype = "text/html";
35:     }
36:     response.setContentType(mimetype);
37:
38:     PrintWriter out = response.getWriter();
39:
40:     try {
41:
42:         Processor processor = Processor.newInstance("xslt");
...
```

Notice first that we've moved this declaration down from the beginning of the method to after we've determined the `media`, so we can take advantage of its value. On line 30, we're creating a `String` variable, then on lines 31 through 35 we're comparing its value to `up`, which is the `media` type for the Up.Simulator (and which is part of the `media.properties` file). If it is the phone, we're setting the value of MIME-type to the `wml` MIME-type, and if it's not we're setting the value to the traditional XHTML version. On line 36, we're actually setting the MIME-type of the response.

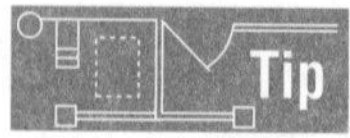

We could have just set the type from within the `if-then` statement, but this will give us more flexibility later if we have more types we want to handle with special instructions.

Next, we need to add the new style sheet (which we have not yet created) to `products.xml`, so the processor will know to look for it. Listing 9.18 shows the changes to `products.xml`.

Listing 9.18—`products.xml`: Adding the New Style Sheet

```
0: <?xml version="1.0" encoding="UTF-8"?>
1: <?xml-stylesheet href="allproducts_wml.xsl"
2:     type="text/xsl" media="up" alternate="yes" ?>
3: <?xml-stylesheet href="allproducts_ns.xsl"
4:     type="text/xsl" media="netscape" alternate="yes" ?>
5: <?xml-stylesheet href="allproducts.xsl" type="text/xsl" ?>
...
```

The actual addition is pretty simple, on lines 1 and 2.

Now we need to create the actual style sheet. Previously, we created a static page for the output we want to see in the browser. Listing 9.19 is the beginning of the corresponding style sheet.

Listing 9.19—`allproducts_wml.xsl`: The WML Style Sheet

```
<?xml version="1.0"?>
<xsl:stylesheet version="1.0"
        xmlns:xsl="http://www.w3.org/1999/XSL/Transform">

<xsl:template match="/">
<wml>
    <card title="ChaseWeb Vendors">
        <p>
            ChaseWeb Furniture vendors:
        </p>
        <p mode="nowrap">
            <select>
                <xsl:apply-templates match="vendor"/>
            </select>
        </p>
    </card>
</wml>
</xsl:template>

<xsl:template match="//vendor">
    <xsl:element name="option">
        <xsl:attribute name="onpick">#<xsl:value-of select="@vendor_id"/>
➥</xsl:attribute>
        <xsl:value-of select="vendor_name"/>
    </xsl:element>
</xsl:template>

</xsl:stylesheet>
```

Line 0 is the XML declaration, and lines 1 and 2 define the namespace for the transformations.

Although the other `allproducts*.xml` style sheets include the `top_include.xsl` style sheet, we've eliminated it here because we don't want the interface elements. Instead, we're taking the document root and using it to create the wml root element and the first card on lines 5, 6, 15, and 16.

Within that card, we've output the descriptive paragraph on lines 7 through 9, and then created the paragraph and the `select` element that holds our options on lines 10 through 14.

On line 12, we're sending the processor off in search of vendor elements that fit the template on lines 19 through 24. This template takes a `vendor` element, no matter where it is in the document, and creates an element for it on lines 20 through 23. As in our static document, this element is an option. On line 21, we're creating the `onpick` attribute, using the value of the vendor's `vendor_id` attribute, and on line 22, we're outputting the `vendor_name` as the content of the element. Save this file as

`C:\files\allproducts_wml.xsl`

We're now prepared to test our WML installation. First, we'll call up

`http://localhost:8080/book/servlet/ShowCatalog`

in either Netscape or Internet Explorer. This behavior should be unchanged, because all we've done is add additional instructions for the Up.Browser. If all is working properly, it's time to move on to actually testing it with the Up.Browser.

Just under the menu bar of the simulator there is a text box marked `Go`. This is the same as the location bar in your browser. Copy and paste the URL from the browser into the location bar of the simulator.

At this point, one of two things will happen. Either the page will be displayed properly, or there will be an error. If there's an error, it will show up in the DOS window that was opened along with the simulator.

Errors generally come in two flavors: MIME-type errors, and translation errors. The former happens when the servlet or Web server doesn't know that it has to send out a MIME-type other than `text/html`. In that case, make sure that you have recompiled the servlet after adding the logic to check for the Up.Browser. The latter happens if there's a mistake in the style sheet. In this case, it might be easiest to save `allproducts.xsl`, and then copy and rename `allproducts_wml.xsl` so that it is processed when you call the servlet from Internet Explorer. If there is a problem actually processing the file, IE tells you exactly what line it's on. If there's something funny about the actual XML that's output, you can see it, because IE just displays it as an XML tree.

Assuming that it worked properly, however, we're ready to create the rest of the style sheet so that the other cards are output as well, as in Listing 9.20.

Listing 9.20—`allproducts_wml.xsl`: Adding the Vendor Cards

```
<?xml version="1.0"?>
<xsl:stylesheet version="1.0"
      xmlns:xsl="http://www.w3.org/1999/XSL/Transform">

<xsl:template match="/">
<wml>
    <card title="ChaseWeb Vendors">
        <p>
            ChaseWeb Furniture vendors:
        </p>
        <p mode="nowrap">
            <select>
                <xsl:apply-templates match="vendor"/>
            </select>
        </p>
    </card>

    <xsl:for-each select="//vendor">
        <xsl:call-template name="vendorcard" />
    </xsl:for-each>

</wml>
</xsl:template>

<xsl:template match="//vendor">
    <xsl:element name="option">
        <xsl:attribute name="onpick">#<xsl:value-of
               select="@vendor_id"/></xsl:attribute>
        <xsl:value-of select="vendor_name"/>
    </xsl:element>
</xsl:template>

<xsl:template name="vendorcard">
    <xsl:element name="card">
        <xsl:attribute name="id">
            <xsl:value-of select="@vendor_id" />
        </xsl:attribute>
        <xsl:attribute name="title">
           <xsl:value-of select="vendor_name" />
        </xsl:attribute>
        <p>
            <xsl:value-of select="vendor_name" />
        </p>
        <p mode="nowrap">
            <select>
                <xsl:for-each select="product">
                    <xsl:call-template name="productchoices" />
```

Listing 9.20—continued

```
47:                </xsl:for-each>
48:            </select>
49:        </p>
50:    </xsl:element>
51:</xsl:template>
52:
53:<xsl:template name="productchoices">
54:    <xsl:element name="option">
55:        <xsl:attribute name="onpick"
56:              >TransformServlet?product_id=<xsl:value-of
57:              select="product_id"/></xsl:attribute>
58:        <xsl:value-of select="short_desc" />
59:    </xsl:element>
60:</xsl:template>
61:
62:</xsl:stylesheet>
```

Because we've already created a template for the `vendor` elements, we'll go ahead and call the template for the `vendor` cards explicitly. On lines 17 through 19, we loop through each of the `vendors` and specifically call the `vendorcard` template.

The `vendorcard` template is defined on lines 32 through 51. Because we want to dynamically create the `id` and `title` attributes, we'll create the `card` element explicitly on lines 33 and 50. On lines 34 through 39, we're creating those two attributes, feeding them values based on the `vendor` node we're processing. On lines 40 through 42, we create the `vendor` name that goes across the top of the page.

On lines 43 through 49, we're creating the product listing, but rather than just creating a template for all products, we're again going to create a named template, `productchoices`, which we'll call for each `product` in the loop on lines 45 through 47.

The `productchoices` template, on lines 53 through 60, is pretty straightforward, simply creating an `option` element for each `product`, with the `onpick` attribute pointing to the `TransformServlet` for this particular `product_id`. (Note that normally this would all be on one line, but it doesn't fit in the book that way!)

To see these changes, you will have to explicitly refresh the deck. Simply re-entering the URL won't do any good, as you can see if you look at the DOS window, because a mobile phone will check its cache to see whether it already has a copy of the file to prevent another trip to the server.

To refresh the Up.Simulator, press the F9 key, or choose Reload from the Edit menu. If your changes still don't seem to be taking effect, shut down the simulator and restart it.

At this point, we should be able to navigate to a specific vendor's page and see their products, but if we choose any of the products, we'll get an error, because `TransformServlet` is not prepared to serve content to a mobile phone.

The principles are the same, however. Create a style sheet, and let the servlet know when to use it! In this way, our entire site can be converted to handle mobile devices by doing little more than creating new style sheets.

More information on WML and WAP can be found in the XML Cover Pages at

`http://www.oasis-open.org/cover/wap-wml.html`

The Simple Object Access Protocol (SOAP)

As useful as XML is for displaying data, perhaps one of the most powerful things that we can do with it is to use it to exchange data between different systems. After all, it's just text, and it's in an agreed-upon format, so that much should be easy.

The Simple Object Access Protocol, or SOAP, is intended as a way to use XML to accomplish Remote Procedure Calls, or RPC. RPC is used to execute some function or procedure on a completely different machine, usually without leaving the original program.

SOAP actually accomplishes this without inventing any new technologies. Instead, it takes the existing technologies of XML and HTTP, the underlying protocol of the Web, and combines them with an agreed-upon way to send messages back and forth.

For instance, we could use SOAP to notify our vendors when one of their products has been sold, possibly triggering a reorder.

Notice that nowhere in those paragraphs did I say anything about an API. There is no SOAP API. Instead, it's a protocol, which basically explains how to do things, but leaves the actual implementation of them up to the programmer. In fact, writing a SOAP engine is fairly straightforward, so to familiarize you with how SOAP works, we'll build one here.

SOAP 1.1 is actually a W3C Note, as opposed to a Recommendation. The most current version can be found at

`http://www.w3.org/TR/SOAP`

9

Of course, our engine will be fairly simple, and you wouldn't want to use it in a production environment without some serious bulletproofing, but it will give you an idea of how this process works.

Because we'll be delving into some of the lower-level mechanics of HTTP, this might be a bit daunting if you haven't done any Java coding before. Not to worry, however; the Apache group has a group of SOAP classes to help you out. You can find them at

`http://xml.apache.org/soap/`

How SOAP Messages Are Passed

Previously in the "Browser Detection" section of this chapter, we looked at an HTTP request:

```
GET /book/servlet/TransformServlet HTTP/1.1
Host: 216.2.13.156
User-Agent: Mozilla/5.0 (Windows; U; Win98; en-US; m18) Gecko/20001108
➥Netscape6/6.0
Accept: */*
Accept-Encoding: gzip,deflate,compress,identity
Host: localhost:8080
Accept-Language: en
Keep-Alive: 300
Connection: keep-alive
```

Although this is a complete request, we can also add information to it. For instance, Listing 9.21 is also a complete request.

Listing 9.21—Sample HTTP Request

```
POST /book/servlet/InventorySold HTTP/1.1
Host: 216.2.13.156
User-Agent: Mozilla/5.0 (Windows; U; Win98; en-US; m18)
➥ Gecko/20001108 Netscape6/6.0
Host: localhost:8080

Hey, we sold something!
```

Notice that we have actual content in the request, and that it's separated from the headers by a blank line.

Of course, that content isn't formatted in such a way that any server would be able to understand it, so it's not doing anybody much good. A similar SOAP request might resemble Listing 9.22.

Listing 9.22—A Sample SOAP Request

```
0: POST /book/servlet/InventorySold HTTP/1.1
1: Host: 216.2.13.156
2: User-Agent: Mozilla/5.0 (Windows; U; Win98; en-US; m18)
➥ Gecko/20001108 Netscape6/6.0
3: Host: localhost:8080
4: Content-Length: 221
5: Content-Type: text/xml
6: SOAPMethodName: http://www.nicholaschase.com/soap#InventorySold
7:
8: <envelope>
9:     <body>
10:        <inv:InventorySold xmlns:inv="http://www.nicholaschase.com/soap">
11:            <product_id>QA3452 </product_id>
12:            <quantity>1</quantity>
13:        </inv:InventorySold>
14:    </body>
15:</envelope>
```

Lines 0 through 5 are standard HTTP headers, which we discussed earlier. Line 6, however, is not standard, although it is a header. The `SOAPMethodName` header serves two purposes. First, it provides information on what we're supposed to do with this message, and second, it saves firewall administrators from having to parse the message, because the message must match this header or be rejected.

Firewall—A firewall is a computer that serves as a kind of gate between an internal network and the Internet at large. It monitors traffic and, in most cases, allows only authorized traffic through.

The `SOAPMethodName` actually consists of two parts: the namespace before the `#` delimiter, and the method name after it.

The actual content of the request is known as the payload, because it's being delivered to the target. A SOAP message must consist of an `<envelope>` and a `<body>`. The body is what actually contains the request itself, with a child element that must satisfy two requirements:

- The name of the element must match the method name in `SOAPMethodName`.
- The namespace URI of the element must match the namespace in `SOAPMethodName`.

Within this child element are parameters that will eventually be passed by and to our engine.

When a SOAP request is processed, the engine will return a response. This response might look something like Listing 9.23.

Listing 9.23—A Sample SOAP Response

```
200 OK
Content-Type: text/xml
Content-Length: 195

<envelope>
    <body>
        <inv:InventorySoldResponse xmlns:inv=
➥"http://www.nicholaschase.com/soap">
            <reorder>false</reorder>
        </inv:InventorySoldResponse>
    </body>
</envelope>
```

In this case, we start out with a standard HTTP result code. 200 means that everything was executed without a problem. Next, we have the MIME-type and length of the content, and then the content itself. Once again, we have the `envelope` and `body`, and then the content. The actual content uses the same name as the request, with `Response` appended to the end of it.

More information on HTTP can be found at `http://www.jmarshall.com/easy/http/`

HTTP Requests and Responses

Throughout this book, we've been dealing with HTTP requests and responses in the context of servlets. Now we're going to combine that with some direct HTTP calls.

First, let's create our SOAP servlet. This will eventually be the servlet that receives all our SOAP requests and passes them on to the appropriate class, so we need it to be able to take input from a calling servlet. In Listing 9.24, we create the basic SOAP servlet.

Listing 9.24—`SOAPServlet.java`: The Basic Structure

```
import java.util.*;
import javax.servlet.http.*;
import java.io.*;

public class SOAPServlet extends HttpServlet
{
    public void doPost(HttpServletRequest request,
                       HttpServletResponse response)
                              throws IOException
    {

```

Listing 9.24—continued

```
11:         response.setContentType("text/html");
12:         PrintWriter out = response.getWriter();
13:
14:         String SOAPMethodName =
15:                     request.getHeader("SOAPMethodName");
16:
17:         StringTokenizer SOAPHeader =
18:                  new StringTokenizer(SOAPMethodName, "#");
19:         String ns = SOAPHeader.nextToken();
20:         String className = SOAPHeader.nextToken();
21:         out.print("The namespace is "+ns+"<br />");
22:         out.print("The className is "+className+"<br />");
23:
24:         InputStream toSOAP = request.getInputStream();
25:         byte[] payloadArr = new byte[request.getContentLength()];
26:         int payloadLength = toSOAP.read(payloadArr);
27:         String payloadStr =
28:                     new String(payloadArr, 0, payloadLength);
29:
30:         out.print("Payload: "+payloadStr);
31:     }
32:
33:}
```

On lines 11 and 12, we're creating the output for this servlet. This output will be sent to whatever the calling program was. This is an important distinction, because that's not always the browser. In Figure 9.10, we see that in a traditional request to a servlet, the output is sent back to the browser, because that's the program that called it. In the case of SOAP, however, this servlet will actually be called by another Java program, so that's where the results will go.

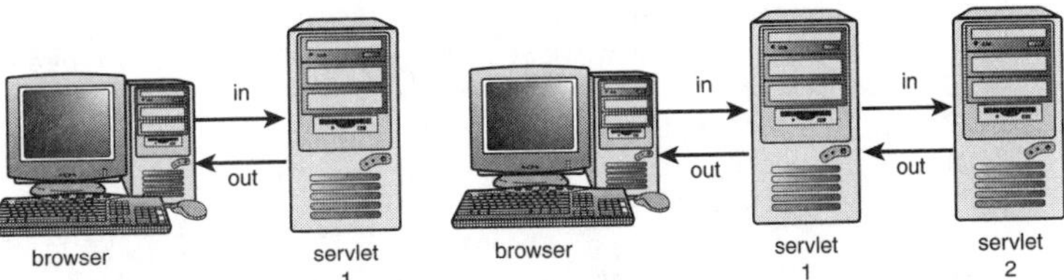

Figure 9.10

When one servlet is called by another, that's where the output goes.

In lines 14 and 15, we're retrieving the `SOAPMethodName` header. As we mentioned, this is the line that will contain the namespace of the payload, as well as the class to call. That information is being retrieved and output on lines 17 through 22.

We've discussed where the output of this servlet will go; now we'll talk about where the input will come from. In line 24, we're creating an `InputStream` from the `request` object. It doesn't matter how the `request` was created, or by what—we just want to create an `InputStream` to read its contents. Until now, we've just been looking at information about the request, such as headers or parameter values. Now we want the actual `request` itself.

`InputStreams` come back to us as arrays of `bytes`, so, on line 25, we'll create the array that will receive the information. Because we need to set a size, we'll retrieve the length of the request from the headers. On line 26, we're actually reading the stream of bytes into payload, returning the actual number of characters. We'll turn that stream into a `String` on lines 27 and 28, reading the array of `bytes` (`payload`) from the start (`0`) to the end (`payloadLength`).

Finally, on line 30, we output the value of the `payload`. That output will go back to the calling servlet.

Now, let's look at the calling servlet. Listing 9.25 shows the call to `SOAPServlet.java`.

Listing 9.25—`SendServlet.java`: The Basic Structure

```
0:import javax.servlet.http.*;
1:import java.net.*;
2:import java.io.*;
3:
4:public class SendServlet extends HttpServlet
5:{
6:    public void doGet(HttpServletRequest request,
7:                      HttpServletResponse response)
8:                            throws IOException
9:    {
10:        String payload = "THE PAYLOAD WILL BE HERE";
11:
12:        URL url =
13:          new URL("http://localhost:8080/book/servlet/SOAPServlet");
14:        HttpURLConnection conn =
15:              (HttpURLConnection)url.openConnection();
16:
17:        conn.setRequestProperty("SOAPMethodName",
18:             "http://www.nicholaschase.com/soap/#InventorySold");
19:
20:        conn.setRequestMethod("POST");
21:        conn.setDoOutput(true);
22:        conn.connect();
23:
24:        OutputStream toSOAP = conn.getOutputStream();
25:        toSOAP.write(payload.getBytes());
26:        toSOAP.close();
27:
28:        InputStream fromSOAP = conn.getInputStream();
29:        byte[] SOAPResult = new byte[5000];
30:        int resultLength = fromSOAP.read(SOAPResult);
31:        String SOAPResultStr =
32:               new String(SOAPResult, 0, resultLength);
33:        fromSOAP.close();
34:
35:        response.setContentType("text/html");
36:        PrintWriter out = response.getWriter();
```

Listing 9.25—continued

```
37:        out.print("The results are: <br />");
38:        out.print(SOAPResultStr);
39:    }
40:
41:}
```

On line 10, we have a sample payload. This is where the SOAP envelope will be defined, but for now let's just look at how the system works.

Lines 12 and 13 create a `URL` object. On the face of it, it looks like just an address string, but remember, this is Java. A `URL` object has specific properties and methods, such as the capability to open a connection, which we're doing on lines 14 and 15.

What we're doing here is essentially the same thing the browser does when we enter a URL into the location bar: We're opening a connection to a particular location, sending a request, including headers, and listening for a response. The `SOAPMethodName` header is set on lines 17 and 18, and the `request` method is set on line 20.

On line 21, we're setting `DoOutput` to `true`. This means that we're going to be receiving information back from this connection.

After we have all our properties set, we actually make the connection on line 22, but that just sends the headers. To actually send the request—specifically, the payload—we are creating a stream from `SendServlet` out to `SOAPServlet` on line 24. The payload actually gets sent on line 25, after which we close the `OutputStream` on line 26.

Although the `OutputStream` is closed, the connection itself is still open, and on line 28 we get ready to receive the response from `SOAPServlet`, creating an `InputStream`. On line 29, we're creating an array of `bytes` for the result, assuming that we won't have more than 5,000 bytes. On line 30, we actually read the `response`, and on lines 31 and 32 we turn it into a `String`, just as we did in `SOAPServlet`. Finally, we close the connection on line 33.

At this point, we've executed `SOAPServlet` and received the result, so we're ready to output it to the browser window. The results look like Figure 9.11.

Figure 9.11

Shown here are the results of sending information to `SOAPServlet`.

Notice that even though `SOAPServlet` is executed before `SendServlet` outputs any text, the `SendServlet` text appears first. This is because all the output from `SOAPServlet` goes not to the browser, but to the `SOAPResult` variable. The only reason that we're seeing it at all is because we're outputting it to the page on line 38. (Don't believe it? Try commenting out line 38 and watch the results disappear.)

> Although Tomcat will automatically reload the servlet that we actually call—`SendServlet`, in this case—it will not check for changes in a servlet that is called indirectly, for instance, the way we're calling `SOAPServlet`. To get changes to take effect, we need to restart Tomcat.

In Listing 9.26, we'll add our payload to `SendServlet`.

Listing 9.26—`SendServlet.java`: Adding the Payload

```
import javax.servlet.http.*;
import java.net.*;
import java.io.*;
import org.apache.xerces.dom.*;
import org.apache.xerces.parsers.*;
import org.w3c.dom.*;
import org.apache.xml.serialize.*;

public class SendServlet extends HttpServlet
{
    public void doGet(HttpServletRequest request,
                      HttpServletResponse response)
                            throws IOException
    {

        Document SOAPReq = new DocumentImpl();
        Element envelope = SOAPReq.createElement("envelope");
        Element body = SOAPReq.createElement("body");
        Element InventorySold = SOAPReq.createElementNS(
                              "http://www.nicholaschase.com/soap/",
                              "InventorySold");
        Element product_id = SOAPReq.createElement("product_id");
        Element quantity = SOAPReq.createElement("quantity");

        quantity.appendChild(SOAPReq.createTextNode("1"));
        product_id.appendChild(SOAPReq.createTextNode("QA3452"));
        InventorySold.appendChild(product_id);
        InventorySold.appendChild(quantity);
        body.appendChild(InventorySold);
        envelope.appendChild(body);
        SOAPReq.appendChild(envelope);

        URL url =
          new URL("http://localhost:8080/book/servlet/SOAPServlet");
        HttpURLConnection conn =
```

Listing 9.26—continued

```
35:             (HttpURLConnection)url.openConnection();
36:
37:         conn.setRequestProperty("SOAPMethodName",
38:              "http://www.nicholaschase.com/soap/#InventorySold");
39:
40:         conn.setRequestMethod("POST");
41:         conn.setDoOutput(true);
42:         conn.connect();
43:
44:
45:         OutputStream toSOAP = conn.getOutputStream();
46:
47:         OutputFormat format =
48:              new OutputFormat(SOAPReq, "UTF-8", false);
49:         XMLSerializer output = new XMLSerializer(toSOAP, format);
50:         output.serialize(SOAPReq);
51:
52:         toSOAP.close();
53:
54:         InputStream fromSOAP = conn.getInputStream();
55:         byte[] SOAPResult = new byte[5000];
56:         int resultLength = fromSOAP.read(SOAPResult);
57:         String SOAPResultStr =
58:                 new String(SOAPResult, 0, resultLength);
59:         fromSOAP.close();
60:
61:         response.setContentType("text/html");
62:         PrintWriter out = response.getWriter();
63:         out.print("The results are: <br />");
64:         out.print(SOAPResultStr);
65:     }
66:
67:}
```

What we're doing here is moving back into the world of XML, creating the payload as an XML document and then serializing it to our destination. On lines 3 through 6, we're adding the Xerces and DOM packages we're going to need.

On line 15, we're creating the empty document, and on lines 16 and 17 we're creating the basic framework of our SOAP request, the envelope and body. Lines 18 through 20 create our actual payload, which is in its own namespace. The elements that will contain our data are created on lines 21 and 22.

On lines 24 and 25, we add the content to data elements, and on lines 26 through 30, we build the rest of the document.

After we've built the XML document, we need to find a way to send a text version of it to the `SOAPServlet`. The means for doing that are already at our disposal; we just need to serialize the document. Previously, we have either serialized a document to a file or to the browser. There's no reason we can't serialize it to another servlet. On lines 47 and 48, we create the `OutputFormat`, just as we've always done, but this time we're setting the indenting to false, because we're going to be reading this as data, so we don't want the indenting that comes with "pretty printing."

On line 49, where we normally create an `XMLSerializer` that goes to a file, we're sending it directly to `toSOAP`, the `OutputStream` to `SOAPServlet`. This way, when we serialize the document on line 50, the servlet receives the information as a text stream.

If we recompile the servlet and run it, we'll see that the payload has changed.

Now that we have the payload, the question becomes What do we do with it?

Well, the first thing that we have to do is give `SOAPServlet` the capability to parse the SOAP envelope and retrieve the information from it, as in Listing 9.27.

Listing 9.27—`SOAPServlet`: Parsing the Payload Envelope

```
import java.util.*;
import javax.servlet.http.*;
import java.io.*;
import org.apache.xerces.dom.*;
import org.apache.xerces.parsers.*;
import org.w3c.dom.*;
import org.apache.xml.serialize.*;
import org.xml.sax.*;

public class SOAPServlet extends HttpServlet
{
     public void doPost(HttpServletRequest request,
                          HttpServletResponse response)
                                  throws IOException
     {

          response.setContentType("text/html");
          PrintWriter out = response.getWriter();

          String SOAPMethodName =
                          request.getHeader("SOAPMethodName");

          StringTokenizer SOAPHeader =
                    new StringTokenizer(SOAPMethodName, "#");
          String ns = SOAPHeader.nextToken();
          String className = SOAPHeader.nextToken();
          out.print("The namespace is "+ns+"<br />");
          out.print("The className is "+className+"<br />");

          Hashtable payload = new Hashtable();
          try {

              DOMParser parser = new DOMParser();
              parser.parse(
                    new InputSource(request.getInputStream()));
```

Listing 9.27—continued

```
35:            Document envelope = parser.getDocument();
36:            Element body =
37:                  (Element)envelope.getElementsByTagName("body").item(0);
38:            Node payloadEl =
39:                  body.getElementsByTagName(className).item(0);
40:            NodeList childElements = payloadEl.getChildNodes();
41:            for (int i=0; i < childElements.getLength(); i++) {
42:                payload.put(childElements.item(i).getLocalName(),
43:                        childElements.item(i).getFirstChild().getNodeValue());
44:            }
45:
46:        } catch (Exception e) {
47:            out.print("Problem parsing payload: "+e.getMessage());
48:        }
49:
50:    }
51:
52:}
```

Here, we've completely changed how we retrieve the payload. First, on line 29, we're creating an empty `Hashtable` to hold our data. A `Hashtable` is perfect for this, because we don't know how many pieces of information we're going to have, but we know they'll all have names associated with them.

On line 32, we're creating a new `DOMParser`. This is what we're going to use to parse the XML coming from `SendServlet`. On lines 33 and 34, we're creating an `InputSource` using the actual `InputStream` for the servlet; this is the string of bytes coming in as the request. It is this `InputSource` that we then parse.

After we've parsed the data, we get the XML document on line 35, and then retrieve the body element on lines 36 and 37. The next thing that we want to do is retrieve the actual payload itself, but this is supposed to be a generic servlet, so we don't want to hard-code in the name of the element. Fortunately, the protocol helps us out here. The payload element will always have the same name as the method specified in the `SOAPMethodName`, so we'll use that on lines 36 and 37.

After we have the payload element, we can simply get all the child nodes and loop through them, inserting them into the `Hashtable`.

Okay, so we have them. Now, what do we do with them?

Well, if this were a full-blown production application, we'd be sending them off to a servlet for processing of some type. The receiver might not even be within our own company. In this case, however, because we're just looking at how to do it, we're going to start with something simple. This application returns the current quantity on hand (after the order), and whether or not it's time to reorder stock. Because this is just a demo, we'll hard-code the data into our SOAP processor, `SOAPProcess.java`. Just remember, in the real world, `SOAPProcess` can be anything.

In Listing 9.28, we'll create the `SOAPProcess` class.

Listing 9.28—`SOAPProcess.java`

```
0: import java.util.*;
1:
2: public class SOAPProcess extends Object {
3:
4:     public static Hashtable InventorySold (Hashtable callparam) {
5:
6:          Hashtable results = new Hashtable();
7:          results.put("quantity", callparam.get("quantity"));
8:          results.put("reorder", "false");
9:
10:         return results;
11:    }
12:}
```

Notice that this is not a servlet. We will not be using URLs to call it. It has a `Hashtable` as both input and output because they're extremely convenient when it comes to XML; we don't have to decide what's in them before we're ready to fill them up, and after they're full, we don't need to know what's in them to start using them.

All that makes it perfect for this system, in which `SOAPServlet` shouldn't have to know anything at all about the program it's calling.

So, on line 6 we create the `Hashtable` we're going to send back to the calling program, and on lines 7 and 8 we fill the `Hashtable`.

Line 7 is data that was input from the SOAP request, and line 8 is a response that normally would have gone through some sort of processing before coming up with an answer. Again, we are inserting an arbitrary value because this is just a demonstration.

Now we need to be able to call `SOAPProcess` from `SOAPServlet`, send it the original `Hashtable`, and retrieve the results. We take care of that in Listing 9.29.

Listing 9.29—`SOAPServlet.java`: Calling `SOAPProcess`

```
...
               for (int i=0; i < childElements.getLength(); i++) {
                   payload.put(childElements.item(i).getLocalName(),
                        childElements.item(i).getFirstChild().getNodeValue());
               }

          } catch (Exception e) {
               out.print("Problem parsing payload: "+e.getMessage());
          }

          Hashtable result = null;
```

Listing 9.29—continued

```
51:        try {
52:
53:            Class calledClass = Class.forName("SOAPProcess");
54:            Class[] parameterTypes = new Class[] {Hashtable.class};
55:            java.lang.reflect.Method SOAPMethod;
56:            Object[] arguments = new Object[] {payload};
57:
58:            SOAPMethod =
59:                calledClass.getMethod(methodName, parameterTypes);
60:            result = (Hashtable) SOAPMethod.invoke(null, arguments);
61:            out.print(result.toString());
62:
63:        } catch (Exception e) {
64:            out.print("Problem calling the work servlet: "
65:                                                  +e.getMessage());
66:        }
67:    }
68:}
```

Let's talk protocol for just a moment. The `SOAPMethodName` header is there to tell us what method to call, but there is no indication of the class. So, while we can indicate any method we want in the actual SOAP request, we want to standardize on the class. That class, in our case, is `SOAPProcess`. But because we don't know what the method will be until we receive the message, we need to use some of the deeper capabilities of Java to build our requests on-the-fly, so to speak.

On line 50, we're creating the `Hashtable` that will hold our ultimate result. On line 53, we're creating a `Class` object specifically by name. This allows us to build a call to the method specified in `SOAPMethodName`.

To build and invoke the method, we're going to need a few things. The first is an array of `Class` objects that represents the parameters the method is going to take. That's what we're creating on line 54. We've made the decision that SOAP-related methods are going to look for `Hashtables`, so our `parameterTypes` array has only one entry, a `Class` object for `Hashtable`. Notice that we had to actually create a `Class` object, as opposed to just referencing `Hashtable` all by itself.

On line 55, we're creating the actual `Method` object, but because there is also a `Method` object in one of the other packages we're importing, we're going to go ahead and specify the version we want right there within the code.

The last piece we need is being created on line 56. Our arguments will be passed in as an array of objects, which, in our case, is just the single payload `Hashtable`.

Now that we have all our pieces, on lines 58 and 59 we can create the method object, feeding `getMethod()` the name (from `SOAPMethodName`) and the `parameterTypes` array.

Finally, we are ready to actually call the method. On line 60, we invoke the method. The first parameter for `invoke()` is to specify an object, but everything we're doing right now is static, so there's no object to reference. The second is the array of arguments we created earlier. This will return a `Hashtable`, which we're converting to a string and printing on line 61.

Compile both classes and restart Tomcat to see the changes when we run `SendServlet` (which we haven't touched).

Now that we're receiving the result, we need to put it back into a form that can be understood by an application following the SOAP protocol. In Listing 9.30, we create the SOAP response.

Listing 9.30—`SOAPServlet.java`: Creating the Response

```
...
59:            result =
60:                 (Hashtable)SOAPMethod.invoke(null, arguments);
61:
62:        } catch (Exception e) {
63:            out.print("Problem calling the work servlet: "
64:                                                +e.getMessage());
65:        }
66:
67:        Document SOAPRes = new DocumentImpl();
68:        Element envelope = SOAPRes.createElement("envelope");
69:        Element body = SOAPRes.createElement("body");
70:        Element returnResult = SOAPRes.createElementNS(
71:                              ns, methodName+"Result");
72:
73:        Enumeration allKeys = result.keys();
74:        while (allKeys.hasMoreElements()) {
75:            String thisKey = (String)allKeys.nextElement();
76:            String thisValue = (String)result.get(thisKey);
77:            Element thisElement =
78:                 SOAPRes.createElement(thisKey);
79:            thisElement.
80:                 appendChild(SOAPRes.createTextNode(thisValue));
81:            returnResult.appendChild(thisElement);
82:        }
83:        body.appendChild(returnResult);
84:        envelope.appendChild(body);
85:        SOAPRes.appendChild(envelope);
86:
87:        OutputFormat format =
88:             new OutputFormat(SOAPRes, "UTF-8", false);
89:        XMLSerializer output = new XMLSerializer(out, format);
90:        output.serialize(SOAPRes);
91:
92:    }
93:}
```

What we're trying to do here is to take the `Hashtable` that holds our results and create an XML document that we can send back to `SendServlet`. On line 67, we're creating that document, and then on lines 68 and 69 we create the envelope and body elements.

On line 70, we begin the actual result. Notice that the namespace is the same as the original namespace, and that the actual element itself is named as the original request element, plus `Result`. This is the standard convention for returning results.

On line 73, we're getting a list of all the keys in our result, and on lines 74 through 82 we're looping through each of them, creating elements and adding them to the result. On line 75, we get the actual key, and then the value on line 76. We can then create the element on lines 77 and 78, and assign it the appropriate value on lines 79 and 80. This leaves us an element that we can add to the result element. This routine will work for any `Hashtable` response. It's not tied to just this case.

Finally, on lines 83 through 85, we finish assembling the document by adding the body and the envelope.

After we have the document, we need to send it back to the calling servlet, which we're doing on lines 87 through 90. Notice that this is the same way we had previously sent XML to the browser, but in this case, our response object is feeding back to the calling servlet, as we have seen.

We've also removed the previous output statements, because we're ready to start analyzing the result. In Listing 9.31, we'll receive the results.

Listing 9.31—`SendServlet.java`: Receiving the Results

```
...
        OutputStream toSOAP = conn.getOutputStream();

        OutputFormat format =
             new OutputFormat(SOAPReq, "UTF-8", false);
        XMLSerializer output = new XMLSerializer(toSOAP, format);
        output.serialize(SOAPReq);

        toSOAP.close();

        response.setContentType("text/html");
        PrintWriter out = response.getWriter();

        Hashtable SOAPRes = new Hashtable();
        try {

            DOMParser parser = new DOMParser();
            parser.parse(
                  new InputSource(conn.getInputStream()));
            Document envelopeDoc = parser.getDocument();
            body =
```

Listing 9.31—continued

```
67:                     (Element)envelopeDoc
68:                     .getElementsByTagName("body").item(0);
69:               Node payloadEl = body
70:                         .getElementsByTagName("InventorySoldResult")
71:                         .item(0);
72:               NodeList childElements = payloadEl.getChildNodes();
73:               for (int i=0; i < childElements.getLength(); i++) {
74:                   SOAPRes.put(childElements.item(i).getLocalName(),
75:                           childElements.item(i)
76:                           .getFirstChild().getNodeValue());
77:               }
78:
79:           } catch (Exception e) {
80:               out.print("Problem parsing SOAPRes: "+e.getMessage());
81:           }
82:
83:           out.print("After this order of "+SOAPRes.get("quantity"));
84:           String reorder = (String)SOAPRes.get("reorder");
85:           if (reorder.equals("false")) {
86:               out.print(" we do not need to reorder.");
87:           } else {
88:               out.print(" we need to reorder.");
89:           }
90:      }
91:
92:}
```

Lines 59 through 81 are virtually identical to this same section in `SOAPServlet`, except that we're reading the InputStream from the connection instead of the request, and we're specifying `InventorySoldResult` instead of reading `methodName` from the headers.

After we've received our response, on lines 83 through 89 we're doing some simple logic and sending output to the page. This is the section where we would be using the results if this weren't a demo.

Taking It a Step Further

So, what did we accomplish here? Although it looks as though we're dealing with a very specific situation—selling a single item—it would be pretty simple to make this generic enough to serve any purpose. For instance, we could incorporate this into the order system, using it to check whether an item is still in stock, and automatically reordering if necessary. `SendServlet.java` is specific only in the sections in which we specify the payload itself, and in which we use the results. Other than that, the code can be used to send any SOAP request to any SOAP server—even one at another company. Because our messages follow the protocol, they could easily be moved to any of the commercial SOAP engines that will have emerged by the time this book is published.

Formatting Objects

Now that we've looked at one of the more powerful ways to use XML for data transfer, let's look at one of the more powerful ways to use it for presentation.

We've done a lot of work through the course of the book in XSL Transformations. Now it's time for us to look at XSL Formatting Objects. We're going to use them to create a PDF file that could be used to precisely control how our site looks in the browser, or even to print a paper catalog.

Downloading, Installing, and Testing FOP

The software that we're going to use for this is a program called *FOP*, available, like the other packages we've been using, from the Apache project. The home page for the product is at

```
http://xml.apache.org/fop
```

and it can be downloaded at

```
http://xml.apache.org/dist/fop/
```

In our case, we're downloading the file `fop-0_15_0-forBeginners.zip`, but you should use the latest version available for your platform.

Installation is simple: Just uncompress the files into a directory. In our case, we'll use

```
C:\fop\
```

All the software we've installed so far was compressed into a single directory, which could then be uncompressed. This is not the case for FOP. You must create the `C:\fop` directory and extract the files into it, or they will be scattered around your drive.

9

After the files are uncompressed, we need to add the .jar files to our classpath. Add the following to the `autoexec.bat` file:

```
set CLASSPATH=%CLASSPATH%c:\fop\build\fop.jar;c:\fop\lib\w3c.jar;
```

To test the installation, we can do the following:

```
\autoexec
Cd \fop
java org.apache.fop.apps.CommandLine test.fo test.pdf
```

You should see a series of statements as the PDF file is built. To view the file when it's done, simply open it with your browser.

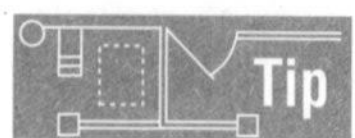

If your installation of FOP doesn't come with the file test.fo, try copying one of the sample *.fo files to the fop directory.

Browsers need the Adobe Acrobat Reader to view a PDF file. The Acrobat Reader can be downloaded from

`http://www.adobe.com/products/acrobat/readstep2.html`

FOP takes advantage of the fact that the PDF format is itself a standard, taking a Formatting Objects file and translating it into PDF. The PDF file can then be read by the PDF reader, which most people already have installed for their browser.

But how do we create the Formatting Objects file? The same way we created XHTML files: using XSL style sheets.

To create a PDF, we need an FO file. Under normal circumstances, we could skip this intermediate step and go directly from XML to PDF using a style sheet, but as of this writing, the FOP samples were written for Xalan 1, so this functionality won't work with our current installation. It is likely that by the time you read this, FOP will have been updated to do the conversion directly.

Before we move into creating `.fo` files with style sheets, let's take a look at what goes into a formatting objects file.

The Structure of a Formatting Objects File

XSLFO has a lot in common with Cascading Style Sheets. For instance, they can be used to programmatically move items to specific areas, group them together, and even format different pages in different ways, depending on whether they are the first page or not.

In this section, we'll create the layout for a PDF version of our catalog. In Listing 9.32, we'll start with the basic structure of a Formatting Objects file, or FO file.

Listing 9.32—`catalog.fo`: The Basic Structure of Our Catalog

```
<?xml version="1.0" encoding="utf-8"?>

<fo:root xmlns:fo="http://www.w3.org/1999/XSL/Format">

    <fo:layout-master-set>
```

Listing 9.32—continued

```

    <fo:simple-page-master master-name="first"
            page-height="11in"
            page-width="8.5in"
            margin-top="1in"
            margin-bottom=".75in"
            margin-left="1in"
            margin-right="1in">
        <fo:region-body margin-top=".75in" />
    </fo:simple-page-master>

    <fo:simple-page-master master-name="rest"
            page-height="11in"
            page-width="8.5in"
            margin-top="1in"
            margin-bottom=".75in"
            margin-left="1in"
            margin-right="1in">
        <fo:region-body margin-top=".75in"/>
        <fo:region-before extent=".5in"/>
        <fo:region-after extent=".75in"/>
    </fo:simple-page-master>

    <fo:page-sequence-master master-name="layout" >
        <fo:repeatable-page-master-alternatives>
            <fo:conditional-page-master-reference
                 master-name="first"
                 page-position="first" />
            <fo:conditional-page-master-reference
                 master-name="rest"
                 page-position="rest" />

            <fo:conditional-page-master-reference
                 master-name="rest" />
        </fo:repeatable-page-master-alternatives>
    </fo:page-sequence-master>

</fo:layout-master-set>

<fo:page-sequence master-name="layout">

    <fo:static-content flow-name="xsl-region-before">
        Header goes here
    </fo:static-content>

    <fo:flow flow-name="xsl-region-body">
        Body goes here
    </fo:flow>

```

Listing 9.32—continued

```
54:        <fo:static-content flow-name="xsl-region-after">
55:            Footer goes here
56:        </fo:static-content>
57:
58:    </fo:page-sequence>
59:
60:</fo:root>
```

This is, of course, a standard XML file, so we have the XML declaration on line 0.

In line 2, we have the `<fo:root>` element. Every FO file must start with the root element. This one also defines the Formatting Objects namespace, `http://www.w3.org/1999/XSL/Format`, which is analogous to `http://www.w3.org/1999/XSL/Transform`.

On lines 4 through 42, we are defining the layout-master-set. This is a group of page layouts and combinations of page layouts that will be used throughout the document. This includes the simple-page-masters on lines 6 through 26 and the page-sequence-master on lines 28 through 40.

Starting with the first simple-page-master on lines 6 through 14, we see that we're specifying a number of properties for the page, specifically the size and margins. We've also given it a master-name on line 6, so we can refer to it later.

Lengths such as the page height or width or margins can be specified in a variety of units, just as they could in CSS. Here we're using inches, but we could just as easily have used centimeters (cm), picas (pc), points (pt), or pixels (px).

On line 13, we're including a region-body in this page. That means that any region-body content will appear on a page that uses this master.

Lines 16 through 26 define a similar simple-page-master, except that on lines 24 and 25 we're defining two additional areas, region-before and region-after, which are analogous to the header and footer of a page.

In this way, we're defining the areas of the respective pages, and what their sizes should be. Each of these measurements affects a different area of the page, as shown in Figure 9.12.

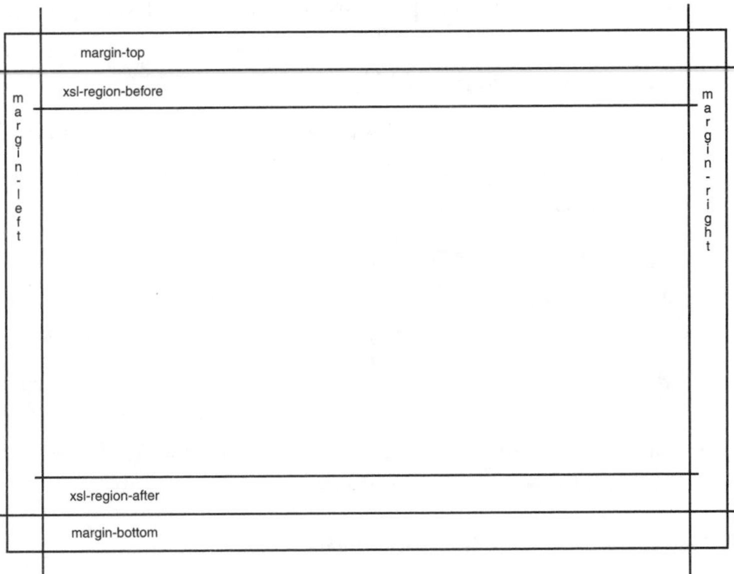

Figure 9.12

Here is the layout of an XSL Formatting Objects page.

Notice that the region-before and region-after are part of the actual content rectangle of the page, and not part of the margins, as might be expected.

On lines 28 through 40, we're defining the sequence of pages that will appear in our document, the repeatable-page-master-alternatives. In lines 30 through 32, we're telling the processor (whatever it might be) that the first page should use the simple-page-master named first, and on lines 33 through 35 we're specifying the simple-page-master for the rest of the pages, rest.

Lines 37 and 38 are a recommended fallback position: If the processor doesn't understand first and rest (perhaps because this is not a paged media), it will use this master.

Now that we've defined the page templates and indicated the order in which we want them to appear, we can begin to define the content of our regions as part of the page-sequence itself. Notice that the page-sequence refers back to the page-sequence-master that we created.

On lines 46 through 48, we're creating a section of static-content. This means that it will appear, in its entirety, on any page that contains this particular region type—in this case, xsl-region-before. That means that it will appear at the top of all our pages—except for the first page, because our simple-page-master does not include the region-before. The static-content on lines 54 through 56 is a similar situation, which appears only as a footer on all pages but the first.

Lines 50 through 52 define a flow object, the xsl-region-body. A flow object will appear once in the document, and will span pages if necessary. This is where the majority of our content will go.

Now we need to convert the FO file to a PDF file. To do this, open a Command Prompt window and change to the directory that contains catalog.fo. Then, type

```
java org.apache.fop.apps.CommandLine catalog.fo cat.pdf
```

This will create a PDF file out of the FO file. We can view this file from the browser, but we can also open it directly by using the Acrobat Reader. Open the reader and then choose File, Open, and navigate to `cat.pdf`.

When we do this, however, we'll notice that even though we put content on the page, it's not appearing in the file. This is because all Formatting Objects content must appear within a block, even if it's within an inline section within the block. We'll add this information in Listing 9.33.

Listing 9.33—`catalog.fo`: Adding Basic Content

```
...
41:
42:     </fo:layout-master-set>
43:
44:     <fo:page-sequence master-name="layout">
45:
46:         <fo:static-content flow-name="xsl-region-before">
47:             <fo:block text-align="end"
48:                 font-size="10pt"
49:                 font-family="sans-serif">
50:
51:                 ChaseWeb Spring Catalog
52:
53:             </fo:block>
54:         </fo:static-content>
55:
56:         <fo:flow flow-name="xsl-region-body">
57:
58:             <fo:block font-size="18pt"
59:                 font-family="sans-serif"
60:                 background-color="red"
61:                 color="yellow"
62:                 text-align="center"
63:                 padding-top="3pt">
64:
65:                 The ChaseWeb Furniture Spring Catalog
66:
67:             </fo:block>
68:
69:             <fo:block font-size="12pt"
70:                 font-family="sans-serif"
```

Listing 9.33—continued

```
71:                space-before.optimum=".25in"
72:                space-before.minimum=".1in"
73:                space-before.maximum=".5in"
74:                text-align="start">
75:
76:                This is where the regular catalog text will go.
77:
78:            </fo:block>
79:
80:        </fo:flow>
81:
82:        <fo:static-content flow-name="xsl-region-after">
83:            <fo:block text-align="center"
84:                font-size="10pt"
85:                font-family="sans-serif">
86:
87:                Page <fo:page-number/>
88:
89:            </fo:block>
90:        </fo:static-content>
91:
92:    </fo:page-sequence>
93:
94:</fo:root>
```

On lines 47 through 53, we're adding a block that will be aligned to the end of the text. Notice that the attribute is `end`, and not `right`. This is because it's only `right` for languages that read from left to right, such as English. We're also setting the font size and family.

There are many, many, attributes that we can set here, as we saw in Chapter 2, but we'll keep it simple and focus on the Formatting Objects themselves.

On lines 58 through 67, we're adding a block of text that will serve as a title for the catalog, and on lines 69 through 78, we're putting in a placeholder for the text itself. Notice that on lines 71 through 73 we're giving the processor a little bit of leeway in where it puts the text, but we're specifying that there must be at least some space between the previous block and this one. If we left that out, we'd wind up with this block flush against the bottom of the title.

Finally, on lines 83 through 89, we're creating the footer for each page. Page 87 shows the page-number object, a built-in function of Formatting Objects.

Now if we convert this to a PDF, we can see our content, as in Figure 9.13. Note that you will have to close the document in the Acrobat Reader in order for `CommandLine` to be able to replace it.

Figure 9.13

This shows basic content in our page.

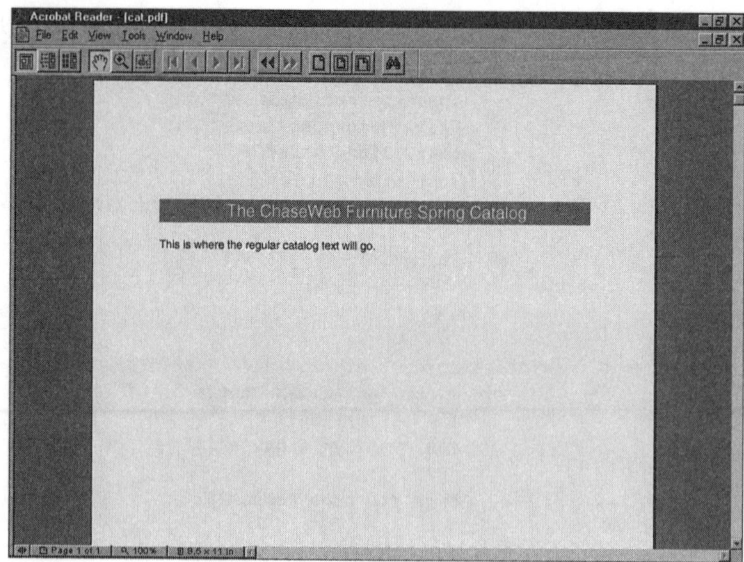

Notice that we don't see the header or footer. This is because we have only one page. After we get more content, they'll appear on the subsequent pages.

Now we're ready to start building the catalog itself. The catalog will consist of a table of contents, followed by a section for each vendor listing each product's information. Before we start building the XSL style sheet, however, we'll build a prototype to work from in Listing 9.34.

Listing 9.34—`catalog.fo`: A Catalog Prototype

```
...
    <fo:page-sequence master-name="layout">

        <fo:static-content flow-name="xsl-region-before">
            <fo:block text-align="end"
                font-size="10pt"
                font-family="sans-serif">

                ChaseWeb Spring Catalog

            </fo:block>
        </fo:static-content>

        <fo:flow flow-name="xsl-region-body">

            <fo:block text-align="center">
                <fo:external-graphic
                   src="file:///c:/files/chasewebfurniture.gif"/>
            </fo:block>

```

Listing 9.34—continued

```
            <fo:block font-size="18pt"
                font-family="sans-serif"
                background-color="red"
                color="yellow"
                text-align="center"
                padding-top="3pt">

                The ChaseWeb Furniture Spring Catalog

            </fo:block>

            <fo:block font-size="24pt"
                font-family="sans-serif"
                space-before.optimum=".25in"
                space-before.minimum=".1in"
                space-before.maximum=".5in"
                text-align="center">

                Table of Contents

            </fo:block>

            <fo:block font-size="18pt"
                font-family="sans-serif"
                space-before.optimum=".25in"
                space-before.minimum=".1in"
                space-before.maximum=".5in"
                text-align="start">

                Conners Chair Company

            </fo:block>

            <fo:block font-size="12pt"
                font-family="sans-serif"
                text-align="start">

                 QA3452 -- Queen Anne Chair

             </fo:block>

             <fo:block font-size="12pt"
                 font-family="sans-serif"
                 text-align="start">

                 RC2342 -- Early American Rocking Chair

             </fo:block>

             <fo:block font-size="12pt"
                 font-family="sans-serif"
                 text-align="start">
```

Listing 9.34—continued

```

                    BR3452 -- Bentwood Rocker

                </fo:block>

                <fo:block font-size="18pt"
                    font-family="sans-serif"
                    space-before.optimum=".25in"
                    space-before.minimum=".1in"
                    space-before.maximum=".5in"
                    text-align="start">

                    Wally's Wonderful World of Furniture

                </fo:block>

                <fo:block font-size="12pt">
                    ...
                </fo:block>

                <fo:block break-before="page"
                    font-size="24pt"
                    font-family="sans-serif"
                    text-align="center"
                    font-weight="bold">

                    Conners Chair Company
                </fo:block>

              <fo:block font-size="14pt"
                    font-family="sans-serif"
                    space-before.optimum=".25in"
                    text-align="start">

                    Conners Chair Company presents their annual big
                    three day only chair sale. We&apos;re making
                    way for our new stock!  All current inventory
                    must go! Regular prices slashed by up to 60%!
              </fo:block>

              <fo:block font-size="14pt"
                    font-family="sans-serif"
                    space-before.optimum=".25in"
                    font-weight="bold"
                    text-align="start">

                    QA3452 --  Queen Anne Chair
              </fo:block>

              <fo:block font-size="12pt"
                    font-family="sans-serif"
```

Listing 9.34—continued

```
            space-before.optimum=".25in"
            text-align="start">

            Price:  $195
        </fo:block>

        <fo:block font-size="12pt"
            font-family="sans-serif"
            space-before.optimum=".25in"
            text-align="start">

            Available in the great colors:
            <fo:list-block>
                <fo:list-item>
                    <fo:list-item-label>
                        <fo:block>&#x2022;</fo:block>
                    </fo:list-item-label>
                    <fo:list-item-body>
                        <fo:block>
                            royal blue
                        </fo:block>
                    </fo:list-item-body>
                </fo:list-item>
                <fo:list-item>
                    <fo:list-item-label>
                        <fo:block>&#x2022;</fo:block>
                    </fo:list-item-label>
                    <fo:list-item-body>
                        <fo:block>
                            flower print
                        </fo:block>
                    </fo:list-item-body>
                </fo:list-item>
                <fo:list-item>
                    <fo:list-item-label>
                        <fo:block>&#x2022;</fo:block>
                    </fo:list-item-label>
                    <fo:list-item-body>
                        <fo:block>
                            seafoam green
                        </fo:block>
                    </fo:list-item-body>
                </fo:list-item>
                <fo:list-item>
                    <fo:list-item-label>
                        <fo:block>&#x2022;</fo:block>
                    </fo:list-item-label>
                    <fo:list-item-body>
                        <fo:block>
                            teal
                        </fo:block>
```

Listing 9.34—continued

```
                        </fo:list-item-body>
                    </fo:list-item>
                </fo:list-block>
            </fo:block>

            <fo:block>
                <fo:leader leader-pattern="rule"
                    space-before.optimum="12pt"
                    space-after.optimum="12pt"/>
            </fo:block>

            <fo:block font-size="14pt"
                 font-family="sans-serif"
                 space-before.optimum=".25in"
                 font-weight="bold"
                 text-align="start">

                 RC2342 --  Early American Rocking Chair with
                 brown and tan plaid upholstery

            </fo:block>

            <fo:block font-size="12pt"
                 font-family="sans-serif"
                 space-before.optimum=".25in"
                 text-align="start">

                 Price:  $120
            </fo:block>

            <fo:block>
                <fo:leader leader-pattern="rule"
                    space-before.optimum="12pt"
                    space-after.optimum="12pt" />
            </fo:block>

            <fo:block font-size="12pt"
                 font-family="sans-serif"
                 space-before.optimum=".25in"
                 text-align="start">

                 ...
            </fo:block>

        </fo:flow>

        <fo:static-content flow-name="xsl-region-after">
...
```

The first thing that we've done, on lines 58 through 61, is add our graphic. The external-graphic formatting object is used to add graphics such as those we might use in a Web page.

Next, on lines 74 through 133, we've added our first page, the table of contents. Although there are different sizes of text, it's all just a series of blocks.

The block on lines 135 through 142 is also just a text block, but on line 135 we've added a special attribute—break-before. This way, we've specified that each vendor will always start a new page. There are several values we could have used for this, such as even-page and odd-page, in case we wanted to make sure that each vendor started on, say, a right-side page.

On lines 178 to 219, we've added another type of item, the list-block. A list-block contains list-items, and each list-item must contain exactly two elements: a list-item-label, which here is a bullet, and a list-item-body, which contains the content.

The block on lines 222 through 226 is also special, containing a horizontal rule between products.

The end result is shown in Figures 9.14 and 9.15.

Figure 9.14

The first page of our prototype catalog is shown.

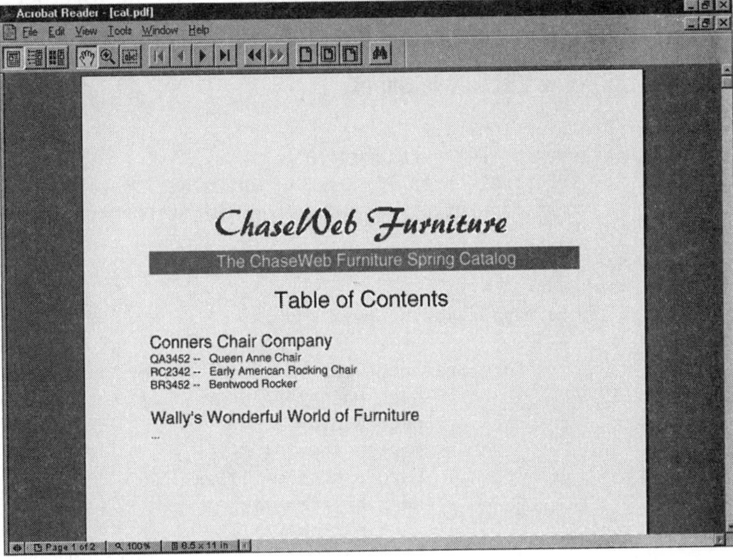

9

Figure 9.15

Subsequent pages of our prototype catalog follow.

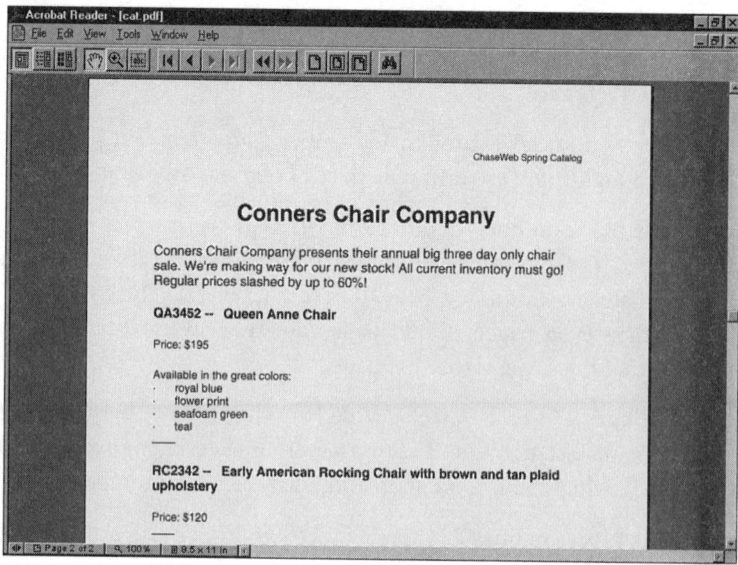

Notice that when you advance to a second page, our header and footer are showing up.

Now that we know what we're building, we can put together an XSLT style sheet that will create the FO file for us. In Listing 9.35, we create the XSL style sheet.

Listing 9.35—The XSLT Style Sheet

```
<?xml version="1.0"?>
<xsl:stylesheet version="1.0"
    xmlns:xsl="http://www.w3.org/1999/XSL/Transform"
    xmlns:fo="http://www.w3.org/1999/XSL/Format">

<xsl:template match="products">
<fo:root>
    <fo:layout-master-set>

        <fo:simple-page-master master-name="first"
                  page-height="11in"
                  page-width="8.5in"
                  margin-top="1in"
                  margin-bottom=".75in"
                  margin-left="1in"
                  margin-right="1in">
            <fo:region-body margin-top=".75in" />
        </fo:simple-page-master>

        <fo:simple-page-master master-name="rest"
                  page-height="11in"
                  page-width="8.5in"
                  margin-top="1in"
                  margin-bottom=".75in"
```

Listing 9.35—continued

```
                margin-left="1in"
                margin-right="1in">
            <fo:region-body margin-top=".75in"/>
            <fo:region-before extent=".5in"/>
            <fo:region-after extent=".75in"/>
        </fo:simple-page-master>

        <fo:page-sequence-master master-name="layout" >
            <fo:repeatable-page-master-alternatives>
                <fo:conditional-page-master-reference
                      master-name="first"
                      page-position="first" />
                <fo:conditional-page-master-reference
                      master-name="rest"
                      page-position="rest" />

                <fo:conditional-page-master-reference
                      master-name="rest" />
            </fo:repeatable-page-master-alternatives>
        </fo:page-sequence-master>

    </fo:layout-master-set>

    <fo:page-sequence master-name="layout">

        <fo:static-content flow-name="xsl-region-before">
            <fo:block text-align="end"
                font-size="10pt"
                font-family="sans-serif">

                ChaseWeb Spring Catalog

            </fo:block>
        </fo:static-content>

        <fo:flow flow-name="xsl-region-body">

            <fo:block text-align="center">
                <fo:external-graphic
                   src="file:///c:/files/chasewebfurniture.gif"/>
            </fo:block>

            <fo:block font-size="18pt"
                font-family="sans-serif"
                background-color="red"
                color="yellow"
                text-align="center"
                padding-top="3pt">

                The ChaseWeb Furniture Spring Catalog

            </fo:block>
```

Listing 9.35—continued

```

            <fo:block font-size="24pt"
                font-family="sans-serif"
                space-before.optimum=".25in"
                space-before.minimum=".1in"
                space-before.maximum=".5in"
                text-align="center">

                Table of Contents

            </fo:block>

            <xsl:for-each select="vendor">

                <fo:block font-size="18pt"
                    font-family="sans-serif"
                    space-before.optimum=".25in"
                    space-before.minimum=".1in"
                    space-before.maximum=".5in"
                    text-align="start">

                    <xsl:value-of select="vendor_name" />

                </fo:block>

                <xsl:for-each select="product | suite">

                    <fo:block font-size="12pt"
                        font-family="sans-serif"
                        text-align="start">

                        <xsl:value-of select="product_id" />
                        --
                        <xsl:value-of select="short_desc" />
                    </fo:block>
                </xsl:for-each>

            </xsl:for-each>

            <xsl:for-each select="vendor">
                <xsl:call-template name="vendor_page" />
            </xsl:for-each>

        </fo:flow>

        <fo:static-content flow-name="xsl-region-after">
            <fo:block text-align="center"
                font-size="10pt"
                font-family="sans-serif">

                Page <fo:page-number/>

```

Listing 9.35—continued

```
            </fo:block>
        </fo:static-content>

    </fo:page-sequence>

</fo:root>

</xsl:template>

<xsl:template name="vendor_page">

    <fo:block break-before="page"
        font-size="24pt"
        font-family="sans-serif"
        text-align="center"
        font-weight="bold">

        <xsl:value-of select="vendor_name" />

    </fo:block>

    <fo:block font-size="14pt"
        font-family="sans-serif"
        space-before.optimum=".25in"
        text-align="start">

        <xsl:value-of select="advertisement" />

    </fo:block>

    <xsl:for-each select="product | suite">
        <xsl:call-template name="product_block" />
    </xsl:for-each>

</xsl:template>

<xsl:template name="product_block">

    <fo:block font-size="14pt"
        font-family="sans-serif"
        space-before.optimum=".25in"
        font-weight="bold"
        text-align="start">

        <xsl:value-of select="product_id" />
        --
        <xsl:value-of select="short_desc" />
        <xsl:value-of select="product_desc" />

    </fo:block>

    <fo:block font-size="12pt"
```

Listing 9.35—continued

```
180:         font-family="sans-serif"
181:         space-before.optimum=".25in"
182:         text-align="start">
183:
184:         Price:  <xsl:value-of select="price[@pricetype='retail']" />
185:
186:     </fo:block>
187:
188:     <xsl:if test="inventory[@location='showroom' and @color]">
189:         <fo:block font-size="12pt"
190:             font-family="sans-serif"
191:             space-before.optimum=".25in"
192:             text-align="start">
193:
194:             Available in these great colors:
195:             <fo:list-block>
196:                 <xsl:for-each
197:                     select="inventory[@location='showroom' and @color]">
198:                     <fo:list-item>
199:                         <fo:list-item-label>
200:                             <fo:block>&#x2022;</fo:block>
201:                         </fo:list-item-label>
202:                         <fo:list-item-body>
203:                             <fo:block>
204:                                 <xsl:value-of select="@color"/>
205:                             </fo:block>
206:                         </fo:list-item-body>
207:                     </fo:list-item>
208:
209:                 </xsl:for-each>
210:             </fo:list-block>
211:
212:         </fo:block>
213:     </xsl:if>
214:
215:     <fo:block>
216:         <fo:leader leader-pattern="rule"
217:             space-before.optimum="12pt"
218:             space-after.optimum="12pt"/>
219:     </fo:block>
220:
221:</xsl:template>
222:
223:</xsl:stylesheet>
```

This is just like all the style sheets we've been using, except that the result is in the Formatting Objects namespace instead of the XHTML namespace, as we can see from line 3.

Our main template, based on products, our root element, is on lines 5 through 135. Lines 6 through 86 are the basic pieces of the FO file, independent of any of our data. On lines 88 through 113, we're looping through each vendor, outputting their name on lines 90 through 99, and then looping through each vendor's products on lines 101 through 111.

That takes care of the first page, but we still need to add each vendor's product pages. Just to make things a bit neater, we'll separate that out into a separate template, `vendor_page`, which we're calling on lines 115 through 117.

Lines 119 through 133 are the rest of our standard FO file.

On line 137, we come to the beginning of the `vendor_page` template. This page displays the `vendor_name` on lines 139 through 147, and the advertisement on lines 149 through 156. We then loop through each product or suite on lines 158 through 160, calling the `product_block` template.

The `product_block` template is on lines 164 through 221. Lines 166 through 177 display the actual product information, to which we add the pricing on lines 179 through 186. Because this is the retail catalog, we'll use the retail pricing instead of the sale pricing.

Also because this is the catalog, we're going to look for products that are currently in the showroom as we test for colors on lines 188 through 213. If there are different colors for the product, we'll display the explanatory text on lines 189 through 194, and then begin our list-block on line 195. In lines 198 through 207, just as we did in our prototype, we're outputting the necessary elements for a list: list-item, list-item-label, and list-item-body.

Finally, on lines 215 through 219, we're outputting the horizontal rule.

That's the entire style sheet, so we can go ahead and create the Formatting Objects file by typing

```
java org.apache.xalan.xslt.Process -IN products.xml
➥ -XSL PDFcatalog.xsl -OUT catalogXSL.fo
```

We can then create the PDF file by typing

```
java org.apache.fop.apps.CommandLine catalogXSL.fo catalogXSL.pdf
```

This is our complete catalog, ready to go to the printer.

XSL Formatting Objects is a Candidate Recommendation at W3C, so it's unlikely to change. It is a huge Recommendation—much more than we can cover in a few sections, so it might be helpful to check the actual Recommendation at

`http://www.w3.org/TR/xsl/`

Where We Go from Here

In the course of this book, we have discussed XML as both a means for storing and manipulating content, and a means for data exchange. We've discussed styling XML with Cascading Style Sheets, and with Extensible Stylesheet Language. We used Java and XML to update SQL databases, and to do remote procedure calls using SOAP. We've taken orders, and we've created browser-specific output, including for wireless devices such as mobile phones. So, what's left?

Plenty! The extensibility of XML means that not a week passes, it seems, without another company announcing another proposed standard or product. Here are some topics to watch for in the coming months:

- **XHTML Modularization**—XHTML 1.0, as an XML version of HTML 4.0, is too much for many devices to handle in its entirety. Watch for different subsets of XHTML to be created, allowing vendors and authors to choose which sets to support. (More information: `http://www.w3.org`.)
- **XML Linking Language (XLink)**—XLink is a means for describing relationships between XML files. For instance, an XHTML link is a one-way link. XLink makes it possible to specify bidirectional links, multiple-destination links, and other ways to make use of a file that you might not have access to change. (More information at `http://www.w3.org`.)
- **XML Pointer Language (XPointer)**—Just as XLink has a counterpart in XHTML, so does XPointer. In XHTML, we can specify not just what page we would like to link to, but also a specific anchor in the page, such as `http://www.nicholaschase.com/pointers.html#future`. XPointer will allow the same sort of specificity with XML files. (More information: `http://www.w3.org`.)
- **XML Signature**—This initiative aims to provide functionality for digital signatures, which provide authentication and verification of messages and their senders. (More information: `http://www.w3.org`.)
- **Industry-Specific Vocabularies**—One of the problems with Electronic Data Exchange has been the difficulty in getting trading partners to agree on precisely how data should be represented. Although XML takes care of many of those problems, there is still the issue of vocabulary. Fortunately, many industries are seeing the development of vocabularies relevant to the work that they do. For instance, if this were a real furniture catalog, we might have used FurnML, a proposed vocabulary for the furniture industry. (More information: `http://www.xml.org/xmlorg_registry/index.shtml`.)
- **XML Application Servers**—With XML as such a powerful language for data exchange, it's only natural that companies will build servers to utilize it. Some

examples are Microsoft's Biztalk Server and the Enhydra Application Server. (More information: `http://www.microsoft.com/biztalk/default.htm` and `http://www.enhydra.org`, respectively.)

Getting More Information

As quickly as XML moves, often the best place for information is on the Web itself. Some good resources are

- **The W3C**—`http://www.w3.org`
- **The XML Cover Pages**—`http://www.oasis-open.org/cover/`
- **XMLHack**—`http://www.xmlhack.com`
- **The XML Frequently Asked Questions List**—`http://www.ucc.ie/xml/`

There are also some good books on the market to help you with some of the deeper XML topics. *XML by Example*, by Benoît Marchal, is an excellent look at the topic, particularly if you want to use JavaScript. If you are more of a Visual Basic programmer, you'll find *XML Web Documents from scratch* by Mike Kraley and Jesse Liberty helpful.

To get much more in depth regarding XML itself, try *XML Unleashed* by Michael Morrison. For more Java instruction, pick up *Sams Teach Yourself Java 2 in 21 Days, Professional Reference, Second Edition* by Laura Lemay.

More Information on This Book

XML moves so fast that it's pretty unlikely that this book will make it to press without something in it changing. Que will have an information page for this book at `www.quecorp.com`. I'll also be maintaining my own information page at `http://www.nicholaschase.com/xmlfs.html`. If you have any questions, or if you just want to let me know what you think, please drop me a line at `xmlfs@nicholaschase.com`. I do try to answer everyone, but please be patient if it takes me a day or two to get to you.

The Last Word

Like a good college survey course, we've covered an awful lot of ground in this book. I've tried to give you a solid footing in all the areas you might need when working with XML using Java, but there is a wealth of information still to explore. You've just begun upon the path.

Enjoy the ride!

Index

Symbols

A

B

C

D

E

O

P-Q

R

T